Collins

KEY WORDS
FOR IELTS

BOOK 3: ADVANCED

HarperCollins Publishers
Westerhill Road
Bishopbriggs
Glasgow
G64 2QT

First edition 2011

10 9

© HarperCollins Publishers 2011

ISBN 978-0-00-736547-0

Collins ® is a registered trademark of
HarperCollins Publishers Limited

www.collinselt.com
www.collinsdictionary.com/cobuild

A catalogue record for this book is
available from the British Library

Typeset by Davidson Publishing
Solutions, Glasgow

Printed and bound by
CPI Group (UK) Ltd, Croydon, CR0 4YY

Editorial staff

Senior editor
Julie Moore

Project manager
Lisa Sutherland

Contributors
Sandra Anderson
Jamie Flockhart
Lucy Hollingworth
Virginia Klein
Claire Newton
Cerwyss O'Hare
Kate Wild

For the publishers
Lucy Cooper
Kerry Ferguson
Gavin Gray
Elaine Higgleton

Computing support
Thomas Callan

The publishers would like to thank
the following for their invaluable
contribution to the series:
Sharon Chalmers
Rachael Clarke
Jane Cursiter
Patrick Hubbuck
Martin Jenkins

contents

Collins COBUILD KeyWords for IELTS: Book 3 Advanced is the final book in the *KeyWords for IELTS* series. It covers the words and phrases that will help you to raise the level of your English to achieve the high IELTS score required by some universities for more challenging courses and postgraduate study. Mastering the vocabulary in this book will give you the skills you need to confidently use Academic English in an English-medium university context.

The first section of the book consists of **word lists** organized by subject and topic area. You can use these lists to help you **revise** sets of vocabulary or when preparing for writing tasks. The words are grouped into academic **subject areas**, such as Science and History, **common topics** such as social issues and the environment, as well as according to **functions**, such as talking about cause and effect or describing trends.

The second section of the book contains alphabetically ordered dictionary-style entries for **key words** and **phrases**. The vocabulary items have been chosen to fully prepare you for the kind of language found in the IELTS exam. The words and phrases regularly appear in the most **common IELTS topics**, and are clearly labelled by subject area. More formal vocabulary has been included so that you can feel confident using a more sophisticated style in IELTS **writing** tasks and **academic** essays.

Each word is illustrated with **examples** of natural English taken from the Collins corpus and reflects the style of language used in IELTS texts. As well as definitions and examples, entries include additional information about **collocations**, as well as **usage notes** to help you put the vocabulary you have learnt into practice.

Words from the same root, for example, *coincide, coincidence, coincidental*, are shown together to help you make these vital **links** between words. By understanding how these words relate to each other, you will be able to vary the way you express your ideas, which will help improve your writing and speaking skills.

There are **synonyms** and **antonyms** at each entry to help you widen your range of vocabulary and create more variety in your writing style. The ***Extend your vocabulary*** boxes help you understand the differences between sets of similar words, so you can be sure that your English is accurate and natural.

We hope you enjoy preparing for IELTS using *Collins COBUILD KeyWords for IELTS*. The vocabulary in these books will help you to not only achieve the IELTS score you are aiming for, but will equip you for success in the future.

We have used the International Phonetic Alphabet (IPA) to show how the words are pronounced.

IPA Symbols

Vowel Sounds

ɑː	calm, ah		
æ	act, mass		
aɪ	dive, cry		
aɪə	fire, tyre		
aʊ	out, down		
aʊə	flour, sour		
e	met, lend, pen		
eɪ	say, weight		
eə	fair, care		
ɪ	fit, win		
iː	seem, me		
ɪə	near, beard		
ɒ	lot, spot		
eʊ	note, coat		
ɔː	claw, more		
ɔɪ	boy, joint		
ʊ	could, stood		
uː	you, use		
ʊə	sure, pure		
ɜː	turn, third		
ʌ	fund, must		
ə	the first vowel in about		

Consonant Sounds

b	bed, rub
d	done, red
f	fit, if
g	good, dog
h	hat, horse
j	yellow, you
k	king, pick
l	lip, bill
m	mat, ram
n	not, tin
p	pay, lip
r	run, read
s	soon, bus
t	talk, bet
v	van, love
w	win, wool
x	loch
z	zoo, buzz
ʃ	ship, wish
ʒ	measure, leisure
ŋ	sing, working
tʃ	cheap, witch
θ	thin, myth
ð	then, bathe
dʒ	joy, bridge

Notes

Primary and secondary stress are shown by marks above and below the line, in front of the stressed syllable. For example, in the word *abbreviation*, /əˌbriːviˈeɪʃən/, the second syllable has secondary stress and the fourth syllable has primary stress.

We do not normally show pronunciations for compound words (words which are made up of more than one word). Pronunciations for the words that make up the compounds are usually found at their entries in other parts of the book. However, compound words do have stress markers.

Headwords are organized in alphabetical order.

Labels tell you more about how and when the word is used

Words from the Academic Word List are highlighted

at|tain /əˈteɪn/ (attains, attaining, attained)   `ACADEMIC WORD`

VERB If you **attain** something, you gain it or achieve it, often after a lot of effort. [FORMAL] ○ *the best way to attain the objectives of our strategy* ○ *Business has yet to attain the social status it has in other countries.*

▸ **COLLOCATIONS:**
attain **enlightenment/perfection**
attain a **status/rank/goal/objective**

Words from the same root are shown together

> **EXTEND YOUR VOCABULARY**
>
> You can talk about **reaching** or **achieving** something like a goal or a level. ○ *The temperature reached the required level.* ○ *There are simpler ways of achieving the same result.*
>
> **Attain** is a more formal verb, used especially to talk about getting to a high or respected level. ○ *a book that in time attained the status of a classic*

at|tain|ment /əˈteɪnmənt/ (attainments)

NOUN ○ [+ *of*] *the attainment of independence* ○ *their educational attainments*

▸ **COLLOCATIONS:**
the attainment **of** *something*
the attainment of a **goal**
educational/academic attainments
▸ **SYNONYMS:** achievement, success
▸ **ANTONYM:** failure

Information boxes help increase your understanding of the word and when to use it

Collocations help you put the word into practice

Synonyms and antonyms help expand your vocabulary

Labels show common grammatical patterns

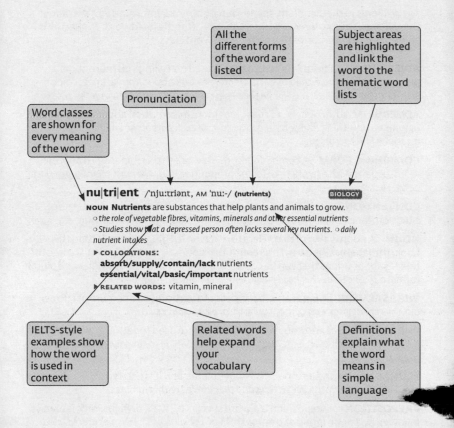

All the different forms of the word are listed

Subject areas are highlighted and link the word to the thematic word lists

Pronunciation

Word classes are shown for every meaning of the word

nu|tri|ent /ˈnjuːtriənt, AM ˈnuː-/ (nutrients)   `BIOLOGY`

NOUN **Nutrients** are substances that help plants and animals to grow.
◦ *the role of vegetable fibres, vitamins, minerals and other essential nutrients*
◦ *Studies show that a depressed person often lacks several key nutrients.* ◦ *daily nutrient intakes*

▶ COLLOCATIONS:
absorb/supply/contain/lack nutrients
essential/vital/basic/important nutrients

▶ RELATED WORDS: vitamin, mineral

IELTS-style examples show how the word is used in context

Related words help expand your vocabulary

Definitions explain what the word means in simple language

All the words in the dictionary section have grammar information given about them. For each word, its word class is shown after the headword. The sections below show more information about each word class.

ADJECTIVE   An adjective is a word that is used for telling you more about a person or thing. You would use an adjective to talk about appearance, colour, size, or other qualities, e.g. *He has been _absent_ from his desk for two weeks*.

ADVERB   An adverb is a word that gives more information about when, how, or where something happens, e.g. *The costs of each part of the process can be measured fairly _accurately_*.

COMBINING FORM   A combining form is a word that is joined with another word, usually with a hyphen, to form compounds, e.g. *the most injury-_prone_ rider on the circuit*.

CONVENTION   A convention is a word or a fixed phrase that is used in a specific situation, for example when greeting someone, apologizing or replying, e.g. _hello_.

NOUN   A noun is a word that refers to a person, a thing, or a quality. In this book, the label *noun* is given to all countable nouns. A countable noun is used for talking about things that can be counted, and that have both singular and plural forms, e.g. *She turned her _head_ away; difficult financial _situations_*.

PHRASAL VERB   A phrasal verb consists of a verb and one or more particles, e.g. *All experiments were _carried out_ by three psychologists*.

PHRASE   Phrases are groups of words which are used together and which have a meaning of their own, e.g. *Most schools are unwilling to cut down on staff _in order to_ cut costs*.

PLURAL NOUN   A plural noun is always plural, and it is used with plural verbs, *He called the _emergency services_ and they arrived within minutes*.

PREPOSITION   A preposition is a word such as *by*, *with*, or *from* which is always followed by a noun group or the *-ing* form of a verb, e.g. *The themes are repeated _throughout_ the film*.

PRONOUN   A pronoun is a word that you use instead of a noun, when you do not need or want to name someone or something directly, e.g. *No one drug will suit everyone and sometimes _several_ may have to be tried*.

QUANTIFIER   A quantifier comes before *of* and a noun group, e.g. *the _bulk_ of the text*.

UNCOUNTABLE NOUN   An uncountable noun is used for talking about things that are not normally counted, or that we do not think of as single items. Uncountable nouns do not have a plural form, and they are used with a singular verb, e.g. *The report has inevitably been greeted with _scepticism_*.

VERB   A verb is a word that is used for saying what someone or something does, or what happens to them, or to give information about them, e.g. *The exhibition _traces_ the history of graphic design*.

Word lists

General science

biochemistry (uncount)
biochemical (adj)
biochemist (noun)
biotechnology (uncount)
biotechnologist (noun)

Scientific research
apparatus (uncount)
gauge (verb, noun)
laser (noun)
Petri dish (noun)
telescope (noun)
test tube (noun)
vacuum (noun)

Scientific processes
accelerate (verb)
acceleration (uncount)
activate (verb)
activation (uncount)
combustion (uncount)
condense (verb)
condensation (uncount)
conduct (verb)
conduction (uncount)
conductive (adj)
conductivity (uncount)
conductor (noun)
contaminate (verb)
contaminated (adj)
contamination (uncount)
contaminant (noun)
contract (verb)
contraction (noun)
dehydrate (verb)
dehydrated (adj)
dehydration (uncount)
deplete (verb)
depletion (uncount)
dilute (verb, adj)
dilution (uncount, noun)
disperse (verb)
dispersal (uncount)
dissolve (verb)
evaporate (verb)
evaporation (uncount)
exhaust (verb, uncount)

extract (verb)
extraction (uncount)
filter (verb, noun)
harness (verb)
synthesize (verb)
synthetic (adj)
synthetically (adv)
yield (verb, noun)

Substances & qualities
constituent (noun, adj)
debris (uncount)
dense (adj)
density (noun)
fibre (noun)
permeable (adj)
porous (adj)
radioactive (adj)
radiation (uncount)
raw (adj)
staple (adj, noun)

The environment
biodiversity (uncount)
ecosystem (noun)
fossil fuel (noun)
landfill (uncount)
refuse (uncount)
unspoiled (adj)

Chemistry

agent (noun)
atom (noun)
atomic (adj)
chain reaction (noun)
compound (noun)
crystal (noun)
dilute (verb, adj)
dilution (uncount, noun)
insoluble (adj)
molecule (noun)
molecular (adj)
periodic table (noun)

Physics

atom (noun)
  atomic (adj)
electron (noun)
neutron (noun)
particle (noun)

dynamic (adj, noun, plural, uncount)
force (noun)
hydraulic (adj)
  hydraulically (adv)
  hydraulics (uncount)
hydroelectric (adj)
  hydroelectricity (uncount)
kinetic (adj)
momentum (uncount)
motion (uncount)
propel (verb, comb)

acoustic (uncount, adj)
analogue (adj)
electrode (noun)
lens (noun)
optical (adj)
reflect (verb)
  reflection (uncount)
sonic (adj)
spectrum (noun)
terminal (adj, noun)

Applied sciences

Engineering
analogue (adj)
propel (verb, comb)
audio (adj)
automate (verb)
  automation (uncount)
conduct (verb)
  conduction (uncount)
  conductive (adj)
  conductivity (uncount)
  conductor (noun)

hydraulic (adj)
  hydraulically (adv)
  hydraulics (uncount)
hydroelectric (adj)
  hydroelectricity (uncount)
laser (noun)
lens (noun)
optical (adj)
prototype (noun)

IT
default (adj, uncount)
erase (verb)
icon (noun)
interactive (adj)
interface (noun, verb)
protocol (noun)
silicon chip (noun)
state-of-the-art (adj)

Maths

constant (noun)
deduct (verb)
  deduction (noun, uncount)
integer (noun)
mean (noun)
median (adj)
power (noun)
prime number (noun)
theorem (noun)
three-dimensional (adj)
two-dimensional (adj)

Biology & medicine

Anatomy
anatomy (uncount, noun)
  anatomical (adj)
  anatomically (adv)
artery (noun)
  arterial (adj)
aural (adj)
cardiovascular (adj)
cognitive (adj)
embryo (noun)
  embryonic (adj)

hemisphere (noun)
immune (adj)
　immunity (uncount)
immune system (noun)
nervous system (noun)
neural (adj)
　neurology (uncount)
　neurologist (noun)
oral (adj)
　orally (adv)
pathology (uncount)
　pathologist (noun)
skull (noun)
spine (noun)
　spinal (adj)
vein (noun)

Biological processes & research

decay (verb, uncount)
dormant (adj)
exhale (verb)
　exhalation (noun)
fertilize (verb)
　fertilization (uncount)
inhale (verb)
　inhalation (uncount)
reproduce (verb)
　reproduction (uncount)
respiration (uncount)
　respiratory (adj)
suppress (verb)
　suppression (uncount)

clone (noun, verb)
DNA (uncount)
gene (noun)
genetics (uncount)
　genetic (adj)
　genetically (adv)
　geneticist (noun)
microbiology (uncount)
　microbiological (adj)
　microbiologist (noun)

Plants & animals

amphibian (noun)
　amphibious (adj)
carnivore (noun)
　carnivorous (adj)
colony (noun)
　colonial (adj)
　colonialism (uncount)
　colonialist (adj, noun)
　colonize (verb)
fauna (noun)
food chain (noun)
fossil (noun)
herbivore (noun)
　herbivorous (adj)
hibernate (verb)
　hibernation (uncount)
host (noun)
hybrid (noun, adj)
larva (noun)
mammal (noun)
marine (adj)
migrate (verb)
　migration (noun)
omnivorous (adj)
　omnivore (noun)
parasite (noun)
　parasitic (adj)
pesticide (noun)
predator (noun)
　predatory (adj)
prey (uncount, verb)
reptile (noun)

biodiversity (uncount)
ecosystem (noun)
flourish (verb)
　flourishing (adj)
indigenous (adj)

flora (uncount)
germinate (verb)
  germination (uncount)
nutrient (noun)
photosynthesis (uncount)
pollen (noun)
  pollinate (verb)
  pollination (uncount)
unspoiled (adj)
vegetation (uncount)

adolescent (adj, noun)
  adolescence (uncount)
breed (noun, verb)
mate (noun, verb)
maternal (adj)
  maternity (adj)
nurture (verb, uncount)
paternal (adj)

Health
appetite (noun)
blood pressure (uncount)
carbohydrate (noun)
immune (adj)
  immunity (uncount)
immune system (noun)
intake (noun)
posture (noun)
  postural (adj)
protein (noun)

Healthcare
administer (verb)
anaesthetic (noun)
  anaesthetize (verb)
  anaesthetist (noun)
antibiotic (noun)
antiseptic (noun, adj)
dilute (verb, adj)
  dilution (uncount, noun)
donate (verb)
  donation (noun)
  donor (noun, adj)
dose (noun)
  dosage (noun)

immunize (verb)
  immunization (noun)
pathology (uncount)
  pathologist (noun)
pharmaceutical (adj, plural)
pharmacology (uncount)
  pharmacological (adj)
  pharmacologist (noun)
physiotherapy (uncount)
  physiotherapist (noun)
practitioner (noun)
psychiatry (uncount)
  psychiatric (adj)
  psychiatrist (noun)
remedy (noun)
therapy (uncount, noun)
  therapist (noun)
  therapeutic (adj)
transplant (noun, verb)
  transplantation (uncount)
vaccine (noun)
  vaccinate (verb)
  vaccination (noun)

Illness
acute (adj)
addict (noun)
  addiction (noun)
  addictive (adj)
allergy (noun)
  allergic (adj)
chronic (adj)
  chronically (adv)
deficient (adj, comb)
  deficiency (noun)
dehydrate (verb)
  dehydrated (adj)
  dehydration (uncount)
epidemic (noun)
obese (adj)
  obesity (uncount)
overweight (adj)
stroke (noun)
syndrome (noun)
terminal (adj, noun)
transmit (verb)
  transmission (uncount)
trauma (uncount)

Geography

Astronomy
galaxy (noun)
lunar (adj)
orbit (noun, verb)
solar system (noun)

Physical geography
condense (verb)
  condensation (uncount)
cyclone (noun)
evaporate (verb)
  evaporation (uncount)
hurricane (noun)
meteorology (uncount)
monsoon (noun)
temperate (adj)
tide (noun)
  tidal (adj)
typhoon (noun)

equator (noun)
hemisphere (noun)
latitude (noun, adj)
longitude (noun, adj)
terrestrial (adj)

arid (adj)
biodiversity (uncount)
crater (noun)
ecosystem (noun)
fauna (noun)
flora (uncount)
glacier (noun)
marine (adj)
porous (adj)
summit (noun)
volcano (noun)
  volcanic (adj)

Sociology

People & family
adolescent (adj, noun)
   adolescence (uncount)
feminine (adj)
marital status (uncount)
maternal (adj)
   maternity (adj)
paternal (adj)
peer (noun)
ritual (noun)
upbringing (uncount)

Population
census (noun)
civilian (noun, adj)
demography (uncount)
   demographic (adj, plural, noun)
indigenous (adj)
migrate (verb)
   migration (noun)
opinion poll (noun)
overpopulation (uncount)
per capita (adj, adv)

Social difference
deprived (adj)
elite (noun)
   elitist (adj)
   elitism (uncount)
inequality (noun)
material (adj)
   materially (adv)
multicultural (adj)
   multiculturalism (uncount)
privilege (noun, uncount)
   privileged (adj, plural)
prosperous (adj)
   prosperity (uncount)
redistribute (verb)
   redistribution (uncount)
underprivileged (adj, plural)

Social issues
addict (noun)
   addiction (noun)
   addictive (adj)

burden (noun)
catastrophe (noun)
   catastrophic (adj)
   catastrophically (adv)
civil rights (plural)
combat (verb)
entitle (verb)
   entitlement (noun)
ethics (plural, uncount)
   ethical (adj)
feminism (uncount)
   feminist (noun, adj)
humanitarian (adj, noun)
refugee (noun)
secular (adj)
   secularized (adj)
sexism (uncount)
unethical (adj)

Politics

Government
ally (noun)
autonomy (uncount)
   autonomous (adj)
Cabinet (noun)
colony (noun)
   colonial (adj)
   colonialism (uncount)
   colonialist (adj, noun)
   colonize (verb)
Congress (noun)
   congressional (adj)
constitution (noun)
   constitutional (adj)
counterpart (noun)
coup (noun)
dictator (noun)
   dictatorship (noun)
empire (noun)
   emperor (noun)
legislature (noun)
monarch (noun)
   monarchy (noun)
regime (noun)
sovereign (adj)

Political activities
administer (verb)
combat (verb)
redistribute (verb)
  redistribution (uncount)
suppress (verb)
  suppression (uncount)

Political beliefs
advocate (verb, noun)
  advocacy (noun)
civil rights (plural)
condemn (verb)
  condemnation (noun)
dogma (noun)
  dogmatic (adj)
  dogmatically (adv)
  dogmatism (uncount)
fascism (uncount)
  fascist (adj)
ideology (noun)
  ideological (adj)
liberal (adj, noun)
liberty (noun)
opinion poll (noun)
propaganda (uncount)
rebel (noun)
  rebellion (noun)
terrorist (noun)
  terrorism (uncount)
unanimous (adj)
  unanimously (adv)

Politics & the law
capital punishment (uncount)
comply (verb)
  compliance (uncount)
protocol (noun)
ratify (verb)
  ratification (uncount)
sanction (verb, uncount, plural, noun)
summit (noun)
treaty (noun)
unrest (uncount)
veto (verb, noun)

Business

Business finance
audit (verb, noun)
  auditor (noun)
compensate (verb)
  compensation (uncount)
creditor (noun)
deduct (verb)
  deduction (noun, uncount)
gross (adj, adv, verb)
levy (noun, verb)
liquidate (verb)
  liquidation (noun)
net (adj, adv)
quarter (noun)
  quarterly (adj, adv)
quota (noun)
reimburse (verb)
  reimbursement (noun)
return (noun)
revenue (uncount)
tariff (noun)
turnover (noun)

Business organizations
enterprise (noun)
entrepreneur (noun)
  entrepreneurial (adj)
  entrepreneurship (uncount)
found (verb)
  foundation (noun)
  founder (noun)
franchise (noun, verb)
Incorporated (adj)
merge (verb)
  merger (noun)
pharmaceutical (adj, plural)
restructure (verb)
  restructuring (noun)
rival (noun)
  rivalry (noun)
share (noun)
stake (noun)
stakeholder (noun)
subsidiary (noun, adj)
takeover (noun)

Work & business

collaborate (verb)
  collaboration (noun)
  collaborative (adj)
commodity (noun)
copyright (noun)
endorse (verb)
monopoly (noun)
  monopolize (verb)
niche (noun, adj)
offset (verb)
patent (noun, verb)

blue-collar (adj)
casual (adj)
commission (verb, noun, uncount)
counterpart (noun)
perk (noun, ph verb)
redundant (adj)
  redundancy (noun)
vocational (adj)
white-collar (adj)

Economics

audit (verb, noun)
  auditor (noun)
boom (noun, verb)
commodity (noun)
creditor (noun)
deficit (noun)
depress (verb)
  depressed (adj)
  depression (noun)
fiscal (adj)
  fiscally (adv)
GDP (noun)
gross (adj, adv, verb)
levy (noun, verb)
macroeconomics (uncount)
  macroeconomic (adj)
microeconomics (uncount)
  microeconomic (adj)
net (adj, adv)
per capita (adj, adv)

prosperous (adj)
  prosperity (uncount)
quarter (noun)
  quarterly (adj, adv)
recession (noun)
return (noun)
revenue (uncount)
share (noun)

Law

abide by (ph verb)
enforce (verb)
  enforcement (uncount)
invoke (verb)
jurisdiction (uncount)
lawsuit (noun)
legislature (noun)
legitimate (adj)
  legitimacy (uncount)
  legitimately (adv)
litigate (verb)
prosecute (verb)
  prosecution (noun)
  prosecutor (noun)
unanimous (adj)
  unanimously (adv)

Criminal law

attorney (noun)
convict (verb)
cross-examine (verb)
  cross-examination (noun)
death penalty (noun)
deter (verb)
  deterrent (noun)
fraud (noun)
  fraudulent (adj)
imprison (verb)
  imprisonment (uncount)
perpetrate (verb)
  perpetrator (noun)
plead (verb)
  plea (noun)
proceedings (plural)
testify (verb)
  testimony (noun)

International & commercial law

clause (noun)
comply (verb)
   compliance (uncount)
copyright (noun)
exempt (adj, verb)
   exemption (noun)
negligent (adj)
   negligence (uncount)
ratify (verb)
   ratification (uncount)
sanction (verb, uncount, plural, noun)
statutory (adj)
treaty (noun)
uphold (verb)
violate (verb)
   violation (noun)

Education

curriculum (noun)
literate (adj)
   literacy (uncount)
scholar (noun)
syllabus (noun)

vocational (adj)
workshop (noun)

Academic subjects

anatomy (uncount, noun)
   anatomical (adj)
   anatomically (adv)
biochemistry (uncount)
   biochemical (adj)
   biochemist (noun)
biotechnology (uncount)
   biotechnologist (noun)
genetics (uncount)
   genetic (adj)
   genetically (adv)
   geneticist (noun)
meteorology (uncount)
microbiology (uncount)
   microbiological (adj)
   microbiologist (noun)
pathology (uncount)
   pathologist (noun)
pharmacology (uncount)
   pharmacological (adj)
   pharmacologist (noun)
physiotherapy (uncount)
   physiotherapist (noun)

Art

aesthetic (adj, noun)
aesthetically (adv)
aesthetics (uncount)
depict (verb)
depiction (noun)
genre (noun)
icon (noun)
iconic (adj)
imagery (uncount)
invoke (verb)
portrait (noun)
sculpture (noun, uncount)
sculptor (noun)
vivid (adj)
vividly (adv)

Literature

biography (noun)
biographical (adj)
depict (verb)
depiction (noun)
drama (noun)
dramatist (noun)
entitle (verb)
evoke (verb)
figurative (adj)
figuratively (adv)
genre (noun)
imagery (uncount)
literal (adj)
manuscript (noun)
metaphor (noun)
metaphorical (adj)
metaphorically (adv)
monologue (noun)
narrative (noun, uncount)
narrate (verb)
narrator (noun)
theme (noun)
thematic (adj)
thematically (adv)

Linguistics

analogy (noun)
analogous (adj)
clause (noun)
coin (verb)
connotation (noun)
dialect (noun)
discourse (uncount)
figurative (adj)
figuratively (adv)
literal (adj)
metaphor (noun)
metaphorical (adj)
metaphorically (adv)
monologue (noun)
mother tongue (noun)
nuance (noun)
oral (adj)
orally (adv)
paraphrase (verb, noun)
rhetoric (uncount)
rhetorical (adj)
sign language (noun)
transcript (noun)
transcribe (verb)
verbal (adj)

History

archive (noun)
archivist (noun)
artefact (noun)
carbon dating (uncount)
excavate (verb)
excavation (noun)
fossil (noun)
manuscript (noun)
Roman numeral (noun)

colony (noun)
colonial (adj)
colonialism (uncount)
colonialist (adj, noun)
colonize (verb)

empire (noun)
  emperor (noun)
monarch (noun)
  monarchy (noun)
ritual (noun)

advent (uncount)
ancestor (noun)
  ancestry (noun)
chronological (adj)
  chronologically (adv)

forerunner (noun)
heritage (noun)
medieval (adj)
Middle Ages (plural)
milestone (noun)
millennium (noun)
predate (verb)
primitive (adj)
Renaissance (noun)

Actions & processes

activate (verb)
 activation (uncount)
proceed (verb)

employ (verb)
expend (verb)

administer (verb)
disperse (verb)
 dispersal (uncount)
displace (verb)
 displacement (uncount)
execute (verb)
 execution (uncount)
fulfil (verb)
 fulfilment (uncount)
imitate (verb)
 imitation (noun)
inflate (verb)
interact (verb)
 interaction (noun)
 interactive (adj)
opt (verb)
reinforce (verb)
 reinforcement (uncount)
replicate (verb)
strive (verb)

accumulate (verb)
 accumulation (noun)
attain (verb)
 attainment (noun)
compile (verb)
 compilation (noun)
secure (verb)
unify (verb)
 unification (uncount)

endure (verb)
exemplify (verb)
exhibit (verb)
flourish (verb)
 flourishing (adj)
incorporate (verb)
permeate (verb)
persist (verb)

prolong (verb)
thrive (verb)
withstand (verb)

assist (verb)
 assistance (uncount)
devote (verb)
 devotion (uncount)
facilitate (verb)
guidance (uncount)
optimize (verb)

arrest (verb)
combat (verb)
curb (verb, noun)
defer (verb)
erase (verb)
exhaust (verb, uncount)
resolve (verb)
 resolution (noun)
stem (verb)
suspend (verb)
 suspension (uncount)
terminate (verb)
 termination (uncount)

aggravate (verb)
counter (verb)
counteract (verb)
deduct (verb)
 deduction (noun, uncount)
exacerbate (verb)
interfere (verb)
 interference (uncount)
neglect (verb, uncount)
obstruct (verb)
 obstruction (noun)
omit (verb)
 omission (noun, uncount)
precaution (noun)
 precautionary (adj)
resist (verb)
 resistance (uncount)
 resistant (adj)
safeguard (verb, noun)
undermine (verb)

abide by (ph verb)
assign (verb)
comply (verb)
  compliance (uncount)
conform (verb)
constrain (verb)
  constraint (noun)
enforce (verb)
  enforcement (uncount)
exert (verb)
grant (noun, verb)
incur (verb)
inhibit (verb)
  inhibition (uncount)
intervene (verb)
  intervention (uncount)
restrain (verb)
  restraint (noun)
scrutinize (verb)
  scrutiny (uncount)

Change

acclimatize (verb)
merge (verb)
restore (verb)
  restoration (uncount)

amend (verb)
  amendment (noun)
deviate (verb)
  deviation (noun)
distort (verb)
  distortion (noun)
divert (verb)
manipulate (verb)
  manipulation (noun)
refine (verb)
  refinement (noun)
transition (noun)
  transitional (adj)

accelerate (verb)
  acceleration (uncount)
boom (noun, verb)
enlarge (verb)
  enlargement (uncount)
perk up (ph verb)

contract (verb)
  contraction (noun)
deplete (verb)
  depletion (uncount)
depress (verb)
  depressed (adj)
  depression (noun)
deteriorate (verb)
  deterioration (uncount)
diminish (verb)
dwindle (verb)
eradicate (verb)
  eradication (uncount)
erode (verb)
  erosion (uncount)
relax (verb)
  relaxation (uncount)
shrink (verb)
tail off (ph verb)

dynamic (adj, noun, plural, uncount)
marked (adj)
  markedly (adv)
status quo (noun)
volatile (adj)
  volatility (uncount)

Mental processes

anticipate (verb)
  in anticipation of (phrase)
appreciate (verb)
  appreciation (noun)
cognitive (adj)
comprehend (verb)
  comprehension (uncount)
conceive (verb)
  conceivable (adj)
  conceivably (adv)
envisage (verb)
expertise (uncount)
formulate (verb)
infer (verb)
  inference (noun, uncount)
intuition (noun)
  intuitive (adj)
  intuitively (adv)

misinterpret (verb)
 misinterpretation (noun)
reassess (verb)
 reassessment (noun)
recall (verb, uncount)

Speech & reporting

clarify (verb)
 clarification (uncount)
 clarity (uncount)
convey (verb)
denote (verb)
depict (verb)
 depiction (noun)
evoke (verb)
explore (verb)
 exploration (noun)
extrapolate (verb)
redefine (verb)
signify (verb)
specify (verb)
 specification (noun)

assert (verb)
 assertion (noun)
contend (verb)
 contention (noun)
point out (ph verb)
speculate (verb)
 speculation (noun)

pose (verb)
query (noun, verb)
respond (verb)
 response (noun)
 respondent (noun)

acknowledge (verb)
 acknowledgement (noun, plural)
attribute (verb)
cite (verb)

advocate (verb, noun)
condemn (verb)
 condemnation (noun)

endorse (verb)

assure (verb)
 assurance (noun)
consent (uncount, verb)
 consensus (noun)
convince (verb)
 convincing (adj)
mediate (verb)
 mediation (uncount)
testify (verb)
 testimony (noun)

compelling (adj)
explicit (adj)
 explicitly (adv)
figurative (adj)
 figuratively (adv)
implicit (adj)
 implicitly (adv)
incoherent (adj)
 incoherently (adv)
 incoherence (uncount)
literal (adj)

Compare & contrast

complement (verb)
 complementary (adj)
converse (noun)
 conversely (adv)
differentiate (verb)
 differentiation (uncount)
discrete (adj)
discriminate (verb)
 discrimination (uncount)
diverse (adj)
 diversity (uncount)
 diversify (verb)
 diversification (noun)
mirror (verb)
resemble (verb)
 resemblance (noun)
synonymous (adj)
tally (verb)

Cause & effect

account for (ph verb)
attribute (verb)
chain reaction (noun)
coincide (verb)
  coincidence (noun)
  coincidental (adj)
derive (verb)
  derivative (noun)
incentive (noun)
induce (verb)
initiate (verb)
  initiation (uncount)
initiative (noun)
interconnect (verb)
  interconnection (noun)
interdependent (adj)
  interdependence (uncount)
interrelate (verb)
motive (noun)
negate (verb)
  negation (noun)
pinpoint (verb)
product (noun)
prompt (verb)
provoke (verb)
rationale (noun)
repercussion (noun)
stem (verb)
whereby (pron)

Time

defer (verb)
endure (verb)
  enduring (adj)
imminent (adj)
prolong (verb)
  prolonged (adj)
thereafter (adv)

forerunner (noun)
precede (verb)
  precedent (noun)
  precedence (uncount)
predate (verb)

foresee (verb)
hindsight (uncount)
in retrospect (phrase)
  retrospective (adj)
  retrospectively (adv)
unforeseen (adj)
unprecedented (adj)

indefinite (adj)
  indefinitely (adv)
inexorable (adj)
  inexorably (adv)
interim (adj)
monotonous (adj)
  monotonously (adv)
  monotony (uncount)
quarter (noun)
  quarterly (adj, adv)
span (noun)
term (noun)
time-consuming (adj)

advent (uncount)
landmark (noun)

coincide (verb)
  coincidence (noun)
  coincidental (adj)
concurrent (adj)
  concurrently (adv)

consecutive (adj)
  consecutively (adv)
penultimate (adj)
successive (adj)

incidence (noun)
intermittent (adj)
  intermittently (adv)
periodic (adj)
  periodical (adj, noun)
  periodically (adv)

Structures

attribute (verb)
constituent (noun, adj)

cross-section (noun)
particle (noun)
trace (verb, ph verb, noun)

inherent (adj)
  inherently (adv)
integral (adj)
interconnect (verb)
  interconnection (noun)
interdependent (adj)
  interdependence (uncount)
intrinsic (adj)
  intrinsically (adv)

hierarchy (noun)
  hierarchical (adj)
interface (noun, verb)
restructure (verb)
  restructuring (noun)

domain (noun)
entity (noun)
medium (noun)
mode (noun)
sphere (noun)
theme (noun)
  thematic (adj)
  thematically (adv)

Shape & position

ellipse (noun)
  elliptical (adj)
hexagon (noun)
  hexagonal (adj)
pentagon (noun)
pyramid (noun)
three-dimensional (adj)
two-dimensional (adj)

adjacent (adj)
axis (noun)
confined (adj)
cross-section (noun)
intersect (verb)
  intersection (noun)
proximity (uncount)

rigid (adj)
  rigidity (uncount)
  rigidly (adv)
texture (noun)
uniform (adj)
  uniformly (adv)
  uniformity (uncount)

Size & amount

abundant (adj)
  abundantly (adv)
appreciable (adj)
  appreciably (adv)
bulk (quant, pron)
dense (adj)
  density (noun)

marginal (adj)
  marginally (adv)
negligible (adj)
scarce (adj)

enlarge (verb)
  enlargement (uncount)
maximize (verb)
  maximization (uncount)
minimize (verb)

aggregate (adj, noun)
dual (adj)

account for (ph verb)
gauge (verb, noun)
magnitude (uncount)
margin (noun)
mean (noun)
median (adj)
per capita (adj, adv)
proportional (adj)
  proportionally (adv)
quantity (noun)
  quantitative (adj)
  quantitatively (adv)
quota (noun)
surpass (verb)
threshold (noun)
underestimate (verb)

Opinion, uncertainty & probability

assertion (noun)
conjecture (noun)
contention (noun)
dogma (noun)
  dogmatic (adj)
  dogmatically (adv)
  dogmatism (uncount)
orthodox (adj)
pragmatic (adj)
  pragmatically (adv)
  pragmatism (uncount)
speculation (noun)
stance (noun)

arbitrary (adj)
  arbitrarily (adv)
compulsory (adj)
  compulsorily (adv)
discretion (uncount)
  discretionary (adj)

apparent (adj)
caution (uncount)
  cautious (adj)
  cautiously (adv)
notional (adj)
  notionally (adv)
prone (adj, comb)
provisional (adj)
  provisionally (adv)
reportedly (adv)
sceptic (noun)
  sceptical (adj)
  scepticism (uncount)
so-called (adj)
tentative (adj)
  tentatively (adv)

credible (adj)
viable (adj)
  viability (uncount)

Importance & degree

acute (adj)
chronic (adj)
  chronically (adv)
core (noun)
crucial (adj)
  crucially (adv)
intense (adj)
  intensity (noun)
  intensify (verb)
  intensification (uncount)
marked (adj)
  markedly (adv)
pervasive (adj)
pivotal (adj)
predominant (adj)
  predominantly (adv)
pressing (adj)
profound (adj)
  profoundly (adv)
prominent (adj)
  prominently (adv)
  prominence (uncount)
pronounced (adj)
rigorous (adj)
  rigorously (adv)
seminal (adj)
striking (adj)

negligible (adj)
subordinate (adj)

Positive qualities

authentic (adj)
  authenticity (uncount)
coherent (adj)
  coherence (uncount)
compatible (adj)
  compatibility (uncount)
compelling (adj)
constructive (adj)
credible (adj)
groundbreaking (adj)

integrity (uncount)
legitimate (adj)
  legitimacy (uncount)
  legitimately (adv)
optimum (adj)
rigorous (adj)
  rigorously (adv)
state-of-the-art (adj)
succinct (adj)
  succinctly (adv)

Negative qualities

abnormal (adj)
  abnormally (adv)
adverse (adj)
  adversely (adv)
catastrophic (adj)
  catastrophically (adv)
deficient (adj, comb)
  deficiency (noun)
deprived (adj)
flaw (noun)
  flawed (adj)
fraudulent (adj)
hostile (adj)
illogical (adj)
incoherent (adj)
  incoherently (adv)
  incoherence (uncount)
incompatible (adj)
  incompatibility (uncount)

inequality (noun)
insufficient (adj)
  insufficiency (uncount)
  insufficiently (adv)
irreparable (adj)
  irreparably (adv)
monotonous (adj)
  monotonously (adv)
  monotony (uncount)
needless (adj)
  needlessly (adv)
negligent (adj)
  negligence (uncount)
obstacle (noun)
obstruction (noun)
prone (adj, comb)
shortcoming (noun)
underprivileged (adj, plural)
unethical (adj)
unpredictable (adj)
volatile (adj)
  volatility (uncount)

Linking words

aforementioned (adj)
nonetheless (adv)
notwithstanding (prep, adv)
regardless of (phrase)
thereafter (adv)
thereby (adv)
whereby (pron)

Research methods

apparatus (uncount)
fieldwork (uncount)
in the field (phrase)
Petri dish (noun)
prototype (noun)
test tube (noun)

catalogue (verb)
chronological (adj)
 chronologically (adv)
collaborate (verb)
 collaboration (noun)
 collaborative (adj)
collate (verb)
 collation (uncount)
correlate (verb)
 correlation (noun)
cross-section (noun)
document (verb)
empirical (adj)
 empirically (adv)
hypothesis (noun)
 hypothesize (verb)
paradigm (noun)
parameter (noun)
peer review (uncount)
pilot study (noun)
qualitative (adj)
 qualitatively (adv)
quantitative (adj)
 quantitatively (adv)
rationale (noun)
schematic (adj)
theorem (noun)
transcript (noun)
 transcribe (verb)

conclusive (adj)
 conclusively (adv)

deduce (verb)
 deduction (noun, uncount)
 deductive (adj)
definitive (adj)
 definitively (adv)
inconclusive (adj)
tentative (adj)
 tentatively (adv)

Texts

abstract (noun)
bibliography (noun)
commentary (noun, uncount)
footnote (noun)
paper (noun)
periodical (adj, noun)
prècis (noun)

Reporting from sources

acknowledge (verb)
 acknowledgement (noun, plural)
cite (verb)
paraphrase (verb, noun)
plagiarism (uncount)
 plagiarize (verb)

Writing conventions

asterisk (noun)
cf.
et al.
ibid (conv)
NB
Roman numeral (noun)

abnormal (adj)
  abnormally (adv)
abstract (noun)
accumulate (verb)
  accumulation (noun)
acknowledge (verb)
  acknowledgement (noun, plural)
adjacent (adj)
advocate (verb, noun)
  advocacy (noun)
aggregate (adj, noun)
amend (verb)
  amendment (noun)
analogy (noun)
  analogous (adj)
anticipate (verb)
  in anticipation of (phrase)
apparent (adj)
appreciable (adj)
  appreciably (adv)
appreciate (verb)
  appreciation (noun)
arbitrary (adj)
  arbitrarily (adv)
assign (verb)
assist (verb)
  assistance (uncount)
assure (verb)
  assurance (noun)
attain (verb)
  attainment (noun)
attribute (verb)
automate (verb)
  automation (uncount)
bulk (quant, pron)
cite (verb)
clarify (verb)
  clarification (uncount)
  clarity (uncount)
clause (noun)
coherent (adj)
  coherence (uncount)
coincide (verb)
  coincidence (noun)
  coincidental (adj)
commentary (noun, uncount)
commission (verb, noun, uncount)
commodity (noun)
compatible (adj)

compatibility (uncount)
compensate (verb)
  compensation (uncount)
compile (verb)
  compilation (noun)
complement (verb)
  complementary (adj)
compound (noun)
conceive (verb)
  conceivable (adj)
  conceivably (adv)
conclusive (adj)
  conclusively (adv)
concurrent (adj)
  concurrently (adv)
confined (adj)
conform (verb)
consent (uncount, verb)
  consensus (noun)
constitution (noun)
  constitutional (adj)
constrain (verb)
  constraint (noun)
contract (verb)
  contraction (noun)
converse (noun)
  conversely (adv)
convince (verb)
  convincing (adj)
core (noun)
coup (noun)
crucial (adj)
  crucially (adv)
crystal (noun)
deduce (verb)
  deduction (noun, uncount)
  deductive (adj)
definitive (adj)
  definitively (adv)
denote (verb)
depress (verb)
  depressed (adj)
  depression (noun)
derive (verb)
  derivative (noun)
deviate (verb)
  deviation (noun)
devote (verb)
  devotion (uncount)

differentiate (verb)
  differentiation (uncount)
diminish (verb)
discrete (adj)
discretion (uncount)
  discretionary (adj)
discriminate (verb)
  discrimination (uncount)
displace (verb)
  displacement (uncount)
distort (verb)
  distortion (noun)
diverse (adj)
  diversity (uncount)
  diversify (verb)
  diversification (noun)
document (verb)
domain (noun)
drama (noun)
  dramatist (noun)
dynamic (adj, noun, plural, uncount)
empirical (adj)
  empirically (adv)
enforce (verb)
  enforcement (uncount)
entity (noun)
erode (verb)
  erosion (uncount)
ethic (plural, uncount)
  ethical (adj)
exhibit (verb)
explicit (adj)
  explicitly (adv)
extract (verb)
  extraction (uncount)
facilitate (verb)
found (verb)
  foundation (noun)
  founder (noun)
grant (noun, verb)
hierarchy (noun)
  hierarchical (adj)
hypothesis (noun)
  hypothesize (verb)
ideology (noun)
  ideological (adj)
illogical (adj)
imagery (uncount)

implicit (adj)
  implicitly (adv)
incentive (noun)
incident (noun)
  incidence (noun)
inclined (adj)
  inclination (noun)
incompatible (adj)
  incompatibility (uncount)
inconclusive (adj)
incorporate (verb)
Incorporated (adj)
indefinite (adj)
  indefinitely (adv)
induce (verb)
inherent (adj)
  inherently (adv)
inhibit (verb)
  inhibition (uncount)
initiate (verb)
  initiation (uncount)
initiative (noun)
insufficient (adj)
  insufficiency (uncount)
  insufficiently (adv)
integral (adj)
integrity (uncount)
intense (adj)
  intensity (noun)
  intensify (verb)
  intensification (uncount)
intervene (verb)
  intervention (uncount)
intrinsic (adj)
  intrinsically (adv)
invoke (verb)
legislature (noun)
levy (noun, verb)
liberal (adj, noun)
manipulate (verb)
  manipulation (noun)
margin (noun)
  marginal (adj)
  marginally (adv)
maximize (verb)
  maximization (uncount)
mediate (verb)
  mediation (uncount)
medium (noun)

migrate (verb)
  migration (noun)
minimize (verb)
misinterpret (verb)
  misinterpretation (noun)
mode (noun)
motion (uncount)
motive (noun)
nonetheless (adv)
notwithstanding (prep, adv)
offset (verb)
orient (verb)
  oriented (adj)
  orientation (noun)
paradigm (noun)
parameter (noun)
passive (adj)
periodic (adj)
  periodical (adj, noun)
  periodically (adv)
persist (verb)
  persistent (adj)
  persistently (adv)
pose (verb)
practitioner (noun)
precede (verb)
  precedent (noun)
  precedence (uncount)
predominant (adj)
  predominantly (adv)
proceed (verb)
proceeding (noun)
proportional (adj)
  proportionally (adv)
protocol (noun)
quality (uncount)
  qualitative (adj)
  qualitatively (adv)
quantity (noun)
  quantitative (adj)
  quantitatively (adv)
reassess (verb)
  reassessment (noun)
redefine (verb)
redistribute (verb)
  redistribution (uncount)
refine (verb)
  refinement (noun)

regime (noun)
reinforce (verb)
  reinforcement (uncount)
relax (verb)
  relaxation (uncount)
resolve (verb)
  resolution (noun)
respond (verb)
  response (noun)
  respondent (noun)
restore (verb)
  restoration (uncount)
restrain (verb)
  restraint (noun)
restructure (verb)
  restructuring (noun)
revenue (uncount)
rigid (adj)
  rigidity (uncount)
  rigidly (adv)
scenario (noun)
schematic (adj)
secure (verb)
signify (verb)
so-called (adj)
sole (adj)
  solely (adv)
specify (verb)
  specification (noun)
sphere (noun)
subordinate (adj)
subsidiary (noun, adj)
successive (adj)
suspend (verb)
  suspension (uncount)
terminal (adj, noun)
terminate (verb)
  termination (uncount)
theme (noun)
  thematic (adj)
  thematically (adv)
thereby (adv)
trace (verb, ph verb, noun)
transition (noun)
  transitional (adj)
transmit (verb)
  transmission (uncount)
underestimate (verb)
unethical (adj)

uniform (adj)
  uniformly (adv)
  uniformity (uncount)
unify (verb)
  unification (uncount)
unpredictable (adj)
unspecified (adj)
utility (uncount)
violate (verb)
  violation (noun)
whereby (pron)

Key to grammatical labels used in word lists

adj	adjective
adv	adverb
comb	combining form
noun	noun
phrase	phrase
ph verb	phrasal verb
plural	plural noun
prep	preposition
pron	pronoun
quant	quantifier
uncount	uncountable noun
verb	verb

Key Words
A–Z

Aa

abide by /əˈbaɪd baɪ/ **(abides by, abiding by, abided by)** `LAW`

PHRASAL VERB If you **abide by** a law, agreement, or decision, you do what it says you should do. ○ *a warning to employees to improve performance levels and abide by organizational rules* ○ *making sure that people abide by the law*

→ see note at **comply**

▶ **COLLOCATIONS:**
abide by a **rule/law/restriction**
abide by a **ceasefire/agreement**

▶ **SYNONYMS:** observe, obey, adhere to

▶ **ANTONYM:** disobey

ab|nor|mal /æbˈnɔːməl/ `ACADEMIC WORD`

ADJECTIVE Someone or something that is **abnormal** is unusual, especially in a way that is worrying. [FORMAL] ○ *abnormal heart rhythms and high anxiety levels* ○ *a child with an abnormal fear of strangers* ○ *Nothing abnormal was detected.*

▶ **COLLOCATIONS:**
abnormal **bleeding/cells/behaviour**
an abnormal **heartbeat/rhythm/smear/mammogram**

▶ **SYNONYMS:** aberrant, deviant, irregular, unusual

▶ **ANTONYM:** normal

ab|nor|mal|ly /æbˈnɔːməli/

ADVERB ○ *abnormally high levels of glucose* ○ *This stops the cells from growing abnormally.*

▶ **COLLOCATIONS:**
abnormally **high/low/large/thin**
grow/behave/develop abnormally

▶ **SYNONYM:** unusually

▶ **ANTONYM:** normally

ab|stract /ˈæbstrækt/ **(abstracts)** `ACADEMIC WORD` `ACADEMIC STUDY`

NOUN An **abstract of** an article, document, or speech is a short piece of writing that gives the main points of it. ○ [+ *of*] *Many scientists only have enough time to read the abstracts of papers.* ○ [+ *of*] *Some indexes also have abstracts or summaries of articles.*

▶ **COLLOCATIONS:**
an abstract **of** *something*
an abstract of a **paper/article**
read/write/review/submit an abstract

▶ **SYNONYMS:** summary, précis

ACADEMIC WRITING: Academic summaries

A **summary** is a general word for a short piece of writing or a spoken account that gives the main points of something longer. You can talk about a **summary** in lots of different contexts. ○ *Each manager receives a summary of this information.* ○ *This article provides a brief summary of some of the main evidence available.*

Précis is a more formal word for a short piece of writing or a spoken account giving only the main points of a longer text. ○ *George gives a succinct oral précis of Fernando Joao's novel.*

An **abstract** is a summary of an academic paper that appears at the beginning of the paper so that readers can see the main points and decide whether to read the full text. It can also be a written summary of an academic presentation, for example, at a conference. An **abstract** usually has a set structure and length. ○ *We reviewed all abstracts and selected relevant, research-based articles.*

---

abun|dant /əˈbʌndənt/

ADJECTIVE Something that is **abundant** is present in large quantities.
○ *There is an abundant supply of cheap labour.* ○ *Birds are abundant in the tall vegetation.* ○ *Hydrogen is the most abundant element in the universe.*

▶ **COLLOCATIONS:**
abundant **wildlife/evidence/resources**
an abundant **supply/element**

▶ **SYNONYM:** plentiful

▶ **ANTONYM:** sparse

abun|dant|ly /əˈbʌndəntli/

ADVERB ○ *a plant that grows abundantly in the United States* ○ *All the pages are abundantly illustrated with colour photographs.*

▶ COLLOCATIONS:
grow/flower abundantly
abundantly **documented/illustrated/demonstrated**
▶ SYNONYM: plentifully
▶ ANTONYM: sparsely

---

ac|cel|er|ate /æk'seləreɪt/ (accelerates, accelerating, accelerated)

1 VERB If the process or rate of something **accelerates** or if something **accelerates** it, it gets faster and faster. ○ [+ to] *Growth will accelerate to 2.9 per cent next year.* ○ *The government is to accelerate its privatisation programme.*

2 VERB When a moving vehicle **accelerates**, it goes faster and faster. ○ *Traffic calming often created extra noise as motorists accelerated and braked around traffic islands.* ○ [+ to] *A police video showed the patrol car accelerating to 115mph.*

▶ COLLOCATIONS:
accelerate **to** x
accelerate **pace/growth**
accelerate a **process/trend/timetable**
accelerate **smoothly/gradually/rapidly/sharply**
a **car/driver** accelerates
inflation/growth/decline accelerates
▶ SYNONYM: hasten
▶ ANTONYM: decelerate

ac|cel|era|tion /æk,selə'reɪʃən/

UNCOUNTABLE NOUN ○ [+ of] *He has also called for an acceleration of political reforms.* ○ [+ in] *the sharp acceleration in job losses* ○ *Acceleration to 60 mph takes a mere 5.7 seconds.* ○ *The flexible engine provides smooth acceleration at low speeds.*

▶ COLLOCATIONS:
acceleration **of/in** something
acceleration of **growth/change/cuts**
quick/rapid/sudden acceleration
provide/show acceleration
▶ ANTONYM: deceleration

---

ac|cli|ma|tize /ə'klaɪmətaɪz/ (acclimatizes, acclimatizing, acclimatized)

VERB When you **acclimatize** or **are acclimatized to** a new situation, place, or climate, you become used to it. [FORMAL; in BRIT, also use

a

acclimatise] ○ [+ to] *Childhood eczema is caused by the body becoming acclimatized to the type of diet that we now eat.* ○ *soldiers struggling to acclimatize themselves* ○ *If you are changing altitudes rapidly, allow time to acclimatize.*

▶ COLLOCATION: acclimatize **to** *something*

▶ SYNONYMS: adapt, adjust

---

ac|count for /əˈkaʊnt fə, STRONG ˌfɔː/
(accounts for, accounting for, accounted for)

1 PHRASAL VERB If a particular thing **accounts for** a part or proportion of something, that part or proportion consists of that thing, or is used or produced by it. ○ *Computers account for 5% of the country's commercial electricity consumption.* ○ *Pension funds currently account for around a third of all equity investment in Britain.*

▶ COLLOCATIONS:
  account for *an* amount **of** *something*
  account for *x* **per cent** of *something*
  account for a **portion/proportion** of *something*
  account for a **third/quarter** of *something*
  account for the **majority/bulk** of *something*
  account for **half/two-thirds** of *something*
  currently/collectively account for *something*

2 PHRASAL VERB If something **accounts for** a particular fact or situation, it causes or explains it. ○ *The blood pressure in veins is less than in arteries, and this accounts for the differences in their structures.*

▶ COLLOCATION: account for a **discrepancy/disparity/difference**

▶ SYNONYM: explain

3 PHRASAL VERB If you can **account for** something, you can explain it or give the necessary information about it. ○ *How do you account for the company's alarmingly high staff turnover?* ○ *Public money has to be properly accounted for.*

▶ COLLOCATION: **properly** account for *something*

▶ SYNONYM: explain

---

ac|cu|mu|late /əˈkjuːmjʊleɪt/   `ACADEMIC WORD`
(accumulates, accumulating, accumulated)

VERB When you **accumulate** things or when they **accumulate**, they collect or are gathered over a period of time. ○ *Households accumulate wealth across a broad spectrum of assets.* ○ [+ in] *Lead can accumulate in the* *body until toxic levels are reached.*

▶ COLLOCATIONS:
accumulate **in** *something*
accumulate in the **body/lungs/brain/atmosphere**
accumulate **wealth/debt/wisdom/knowledge**
accumulated **losses**
an accumulated **deficit**
evidence/fluids/toxins accumulate

▶ SYNONYMS: gather, amass

ac|cu|mu|la|tion /əˌkjuːmjʊˈleɪʃən/ (accumulations)

NOUN ○ [+ *of*] *technological advance and the accumulation of scientific knowledge* ○ [+ *of*] *an accumulation of fluid in the lungs* ○ *No economy can sustain such a colossal rate of capital accumulation.*

▶ COLLOCATIONS:
the accumulation **of** *something*
the accumulation of **wealth/capital/fluid/knowledge**
cause/prevent/increase/reduce accumulation

▶ SYNONYM: increase

▶ ANTONYMS: reduction, decrease

---

ac|knowl|edge /ækˈnɒlɪdʒ/ ACADEMIC STUDY ACADEMIC WORD
(acknowledges, acknowledging, acknowledged)

1 VERB If you **acknowledge** a fact or a situation, you accept or admit that it is true or that it exists. [FORMAL] ○ [+ *that*] *It is widely acknowledged that transferring knowledge in a classroom environment is very inefficient.* ○ *Belatedly, the government has acknowledged the problem.* ○ *There is an acknowledged risk of lung cancer from radon.*

2 VERB If someone's achievements, status, or qualities **are acknowledged**, they are known about and recognized by a lot of people, or by a particular group of people. ○ [+ *as*] *Davies is now widely acknowledged as one of the world's leading virtual reality artists.* ○ *Some of the clergy refused to acknowledge the new king's legitimacy.*

▶ COLLOCATIONS:
acknowledge *someone* **as** *something*
acknowledge the **existence/importance** of *something*
acknowledge the **need** for *something*
acknowledge **difficulties**
acknowledge a **fact/contribution/mistake/debt/risk**
publicly/readily acknowledge

a

widely/universally acknowledged
a **president/government/official** acknowledges
▶ SYNONYMS: accept, recognize, grant

3 VERB If you **acknowledge** the source of some information in a piece of academic writing, you state clearly where the information came from. ○ *Every time you borrow the words, facts, or ideas of others, you must acknowledge the source.*
▶ COLLOCATION: acknowledge a **source**
▶ RELATED WORDS: reference, cite

ac|knowl|edge|ment /æk'nɒlɪdʒmənt/ (acknowledgements)
also **acknowledgment**

1 NOUN An **acknowledgement** is a statement or action which recognizes that something exists or is true. ○ [+ *that*] *The President's resignation appears to be an acknowledgment that he has lost all hope of keeping the country together.* ○ [+ *of*] *This is a clear acknowledgement of the need to improve corporate governance.*
▶ COLLOCATIONS:
an acknowledgement **of** *something*
an acknowledgement of a **fact/need**
make an acknowledgement
a **public/official/tacit/formal** acknowledgement
▶ SYNONYM: recognition

2 PLURAL NOUN The **acknowledgements** in a book are the section in which the author thanks all the people who have helped him or her. ○ *In the acknowledgements, Weis lists five people who acted as research assistants.*

acous|tic /ə'kuːstɪk/ (acoustics)　PHYSICS

1 UNCOUNTABLE NOUN Acoustics is the scientific study of sound. ○ [+ *of*] *studying the acoustics of underwater volcanoes* ○ *simple laws of acoustics*

2 ADJECTIVE Acoustic means relating to sound or hearing. ○ *acoustic signals* ○ *acoustic sensors used to detect promising formations for drilling offshore*
▶ COLLOCATION: an acoustic **sensor/signal**
▶ RELATED WORD: aural

ac|ti|vate /'æktɪveɪt/ (activates, activating, activated)　SCIENCE

VERB If a device or process **is activated**, something causes it to start working. ○ *Video cameras with night vision can be activated by movement.*

○ *a voice-activated computer* ○ *Heat also activates enzymes which further destroy vitamins.*

▶ COLLOCATIONS:
activated **by** *something*
activate a **system/alarm/light/gene/enzyme**
voice/electronically/automatically activated

▶ SYNONYMS: trigger, initiate

▶ ANTONYM: deactivate

ac|ti|va|tion /ˌæktɪˈveɪʃən/

UNCOUNTABLE NOUN ○ [+ of] *A computer controls the activation of an air bag.* ○ *The activation code must be entered into the computer to print copies.*

▶ COLLOCATIONS:
the activation **of** *something*
trigger/require activation
an activation **code/fee**

acute /əˈkjuːt/ MEDICINE

1 ADJECTIVE You can use **acute** to indicate that an undesirable situation or feeling is very severe or intense. ○ *The war has aggravated an acute economic crisis.* ○ *The report has caused acute embarrassment to the government.* ○ *The labour shortage is becoming acute.*

2 ADJECTIVE An **acute** illness is one that becomes severe very quickly but does not last very long. ○ *a patient with acute rheumatoid arthritis* ○ *an acute case of dysentery*

▶ COLLOCATIONS:
acute **pain/embarrassment/symptoms/leukaemia**
an acute **shortage/problem/illness/infection**

▶ SYNONYM: severe

▶ ANTONYM: mild

▶ RELATED WORD: chronic

ad|dict /ˈædɪkt/ (addicts) MEDICINE

NOUN An **addict** is someone who takes harmful drugs and cannot stop taking them. ○ *The finding could help understand why recovering drug addicts relapse.* ○ *alcoholics and drug addicts*

▶ COLLOCATIONS:
a **drug/cocaine/heroin** addict
a **recovering/former/reformed** addict

ad|dic|tion /əˈdɪkʃən/ (addictions)

NOUN **Addiction** is the condition of taking harmful drugs and being unable to stop taking them. ○ *a model showing the transition from drug usage to drug addiction* ○ [+ *to*] *long-term addiction to nicotine*

▶ COLLOCATIONS:
addiction **to** *something*
drug/heroin/cocaine/nicotine/alcohol addiction
a **long-term/chronic/serious** addiction
cure/treat/overcome/fight against/feed an addiction
an addiction **problem/clinic/counsellor**

▶ SYNONYMS: dependence, habit

ad|dic|tive /əˈdɪktɪv/

ADJECTIVE If a drug is **addictive**, people who take it cannot stop taking it. ○ *Cigarettes are highly addictive.* ○ *Crack is the most addictive drug on the market.*

▶ COLLOCATIONS:
highly/potentially addictive
psychologically/physically addictive
an addictive **drug/substance**

▶ SYNONYM: habit-forming

ad|ja|cent /əˈdʒeɪsənt/ `ACADEMIC WORD`

ADJECTIVE If one thing is **adjacent to** another, the two things are next to each other. ○ *plans to redevelop the railway station and adjacent land* ○ [+ *to*] *surveys to monitor toxin levels in the areas adjacent to the incinerators*

▶ COLLOCATIONS:
adjacent **to** *something*
a **site/area** adjacent to *something*
an adjacent **building/neighbourhood**
adjacent **land**

▶ SYNONYMS: neighbouring, near

ad|min|is|ter /ædˈmɪnɪstə/ `POLITICS` `MEDICINE`
(administers, administering, administered)

1 VERB If someone **administers** something such as a country, the law, or a test, they take responsibility for organizing and supervising it. ○ *The plan calls for the U.N. to administer the country until elections can be held.* ○ *In some states these laws are administered by state agencies, and in others they are administered on a municipal level.*

▶ COLLOCATIONS:
administered **by** *someone/something*
administered by a **body/agency/committee**
administer **justice/punishment**
administer a **rite/oath/questionnaire**
administer a **law/country**
federally/centrally/jointly administered

▶ SYNONYMS: manage, oversee, supervise

2 VERB If a doctor or a nurse **administers** a drug, they give it to a patient. [FORMAL] ○ *Paramedics are trained to administer certain drugs.* ○ *Vitamins are administered orally or by injection into the veins or muscles.*

▶ COLLOCATIONS:
administer *something* **to** *someone*
administered **by** *someone/something*
administered by **injection**
administer a **dose/injection/vaccine/drug**
administer **medication/antibiotics/morphine**
orally/intravenously administered

▶ SYNONYM: dispense

---

ado|les|cent /ˌædəˈlesənt/ (adolescents)

ADJECTIVE Adolescent is used to describe young people who are no longer children but who have not yet become adults. It also refers to their behaviour. ○ *an area where early marriage and adolescent pregnancy are common* ○ *Nearly 1 percent of adolescent girls suffer from anorexia.*

▶ COLLOCATIONS:
an adolescent **boy/girl/male**
adolescent **psychiatry/sexuality**
adolescent **angst/rebellion**

▶ SYNONYMS: teenage, juvenile

• An **adolescent** is an adolescent boy or girl. ○ *Young adolescents are happiest with small groups of close friends.* ○ *Lack of sleep in humans, especially adolescents and young adults, might exacerbate skin problems.*

▶ SYNONYMS: teenager, young adult, youth

ado|les|cence /ˌædəˈlesəns/

UNCOUNTABLE NOUN Adolescence is the period of your life in which you develop from being a child into being an adult. ○ *The need for sleep is even greater during adolescence than at younger ages.* ○ *When the child reaches adolescence, this bond between mother and child faces its ultimate test.*

a

▶ COLLOCATIONS:
in/during adolescence
enter/reach/approach adolescence
early/protracted/extended adolescence
▶ SYNONYMS: puberty, youth

---

ad|vent /ˈædvent/

UNCOUNTABLE NOUN The advent of an important event, invention,
or situation is the fact of it starting or coming into existence. [FORMAL]
○ [+ of] *the leap forward in communication made possible by the advent of the
mobile phone* ○ [+ of] *The advent of war led to a greater austerity.*

▶ COLLOCATIONS:
the advent **of** *something*
the advent of **war/Christianity/capitalism**
mark/herald/celebrate/welcome the advent of *something*
▶ SYNONYMS: beginning, arrival

---

ad|verse /ˈædvɜːs, AM ædˈvɜːrs/

ADJECTIVE Adverse decisions, conditions, or effects are unfavourable to
you. ○ *There were no significant adverse effects attributable to the dosage of the
vitamin.* ○ *Despite the adverse conditions, the road was finished in just eight
months.*

▶ COLLOCATIONS:
adverse **conditions/findings/weather/publicity**
an adverse **comment/effect/impact/reaction**
materially/potentially adverse
▶ SYNONYMS: negative, unfavourable
▶ ANTONYMS: favourable, advantageous

ad|verse|ly /ˈædvɜːsli, AM ædˈvɜːrsli/

ADVERB ○ *Price changes must not adversely affect the living standards of the
people.* ○ *people who react adversely to foods*

▶ COLLOCATIONS:
adversely **affect/impact** *something*
react adversely
▶ SYNONYMS: negatively, unfavourably
▶ ANTONYMS: favourably, advantageously

ad|vo|cate (advocates, advocating, advocated) `ACADEMIC WORD`

> The verb is pronounced /'ædvəkeɪt/. The noun is pronounced /'ædvəkət/.

1 VERB If you **advocate** a particular action or plan, you recommend it publicly. [FORMAL] ○ *Mr Williams is a conservative who advocates fewer government controls on business.* ○ *the tax policy advocated by the Opposition*

▶ **COLLOCATIONS:**
  advocated **by** *someone*
  advocate **reform/legislation/violence**
  openly/strongly/publicly advocate
  long advocated

▶ **SYNONYM:** advance

▶ **ANTONYM:** oppose

EXTEND YOUR VOCABULARY

If you **support** an idea, a plan or an action, you agree with it and think it is right. You might or might not express your views publicly. ○ *Some ministers have openly supported positive discrimination.*

If you **recommend** something, you tell other people that you think it is good or that they should do it. You can **recommend** something to an individual privately, or you can **recommend** something more formally, for example, in an official report. ○ *A high-carbohydrate, low-fat diet is also recommended by many diabetes experts.*

If you **advocate** something, you strongly agree with it and you express your support publicly. ○ *The center advocates the use of rehabilitation programs instead of prison.*

Condone is usually used in negative constructions to say that you do not support something that is morally wrong. ○ *He stated that he does not condone violence of any kind.*

Endorse is used especially to talk about recommending something or someone in an advertising or political campaign. ○ *The newspaper stopped short of endorsing either candidate.*

---

2 NOUN An **advocate of** a particular action or plan is someone who recommends it publicly. [FORMAL] ○ [+ of] *He was a strong advocate of free market policies and a multi-party system.* ○ [+ of] *The advocates of active citizenship are hostile to such institutionalized apathy.*

a

▶ **COLLOCATIONS:**
an advocate **of** *something*
an advocate of **reform/privatization/independence**
a **leading/strong/passionate/staunch** advocate
a **privacy** advocate
▶ **SYNONYMS:** supporter, proponent
▶ **ANTONYM:** opponent

ad|vo|ca|cy /ˈædvəkəsi/

NOUN [FORMAL] ○ [+ *of*] *the party's advocacy of reform* ○ *His advocacy helped persuade the Royal Society to back the project.*

▶ **COLLOCATIONS:**
advocacy **of** *something*
advocacy of **reform/rights**
strong/passionate advocacy
▶ **SYNONYM:** support
▶ **ANTONYM:** opposition

---

aes|thet|ic /iːsˈθetɪk, AM es-/ `ARTS`

ADJECTIVE Aesthetic is used to talk about beauty or art, and people's appreciation of beautiful things. [in AM, also use **esthetic**] ○ *products chosen for their aesthetic appeal as well as their durability and quality* ○ *an aesthetic stance toward the reading of literature*

▶ **COLLOCATIONS:**
aesthetic **appeal/merit/considerations/sensibility**
an aesthetic **judgement/stance/response**
purely aesthetic
▶ **SYNONYMS:** artistic, creative

● **The aesthetic** of a work of art is its aesthetic quality. ○ [+ *of*] *He responded very strongly to the aesthetic of this particular work.*

▶ **COLLOCATIONS:**
the aesthetic **of** *something*
appreciate the aesthetic
▶ **SYNONYM:** beauty

aes|theti|cal|ly /iːsˈθetɪkli, AM es-/

ADVERB [in AM, also use **esthetically**] ○ *There is nothing aesthetically pleasing about this bridge.* ○ *a country that was aesthetically and intellectually multicultural*

▶ **COLLOCATIONS:**
  aesthetically **pleasing/appealing**
  aesthetically **unappealing/offensive**
▶ **SYNONYMS:** visually, artistically

aes|thet|ics /iːsˈθetɪks, AM es-/

UNCOUNTABLE NOUN **Aesthetics** is a branch of philosophy concerned with the study of the idea of beauty. [in AM, also use **esthetics**] ○ *questions of ethics and aesthetics* ○ *The fact that there are works of art is a given in aesthetics.*

afore|men|tioned /əˈfɔːmenʃənd/

ADJECTIVE If you refer to **the aforementioned** person or subject, you mean the person or subject that has already been mentioned. [FORMAL] ○ *A declaration will be issued at the end of the aforementioned U.N. conference.* ○ *a variation of the aforementioned method*

> **USAGE:** Very formal language
>
> The word **aforementioned** is only used in very formal contexts, especially official and legal documents. ○ *The aforementioned Funds may invest in convertible preferred stocks.*
>
> A more neutral word that is common in academic writing is **above** used to refer to something already mentioned in the text. ○ *Several conclusions could be drawn from the results described above.* ○ *Full details are in the table above.*

agent /ˈeɪdʒənt/ (agents)   CHEMISTRY

NOUN A chemical that has a particular effect or is used for a particular purpose can be referred to as a particular kind of **agent**. ○ *the bleaching agent in white flour* ○ *a chemical agent that can produce birth defects*

▶ **COLLOCATIONS:**
  a **chemical/biological** agent
  a **bleaching/clotting/bonding** agent

ag|gra|vate /ˈæɡrəveɪt/ (aggravates, aggravating, aggravated)

VERB If someone or something **aggravates** a situation, they make it worse. ○ *Stress and lack of sleep can aggravate the situation.* ○ *irritants which cause or aggravate eczema*

a

▶ **COLLOCATIONS:**
  aggravate a **situation/injury/strain**
  stress/heat/caffeine/alcohol aggravates *something*
▶ **SYNONYM:** exacerbate
▶ **ANTONYM:** alleviate

---

ag|gre|gate /'ægrɪgət/ ACADEMIC WORD

ADJECTIVE An **aggregate** amount or score is made up of several smaller amounts or scores added together. ○ *The rate of growth of GNP will depend upon the rate of growth of aggregate demand.* ○ *a total of 57 investments with an aggregate value of $1.47 billion*

▶ **COLLOCATIONS:**
  aggregate **demand/supply/income**
  an aggregate **score/result/value**
▶ **SYNONYMS:** total, combined
▶ **ANTONYM:** individual

● **Aggregate** is also a noun. ○ *earlier estimates of the monetary aggregates*
▶ **COLLOCATION:** **monetary** aggregates
▶ **SYNONYMS:** total, sum

---

al|ler|gy /'ælədʒi/ **(allergies)** MEDICINE

NOUN If you have a particular **allergy**, you become ill or get a rash when you eat, smell, or touch something that does not normally make people ill. ○ *Food allergies can result in an enormous variety of different symptoms.* ○ *[+ to] Allergy to cats is one of the commonest causes of asthma.* ○ *protecting infants against developing allergies*

▶ **COLLOCATIONS:**
  an allergy **to** *something*
  develop/diagnose/treat/trigger/cause an allergy
  a **severe/common/serious/life-threatening** allergy
  a **food/peanut/penicillin/skin** allergy
  allergy **sufferers/symptoms**
▶ **SYNONYMS:** sensitivity, reaction

al|ler|gic /ə'lɜːdʒɪk/

ADJECTIVE ○ *[+ to] people with asthma who are allergic to dust mites* ○ *Soya milk can cause allergic reactions in some children.*

▶ **COLLOCATIONS:**
  allergic **to** *something*

an allergic **reaction/response**
violently/severely/highly allergic

---

ally /ˈælaɪ/ (allies)

1 NOUN A country's **ally** is another country that has an agreement to support it, especially in war. ○ *Washington would not take such a step without its allies' approval.* ○ [+ *of*] *The United States is a close ally of South Korea.* ○ [+ *in*] *Russia has since become a key American ally in the fight against terrorism.*

2 NOUN If you describe someone as your **ally**, you mean that they help and support you, especially when other people are opposing you. ○ [+ *of*] *He is a close ally of the Prime Minister.* ○ *She will regret losing a close political ally.*

▶ **COLLOCATIONS:**
an ally **of** *someone/somewhere*
an ally **in** *something*
an ally in a **war/battle/fight/struggle/campaign**
a **former/staunch/close/long-time** ally
a **powerful/political/key/war-time/coalition** ally

▶ **SYNONYMS:** supporter, friend

▶ **ANTONYMS:** enemy, adversary

---

amend /əˈmɛnd/ (amends, amending, amended)   ACADEMIC WORD

VERB If you **amend** something that has been written such as a law, or something that is said, you change it in order to improve it or make it more accurate. ○ *The president agreed to amend the constitution and allow multi-party elections.* ○ *the amended version of the Act*

▶ **COLLOCATIONS:**
amend a **law/act/bill/plan/treaty**
amend **legislation**
amend the **constitution**
parliament/government amends *something*

> **EXTEND YOUR VOCABULARY**
>
> If you **change** something slightly, you can say that you **alter** or **modify** it. ○ *The original specification was altered/modified.*
>
> You can you **revise**, **amend** or **edit** to talk specifically about making changes to something written. **Editing** is usually part of the process of creating a new text, making small changes and corrections to early drafts. ○ *Prepare the final draft of your paper when you have edited the text.*

a

> You use **revise** and **amend** when you go back later to make changes
> to something written. **Amend** is used particularly to talk about laws
> and rules.
> ▶ revise a **version/edition/paragraph/guideline/proposal**
> ▶ amend the **constitution/legislation/law/rules**

amend|ment /ə'mendmənt/ (amendments)

NOUN An **amendment** is a section that is added to a law or rule in order to
change it. ○ [+ to] *In the United States, press freedom is entrenched in the first
amendment to the U.S. Constitution.* ○ *hundreds of amendments proposed by
private members* ○ *Parliament gained certain rights of amendment.*

▶ **COLLOCATIONS:**
an amendment **to** *something*
propose/draft/introduce/table an amendment
approve/adopt/pass/back an amendment
a **constitutional/proposed/balanced/budget** amendment
the **first/second** amendment

▶ **SYNONYMS:** alteration, change, correction

---

am|phib|ian /æm'fɪbiən/ (amphibians) `BIOLOGY`

NOUN **Amphibians** are animals such as frogs and toads that can live both
on land and in water. ○ *Alligators and crocodiles may not have evolved from
lizards or amphibians.*

▶ **PHRASE:** reptiles and amphibians
▶ **RELATED WORD:** reptile

am|phibi|ous /æm'fɪbiəs/

ADJECTIVE ○ *The area teemed with birdlife and all manner of insects, otters and
amphibious creatures.* ○ *Amphibious creatures feature prominently in ancient
legends.*

---

an|aes|thet|ic /ˌænɪs'θetɪk/ (anaesthetics) `MEDICINE`
also **anesthetic**

NOUN **Anaesthetic** is a substance that doctors use to stop you feeling pain
during an operation, either in the whole of your body when you are
unconscious, or in a part of your body when you are awake. ○ *The
operation is carried out under a general anaesthetic.* ○ *73 percent of women
surveyed had an epidural anaesthetic administered during labour.*

▶ COLLOCATIONS:
under anaesthetic
a **general/local** anaesthetic
inject/administer/require/use an anaesthetic

anaes|the|tize /əˈniːsθətaɪz/ (anaesthetizes, anaesthetizing, anaesthetized)

> The spellings **anesthetize** in American English, and **anaesthetise** in British English are also used.

VERB When a doctor or other trained person **anaesthetizes** a patient, they make the patient unconscious or unable to feel pain by giving them an anaesthetic. ○ *the patient's anaesthetized lung* ○ *The operation involves anaesthetising the eye.*

anaes|the|tist /əˈniːsθətɪst/ (anaesthetists)

NOUN An **anaesthetist** is a doctor who specializes in giving anaesthetics to patients. [BRIT; in AM, use **anesthesiologist**] ○ *a consultant paediatric anaesthetist* ○ *The anaesthetist ordered premedication, which included morphine.*

▶ COLLOCATIONS:
a **consultant/paediatric** anaesthetist
a **junior/senior** anaesthetist

---

ana|logue /ˈænəlɒg, AM -lɔːg/ also **analog** `SCIENCE`

ADJECTIVE **Analogue** technology involves measuring, storing, or recording an infinitely variable amount of information by using physical quantities such as voltage. ○ *The analogue signals from the video tape are converted into digital code.* ○ *Digital television is a more efficient means of delivering high-quality sound and images than conventional analogue transmissions.*

▶ COLLOCATIONS:
an analogue **signal/cassette**
analogue **recording/technology/transmission/broadcasting**
▶ ANTONYM: digital

---

anal|ogy /əˈnælədʒi/ (analogies) `ACADEMIC WORD`

NOUN If you make or draw an **analogy between** two things, you show that they are similar in some way. ○ [+ between] *It is probably easier to make an analogy between the courses of the planets, and two trains travelling in the same direction.* ○ [+ with] *The term 'social capital' was coined by analogy with*

a

the conventional use of the word capital to mean financial assets.

▶ **COLLOCATIONS:**
by analogy
an analogy **between** *things*
by analogy **with** *something*
make/draw/use an analogy
a **false/appropriate/useful/obvious** analogy

▶ **SYNONYMS:** comparison, similarity, resemblance

analo|gous /ə'næləgəs/

ADJECTIVE If one thing is **analogous to** another, the two things are similar in some way. [FORMAL] ○ [+ *to*] *Marine construction technology like this is very complex, somewhat analogous to trying to build a bridge under water.*
○ [+ *to*] *a new conflict situation analogous to the one on the Korean peninsula*

▶ **COLLOCATIONS:**
analogous **to** *something*
a **manner/situation/process/position** is analogous
somewhat/closely/roughly/directly analogous

▶ **SYNONYM:** similar

▶ **ANTONYM:** different

anato|my /ə'nætəmi/ (anatomies)   `MEDICINE` `BIOLOGY`

1 UNCOUNTABLE NOUN Anatomy is the study of the structure of the bodies of people or animals. ○ *an anatomy professor at Naples University*

2 NOUN An animal's **anatomy** is the structure of its body. ○ *It is hard to determine whether an animal's anatomy or physiology has been altered by environmental problems.* ○ [+ *of*] *He had worked extensively on the anatomy of living animals.*

▶ **COLLOCATIONS:**
the anatomy **of** *something*
an anatomy **professor/textbook/lesson/department**
teach/study anatomy

▶ **PHRASE:** anatomy and physiology

ana|tomi|cal /ˌænə'tɒmɪkəl/

ADJECTIVE ○ *minute anatomical differences between insects* ○ *the anatomical structure of the heart*

▶ **COLLOCATIONS:**
anatomical **studies/structures**
an anatomical **specimen/drawing/abnormality**

▶ **SYNONYM:** bodily

a

ana|tomi|cal|ly /ˌænə'tɒmɪkli/

ADVERB ○ *an anatomically correct drawing* ○ *Homo sapiens became anatomically modern in Africa about 100,000 years ago.*

▶ **COLLOCATION:** anatomically **correct/modern**

an|ces|tor /'ænsestə/ (ancestors)   HISTORY

NOUN Your **ancestors** are the people from whom you are descended.
○ *Modern humans and great apes both descend from one common ancestor.*
○ *Chinese traditions, including ancestor worship*

▶ **COLLOCATIONS:**
a **common/distant/human** ancestor
ancestor **worship**

▶ **SYNONYM:** forefather

▶ **ANTONYM:** descendant

an|ces|try /'ænsestri/ (ancestries)

NOUN Your **ancestry** is the fact that you are descended from certain people. ○ *a family who could trace their ancestry back to the sixteenth century* ○ *people of Japanese ancestry*

▶ **COLLOCATIONS:**
trace/claim ancestry
maternal/paternal ancestry
Japanese/Jewish/Indian/mixed ancestry

▶ **SYNONYMS:** heritage, roots

anti|bi|ot|ic /ˌæntibaɪ'ɒtɪk/ (antibiotics)   MEDICINE

NOUN **Antibiotics** are medical drugs used to kill bacteria and treat infections. ○ *Approximately 60% of antibiotics are prescribed for respiratory infections.* ○ *A 10-day course of oral antibiotics is the usual treatment mode for cellulitis.*

▶ **COLLOCATIONS:**
prescribe/administer antibiotics
potent/powerful/oral/intravenous antibiotics

an|tici|pate /æn'tɪsɪpeɪt/   ACADEMIC WORD
(anticipates, anticipating, anticipated)

VERB If you **anticipate** an event, you realize in advance that it may happen and you are prepared for it. ○ *Surveyors anticipate further price declines over coming months.* ○ *[+ that] It is anticipated that the equivalent of 192 full-time jobs will be lost.* ○ *[+ that] Officials anticipate that rivalry between leaders of the*

a

various drug factions could erupt into full scale war.

▶ **COLLOCATIONS:**
anticipate a **decline/slowdown/surge/advance/reaction**
widely anticipated

▶ **SYNONYM:** expect

an|tici|pa|tion /æn,tɪsɪ'peɪʃən/

PHRASE If something is done **in anticipation of** an event, it is done because people believe that event is going to happen. ○ *Troops in the Philippines have been put on full alert in anticipation of trouble during a planned general strike.* ○ *the company's ability to constantly renew itself in anticipation of future technology trends*

▶ **SYNONYMS:** in advance of, in expectation of, in preparation for

anti|sep|tic /,ænti'septɪk/ (antiseptics)   MEDICINE

1 NOUN Antiseptic is a substance that kills germs and harmful bacteria. ○ *Chlorine is a natural antiseptic.*

▶ **COLLOCATIONS:**
a **powerful/strong/natural** antiseptic
apply/contain antiseptic

▶ **SYNONYM:** disinfectant

2 ADJECTIVE Something that is **antiseptic** kills germs and harmful bacteria. ○ *These vegetables and herbs have strong antiseptic qualities.* ○ *the antiseptic properties of eucalyptus*

▶ **COLLOCATIONS:**
an antiseptic **cream/soap/mouthwash**
antiseptic **properties/qualities**

▶ **SYNONYM:** antibacterial

ap|pa|rat|us /,æpə'reɪtəs, -'ræt-/   SCIENCE

UNCOUNTABLE NOUN Apparatus is the equipment, such as tools and machines, which is used to do a particular job or activity. ○ *firefighters wearing breathing apparatus* ○ *a standard piece of laboratory apparatus, the spectrometer*

▶ **COLLOCATION: breathing/electrical/underwater** apparatus

▶ **SYNONYM:** equipment

ap|par|ent /ə'pærənt/   ACADEMIC WORD

1 ADJECTIVE An **apparent** situation, quality, or feeling seems to exist, although you cannot be certain that it does exist. ○ *the apparent government lack of concern for the advancement of science* ○ *There are two reasons for this apparent contradiction.*

▶ **COLLOCATIONS:**
an apparent **contradiction/lack**
an apparent **failure/inability**
an apparent **reason/attempt**

▶ **SYNONYMS:** seeming, supposed

▶ **ANTONYM:** actual

2 ADJECTIVE If something is **apparent** to you, it is clear and obvious to you. ○ *It has been apparent that in other areas standards have held up well.* ○ [+ *that*] *It will be readily apparent from Fig. 108a that there is a link between the monetary side of the economy and the real economy.* ○ [+ *from*] *The shrinkage of the tissue is not immediately apparent.*

▶ **COLLOCATIONS:**
apparent **to** *someone*
apparent **from** *something*
readily/immediately/increasingly apparent

▶ **SYNONYMS:** clear, obvious

▶ **ANTONYM:** unclear

---

ap|pe|tite /ˈæpɪtaɪt/ (appetites) `MEDICINE`

NOUN Your **appetite** is your desire to eat. ○ *He has a healthy appetite.* ○ *Symptoms are a slight fever, headache and loss of appetite.* ○ *stomach hormones that normally increase appetite*

▶ **COLLOCATIONS:**
a **healthy/hearty** appetite
loss of appetite

▶ **SYNONYM:** hunger

▶ **RELATED WORD:** thirst

---

ap|pre|ci|able /əˈpriːʃəbəl/ `ACADEMIC WORD`

ADJECTIVE An **appreciable** amount or effect is large enough to be important or clearly noticed. [FORMAL] ○ *It contains less than 1 per cent fat, an appreciable amount of protein, and a high content of minerals.* ○ *This has not had an appreciable effect on production.* ○ *There was no appreciable difference in test results.*

▶ **COLLOCATIONS:**
an appreciable **amount/proportion**

an appreciable **effect/difference**

▶ **ANTONYM:** insignificant

EXTEND YOUR VOCABULARY

If an effect or a difference is **appreciable**, **noticeable** or **discernable**, it is large enough to be clearly noticed. ○ *This distinction makes no appreciable difference in our analysis.*

You can talk about a **visible** effect or change, if you can physically see it. ○ *There may be no visible signs of infection.*

A **significant** change or difference is large enough to be important. In academic writing, we often use **significant** to describe a change that is large enough according to a statistical measure to be considered more than just due to chance or normal variation. ○ *Numerous studies appear to show a statistically significant increase in risk.*

---

ap|pre|ci|ably /əˈpriːʃəbli/

ADVERB ○ *The average earnings of women have risen appreciably since the 1970 Equal Pay Act.* ○ *The calculations would not change appreciably if we included future generations.*

▶ **COLLOCATION: change/differ/rise** appreciably

▶ **SYNONYMS:** noticeably, significantly

---

ap|pre|ci|ate /əˈpriːʃieɪt/   ACADEMIC WORD
(appreciates, appreciating, appreciated)

VERB If you **appreciate** a situation or problem, you understand it and know what it involves. ○ *Those arguing the case often do not appreciate the difference between an island nation and a continental one.* ○ *[+ that] It is essential to appreciate that addictive behaviour can compromise energy levels.*

▶ **COLLOCATIONS:**
appreciate the **importance/significance** of *something*
appreciate the **seriousness/extent** of *something*
appreciate a **fact**
fully appreciate

▶ **SYNONYMS:** acknowledge, recognize

ap|pre|cia|tion /əˌpriːʃiˈeɪʃən/ **(appreciations)**

NOUN An **appreciation of** a situation or problem is an understanding of what it involves. ○ *[+ of] They have a stronger appreciation of the importance* *of economic incentives.* ○ [+ *of*] *The WTO showed a deeper appreciation of the need for environmental exemptions.*

▶ **COLLOCATIONS:**
appreciation **of** *something*
appreciation of the **importance/significance** of *something*
appreciation of the **need** for *something*
show appreciation

▶ **SYNONYMS:** grasp, understanding

ar|bi|trary /ˈɑːbɪtri, ᴀᴍ -treri/ ACADEMIC WORD

ADJECTIVE If you describe an action, rule, or decision as **arbitrary**, you think that it is not based on any principle, plan, or system. It often seems unfair because of this. ○ *Arbitrary arrests and detention without trial were common.* ○ *a seemingly arbitrary deadline*

▶ **COLLOCATIONS:**
an arbitrary **arrest/imprisonment/execution**
an arbitrary **limit/deadline/distinction/code**
seemingly/purely arbitrary

▶ **SYNONYMS:** random, unfounded
▶ **ANTONYMS:** logical, reasonable

ar|bi|trari|ly /ˌɑːbɪˈtreərɪli/

ADVERB ○ *The victims were not chosen arbitrarily.* ○ *It would be wrong arbitrarily to exclude any particular groups of people from consideration.*

▶ **COLLOCATION:** **choose/select/decide** arbitrarily
▶ **SYNONYMS:** randomly, unreasonably

ar|chive /ˈɑːkaɪv/ (archives) HISTORY

NOUN The **archive** or **archives** are a collection of documents and records that contain historical information. You can also use **archives** to refer to the place where archives are stored. ○ [+ *of*] *the archives of the Imperial War Museum* ○ [+ *of*] *The state now has an online archive of records, including birth, marriage, death, census and military information.*

▶ **COLLOCATIONS:**
an archive **of** *something*
an archive of **photographs/documents/reviews/material**
a **digital/online/central/vast/extensive** archive
a **film/family/newspaper/video** archive

▶ **SYNONYMS:** collection, library, repository

a

archi|vist /ˈɑːkɪvɪst/ (archivists)

NOUN An **archivist** is a person whose job is to collect, sort, and care for historical documents and records. ○ *an archivist at the National Library of Medicine*

▶ **SYNONYM:** librarian

arid /ˈærɪd/　　　　　　　　　　　GEOGRAPHY

ADJECTIVE **Arid** land is so dry that very few plants can grow on it. ○ *new strains of crops that can withstand arid conditions* ○ *the arid zones of the country*

▶ **COLLOCATIONS:**
an arid **land/region/landscape/zone/desert**
arid **conditions/plains**

▶ **SYNONYMS:** dry, barren

▶ **ANTONYMS:** lush, fertile

ar|rest /əˈrest/ (arrests, arresting, arrested)

VERB If something or someone **arrests** a process, they stop it continuing. [FORMAL] ○ *The sufferer may have to make major changes in his or her life to arrest the disease.* ○ *The law could arrest the development of good research if applied prematurely.*

▶ **COLLOCATION:** arrest the **decline/development** of *something*

▶ **SYNONYMS:** stop, hinder, impede

ar|te|fact /ˈɑːtɪfækt/ (artefacts) also artifact　　HISTORY

NOUN An **artefact** is an ornament, tool, or other object that is made by a human being, especially one that is historically or culturally interesting. ○ *The museum holds more than 7000 artefacts collected from the Pandora.* ○ *illegal traders in ancient artefacts*

▶ **COLLOCATIONS:**
a **cultural/historical/archaeological** artefact
a **priceless/precious/rare/ancient** artefact
Roman/Egyptian artefacts
collect/display/recover artefacts

ar|tery /ˈɑːtəri/ (arteries)　　　　MEDICINE BIOLOGY

NOUN **Arteries** are the tubes in your body that carry blood from your heart to the rest of your body. ○ *patients suffering from blocked arteries* ○ *a blood clot which obstructs a coronary artery*

▶ **COLLOCATIONS:**
a **blocked/clogged/diseased/narrowed** artery
a **coronary/main** artery
sever/obstruct/clear/widen an artery
an artery **blockage**

▶ **RELATED WORD:** vein

ar|te|rial /ɑːˈtɪəriəl/

ADJECTIVE ○ *people with arterial disease* ○ *damage in brain cells and arterial walls*

▶ **COLLOCATIONS:**
arterial **disease/blood**
an arterial **blockage/wall**

---

as|sert /əˈsɜːt/ (asserts, asserting, asserted)

VERB If someone **asserts** a fact or belief, they state it firmly. [FORMAL]
○ [+ that] *Mr. Helm plans to assert that the bill violates the First Amendment.*
○ *The defendants, who continue to assert their innocence, are expected to appeal.*
○ *Altman asserted, 'We were making a political statement about western civilisation and greed.'*

▶ **COLLOCATION:** **confidently/bluntly/boldly/repeatedly** assert

▶ **SYNONYMS:** declare, state

▶ **ANTONYM:** deny

> **ACADEMIC WRITING: Reporting beliefs and opinions**
>
> Some reporting verbs are fairly neutral and simply show that someone has said or written something. ○ *Men were more likely to **state** the reason for wanting to work overseas as higher salary.* ○ *Hughes **points out** that this is only a preliminary trial.*
>
> Reporting verbs such as **assert**, **declare** and **contend** show that someone is expressing a strongly held belief or position. ○ *The American sugar industry has repeatedly asserted that quotas ensure a reliable supply of sugar.* ○ *In a speech on 5 January 1950 Truman publicly declared that the United States would not intervene.* ○ *Critics contend that the cameras will not reduce accidents.*

as|ser|tion /əˈsɜːʃən/ (assertions)

NOUN ○ [+ that] *There is no concrete evidence to support assertions that the recession is truly over.* ○ [+ that] *Miedzian (1991) challenges the assertion that* *participation in organized sports teaches children the importance of teamwork.*

▶ **COLLOCATIONS:**
contradict/refute/reject/challenge an assertion
make/repeat an assertion
a **repeated/bold/confident** assertion

▶ **SYNONYMS:** statement, argument

▶ **ANTONYM:** denial

---

as|sign /əˈsaɪn/ (assigns, assigning, assigned)   ACADEMIC WORD

1 VERB If you **assign** a piece of work **to** someone, you give them the work to do. ○ [+ *to*] *The task is sometimes jointly assigned to accounting and engineering departments.* ○ *Workers felt forced to work late because managers assigned them more work than they could complete in a regular shift.* ○ *When teachers assign homework, students usually feel an obligation to do it.*

2 VERB If you **assign** a particular function or value **to** someone or something, you say they have it. ○ [+ *to*] *Under Mr. Harel's system, each business must assign a value to each job.* ○ *Assign the letters of the alphabet their numerical values – A equals 1, B equals 2, etc.*

▶ **COLLOCATIONS:**
assign *something* **to** *someone/something*
assign a **task/chore/duty**
assign **homework**
assign a **value/score/meaning/role**

▶ **SYNONYMS:** allot, allocate

---

as|sist /əˈsɪst/ (assists, assisting, assisted)   ACADEMIC WORD

1 VERB If you **assist** someone, you help them to do a job or task by doing part of the work for them. ○ [+ *with*] *The family decided to assist me with my chores.* ○ *Dr Amid was assisted by a young Asian nurse.*

2 VERB If you **assist** someone, you give them information, advice, or money. ○ [+ *in*] *The public is urgently requested to assist police in tracing this man.* ○ [+ *with*] *Foreign Office officials assisted with transport and finance problems.*

3 VERB If something **assists in** doing a task, it makes the task easier to do. ○ [+ *in*] *a chemical that assists in the manufacture of proteins* ○ [+ *in*] *an increasing number of techniques to assist people in creating successful strategies* ○ *Salvage operations have been greatly assisted by the good weather conditions.*

▶ **COLLOCATIONS:**
assisted **by** *someone/something*

assist *someone* **with/in** *something*
assist in/with a **search/rescue/investigation/inquiry**
ably/greatly/materially/financially assisted
assisted **suicide/living**
assist a **victim/refugee**
assist the **police**

▶ **SYNONYMS:** help, aid, back
▶ **ANTONYM:** hinder

as|sis|tance /ə'sɪstəns/

UNCOUNTABLE NOUN ○ [+ *of*] *Since 1976 he has been operating the shop with the assistance of volunteers.* ○ [+ *in*] *Employees are being offered assistance in finding new jobs.* ○ *a viable programme of economic assistance*

▶ **COLLOCATIONS:**
assistance **with/in** *something*
assistance **from** *someone*
assistance with/in a **matter/investigation/case**
assistance from the **community/police/government**
provide/offer/seek/receive assistance
humanitarian/financial/technical/medical assistance
emergency/disaster/development assistance
an assistance **package/programme**

▶ **PHRASES:**
advice and assistance
aid and assistance
with the assistance of

▶ **SYNONYMS:** help, aid, hindrance

as|sure /ə'ʃʊə/ (assures, assuring, assured)　ACADEMIC WORD

1 VERB If you **assure** someone **that** something is true or will happen, you tell them that it is definitely true or will definitely happen, often in order to make them less worried. ○ [+ *that*] *Russia has assured us that it maintains robust command and control arrangements for its nuclear weapons.* ○ [+ *that*] *Assure yourself that the assertion of your paper is both clear and worth supporting.* ○ [+ *of*] *Government officials recently assured Hindus of protection.*

▶ **COLLOCATIONS:**
assure *someone* **of** *something*
assure the **public**

▶ **SYNONYM:** reassure

2 VERB To **assure** someone **of** something means to make certain that they

a

will get it. ○ [+ of] Henry VII's Welsh ancestry assured him of the warmest support in Wales. ○ a retraining programme to assure laid off employees new work ○ A level of self-containment renders us immune to criticism or disapproval, thus assuring our serenity of mind.

▶ COLLOCATIONS:
assure someone **of** something
assure the **victory/success** of something
assure the **discretion** of someone

▶ SYNONYM: guarantee

as|sur|ance /əˈʃʊərəns/ (assurances)

NOUN If you give someone an **assurance that** something is true or will happen, you say that it is definitely true or will definitely happen, in order to make them feel less worried. ○ [+ that] He would like an assurance that other forces will not move into the territory that his forces vacate. ○ [+ of] He will have been pleased by Marshal Yazov's assurance of the armed forces' loyalty.

▶ COLLOCATIONS:
an assurance **of** something
an assurance of **safety/security/support/loyalty**
obtain/seek/give/receive assurance
satisfactory/repeated/written assurance

▶ SYNONYM: guarantee

as|ter|isk /ˈæstərɪsk/ (asterisks) `ACADEMIC STUDY`

NOUN An **asterisk** is the sign *. It is used especially to indicate that there is further information about something in another part of the text. ○ An asterisk indicates a title that is the same in both English and French editions. ○ In Table 2, those crops marked with an asterisk are sown or planted out in the summer.

▶ COLLOCATION: an asterisk **indicates** something

atom /ˈætəm/ (atoms) `CHEMISTRY` `PHYSICS`

NOUN An **atom** is the smallest amount of a substance that can take part in a chemical reaction. ○ A methane molecule is composed of one carbon atom attached to four hydrogens. ○ the scientist who first split the atom

▶ COLLOCATIONS:
split the atom
a **carbon/hydrogen/oxygen/charged** atom
an atom **bomb**

▶ SYNONYM: molecule

atom|ic /ə'tɒmɪk/

1 ADJECTIVE Atomic means relating to power that is produced from the energy released by splitting atoms. ○ *uses of atomic energy* ○ *fears about the spread of atomic weapons*

▶ COLLOCATIONS:
atomic **energy/weapons**
the atomic **bomb**

▶ SYNONYM: nuclear

2 ADJECTIVE Atomic means relating to the atoms of substances. ○ *the complex structure of atomic nuclei* ○ *a device used to study the reactions of atomic particles*

▶ COLLOCATIONS:
an atomic **nucleus/particle**
atomic **physics**

▶ SYNONYM: molecular

at|tain /ə'teɪn/ (attains, attaining, attained) `ACADEMIC WORD`

VERB If you **attain** something, you gain it or achieve it, often after a lot of effort. [FORMAL] ○ *the best way to attain the objectives of our strategy* ○ *Business has yet to attain the social status it has in other countries.*

▶ COLLOCATIONS:
attain **enlightenment/perfection**
attain a **status/rank/goal/objective**

> **EXTEND YOUR VOCABULARY**
>
> You can talk about **reaching** or **achieving** something like a goal or a level. ○ *The temperature reached the required level.* ○ *There are simpler ways of achieving the same result.*
>
> **Attain** is a more formal verb, used especially to talk about getting to a high or respected level. ○ *a book that in time attained the status of a classic*

at|tain|ment /ə'teɪnmənt/ (attainments)

NOUN ○ [+ *of*] *the attainment of independence* ○ *their educational attainments*

▶ COLLOCATIONS:
the attainment **of** *something*
the attainment of a **goal**
educational/academic attainments

▶ **SYNONYMS:** achievement, success

▶ **ANTONYM:** failure

---

at|tor|ney /əˈtɜːni/ (attorneys)   LAW

NOUN In the United States, an **attorney** or **attorney at law** is a lawyer.
  ○ *a prosecuting attorney* ○ *an attorney representing families of 319 victims*

▶ **COLLOCATIONS:**
  a **prosecuting/defence** attorney
  a **district/court/deputy** attorney
  an attorney **represents** *someone*
  an attorney **argues/contends** *something*
  hire/consult/appoint an attorney

▶ **SYNONYMS:** lawyer, barrister

---

at|trib|ute /əˈtrɪbjuːt/   ACADEMIC WORD
(attributes, attributing, attributed)

1 VERB If you **attribute** something **to** an event or situation, you think that it was caused by that event or situation. ○ [+ *to*] *Women tend to attribute their success to external causes such as luck.* ○ [+ *to*] *The rising death toll is attributed largely to the growing number of elderly people, who are especially vulnerable to the flu.*

2 VERB If you **attribute** a particular quality or feature **to** someone or something, you think that they have got it. ○ [+ *to*] *the tendency to attribute more positive characteristics to physically attractive people*

3 VERB If a piece of writing, a work of art, or a remark **is attributed to** someone, people say that they wrote it, created it, or said it.
  ○ [+ *to*] *This, and the remaining frescoes, are not attributed to Giotto.*
  ○ [+ *to*] *The article incorrectly attributed some quotes to evangelist Billy Graham.*

▶ **COLLOCATIONS:**
  attribute *something* **to** *something/someone*
  attribute a **success/rise/increase**
  attribute a **quality/characteristic**
  incorrectly/falsely/wrongly attribute
  partly/largely/directly attributed

▶ **SYNONYMS:** ascribe, assign, accredit

---

audio /ˈɔːdiəʊ/

ADJECTIVE **Audio** equipment is used for recording and reproducing sound.
  ○ *a digital audio tape* ○ *downloadable audio files of books*

▶ **COLLOCATIONS:**
an audio **cassette/tape/CD/file/recording**
audio **equipment/footage**

▶ **RELATED WORD:** video

---

audit /ˈɔːdɪt/ (audits, auditing, audited)   BUSINESS ECONOMICS

VERB When an accountant **audits** an organization's accounts, he or she
examines the accounts officially in order to make sure that they have
been done correctly. ○ *Each year they audit our accounts and certify them as
being true and fair.* ○ *plans to audit the company*

▶ **COLLOCATIONS:**
a **firm/accountant** audits *something*
audit a **company/account**
independently/routinely/annually audit

▶ **SYNONYMS:** investigate, inspect

• **Audit** is also a noun. ○ *The bank first learned of the problem when it carried out
an internal audit.* ○ *[+ of] an independent audit of the organization*

▶ **COLLOCATIONS:**
an audit **of** *something*
conduct/carry out an audit
a **routine/internal/external/independent** audit
an audit **committee/report**
an audit **finds/shows** *things*

▶ **SYNONYMS:** investigation, inspection

audi|tor /ˈɔːdɪtə/ (auditors)

NOUN An **auditor** is an accountant who officially examines the accounts of
organizations. ○ *the company's external auditor* ○ *The misdirected spending
was uncovered by the state auditor.*

▶ **COLLOCATIONS:**
appoint/hire an auditor
a **city/state/internal/external/outside** auditor
an auditor **finds/discovers/uncovers/reviews** *something*

---

aural /ˈɔːrəl, ˈaʊrəl/   MEDICINE BIOLOGY

ADJECTIVE Aural means related to the sense of hearing. ○ *He became famous
as an inventor of astonishing visual and aural effects.* ○ *Low's music is the aural
equivalent of a Rothko painting.*

▶ **RELATED WORDS:** visual, oral, acoustic

a

authen|tic /ɔː'θentɪk/

1 ADJECTIVE An **authentic** person, object, or emotion is genuine.
○ *authentic Italian food* ○ *a demand for reliable, authentic information on which to base investment decisions*

2 ADJECTIVE If you describe something as **authentic**, you mean that it is such a good imitation that it is almost the same as or as good as the original. ○ *patterns for making authentic frontier-style clothing*

▶ **COLLOCATIONS:**
  authentic **cuisine**
  an authentic **portrayal/replica/flavour**
  the authentic **voice** of *a group of people*
  historically authentic
  look/sound/feel authentic

▶ **SYNONYMS:** genuine, real

▶ **ANTONYMS:** fake, false, imitation, inauthentic

au|then|tic|ity /ˌɔːθen'tɪsɪti/

UNCOUNTABLE NOUN ○ *There are factors, however, that have cast doubt on the statue's authenticity.* ○ *[+ of] efforts to determine the authenticity of the documents*

▶ **COLLOCATIONS:**
  the authenticity **of** *something*
  the authenticity of a **document/photograph/statement**
  guarantee/lend/check/determine authenticity

▶ **ANTONYM:** artifice

auto|mate /'ɔːtəmeɪt/ `ACADEMIC WORD` `ENGINEERING`
(automates, automating, automated)

VERB To **automate** a factory, office, or industrial process means to put in machines which can do the work instead of people. ○ *an initiative that involved automating a manual process* ○ *a self-service, fully automated programme*

▶ **COLLOCATIONS:**
  automate a **system/process/task/function**
  fully/highly/completely/entirely automated

▶ **SYNONYM:** mechanize

auto|ma|tion /ˌɔːtə'meɪʃən/

UNCOUNTABLE NOUN ○ *In the last ten years automation has reduced the work force here by half.* ○ *[+ of] the automation of everyday business transactions*

▶ **COLLOCATIONS:**
the automation **of** *something*
increase automation
factory/design/office/marketing automation
automation **savings/equipment/software/technology**

▶ **SYNONYMS:** mechanization, industrialization

autono|my /ɔːˈtɒnəmi/

1 UNCOUNTABLE NOUN Autonomy is the control or government of a country, organization, or group by itself rather than by others. ○ *Activists stepped up their demands for local autonomy last month.* ○ [+ *of*] *the increased autonomy of foundation hospitals*

2 UNCOUNTABLE NOUN Autonomy is the ability to make your own decisions about what to do rather than being influenced by someone else or told what to do. [FORMAL] ○ [+ *in*] *Each of the area managers enjoys considerable autonomy in the running of his own area.* ○ [+ *of*] *Consent is important to respect the autonomy of mature people.*

▶ **COLLOCATIONS:**
the autonomy **of** *someone/something*
autonomy **in** *doing something*
local/regional/political/fiscal autonomy
considerable/limited autonomy
grant/demand/exercise/respect autonomy
an autonomy **plan/package**

▶ **SYNONYMS:** independence, self-rule, self-determination, self-government, freedom

▶ **ANTONYM:** dependence

autono|mous /ɔːˈtɒnəməs/

ADJECTIVE ○ *They proudly declared themselves part of a new autonomous province.* ○ *the liberal idea of the autonomous individual*

▶ **COLLOCATIONS:**
an autonomous **individual**
an autonomous **region/republic/province/unit**
fiercely/relatively/largely autonomous

▶ **SYNONYMS:** independent, self-governing, self-determining

▶ **ANTONYM:** dependent

axis /ˈæksɪs/ (axes) `SCIENCE`

NOUN An **axis** is an imaginary line through the middle of something.

a

○ *The reason for the solstice is the 23.5 degrees tilt of the Earth's axis towards the Sun.*

▶ **COLLOCATIONS:**
the **Earth's** axis
the **principal/central** axis
a **north-south/east-west** axis

▶ **SYNONYM:** pivot

Bb

bib|li|og|ra|phy /ˌbɪbliˈɒɡrəfi/ **(bibliographies)** `ACADEMIC STUDY`

NOUN A **bibliography** is a list of the books and articles that are referred to in a particular book. ○ *Those readers interested in further readings on the subject should refer to the bibliography at the end of the book.* ○ *I have supplied an extensive bibliography containing all of the principal sources consulted during the book's preparation.*

▶ COLLOCATIONS:
annotate/append/compile/supply a bibliography
check/consult/view/refer to a bibliography
a **specialized/extensive** bibliogrpahy
a **detailed/comprehensive** bibliography

---

bio|chem|is|try /ˌbaɪəʊˈkemɪstri/ `SCIENCE`

1 UNCOUNTABLE NOUN Biochemistry is the study of the chemical processes that happen in living things. ○ *He made forays into several areas of clinical biochemistry.* ○ *Richard Axel is professor of biochemistry and molecular biophysics at Columbia University.*

▶ COLLOCATIONS:
study/teach biochemistry
microbial/pathological biochemistry
comparative/clinical biochemistry
a biochemistry **professor/lecturer**
a biochemistry **student/graduate/degree**

▶ PHRASES:
biochemistry and biophysics
biochemistry and immunology

2 UNCOUNTABLE NOUN The **biochemistry** of a living thing is the chemical processes that happen in it or are involved in it. ○ [+ *of*] *the biochemistry of cerebral ischemia* ○ [+ *of*] *That may have been the result of lower levels of CO_2 in the atmosphere, changing the biochemistry of photosynthesis.*

▶ COLLOCATION: the biochemistry **of** *something*

bio|chemi|cal /ˌbaɪəʊˈkemɪkəl/

ADJECTIVE Biochemical changes, reactions, and mechanisms relate to the chemical processes that happen in living things. ○ *In contrast, xenoestrogens tend to move down harmful biochemical pathways that ultimately lead to the types of damage to DNA that can lead to cancer.* ○ *a slight drop in internal heat can slow biochemical reactions*

▶ COLLOCATIONS:
a biochemical **reaction/mechanism/function/pathway**
a biochemical **change/imbalance/abnormality**
biochemical **engineering/weapons/warfare**

bio|chem|ist /ˌbaɪəʊˈkemɪst/ (biochemists)

NOUN A **biochemist** is a scientist or student who studies biochemistry. ○ *the biochemist who discovered p53, the gene that acts as a brake on cancer* ○ *as a clinical biochemist working in a hospital laboratory*

▶ COLLOCATIONS:
a biochemist **formulates/researches** something
a biochemist **discovers/studies** something
a **nutritional/clinical/trained** biochemist

▶ PHRASES:
a biochemist and biophysicist
a biochemist and pharmacologist

bio|di|ver|sity /ˌbaɪəʊdaɪˈvɜːsɪti/ BIOLOGY GEOGRAPHY

UNCOUNTABLE NOUN **Biodiversity** is the existence of a wide variety of plant and animal species living in their natural environment. ○ *The national environment management program encourages farmers to preserve biodiversity.* ○ [+ of] *We must protect the great biodiversity of the oceans.*

▶ COLLOCATIONS:
the biodiversity **of** something
the biodiversity of a **reef/ecosystem/ocean**
conserve/preserve/protect biodiversity
threaten/reduce/diminish biodiversity
marine/regional/global biodiversity

▶ PHRASES:
biodiversity and sustainability
biodiversity and ecology

bi|og|ra|phy /baɪˈɒɡrəfi/ (biographies) LITERATURE

NOUN A **biography** of someone is an account of their life, written by someone else. ○ [+ of] *Cassanovi's acclaimed biography of legendary film producer Sam Spiegel* ○ *a very comprehensive and thoroughly researched biography*

b

▶ COLLOCATIONS:
a biography **of** *someone*
a **definitive/acclaimed/authoritative** biography
an **authorized/unauthorized** biography
research/publish a biography
a biography **reveals/describes** *something*

bio|graphi|cal /ˌbaɪəˈɡræfɪkəl/

ADJECTIVE Biographical facts, notes, or details are concerned with the events in someone's life. ○ *The book contains few biographical details.*
○ *The book opens with a biographical essay.*

▶ COLLOCATIONS:
a biographical **essay/memoir/anecdote/dictionary**
a biographical **documentary/drama/film**
biographical **details/material/information**

---

bio|tech|nol|ogy /ˌbaɪəʊtekˈnɒlədʒi/ SCIENCE

UNCOUNTABLE NOUN Biotechnology is the use of living parts such as cells or bacteria in industry and technology. **Biotech** is also used in informal and spoken English. ○ *This centre will provide opportunities for local biotechnology companies to benefit from its knowledge, innovative research and highly developed skills and expertise.* ○ *The second generation of agricultural biotechnology will market seeds offering benefits for farmers such as increased yields and drought resistance.*

▶ COLLOCATIONS:
a biotechnology **company/start-up/firm/laboratory**
molecular/pharmaceutical biotechnology
industrial/agricultural biotechnology

bio|tech|nolo|gist /ˌbaɪəʊtekˈnɒlədʒɪst/ **(biotechnologists)**

NOUN ○ *biotechnologists turning proteins into pharmaceuticals*
○ *Agricultural biotechnologists have copied genes into seed corn to help make crops resist corn borers and reduce the need for insecticides.*
○ [+ *at*] *Dr Jeffrey Newman, consultant biotechnologist at Cranfield University*

▶ COLLOCATIONS:
a biotechnologist **with/at/from** *somewhere*
a **consultant/principal** biotechnologist
a **plant/agricultural** biotechnologist

b

blood pres|sure /ˈblʌd ˌpreʃə/ MEDICINE

UNCOUNTABLE NOUN Your **blood pressure** is the amount of force with which your blood flows around your body. ○ *Your doctor will monitor your blood pressure.* ○ *Chromium also appears to help prevent and lower high blood pressure.*

▶ **COLLOCATIONS:**
   high/raised/low/normal blood pressure
   reduce/increase blood pressure
   take/check/monitor *someone's* blood pressure
   blood pressure **drops/stabilises/rises**

▶ **PHRASE:** suffer from high blood pressure

blue-collar /ˈbluːˌkɒlə/ BUSINESS

ADJECTIVE Blue-collar workers work in industry, doing physical work, rather than in offices. ○ *By 1925, blue-collar workers in manufacturing industry had become the largest occupational group.* ○ *Industry analysts are calling for a structural shift away from blue-collar factory jobs to a value-added research and development focus.*

▶ **COLLOCATIONS:**
   a blue-collar **job/worker/labourer/voter**
   a blue-collar **neighbourhood/suburb/consituency**

▶ **ANTONYM:** white-collar

boom /buːm/ (booms, booming, boomed) BUSINESS ECONOMICS

1 NOUN If there is a **boom** in the economy, there is an increase in economic activity, for example in the amount of things that are being bought and sold. ○ *[+ in] An economic boom followed, especially in housing and construction.* ○ *The 1980s were indeed boom years.* ○ *the cycle of boom and bust which has damaged us for 40 years*

2 NOUN A **boom in** something is an increase in its amount, frequency, or success. ○ *[+ in] The boom in the sport's popularity has meant more calls for stricter safety regulations.* ○ *Public transport has not been able to cope adequately with the travel boom.* ○ *the collapse of the dotcom boom*

▶ **COLLOCATIONS:**
   a boom **in** *something*
   the boom **of** *a period of time*
   a boom in **spending/tourism/travel/housing**
   the boom of the **1960s/1990s**
   the boom **years**
   a **consumer/economic** boom

the **property/dotcom/tech/telecom** boom
the **baby** boom
a boom **collapses/subsides/peaks/ends**

▶ **PHRASE:** boom and bust

▶ **ANTONYM:** slump

3 VERB If the economy or a business **is booming**, the amount of things being bought or sold is increasing. ○ *By 2008 the economy was booming.* ○ [V-ing] *a booming global consumer electronics market* ○ [V-ing] *It has a booming tourist industry.*

▶ **COLLOCATIONS:**
the **economy** is booming
business is booming
sales are booming
a booming **market/industry/population**

▶ **ANTONYM:** crash

---

breed /briːd/ (breeds, breeding, bred)   `BIOLOGY`

1 NOUN A **breed** of a pet animal or farm animal is a particular type of it. For example, terriers are a breed of dog. ○ [+ of] *rare breeds of cattle* ○ *Certain breeds are more dangerous than others.*

▶ **COLLOCATIONS:**
a breed **of** something
a breed of **sheep/cattle/dog**
a **rare/dangerous/endangered/exotic** breed
research/identify/recognize a breed
domesticate/introduce/create a breed

2 VERB If you **breed** animals or plants, you keep them for the purpose of producing more animals or plants with particular qualities, in a controlled way. ○ *They are the first of their kind to be bred successfully in captivity.* ○ [+ for] *Australians must now focus on breeding sheep for three specific purposes: wool, meat and maternal traits.* ○ [+ to-inf] *These dogs are bred to fight.*

▶ **COLLOCATIONS:**
breed something **for** something
breed **animals/plants/horses/dogs**
bred **successfully/selectively/artificially**

▶ **PHRASE:** bred in captivity

3 VERB When animals **breed**, they have babies. ○ [+ in] *Frogs will usually breed in any convenient pond.* ○ [V-ing] *The area now attracts over 60 species of breeding birds.* ○ *Scientists want to establish breeding colonies of transgenic monkeys with disorders such as diabetes.*

b

▶ COLLOCATIONS:
breed **in** *a place*
animals/mosquitoes breed
a breeding **colony**
breed **freely**

---

bulk /bʌlk/   `ACADEMIC WORD`

QUANTIFIER The **bulk of** something is most of it. ○ [+ *of*] *The bulk of the text is essentially a review of these original documents.* ○ [+ *of*] *The vast bulk of imports and exports are carried by sea.*

• **Bulk** is also a pronoun. ○ *They come from all over the world, though the bulk is from the Indian subcontinent.* ○ *from 1992 the bulk came from Bosnia*

▶ COLLOCATIONS:
the bulk **of** *something*
the bulk of the **population/funding**
the **vast/main/overwhelming** bulk
constitute/form/comprise the bulk
provide/supply the bulk

> **EXTEND YOUR VOCABULARY**
>
> You talk about **the bulk** or **the majority of** people or things in a group to refer to a large proportion or most of them. ○ *The vast bulk/ majority of people driving in the city are residents.*
>
> You do not use **the majority** when you talk about an amount or part of something. ○ *The state provides the bulk of school funding.*
>
> **A majority of** people or things can also refer more precisely to more than 50% of them. ○ *A majority of delegates voted to approve the change.*

---

bur|den /ˈbɜːdən/ (burdens)

NOUN If you describe a problem or a responsibility as a **burden**, you mean that it causes someone a lot of difficulty, worry, or hard work. ○ [+ *of*] *The developing countries bear the burden of an enormous external debt.* ○ *The financial burden will be more evenly shared.* ○ [+ *on*] *Its purpose is to ease the burden on accident and emergency departments by filtering out non-emergency calls.*

▶ COLLOCATIONS:
the burden **of** *something*
a burden **on** *someone/something*
a burden on **society/taxpayers/employers**

the burden of **responsibility/debt/disease**
shoulder/bear/carry a burden
place/impose/shift a burden
ease/lighten/alleviate a burden
a **heavy/financial** burden

b

Cc

Cabi|net /ˈkæbɪnɪt/ (Cabinets)

POLITICS

NOUN The **Cabinet** is a group of the most senior ministers in a government, who meet regularly to discuss policies. ○ *The announcement came after a three-hour Cabinet meeting in Downing Street.* ○ *a former Cabinet Minister*

▶ **COLLOCATIONS:**
a Cabinet **minister/meeting/reshuffle**
appoint/dissolve a Cabinet
a Cabinet **convenes/votes**
a Cabinet **debates/rejects/decides** *something*
a **two-tier/all-male/civic** Cabinet

capi|tal pun|ish|ment /ˌkæpɪtəl ˈpʌnɪʃmənt/

POLITICS

UNCOUNTABLE NOUN **Capital punishment** is punishment which involves the legal killing of a person who has committed a serious crime such as murder. ○ *Most democracies have abolished capital punishment.* ○ *a majority of Americans support capital punishment*

▶ **COLLOCATIONS:**
favour/support/advocate capital punishment
reintroduce/restore capital punishment
abolish/oppose/reject capital punishment

▶ **SYNONYM:** the death penalty

car|bo|hy|drate /ˌkɑːbəʊˈhaɪdreɪt/ (carbohydrates)

MEDICINE

NOUN **Carbohydrates** are substances, found in certain kinds of food, that provide you with energy. Foods such as sugar and bread that contain these substances can also be referred to as **carbohydrates**. **Carbs** is also used in informal and spoken English. ○ *Food is made up of carbohydrates, proteins and fats.* ○ *Fibre is automatically present in complex carbohydrates.*

▶ **COLLOCATIONS:**
digest/consume/absorb/process carbohydrates
limit/restrict/eliminate carbohydrates
refined/unrefined carbohydrates
complex/starchy/slow-release carbohydrates

▶ **RELATED WORDS:** protein, fat

---

car|bon da|ting /ˌkɑːbən ˈdeɪtɪŋ/ HISTORY

UNCOUNTABLE NOUN **Carbon dating** is a system of calculating the age of a very old object by measuring the amount of radioactive carbon it contains. ○ *Carbon dating indicated its age to be around 2500 years.* ○ *The two methods widely used at present are carbon dating and potassium-argon dating.*

▸ **COLLOCATIONS:**
the carbon dating **of** *something*
carbon dating **reveals/indicates/confirms** *something*
carbon dating **tests/methods/techniques**

---

car|dio|vas|cu|lar /ˌkɑːdiəʊˈvæskjʊə/ BIOLOGY MEDICINE

ADJECTIVE **Cardiovascular** means relating to the heart and blood vessels. ○ *Smoking places you at serious risk of cardiovascular and respiratory disease.* ○ *Mercury may cause neurological, respiratory, cardiovascular and digestive disorders.* ○ *exercise contributes to cardiovascular fitness*

▸ **COLLOCATIONS:**
cardiovascular **disease/medicine/fitness**
cardiovascular **toxicity/reactivity/mortality**
a cardiovascular **surgeon/disorder/problem**

---

car|ni|vore /ˈkɑːnɪvɔː/ (carnivores) BIOLOGY

NOUN A **carnivore** is an animal that eats meat. ○ *The researchers conclude that wide-ranging carnivores should not be kept in captivity.* ○ *A herbivore and a carnivore may share the same habitat but their different feeding methods mean that they occupy different niches.*

▸ **RELATED WORDS:** herbivore, omnivore, insectivore

---

car|nivo|rous /kɑːˈnɪvərəs/

ADJECTIVE ○ *Snakes are carnivorous.* ○ *It is the carnivorous species which is of main interest to the gardener.*

▸ **COLLOCATION:** a carnivorous **animal/mammal/species**

▸ **RELATED WORDS:** herbivorous, omnivorous

---

cas|ual /ˈkæʒʊəl/ BUSINESS

ADJECTIVE **Casual** work is done for short periods and not on a permanent or regular basis. ○ *establishments which employ people on a casual basis, such as pubs and restaurants* ○ *It became increasingly expensive to hire casual workers.*

▸ **COLLOCATION:** casual **work/workers**

> ▶ **PHRASE:** on a casual basis
> ▶ **SYNONYM:** temporary
> ▶ **ANTONYM:** permanent

---

cata|logue /ˈkætəlɒg/ (catalogues, cataloguing, catalogued)

VERB To **catalogue** things means to make a list of them. [in AM, usually use **catalog**] ○ *The Royal Greenwich Observatory was founded to observe and catalogue the stars.* ○ *The report catalogues a long list of extreme weather patterns.*

→ see note at **document**

▶ **COLLOCATIONS:**
catalogue **items**
a **report** catalogues *things*
catalogue *things* **carefully/meticulously/properly**

▶ **SYNONYM:** list

---

ca|tas|tro|phe /kəˈtæstrəfi/ (catastrophes)

NOUN A **catastrophe** is an unexpected event that causes great suffering or damage. ○ *From all points of view, war would be a catastrophe.* ○ *If the world is to avoid environmental catastrophe, advanced economies must undergo a profound transition.*

▶ **COLLOCATIONS:**
a **humanitarian/environmental/economic** catastrophe
a **major/imminent/unprecedented** catastrophe
avert/avoid/prevent a catastrophe
trigger/cause/face a catastrophe

▶ **SYNONYM:** disaster

cata|stroph|ic /ˌkætəˈstrɒfɪk/

ADJECTIVE Something that is **catastrophic** involves or causes a sudden terrible disaster. ○ *A tidal wave caused by the earthquake hit the coast causing catastrophic damage.* ○ *The water shortage in this country is potentially catastrophic.* ○ *[+ for] The minister warned that if war broke out, it would be catastrophic for the whole world.*

▶ **COLLOCATIONS:**
catastrophic **for** *someone/something*
potentially/environmentally/financially catastrophic
catastrophic **damage/consequences/repercussions**
a catastrophic **famine/earthquake/tsunami**

▶ **SYNONYM:** disastrous

cata|strophi|cal|ly /ˌkætəˈstrɒfɪkli/

ADVERB ○ *The faulty left-hand engine failed catastrophically as the aircraft approached the airport.* ○ *catastrophically injured people*

▶ **COLLOCATION: fail** catastrophically

▶ **SYNONYM:** disastrously

---

cau|tion /ˈkɔːʃən/

UNCOUNTABLE NOUN Caution is great care which you take in order to avoid possible danger. ○ *Extreme caution should be exercised when buying part-worn tyres.* ○ *The Chancellor is a man of caution.*

▶ **COLLOCATIONS:**
  extreme/considerable caution
  exercise/advocate/urge caution

▶ **SYNONYMS:** care, prudence

cau|tious /ˈkɔːʃəs/

1 ADJECTIVE Someone who is **cautious** acts very carefully in order to avoid possible danger. ○ [+ about] *The scientists are cautious about using enzyme therapy on humans.* ○ *Many Canadians have become overly cautious when it comes to investing.*

2 ADJECTIVE If you describe someone's attitude or reaction as **cautious**, you mean that it is limited or careful. ○ *He has been seen as a champion of a more cautious approach to economic reform.* ○ *There may have been good reasons for this cautious attitude.*

▶ **COLLOCATIONS:**
  cautious **about** *something*
  a cautious **attitude/reaction/approach/outlook**
  scientists/investors/analysts/experts are cautious
  remain/appear cautious
  overly/excessively/relatively/understandably cautious

▶ **SYNONYMS:** careful, circumspect

▶ **ANTONYM:** rash

cau|tious|ly /ˈkɔːʃəsli/

ADVERB ○ *These borderline differences should be interpreted cautiously given the number of outcomes examined.* ○ *I am cautiously optimistic that a new government will be concerned and aware about the environment.* ○ *Rebel sources have so far reacted cautiously to the threat.*

▶ **COLLOCATIONS:**
  cautiously **optimistic/hopeful**

c

proceed/react/move cautiously
interpret/approach *something* cautiously

▸ **SYNONYMS:** circumspectly, carefully

▸ **ANTONYM:** rashly

---

cen|sus /ˈsensəs/ (censuses)   SOCIOLOGY

NOUN A **census** is an official survey of the population of a country that is carried out in order to find out how many people live there and to obtain details of such things as people's ages and jobs. ○ *Population censuses in India show that the number of girls has been falling steadily for the past 20 years relative to the number of boys.* ○ *In the new study, Kaplan studied census data collected between 2007 and 2009.*

▸ **COLLOCATIONS:**
census **figures/data/statistics**
a **population/nationwide** census
conduct/carry out/study a census
a census **reveals/finds/confirms** *something*

---

cf.   ACADEMIC STUDY

cf. is used in writing to introduce something that should be considered in connection with the subject you are discussing. ○ *For the more salient remarks on the matter, cf. Isis Unveiled, Vol. I.* ○ *the beneficial effects of isolation from foreign capital (cf. Taylor, 1975, p.225)*

▸ **SYNONYM:** compare

> **ACADEMIC WRITING: Academic abbreviations**
>
> There are a number of Latin abbreviations that are used in academic writing.
>
> **cf.** means *compare with*
>
> **NB** is used to draw attention to something important, especially in notes and footnotes. ○ *NB The above course is subject to approval.*
>
> Several abbreviations are used when giving academic references. **et al.** is used when a book or an article was written by several people to avoid repeating all the names. You write the name of one writer, then **et al.** in your text and show the names of all the writers in the bibliography. ○ *A research review by Werry et al. (1983) indicates that …*
>
> You use **ibid.** to avoid repeating a full reference. It shows that a reference (a quotation or a paraphrase etc.) comes from the same

source cited directly above. So for example, both of the quotations below are from Krause; the first from page 67, the second from page 70. ○ "... *itself quite new*" (Krause, 1983, p.67). *He came to see America as "the land of political culture*" (ibid., p. 70)

---

chain re|ac|tion /ˌtʃeɪn riˈækʃən/ (chain reactions) CHEMISTRY

1 NOUN A **chain reaction** is a series of chemical changes, each of which causes the next. ○ *Chain reactions triggered by bromine oxide are known to destroy ozone.* ○ *damaging chain reactions caused by free radicals*

2 NOUN A **chain reaction** is a series of events, each of which causes the next. ○ *Whenever recession strikes, a chain reaction is set into motion.* ○ [+ of] *The powder immediately ignited and set off a chain reaction of explosions.*

▶ COLLOCATIONS:
  a chain reaction **of** things
  a chain reaction of **events/damage/explosions**
  cause/set off/trigger/initiate a chain reaction
  a chain reaction **occurs**

---

chron|ic /ˈkrɒnɪk/ MEDICINE

1 ADJECTIVE A **chronic** illness or disability lasts for a very long time. ○ *chronic back pain* ○ *the condition is often chronic*

▶ COLLOCATIONS:
  chronic **pain/stress/depression**
  a chronic **illness/disease/condition/disorder**

▶ PHRASES:
  chronic and degenerative
  chronic and inflammatory

▶ SYNONYM: long-term

▶ RELATED WORD: acute

2 ADJECTIVE A **chronic** situation or problem is very severe and unpleasant. ○ *One cause of the artist's suicide seems to have been chronic poverty.* ○ *There is a chronic shortage of patrol cars in this police district.*

▶ COLLOCATIONS:
  chronic **poverty**
  a chronic **shortage**

▶ SYNONYM: severe

chroni|cal|ly /ˈkrɒnɪkli/

ADVERB ○ *hospitalisation rates for chronically ill patients* ○ *Research and technology are said to be chronically underfunded.*

▶ **COLLOCATIONS:**
chronically **ill/sick/depressed/malnourished**
chronically **underfunded/understaffed**

▶ **SYNONYM:** severely

---

chrono|logi|cal /ˌkrɒnəˈlɒdʒɪkəl/ HISTORY

ADJECTIVE If things are described or shown in **chronological** order, they are described or shown in the order in which they happened. ○ *Such a paper might present a chronological sequence of events.* ○ *The play is in strict chronological order, and attention is paid to demographic and statistical details.*

▶ **COLLOCATION:** a chronological **sequence/arrangement**
▶ **PHRASE:** in chronological order

chrono|logi|cal|ly /ˌkrɒnəˈlɒdʒɪkli/

ADVERB ○ *The exhibition is organised chronologically.* ○ *the museum's chronologically arranged exhibit*

▶ **COLLOCATIONS:**
arrange/organize/order something chronologically
display something chronologically

---

cite /saɪt/ (cites, citing, cited) ACADEMIC WORD ACADEMIC STUDY

VERB If you **cite** something, you quote it or mention it, especially as an example or proof of what you are saying. [FORMAL] ○ *She cites a favourite poem by George Herbert.* ○ *The author cites just one example.* ○ [+ as] *How can we account for the data cited as evidence for that theory?* ○ [+ as] *Spain was cited as the most popular holiday destination.*

▶ **COLLOCATIONS:**
cited **as** something
cited as **proof/evidence/justification**
cite a **source/example/statistic/case**
cite a **report/study/passage/poll**
a **report/article/author/analyst** cites something

▶ **SYNONYMS:** quote, mention

USAGE: cite or quote?

You use both of these words to talk about references and sources. **Quote** always refers to the use of the exact words from another source. In the example below, Ellis uses Harris's exact words in her article. ○ *In the article, Ellis quotes from Harris's personal letters.*

Cite can refer to the use of the exact words, a paraphrase, an idea or data from another source. In the example below, Blum uses the results of the study as evidence. ○ *Blum cites a study done by the California Energy Commission that showed …*

---

ci|vil|ian /sɪ'vɪlɪən/ (civilians) SOCIAL SCIENCE

1 NOUN In a military situation, a **civilian** is anyone who is not a member of the armed forces. ○ *The safety of civilians caught up in the fighting must be guaranteed.* ○ *their total disregard for the lives of innocent civilians*

▶ **COLLOCATIONS:**
 attack/target/wound/massacre civilians
 protect/evacuate civilians
 civilians **march/gather/demonstrate**
 civilians **flee/suffer/die**
 innocent/unarmed/wounded civilians

▶ **ANTONYM:** soldier

2 ADJECTIVE In a military situation, **civilian** is used to describe people or things that are not military. ○ *the country's civilian population* ○ *Inevitably there were also innocent civilian casualties.* ○ *a soldier in civilian clothes*

▶ **COLLOCATIONS:**
 civilian **casualties/targets/deaths**
 civilian **clothes/personnel/aircraft**
 the civilian **population**

▶ **ANTONYM:** military

---

civ|il rights /ˌsɪvəl 'raɪts/ POLITICS SOCIOLOGY

PLURAL NOUN **Civil rights** are the rights that people have in a society to equal treatment and equal opportunities, whatever their race, sex, or religion. ○ *new laws guaranteeing civil rights such as free expression and private business ownership* ○ *violations of civil rights*

▶ **COLLOCATIONS:**
 civil rights **for** *people*
 grant/extend civil rights to *people*
 guarantee/protect/support/promote civil rights

c

violate civil rights
sexual/individual/black/gay civil rights
a civil rights **activist/lawyer/group/campaign/bill**
▶ PHRASE: the civil rights movement

---

clari|fy /ˈklærɪfaɪ/ (clarifies, clarifying, clarified) `ACADEMIC WORD`

VERB To **clarify** something means to make it easier to understand, usually
by explaining it in more detail. [FORMAL] ○ *It is important to clarify the
distinction between the relativity of values and the relativity of truth.* ○ *A bank
spokesman was unable to clarify the situation.* ○ *[+ what] you will want to
clarify what your objectives are*

▶ COLLOCATIONS:
clarify a **position/situation/remark/distinction**
clarify the **meaning** of *something*
a **statement/amendment** clarifies *something*
legislation/guidelines clarify *something*

clari|fi|ca|tion /ˌklærɪfɪˈkeɪʃən/

UNCOUNTABLE NOUN ○ *[+ of] The union has written to Zurich asking for
clarification of the situation.* ○ *[+ on] Please provide clarification on "conflict
of interest" concerning the awarding of contracts by the board of directors.*

▶ COLLOCATIONS:
clarification **of/on** *something*
seek/ask for/request/await clarification
issue/provide/obtain clarification
further/additional/legal clarification

clar|ity /ˈklærɪti/

UNCOUNTABLE NOUN The **clarity** of something such as a book or argument
is its quality of being well explained and easy to understand. ○ *the ease and
clarity with which the author explains difficult technical and scientific subjects*
○ *[+ of] our need as social scientists to strive for clarity of analysis*

▶ COLLOCATIONS:
clarity **of** *something*
clarity of **thought/vision/purpose/focus**
clarity of **argument/expression/analysis/structure**
bring/lend/introduce clarity to *something*
provide/enhance/increase clarity
startling/exceptional/absolute clarity

▶ PHRASES:
clarity and distinctness

clarity and simplicity

▶ SYNONYM: lucidity

---

clause /klɔːz/ (clauses)   ACADEMIC WORD   LANGUAGE   LAW

1 NOUN A **clause** is a section of a legal document. ○ [+ in] *He has a clause in his contract which entitles him to a percentage of the profits.* ○ *a complaint alleging a breach of clause 4 of the code*

  ▶ COLLOCATIONS:
    a clause **in** something
    a **breach/violation/amendment** of a clause
    violate/invoke/amend/abolish a clause
    a clause **stipulates/states/specifies** something
    a clause **permits/guarantees/prevents** something
    a **contractual/opt-out** clause

2 NOUN In grammar, a **clause** is a group of words containing a verb. Sentences contain one or more clauses. There are finite clauses and non-finite clauses. ○ *In both cases it is the subordinate clause which is the governing sentence.* ○ *A subordinate or dependent clause cannot stand by itself but must be connected to another clause.*

  ▶ COLLOCATIONS:
    a **main/relative/subordinate** clause
    a **dependent/independent/restrictive** clause
    a **finite/non-finite** clause

---

clone /kləʊn/ (clones, cloning, cloned)   BIOLOGY

1 NOUN A **clone** is an animal or plant that has been produced artificially, for example in a laboratory, from the cells of another animal or plant. A clone is exactly the same as the original animal or plant. ○ *a Chicago scientist who wants to create human clones* ○ [+ of] *Each colony represents a clone of bacterial cells.*

  ▶ COLLOCATIONS:
    a clone **of** something
    breed/produce/create/generate a clone
    a **genetic/embryonic/T-cell/human** clone

2 VERB To **clone** an animal or plant means to produce it as a clone. ○ *highly controversial proposals to clone humans* ○ *The scientists will clone embryos from the skin cells of motor neurone disease sufferers.*

  ▶ COLLOCATIONS:
    clone a **plant/animal/embryo/cell**
    a **scientist** clones something

cog|ni|tive /ˈkɒgnɪtɪv/

ADJECTIVE Cognitive means relating to the mental process involved in knowing, learning, and understanding things. [FORMAL] ○ *As children grow older, their cognitive processes become sharper.* ○ *Vygotsky's theory of cognitive development*

▶ **COLLOCATIONS:**
cognitive **development/dissonance/therapy/impairment**
cognitive **errors/processes/skills**
cognitive **neuroscience/psychology**

co|her|ent /kəʊˈhɪərənt/ `ACADEMIC WORD`

ADJECTIVE If something is **coherent**, it is well planned, so that it is clear and sensible and all its parts go well with each other. ○ *He has failed to work out a coherent strategy for modernising the service.* ○ *The President's policy is perfectly coherent.*

▶ **COLLOCATIONS:**
a coherent **strategy/policy/plan**
a coherent **vision/approach**
a coherent **presentation/narrative/theory/critique**
intellectually/perfectly coherent

▶ **SYNONYM:** cohesive

▶ **ANTONYM:** muddled

co|her|ence /kəʊˈhɪərəns/

UNCOUNTABLE NOUN ○ *The campaign was widely criticised for making tactical mistakes and for a lack of coherence.* ○ *The three interlocking narratives achieve an overall coherence.* ○ *The anthology has a surprising sense of coherence.*

▶ **COLLOCATIONS:**
the coherence **of** *something*
lack/possess/achieve coherence
lend/bring coherence to *something*
stylistic/thematic/logical/structural coherence

▶ **PHRASES:**
a sense of coherence
coherence and consistency

▶ **SYNONYM:** cohesion

coin /kɔɪn/ (coins, coining, coined)

VERB If you **coin** a word or a phrase, you are the first person to say it.
○ *Jaron Lanier coined the term 'virtual reality' and pioneered its early*

development. ○ *Simone de Beauvoir first coined the phrase 'women's liberation' in her book, The Second Sex.*

▶ **COLLOCATIONS:**
coined **by** *someone*
coin a **term/phrase/word/name/expression**
first/originally coined
a **writer/academic/scientist** coins *something*

---

co|in|cide /ˌkəʊɪnˈsaɪd/ `ACADEMIC WORD`
(coincides, coinciding, coincided)

1 VERB If one event **coincides with** another, they happen at the same time. ○ [+ with] *Although his mental illness had coincided with his war service it had not been caused by it.* ○ *The beginning of the solar and lunar years coincided every 13 years.*

2 VERB If the ideas or interests of two or more people **coincide**, they are the same. ○ *a case in which public and private interests coincide* ○ [+ with] *He gave great encouragement to his students, especially if their passions happened to coincide with his own.*

▶ **COLLOCATIONS:**
coincide **with** *something*
broadly/conveniently/frequently coincide
rarely coincide

co|in|ci|dence /kəʊˈɪnsɪdəns/ **(coincidences)**

NOUN A **coincidence** is when two or more similar or related events occur at the same time by chance and without any planning. ○ *It is, of course, a mere coincidence that the author of this piece is also a pathologist.* ○ *It is no coincidence that so many of the romantic poets suffered from tuberculosis.*

▶ **COLLOCATIONS:**
by coincidence
pure/mere/sheer/no coincidence
a **happy/remarkable/strange** coincidence

co|in|ci|dent|al /ˌkəʊɪnsɪˈdentəl/

ADJECTIVE Something that is **coincidental** is the result of a coincidence and has not been deliberately arranged. ○ *Any resemblance to actual persons, places or events is purely coincidental.* ○ [+ that] *I think that it is not coincidental that we now have arguably the best bookshops in the world.*

▶ **COLLOCATIONS:**
timing is coincidental
purely/entirely coincidental

c

col|labo|rate /kəˈlæbəreɪt/ (collaborates, collaborating, collaborated)

VERB When one person or group **collaborates with** another, they work together, especially on a book or on some research. ○ [+ *with*] *He collaborated with his son Michael on the English translation of a text on food production.* ○ [+ *in*] *a place where professionals and amateurs collaborated in the making of music* ○ [+ *on*] *Kodak and Chinon will continue to collaborate on the engineering and development of digital cameras and scanners.*

▶ **COLLOCATIONS:**
collaborate **with** *someone*
collaborate **in/on** *something*
scientists/architects/engineers collaborate
universities/researchers/organizations collaborate
collaborate **closely/extensively/effectively**

col|labo|ra|tion /kəˌlæbəˈreɪʃən/ (collaborations)

1 NOUN Collaboration is the act of working together to produce a piece of work, especially a book or some research. ○ [+ *with*] *There is substantial collaboration with neighbouring departments.* ○ [+ *between*] *Close collaboration between the Bank and the Fund is not merely desirable, it is essential.* ○ *scientific collaborations* ○ [+ *with*] *Drummond was working on a book in collaboration with Zodiac Mindwarp.*

2 NOUN A **collaboration** is a piece of work that has been produced as the result of people or groups working together. ○ [+ *with*] *He was also a writer of beautiful stories, some of which are collaborations with his fiancee.* ○ *one of their collaborations from the second album*

▶ **COLLOCATIONS:**
a collaboration **with** *someone*
in collaboration
a collaboration **between** *people/things*
collaboration **on** *something*
promote/encourage/promote collaboration
a **scientific/technical/musical** collaboration

col|labo|ra|tive /kəˈlæbərətɪv, AM -reɪt-/

ADJECTIVE A **collaborative** piece of work is done by two or more people or groups working together. [FORMAL] ○ *a collaborative research project* ○ *This work is a collaborative effort with other health care workers, including paediatricians, physiotherapists, and nurses.*

▶ **COLLOCATIONS:**
a collaborative **project/partnership/process/effort**
collaborative **working/learning/research**
highly collaborative

col|late /kəˈleɪt/ (collates, collating, collated)

VERB When you **collate** pieces of information, you gather them all together and examine them. ○ *Roberts has spent much of his working life collating the data on which the study was based.* ○ *They have begun to collate their own statistics on racial abuse.*

▶ **COLLOCATIONS:**
collate **information/data**
collate **figures/statistics**

col|la|tion /kəˈleɪʃən/

UNCOUNTABLE NOUN ○ [+ *of*] *Many countries have no laws governing the collation of personal information.* ○ *The completed surveys are now with Queensland Transport for a more thorough collation and analysis.*

▶ **COLLOCATION:** the collation **of** *something*

colo|ny /ˈkɒləni/ (colonies)   POLITICS   HISTORY   BIOLOGY

1 NOUN A **colony** is a country which is controlled by a more powerful country. ○ *In France's former North African colonies, anti-French feeling is growing.* ○ *Puerto Rico, though it calls itself a Commonwealth, is really a self-governing American colony.*

▶ **COLLOCATIONS:**
a **former/Dutch/Portuguese/British** colony
found/establish/administer/govern a colony
annex/invade a colony

2 NOUN A **colony of** birds, insects, or animals is a group of them that live together. ○ [+ *of*] *The Shetlands are famed for their colonies of sea birds.* ○ *The caterpillars feed in large colonies.*

▶ **COLLOCATIONS:**
a colony **of** *something*
a colony of **bacteria/bats**
a **penguin/ant/seal** colony
a colony **inhabits/nests/breeds/grows**
a **large/breeding** colony

co|lo|nial /kəˈləʊniəl/

1 ADJECTIVE Colonial means relating to countries that are colonies, or to colonialism. ○ *the 31st anniversary of Jamaica's independence from British colonial rule.* ○ *the colonial civil service*

▶ **COLLOCATION:** colonial **rule/power/occupation**

2 ADJECTIVE A **Colonial** building or piece of furniture was built or made in a

style that was popular in America in the 17th and 18th centuries. [mainly AM]
○ *the white colonial houses on the north side of the campus* ○ *There is a lot of old colonial architecture left and it is well preserved.*

▶ COLLOCATIONS:
colonial **architecture/furniture**
a colonial **house/mansion**

co|lo|ni|al|ism /kəˈləʊniəlɪzəm/

UNCOUNTABLE NOUN **Colonialism** is the practice by which a powerful country directly controls less powerful countries and uses their resources to increase its own power and wealth. ○ *the bitter oppression of slavery and colonialism* ○ *It is interesting to reflect why European colonialism ended.*

▶ COLLOCATION: **Western/19th-century/European** colonialism

▶ PHRASES:
colonialism and imperialism
slavery and colonialism

co|lo|ni|al|ist /kəˈləʊniəlɪst/ (colonialists)

1 ADJECTIVE **Colonialist** means relating to colonialism. ○ *Earlier, the Cuban government had accused the Spanish Foreign Minister of colonialist attitudes.* ○ *the European colonialist powers*

2 NOUN A **colonialist** is a person who believes in colonialism or helps their country to get colonies. ○ *rulers who were imposed on the people by the colonialists* ○ *the British colonialists were brutal in the extreme*

▶ COLLOCATION: a **Portuguese/British/18th-century** colonialist

colo|nize /ˈkɒlənaɪz/ (colonizes, colonizing, colonized)

1 VERB If people **colonize** a foreign country, they go to live there and take control of it. [in BRIT, also use **colonise**] ○ *The first British attempt to colonize Ireland was in the twelfth century.* ○ *Liberia was never colonised by the European powers.*

▶ COLLOCATIONS:
colonized **by** *people*
colonize a **land/territory/region/island**

2 VERB When large numbers of animals **colonize** a place, they go to live there and make it their home. [in BRIT, also use **colonise**] ○ *If the bats colonize a new cave, it soon becomes infested with ticks.* ○ *golden eagles colonized the island*

▶ COLLOCATIONS:
colonized **by** *things*
colonize an **area/island/cave**

com|bat /kəmˈbæt/

(**combats, combating** or **combatting, combated** or **combatted**)

VERB If people in authority **combat** something, they try to stop it happening. ○ *Congress has criticised new government measures to combat crime.* ○ *drugs used to combat infectious diseases*

▶ **COLLOCATIONS:**
combat **terrorism/racism/corruption**
combat **pollution/disease**
effectively/successfully combat *something*

com|bus|tion /kəmˈbʌstʃən/ `SCIENCE`

UNCOUNTABLE NOUN Combustion is the act of burning something or the process of burning. ○ *The energy is released by combustion on the application of a match.* ○ *The two principal combustion products are water vapor and carbon dioxide.*

▶ **COLLOCATIONS:**
the combustion **of** *something*
a combustion **product/process/plant/engine**

com|men|tary /ˈkɒməntri, `ACADEMIC STUDY` `ACADEMIC WORD`
AM -teri/ (**commentaries**)

1 NOUN A **commentary** is an article or book which explains or discusses something. ○ [+ *on*] *Mr Rich will be writing a twice-weekly commentary on American society and culture.* ○ [+ *about*] *an insightful weekly commentary about life in the United States*

▶ **COLLOCATIONS:**
a commentary **on/about** *something*
a commentary **by** *someone*
an **informative/insightful** commentary

2 UNCOUNTABLE NOUN Commentary is discussion or criticism of something. ○ *The show mixed comedy with social commentary.* ○ *He provides virtually continuous commentary to his passengers.*

▶ **COLLOCATION: social/ironic/wry** commentary

com|men|ta|tor /ˈkɒmənteɪtə/ (**commentators**)

NOUN A **commentator** is someone who often writes or broadcasts about a particular subject. ○ *a political commentator* ○ [+ *on*] *A. M. Babu is a commentator on African affairs.*

▶ **COLLOCATIONS:**
a commentator **on** *something*

a **political/cultural/left-wing** commentator
a commentator **notes/observes/interprets** something
a commentator **criticizes** something

---

com|mis|sion /kəˈmɪʃən/   [ACADEMIC WORD] [BUSINESS]
(commissions, commissioning, commissioned)

1 VERB If you **commission** something or **commission** someone **to** do
something, you formally arrange for someone to do a piece of work for
you. ○ *The Ministry of Agriculture commissioned a study into low-input
farming.* ○ [+ to-inf] *You can commission them to paint something especially
for you.* ○ *specially commissioned reports*

▶ COLLOCATIONS:
commissioned **by** someone
commission a **study/report/survey**
commission **research**
commission a **composer/architect**
specially commissioned

● **Commission** is also a noun. ○ [+ to-inf] *He approached John Wexley with a
commission to write the screenplay of the film.* ○ [+ to-inf] *Armitage won a
commission to design the war memorial.*

▶ COLLOCATION: **gain/receive/win** a commission

2 NOUN Commission is a sum of money paid to a salesperson for every
sale that he or she makes. If a salesperson is paid **on commission**, the
amount they receive depends on the amount they sell. ○ *The salesmen
work on commission only.* ○ [+ for] *He also got a commission for bringing in
new clients.*

▶ COLLOCATIONS:
on commission
a commission **for** something

3 UNCOUNTABLE NOUN If a bank or other company charges **commission**,
they charge a fee for providing a service, for example for exchanging
money or issuing an insurance policy. ○ [+ on] *Travel agents charge 1 per cent
commission on sterling cheques.* ○ *Sellers pay a fixed commission fee.*

▶ COLLOCATIONS:
commission **on** something
charge/pay commission
a commission **fee**
x **per cent** commission

4 NOUN A **commission** is a group of people who have been appointed to
find out about something or to control something. ○ [+ to-inf] *The*

authorities have been asked to set up a commission to investigate the murders.
○ the Press Complaints Commission

▶ COLLOCATIONS:
   set up/appoint a commission
   a **complaints/independent** commission
   a **special/electoral** commission

---

com|mod|ity /kə'mɒdɪti/ `ACADEMIC WORD` `BUSINESS` `ECONOMICS`
(commodities)

NOUN A **commodity** is something that is sold for money. ○ *The government increased prices on several basic commodities like bread and meat.* ○ *Unlike gold, most commodities are not kept solely for investment purposes.*

▶ COLLOCATIONS:
   a commodity **market/exchange**
   commodity **trading/futures/prices**
   a **tradeable/marketable/valuable/rare** commodity
   a **basic** commodity

---

com|pat|ible /kəm'pætɪbəl/ `ACADEMIC WORD`

1 ADJECTIVE If things, for example systems, ideas, and beliefs, are **compatible**, they work well together or can exist together successfully. ○ [+ with] *Free enterprise, he argued, was compatible with Russian values and traditions.* ○ *The two aims are not necessarily compatible.*

▶ COLLOCATIONS:
   compatible **with** something
   compatible **aims/ideas/beliefs**

2 ADJECTIVE If a make of computer or equipment is **compatible with** another make, they can be used together and can use the same software. ○ [+ with] *iTunes is only compatible with the iPod while Microsoft and Sony are offering rival technologies.* ○ [+ with] *Only Windows-based desktop computers less than 4 years old are compatible with the software.*

▶ COLLOCATIONS:
   compatible **with** something
   compatible with a **device/browser/pc/system**
   compatible with **software**

▶ ANTONYM: incompatible

com|pat|ibil|ity /kəm,pætɪ'bɪlɪti/

UNCOUNTABLE NOUN ○ [+ with] *National courts can freeze any law while its compatibility with European legislation is being tested.* ○ [+ between] *the* *compatibility between a certain job and a candidate* ○ [+ *of*] *chapter 13 describes the compatibility of reincarnation with the Christian faith*

▶ COLLOCATIONS:
compatibility **with** *something/someone*
compatibility **between** *things/people*
the compatibility **of** *something* with *something*

▶ ANTONYM: incompatibility

com|pel|ling /kəmˈpelɪŋ/ `ACADEMIC WORD`

ADJECTIVE A **compelling** argument or reason is one that convinces you that something is true or that something should be done. ○ *Factual and forensic evidence makes a suicide verdict the most compelling answer to the mystery of his death.* ○ *The evidence was so compelling that the central Government did not have to force this change; it was willingly accepted.*

▶ COLLOCATIONS:
a compelling **argument/reason/testimony**
compelling **data/results/evidence**

com|pen|sate /ˈkɒmpənseɪt/
(compensates, compensating, compensated)

1 VERB To **compensate** someone **for** money or things that they have lost means to pay them money or give them something to replace that money or those things. ○ [+ *for*] *To ease financial difficulties, farmers could be compensated for their loss of subsidies.* ○ *the Anglican Church has pledged to fully compensate sex abuse victims in South Australia*

▶ COLLOCATIONS:
compensate *someone* **for** *something*
financially compensated
adequately/amply/generously/fully compensated

2 VERB Something that **compensates for** something else balances it or reduces its effects. ○ [+ *for*] *MPs say it is crucial that a system is found to compensate for inflation.* ○ [+ *for*] *The drug may compensate for prostaglandin deficiency.*

▶ COLLOCATIONS:
compensate **for** *something*
compensate for a **deficiency/imbalance**
compensate for a **loss/absence**

com|pen|sa|tion /ˌkɒmpənˈseɪʃən/ (compensations)

UNCOUNTABLE NOUN **Compensation** is money that someone who has experienced loss or suffering claims from the person or organization responsible, or from the state. ○ [+ *for*] *He received one year's salary as compensation for loss of office.* ○ *The Court ordered Dr Williams to pay £300 compensation and £100 costs after admitting assault.*

▶ **COLLOCATIONS:**
   compensation **for** *something*
   compensation for **unfair dismissal/loss of earnings**
   pay/award/grant/deny/refuse compensation
   demand/seek/claim/receive compensation
   a compensation **payout/package/payment**

com|pile /kəmˈpaɪl/ (compiles, compiling, compiled) `ACADEMIC WORD`

VERB When you **compile** something such as a report, book, or programme, you produce it by collecting and putting together many pieces of information. ○ *The book took 10 years to compile.* ○ *The report was compiled by 240 scientists from 96 countries to assess the status of coral reefs worldwide.*

▶ **COLLOCATIONS:**
   compiled **by** *someone*
   compile a **report/register/list**
   compile a **dictionary/anthology**
   compile **records/data/figures/statistics**

com|pi|la|tion /ˌkɒmpɪˈleɪʃən/ (compilations)

NOUN ○ [+ *of*] *a compilation of essays and articles on a wide range of topics* ○ [+ *of*] *the compilation of research data*

▶ **COLLOCATIONS:**
   a compilation **of** *things*
   a compilation of **songs/clips**
   the compilation of **data/material**

▶ **SYNONYM:** collection

com|ple|ment /ˈkɒmplɪmənt/ `ACADEMIC WORD`
(complements, complementing, complemented)

VERB If people or things **complement** each other, they are different or do something different, which makes them a good combination. ○ *There will be a written examination to complement the practical test.* ○ *Their academic program is complemented by a wide range of sporting, recreational and cultural activities.*

▶ COLLOCATIONS:
complemented **by** *something*
complement the **menu/architecture/setting**
perfectly complement *something*

com|ple|men|tary /ˌkɒmplɪˈmentri/

ADJECTIVE Complementary things are different from each other but make a good combination. [FORMAL] ○ *To improve the quality of life through work, two complementary strategies are necessary.* ○ [+ to] *He has done experiments complementary to those of Eigen.*

▶ COLLOCATIONS:
complementary **to** *something*
complementary **strategies/skills**
complementary **colours/shades**

USAGE: complement or **compliment**?

Be careful, it is easy to confuse these two words.

If two things **complement** each other or are **complementary**, they combine well together. ○ *modern design features that complement the original style of the house*

If you **compliment** someone, you say something nice about them; a **complimentary** remark. ○ *He complimented Tania on her cooking.*

---

com|ply /kəmˈplaɪ/ (complies, complying, complied)

VERB If someone or something **complies with** an order or set of rules, they are in accordance with what is required or expected. ○ [+ with] *The commander said that the army would comply with the ceasefire.* ○ [+ with] *Some beaches had failed to comply with European directives on bathing water.*

▶ COLLOCATIONS:
comply **with** *something*
comply with **requirements/regulations/laws**
fully/willingly comply

EXTEND YOUR VOCABULARY

You can say that someone **obeys**, **abides by** or **complies with** rules, regulations or the law, if they act according to them. ○ *All employees are expected to obey/abide by/comply with the rules on safety.*

You can say that someone **obeys** a rule or another person. You can only say that someone **abides by** or **complies with** a rule. ○ *He was charged with failure to obey a police officer.*

You often say that something, such as a product or a system, **complies with** regulations, whereas it is usually a person who **obeys** or **abides by** something. ○ *New vehicles must comply with emission standards.*

com|pli|ance /kəmˈplaɪəns/

UNCOUNTABLE NOUN Compliance with something, for example a law, treaty, or agreement means doing what you are required or expected to do. [FORMAL] ○ [+ *with*] *The company says it is in full compliance with U.S. labor laws.* ○ [+ *by*] *The Security Council aim to ensure compliance by all sides, once an agreement is signed.*

▶ COLLOCATIONS:
compliance **with** something
compliance **by** someone
compliance with **requirements/regulations/laws**
full/strict/voluntary/non- compliance

com|pound /ˈkɒmpaʊnd/ ACADEMIC WORD CHEMISTRY
(compounds)

NOUN In chemistry, a **compound** is a substance that consists of two or more elements. ○ *Organic compounds contain carbon in their molecules.* ○ [+ *of*] *Gasoline is essentially a compound of carbon and hydrogen.*

▶ COLLOCATIONS:
a compound **of** something
a **synthetic/organic/inorganic** compound
a **chemical/toxic** compound
a **sulphur/nitrogen/chlorine** compound

com|pre|hend /ˌkɒmprɪˈhend/ (comprehends, comprehending, comprehended)

VERB If you cannot **comprehend** something, you cannot understand it. [FORMAL] ○ *Patients may not be mentally focused enough to comprehend the full significance of the diagnosis.* ○ *Wilson did not comprehend the intricacies of his own government's policy and decision-making.*

▶ COLLOCATIONS:
fully/adequately/scarcely comprehend
comprehend the **importance/magnitude/meaning**
comprehend the **implications/intricacies/complexities**

▶ SYNONYM: understand

c

com|pre|hen|sion /ˌkɒmprɪˈhenʃən/ (comprehensions)

1 UNCOUNTABLE NOUN Comprehension is the ability to understand something. [FORMAL] ○ *a devastating and barbaric act that defies all comprehension* ○ *It is an act of cruelty beyond all human comprehension.*

2 UNCOUNTABLE NOUN Comprehension is full knowledge and understanding of the meaning of something. [FORMAL] ○ *They turned to one another with the same expression of dawning comprehension, surprise, and relief.* ○ [+ of] *They have no comprehension of the complexities of law.*

▶ **COLLOCATIONS:**
   comprehension **of** something
   comprehension of **language/complexities**
   comprehension of a **text/passage/concept**
   defy/facilitate/improve/enhance comprehension
   verbal/human/intellectual comprehension
   mutual/limited comprehension

▶ **PHRASE:** beyond comprehension

▶ **SYNONYM:** understanding

---

com|pul|so|ry /kəmˈpʌlsəri/

ADJECTIVE If something is **compulsory**, you must do it or accept it, because it is the law or because someone in a position of authority says you must. ○ *Many companies ask workers to accept voluntary redundancy as opposed to compulsory redundancy.* ○ *Many young men are trying to get away from compulsory military conscription.*

▶ **COLLOCATIONS:**
   compulsory **for** someone
   make something compulsory
   compulsory **vaccination/voting/schooling**
   compulsory **retirement/redundancy**
   compulsory **insurance/superannuation**

▶ **SYNONYM:** mandatory

com|pul|so|ri|ly /kəmˈpʌlsərɪli/

ADVERB ○ *Five of the company's senior managers have been made compulsorily redundant.* ○ *abandon plans to impose the system compulsorily*

▶ **COLLOCATION:** compulsorily **acquire/purchase**

▶ **ANTONYM:** voluntarily

con|ceive /kənˈsiːv/ (conceives, conceiving, conceived) `ACADEMIC WORD`

1 VERB If you cannot **conceive of** something, you cannot imagine it or believe it. ○ [+ of] *Western leaders could not conceive of the idea that there might be traitors at high levels in their own governments.* ○ [+ of] *He was immensely ambitious but unable to conceive of winning power for himself.* ○ [+ that] *We cannot conceive that he will die at home.*

▶ **COLLOCATIONS:**
conceive **of** *something*
not conceive of *something*
not conceive of a **circumstance/idea/situation/possibility**

2 VERB If you **conceive** something **as** a particular thing, you consider it to be that thing. ○ [+ as] *The ancients conceived the Earth as afloat in water.* ○ [+ of] *We conceive of the family as being in a constant state of change.* ○ [+ of] *She cannot conceive of herself being anything else but a doctor.*

▶ **COLLOCATIONS:**
conceive *something* **as** *something*
conceive **of** *something* as *something*

con|ceiv|able /kənˈsiːvəbəl/

ADJECTIVE If something is **conceivable**, you can imagine it or believe it. ○ *Without their support the project would not have been conceivable.* ○ *Through the centuries, flowers have been used for cooking in every conceivable way.*

▶ **COLLOCATIONS:**
every conceivable *something*
every conceivable **angle/way**

▶ **ANTONYM:** inconceivable

con|ceiv|ably /kənˈsiːvəbli/

ADVERB ○ *The mission could conceivably be accomplished within a week.* ○ *A series of interest-rate rises might conceivably affect buyers' confidence at the upper end of the market.*

con|clu|sive /kənˈkluːsɪv/ `ACADEMIC WORD`

ADJECTIVE **Conclusive** evidence shows that something is certainly true. ○ *Her attorneys claim there is no conclusive evidence that any murders took place.* ○ *Research on the matter is far from conclusive.*

▶ **COLLOCATIONS:**
conclusive **evidence/proof**
conclusive **results/tests**

▶ **ANTONYM:** inconclusive

con|clu|sive|ly /kənˈkluːsɪvli/

ADVERB ○ *A new study proved conclusively that smokers die younger than non-smokers.* ○ *By 1 October they had conclusively established the existence of the antiparticle.*

▶ COLLOCATIONS:
conclusively **prove/demonstrate**
conclusively **determine/answer**

ACADEMIC WRITING: Degrees of certainty

In academic writing, it is often important to show how clear or certain something is. You can say that evidence or the results of a study are **conclusive** or **definitive** to mean that they are clear and there is no doubt about them. ○ *There is as yet no conclusive/ definitive proof.*

You can say that someone or something is **credible** is if you think they can be trusted, for example based on reputation. ○ *There is no credible evidence that establishes a causal link.*

---

con|cur|rent /kənˈkʌrənt, AM -ˈkɜːr-/ `ACADEMIC WORD`

ADJECTIVE **Concurrent** events or situations happen at the same time.
○ *There remains a large area of concurrent jurisdiction where a plaintiff may still sue in either a provincial or the Federal Court.* ○ *He will actually be serving three concurrent five-year sentences.* ○ *[+ with] toll-free Web access concurrent with paper publication*

▶ COLLOCATIONS:
concurrent **with** *something*
concurrent **sentences/events/jurisdiction**
concurrent **symptoms/infections/medication**
serve concurrent sentences

con|cur|rent|ly /kənˈkʌrəntli, AM -ˈkɜːr-/

ADVERB ○ *He was jailed for 33 months to run concurrently with a sentence he is already serving for burglary.* ○ *[+ with] It is unethical for human trials to run concurrently with chronic toxicity tests on animals.*

▶ COLLOCATIONS:
concurrently **with** *something*
run/occur/exist concurrently with *something*

con|demn /kən'dem/ (condemns, condemning, condemned)

VERB If you **condemn** something, you say that it is very bad and unacceptable. ○ *Political leaders united yesterday to condemn the latest wave of violence.* ○ [+ *for*] *He publicly condemned the US for moving without the UN to invade Iraq.* ○ [+ *as*] *a document that condemns sexism as a moral and social evil*

▶ **COLLOCATIONS:**
condemn someone **for** something
condemn something **as** something
condemned **by** someone
strongly/unequivocally/unreservedly/publicly condemn

▶ **SYNONYM:** denounce
▶ **ANTONYM:** condone

con|dem|na|tion /ˌkɒndem'neɪʃən/ (condemnations)

NOUN ○ [+ *of*] *There was widespread condemnation of Saturday's killings.* ○ [+ *from*] *The raids have drawn a strong condemnation from the United Nations Security Council.*

▶ **COLLOCATIONS:**
condemnation **of** something
condemnation **from** someone
international/moral/widespread condemnation
condemnation of the **violence/killing/attack/invasion**
provoke/spark/draw/incur condemnation

con|dense /kən'dens/ SCIENCE GEOGRAPHY
(condenses, condensing, condensed)

VERB When a gas or vapour **condenses**, or **is condensed**, it changes into a liquid. ○ [+ *to-inf*] *Water vapour condenses to form clouds.* ○ [+ *into*] *The compressed gas is cooled and condenses into a liquid.* ○ [+ *out of*] *As the air rises it becomes colder and moisture condenses out of it.*

▶ **COLLOCATIONS:**
condense **into/out of** something
condense into **rain/liquid/droplets**
vapour/moisture/steam/gas condenses
a **cloud** condenses

con|den|sa|tion /ˌkɒnden'seɪʃən/

UNCOUNTABLE NOUN **Condensation** consists of small drops of water which form when warm water vapour or steam touches a cold surface such as a window. ○ [+ *of*] *Silicon carbide crystals are formed by the condensation of supersaturated vapour.*

▶ **COLLOCATIONS:**
condensation **on** *something*
the condensation **of** *something*
condensation on a **window/windscreen/surface**
prevent/eliminate/avoid condensation
water/steam/vapour condensation

▶ **PHRASE:** dampness and condensation

---

con|duct /kən'dʌkt/   ENGINEERING   SCIENCE

(conducts, conducting, conducted)

VERB If something **conducts** heat or electricity, it allows heat or electricity to pass through it or along it. ○ *Water conducts heat faster than air.* ○ *The molecule did not conduct electricity.*

▶ **COLLOCATION:** conduct **heat/electricity**

con|duc|tion /kən'dʌkʃən/

UNCOUNTABLE NOUN ○ *Temperature becomes uniform by heat conduction until finally a permanent state is reached.* ○ [+ *of*] *best known for his work on the conduction of electricity by gases*

▶ **COLLOCATIONS:**
conduction **of** *something*
conduction of **electricity/energy/heat**
electron/electrical conduction

con|duc|tive /kən'dʌktɪv/

ADJECTIVE A **conductive** substance is able to conduct things such as heat and electricity. ○ *Salt water is much more conductive than fresh water is.* ○ *electrically conductive polymers*

▶ **COLLOCATIONS:**
electrically conductive
conductive **fibres/threads**

con|duc|tiv|ity /ˌkɒndʌk'tɪvɪti/

UNCOUNTABLE NOUN ○ *a device which monitors electrical conductivity* ○ [+ *of*] *Small electrodes are taped to the fingers, and attached to a device which monitors the electrical conductivity of the skin.*

▶ **COLLOCATIONS:**
the conductivity **of** *something*
electrical/hydraulic conductivity

con|duc|tor /kən'dʌktə/ (conductors)

NOUN A **conductor** is a substance that heat or electricity can pass through or along. ○ *Because this channel is an electrical conductor, it provides a place for surrounding electrons to go.* ○ [+ of] *good conductors of heat and electricity*

▶ **COLLOCATIONS:**
a conductor **of** something
a conductor of **heat/electricity**
a **lightning/electrical** conductor

▶ **RELATED WORD:** semiconductor

con|fined /kən'faɪnd/   ACADEMIC WORD

1 ADJECTIVE If something is **confined to** a particular place, it exists only in that place. If it is **confined to** a particular group, only members of that group have it. ○ [+ to] *The problem is not confined to Germany.* ○ [+ to] *These dangers are not confined to smokers.*

▶ **COLLOCATIONS:**
confined **to** someone/somewhere
largely/exclusively confined to someone/somewhere

▶ **SYNONYMS:** restricted, limited

2 ADJECTIVE A **confined** space or area is small and enclosed by walls. ○ *The drill connects to all 12 volt batteries and is useful for working in confined spaces.* ○ *the confined area of the crash site made rescue operations difficult*

▶ **COLLOCATION:** a confined **space/area**

▶ **SYNONYM:** enclosed

con|form /kən'fɔːm/   ACADEMIC WORD
(conforms, conforming, conformed)

1 VERB If something **conforms to** something such as a law or someone's wishes, it is of the required type or quality. ○ [+ to] *The Night Rider lamp has been designed to conform to new British Standard safety requirements.* ○ [+ with] *The meat market can continue only if it is radically overhauled to conform with strict European standards.*

▶ **COLLOCATIONS:**
conform **to/with** something
conform to/with **requirements/standards/laws**
conform **closely/strictly/exactly**

2 VERB If someone or something **conforms to** a pattern or type, they are very similar to it. ○ [+ to] *I am well aware that we all conform to one stereotype or another.* ○ [+ to] *Like most 'peacetime wars' it did not conform to preconceived ideas.*

▶ **COLLOCATIONS:**
conform **to** *something*
conform to a **pattern/idea/stereotype/model**

con|form|ity /kənˈfɔːmɪti/

1 UNCOUNTABLE NOUN If something happens **in conformity with** something such as a law or someone's wishes, it happens as the law says it should, or as the person wants it to. ○ [+ with] *The prime minister is, in conformity with the constitution, chosen by the president.* ○ [+ with] *Any action it takes has to be in conformity with international law.*

▶ **COLLOCATIONS:**
in conformity with the **law/constitution**
in conformity with the **principles/ideology** of *something*
in conformity with **standards/regulations/requirements**

▶ **PHRASE:** in conformity with something

2 UNCOUNTABLE NOUN **Conformity** means behaving in the same way as most other people. ○ *Excessive conformity is usually caused by fear of disapproval.* ○ [+ in] *Pressure appears to be mounting for conformity in how people speak English.*

▶ **COLLOCATIONS:**
conformity **of/in** *something*
enforce/compel/impose conformity
defy/reject/resist conformity
ideological/mindless/intellectual conformity

Con|gress /ˈkɒŋgres/　[POLITICS]

NOUN **Congress** is the elected group of politicians that is responsible for making the law in the United States. It consists of two parts: the House of Representatives and the Senate. ○ *We want to cooperate with both the administration and Congress.* ○ *and became Tennessee's first representative to Congress*

▶ **COLLOCATIONS:**
Congress **convenes/adjourns**
Congress **approves/adopts/rejects** *something*
elect/dissolve/disband Congress
a **biennial/triennial** Congress

con|gres|sion|al /kənˈgreʃənəl/ also **Congressional**

ADJECTIVE A **congressional** policy, action, or person relates to the United States Congress. ○ *The president explained his plans to congressional leaders.* ○ *a congressional report published on September 5th*

▶ **COLLOCATIONS:**
congressional **approval/authorization**
a congressional **report/policy/hearing**
a congressional **leader/committee**

---

con|jec|ture /kən'dʒektʃə/ (conjectures)

NOUN A **conjecture** is a conclusion that is based on information that is not certain or complete. [FORMAL] ○ *That was a conjecture, not a fact.* ○ *Ozone creation is a very large-scale natural process and the importance of human-generated CFCs in reducing it is largely a matter of conjecture.*

→ see note at **speculate**

▶ **COLLOCATIONS:**
a matter **of/for** conjecture
conjecture **about** *something*
fuel/spark/prompt conjecture
scientific/historical conjecture

▶ **SYNONYM:** surmise

---

con|no|ta|tion /ˌkɒnə'teɪʃən/ (connotations) LANGUAGE

NOUN The **connotations** of a particular word or name are the ideas or qualities which it makes you think of. ○ *In Norse mythology, Hel is the realm of the dead, but the name does not carry the negative connotations which Christianity later placed upon it.* ○ [+ of] *'Urchin', with its connotation of mischievousness, may not be a particularly apt word.*

▶ **COLLOCATIONS:**
the connotations **of** *something*
the connotations of a **word/term**
negative/pejorative connotations
sexual/racist/religious connotations

▶ **SYNONYM:** association

---

con|secu|tive /kən'sekjʊtɪv/

ADJECTIVE **Consecutive** periods of time or events happen one after the other without interruption. ○ *This is the third consecutive year that these countries achieved economic growth.* ○ *Photographs taken at the same time on two consecutive sunny days can be quite different from one another.*

▶ **COLLOCATIONS:**
consecutive **days/nights/months/years**
the **second/third/fourth** consecutive *day/year*
two/three/four consecutive *days/years*

▶ **SYNONYM:** successive

c

con|secu|tive|ly /kən'sekjʊtɪvli/

ADVERB ○ *The judge decided yesterday that the sentences for the three murders should run consecutively, not concurrently as requested by the prosecution.* ○ *He will face two further prison sentences, totalling 11 years, to be served consecutively.*

▶ **COLLOCATION: run/serve** consecutively

▶ **SYNONYM:** successively

▶ **RELATED WORD:** concurrently

---

con|sent /kən'sent/ (consents, consenting, consented) `ACADEMIC WORD`

1 UNCOUNTABLE NOUN If you give your **consent to** something, you give someone permission to do it. [FORMAL] ○ [+ to] *Patients must give their signed consent to an operation.* ○ *Can my child be medically examined without my consent?*

▶ **COLLOCATIONS:**
consent **to** *something*
with/without *someone's* consent
seek/solicit/obtain/grant/refuse consent
written/unanimous/mutual/parental consent

2 VERB If you **consent to** something, you agree to do it or to allow it to be done. [FORMAL] ○ [+ to-inf] *Doctors failed to fully inform patients before they consented to participate.* ○ [+ to] *She had consented to a laparotomy, fibroid removal, and the reconstruction of her uterus.* ○ *Churchill proposed to Stalin a division of influence in the Balkan states. Stalin readily consented.*

▶ **COLLOCATIONS:**
consent **to** *something*
consent to **marry** *someone*
consent to **allow** *something*

▶ **SYNONYM:** agree

con|sen|sus /kən'sensəs/

NOUN A **consensus** is general agreement among a group of people. ○ [+ amongst] *The consensus amongst the world's scientists is that the world is likely to warm up over the next few decades.* ○ [+ on] *So far, the Australians have been unable to come to a uniform consensus on the issue.*

▶ **COLLOCATIONS:**
the consensus **amongst** *people*
a consensus **on/about** *something*
reach/build/achieve a consensus
seek/establish a consensus
a **scientific/cross-party/broad/general** consensus

con|stant /ˈkɒnstənt/ (constants)

`MATHS` `SCIENCE`

NOUN A **constant** is a thing or value that always stays the same. ○ [+ of] *The constants of nature are certain numbers that enter into the mathematical equations that describe the laws of physics.* ○ *Two significant constants have been found in a number of research studies.*

▶ **COLLOCATIONS:**
   a constant **of** something
   a **fundamental/universal** constant
   a **mathematical/physical** constant

▶ **PHRASE:** the constants of nature

▶ **ANTONYM:** variable

con|stitu|ent /kənˈstɪtʃʊənt/ (constituents)

1 NOUN A **constituent of** a mixture, substance, or system is one of the things from which it is formed. ○ [+ of] *Caffeine is the active constituent of drinks such as tea and coffee.* ○ *The main constituents were lemon juice and syrup of radish.*

▶ **COLLOCATIONS:**
   a constituent **of** something
   a **major/active** constituent

2 ADJECTIVE The **constituent** parts of something are the things from which it is formed. [FORMAL] ○ *a plan to split the company into its constituent parts and sell them separately* ○ *These constraints force its constituent minerals to change their atomic structure.*

▶ **COLLOCATIONS:**
   a constituent **part/element/atom/mineral**
   a constituent **assembly/republic**

con|sti|tu|tion /ˌkɒnstɪˈtjuːʃən, AM -ˈtuː-/ (constitutions)

`ACADEMIC WORD` `POLITICS`

NOUN The **constitution** of a country or organization is the system of laws which formally states people's rights and duties. ○ *The transitional authority will draft a constitution.* ○ *The constitution enshrined religious freedom, civil liberties and the right to form unions.*

▶ **COLLOCATIONS:**
   a **written/permanent/interim/democratic** constitution
   draft/write/amend/ratify a constitution
   uphold/violate/suspend the constitution
   the constitution **guarantees/protects** something
   the constitution **forbids/prohibits** something
   the **American/Cuban/Afghan** Constitution

NOUN Your **constitution** is your health. ○ *He must have an extremely strong constitution.* ○ *Cross's insulin requirements will be plotted carefully and the effect of the exercise on his constitution will be monitored.*

▶ **COLLOCATION:** a **strong/hardy** constitution

▶ **SYNONYM:** health

con|sti|tu|tion|al /ˌkɒnstɪˈtjuːʃənəl, AM -ˈtuː-/

ADJECTIVE ○ *Political leaders are making no progress in their efforts to resolve the country's constitutional crisis.* ○ *A Romanian judge has asked for a Constitutional Court ruling on the law.*

▶ **COLLOCATIONS:**
a constitutional **court/right/amendment/change**
a constitutional **crisis**

---

con|strain /kənˈstreɪn/   ACADEMIC WORD
(constrains, constraining, constrained)

VERB To **constrain** someone or something means to limit their development or force them to behave in a particular way. [FORMAL]
○ *Women are too often constrained by family commitments and by low expectations.* ○ *It's the capacity of those roads which is going to constrain the amount of travel by car that can take place.*

▶ **COLLOCATIONS:**
constrained **by** *something*
constrained by **limits**

▶ **SYNONYM:** limit

con|straint /kənˈstreɪnt/ (constraints)

NOUN A **constraint** is something that limits or controls what you can do.
○ *Their decision to abandon the trip was made because of financial constraints.*
○ *[+ on] Water shortages in the area will be the main constraint on development.*

▶ **COLLOCATIONS:**
a constraint **on** *something/someone*
the constraints **of** *something*
financial/budgetary constraints
capacity/budget constraints
constraints **limit** *something*
face/impose/remove/relax constraints

▶ **SYNONYM:** limitation

con|struc|tive /kən'strʌktɪv/

ADJECTIVE A **constructive** discussion, comment, or approach is useful and helpful rather than negative and unhelpful. ○ *The Americans have already praised what they call Syria's constructive approach to ending terrorism.* ○ *After their meeting, both men described the talks as frank, friendly and constructive.* ○ *The Prime Minister has promised that Israel will play a constructive role.*

▶ **COLLOCATIONS:**
constructive **talks/dialogue/criticism**
a constructive **role/comment/approach/discussion**

▶ **SYNONYM:** positive

▶ **ANTONYM:** negative

---

con|tami|nate /kən'tæmɪneɪt/ SCIENCE
(contaminates, contaminating, contaminated)

VERB If something **is contaminated by** dirt, chemicals, or radiation, they make it dirty or harmful. ○ *Have any fish been contaminated in the Arctic Ocean?* ○ *vast tracts of empty land, much of it contaminated by years of army activity*

▶ **COLLOCATIONS:**
contaminated **by** *something*
contaminated by **sewage/bacteria/chemicals**
contaminate **water/blood/food/land**

con|tami|nat|ed /kən'tæmɪneɪtɪd/

ADJECTIVE ○ [+ *with*] *Nuclear weapons plants across the country are heavily contaminated with toxic wastes.* ○ *More than 100,000 people could fall ill after drinking contaminated water.*

▶ **COLLOCATIONS:**
contaminated **with** *something*
widely/heavily/seriously contaminated
contaminated **water/blood/food/land**

con|tami|na|tion /kən,tæmɪ'neɪʃən/

UNCOUNTABLE NOUN ○ [+ *of*] *The contamination of the sea around Capri may be just the beginning.* ○ *There is a slight danger of bacterial contamination.* ○ *The water that does run into the park is contaminated by chemicals.*

▶ **COLLOCATIONS:**
the contamination **of** *something*
contamination **by** *something*
contamination by **sewage/bacteria/chemicals**
bacterial/chemical/radioactive contamination

c

con|tami|nant /kənˈtæmɪnənt/ (contaminants)

NOUN A **contaminant** is something that contaminates a substance such as water or food. [FORMAL] ○ *Contaminants found in poultry will also be found in their eggs.* ○ [+ in] *We are exposed to an overwhelming number of chemical contaminants every day in our air, water and food.*

▶ COLLOCATIONS:
a contaminant **in** *something*
contaminants in **food**
contain/remove a contaminant
a **carcinogenic/toxic/chemical** contaminant

---

con|tend /kənˈtend/ (contends, contending, contended)

VERB If you **contend that** something is true, you state or argue that it is true. [FORMAL] ○ [+ that] *The government contends that he is fundamentalist.* ○ [+ that] *The Government strongly contends that no student should be compelled to pay a fee to support political activism.*

→ see note at **assert**

▶ COLLOCATIONS:
seriously/strongly contend
a **prosecutor/attorney/critic/opponent** contends

▶ SYNONYMS: state, argue

con|ten|tion /kənˈtenʃən/ (contentions)

NOUN Someone's **contention** is the idea or opinion that they are expressing in an argument or discussion. ○ [+ that] *This evidence supports their contention that the outbreak of violence was prearranged.* ○ *Sufficient research evidence exists to support this contention.*

▶ COLLOCATIONS:
support/accept a contention
dispute/refute/challenge a contention
the **prosecution's/author's/government's** contention

▶ SYNONYM: claim

---

con|tract /kənˈtrækt/   ACADEMIC WORD
(contracts, contracting, contracted)

VERB When something **contracts** or when something **contracts** it, it becomes smaller or shorter. ○ *Blood is only expelled from the heart when it contracts.* ○ *New research shows that an excess of meat and salt can contract muscles.*

▶ **COLLOCATIONS:**
the **throat** contracts
the **muscles/ventricles** contract
contract **rhythmically/rapidly**

▶ **ANTONYM:** expand

con|trac|tion /kənˈtrækʃən/ (contractions)

NOUN ○ [+ of] *the contraction and expansion of blood vessels* ○ *Foods and fluids are mixed in the stomach by its muscular contractions.*

▶ **COLLOCATIONS:**
the contraction **of** *something*
isometric/isotonic contractions
uterine/muscular contractions
induce/stimulate/trigger contractions
prevent/inhibit/control contractions

▶ **ANTONYM:** expansion

---

con|verse /ˈkɒnvɜːs/   ACADEMIC WORD

NOUN **The converse** of a statement is its opposite or reverse. [FORMAL]
○ *What you do for a living is critical to where you settle and how you live – and the converse is also true.* ○ *Similarly, the converse applies to coming upright from a bent position with the eyes looking downward.*

▶ **COLLOCATIONS:**
the converse **of** *something*
the converse is **true**

▶ **SYNONYM:** opposite

con|verse|ly /ˈkɒnvɜːsli, kənˈvɜːsli/

ADVERB You say **conversely** to indicate that the situation you are about to describe is the opposite or reverse of the one you have just described. [FORMAL] ○ *If government saving is high private saving will be low. Conversely if government saving is negative then private saving will be high.* ○ *That makes Chinese products even cheaper and, conversely, makes American-made goods more expensive to export.*

> **EXTEND YOUR VOCABULARY**
>
> In academic writing, you are often asked to compare and contrast two things; to talk about the ways in which they are similar and the ways in which they are different.

c

> To make a **contrast**, you can use phrases such as **in contrast** and
> **by contrast** to show that two things are very different. ○ *These figures*
> *are in sharp contrast to the findings of a similar survey in the summer.*
> ○ *Canada's 7.5% of rural land in agriculture contrasts markedly with the*
> *situation in smaller European states.*
>
> You can use **conversely** to introduce a completely opposite idea or
> situation. ○ *They may reduce the activity of certain hormones or, conversely,*
> *they may cause excessive hormonal activity.*

---

con|vey /kənˈveɪ/ (conveys, conveying, conveyed)

VERB To **convey** information or feelings means to cause them to be known
or understood by someone. ○ *Semiological analysis sees a sign as any cultural*
symbol which conveys a meaning. ○ *In every one of her pictures she conveys a*
sense of immediacy. ○ *He also conveyed his views and the views of the*
bureaucracy.

▶ COLLOCATIONS:
  convey a **sense/impression** of *something*
  convey the **meaning** of *something*
  convey *something* **vividly/powerfully/accurately**
  convey **information/emotion**
  convey a **message**

---

con|vict /kənˈvɪkt/ (convicts, convicting, convicted)   `LAW`

VERB If someone **is convicted of** a crime, they are found guilty of that
crime in a law court. ○ [+ *of*] *In 2007 he was convicted of murder and*
sentenced to life imprisonment. ○ *There was insufficient evidence to convict*
him. ○ *a convicted drug dealer*

▶ COLLOCATIONS:
  convict *someone* **of** *something*
  convict *someone* **on** a *charge/count*
  a convicted **felon/murderer/rapist**
  a **jury/juror/magistrate/court** convicts *someone*
  wrongly/falsely/unfairly convicted

con|vic|tion /kənˈvɪkʃən/ (convictions)

NOUN If someone has a **conviction**, they have been found guilty of a crime
in a court of law. ○ *He will appeal against his conviction.* ○ *The man was*
known to the police because of previous convictions.

▶ COLLOCATIONS:
  a conviction **for** *something*

a **criminal/wrongful/previous** conviction
appeal/quash/overturn a conviction
uphold/secure a conviction

---

con|vince /kən'vɪns/ ACADEMIC WORD
(convinces, convincing, convinced)

VERB If someone or something **convinces** you **of** something, they make you believe that it is true or that it exists. ○ [+ of] *We remain to be convinced of the validity of some of the research.* ○ [+ that] *The waste disposal industry is finding it difficult to convince the public that its operations are safe.*

▶ **COLLOCATIONS:**
   convince *someone* **of** *something*
   convinced **by** *something/someone*
   convinced by the **argument/evidence**
   convinced of the **merit/importance**
   convince the **public/electorate/jury**

con|vinc|ing /kən'vɪnsɪŋ/

ADJECTIVE If you describe someone or something as **convincing**, you mean that they make you believe that a particular thing is true, correct, or genuine. ○ *Scientists say there is no convincing evidence that power lines have anything to do with cancer.* ○ *The first explanation appears more convincing.*

▶ **COLLOCATIONS:**
   convincing **evidence**
   a convincing **argument/explanation**
   sound/look/appear/seem convincing

▶ **ANTONYM:** unconvincing

---

copy|right /'kɒpiraɪt/ (copyrights) BUSINESS LAW

NOUN If someone has **copyright** on a piece of writing or music, it is illegal to reproduce or perform it without their permission. ○ *To order a book one first had to get permission from the monastery that held the copyright.* ○ *She threatened legal action against the Sun for breach of copyright.*

▶ **COLLOCATIONS:**
   a copyright **on** *something*
   a copyright **infringement/violation**
   copyright **protection/law**
   infringe/violate a copyright
   hold/protect a copyright

▶ **PHRASE:** breach of copyright

core /kɔː/ (cores) ACADEMIC WORD

1 NOUN The **core** of an object, building, or city is the central part of it. ○ *the earth's core* ○ [+ *of*] *The core of the city is a series of ancient squares.*

▶ **COLLOCATIONS:**
the core **of** *something*
the **city's/planet's** core

▶ **PHRASE:** the earth's core

▶ **SYNONYM:** centre

2 NOUN The **core of** something such as a problem or an issue is the part of it that has to be understood or accepted before the whole thing can be understood or dealt with. ○ [+ *of*] *the ability to get straight to the core of a problem* ○ [+ *of*] *At the core of this ideology was an ethnic nationalism.*

▶ **COLLOCATIONS:**
the core **of** *something*
the core of a **theory/dispute/problem**

▶ **SYNONYM:** heart

3 NOUN The **core** businesses or the **core** activities of a company or organization are their most important ones. ○ *The core activities of local authorities were reorganised.* ○ *The group plans to concentrate on six core businesses.* ○ [+ *of*] *However, the main core of the company performed outstandingly.*

▶ **COLLOCATIONS:**
the core **of** *something*
the core **activities/businesses/areas**

---

cor|re|late /'kɒrəleɪt, AM 'kɔːr-/ (correlates, correlating, correlated)

VERB If one thing **correlates with** another, there is a close similarity or connection between them, often because one thing causes the other. You can also say that two things **correlate**. [FORMAL] ○ [+ *with*] *Obesity correlates with increased risk for hypertension and stroke.* ○ *The political opinions of spouses correlate more closely than their heights.* ○ [+ *to*] *The loss of respect for British science is correlated to reduced funding.* ○ *At the highest executive levels earnings and performance aren't always correlated.*

▶ **COLLOCATIONS:**
something correlates **with/to** *something*
inversely/negatively correlated
correlate **closely/strongly**

cor|re|la|tion /,kɒrə'leɪʃən, AM ,kɔːr-/ (correlations)

NOUN A **correlation between** things is a connection or link between

them. [FORMAL] ○ [+ *between*] *the correlation between smoking and disease*
○ [+ *between*] *Studies have shown that there is a direct correlation between poor*
education and disposition to crime.

▶ COLLOCATIONS:
a correlation **between** *two things*
a **strong/direct/negative** correlation
find/establish a correlation

---

coun|ter /ˈkaʊntə/ (counters, countering, countered)

VERB If you do something to **counter** a particular action or process, you do
something which has an opposite effect to it or makes it less effective.
○ *The leadership discussed a plan of economic measures to counter the effects of*
such a blockade. ○ *It should allow international observers to monitor them, to*
counter claims that the ballots are rigged. ○ [+ *by*] *Sears then countered by filing*
an antitrust lawsuit.

▶ COLLOCATIONS:
counter **with** *something*
counter **by** *doing something*
counter a **threat/accusation/claim/argument**
counter the **effect** of *something*

---

counter|act /ˈkaʊntərækt/ (counteracts, counteracting, counteracted)

VERB To **counteract** something means to reduce its effect by doing
something that produces an opposite effect. ○ *My husband has to take*
several pills to counteract high blood pressure. ○ *The vitamin counteracts the*
harmful effect of allergens in the body.

▶ COLLOCATIONS:
counteract **stress**
counteract **the effects** of *something*

---

counter|part /ˈkaʊntəpɑːt/ (counterparts)

NOUN Someone's or something's **counterpart** is another person or thing
that has a similar function or position in a different place. ○ *The Foreign*
Secretary telephoned his Italian counterpart to protest. ○ [+ *in*] *The Finnish*
organization was very different from that of its counterparts in the rest of the
Nordic region.

▶ COLLOCATIONS:
someone's/something's counterpart **in** *somewhere*
someone's counterpart in a **country**
a **male/continental/European** counterpart

c

coup /kuː/ (coups)   ACADEMIC WORD   POLITICS

NOUN When there is a **coup**, a group of people seize power in a country. ○ *a military coup* ○ *They were sentenced to death for their part in April's coup attempt.*

▸ COLLOCATIONS:
 a **military/attempted/failed/bloodless** coup
 a coup **overthrows/ousts/topples** *something*
 stage/plot/mount/provoke a coup

▸ SYNONYM: coup d'état

cra|ter /ˈkreɪtə/ (craters)   GEOGRAPHY

NOUN A **crater** is a very large hole in the ground, which has been caused by something hitting it or by an explosion. ○ *Experts calculate that a 3km asteroid could gouge a crater 60km across, and destroy an area the size of Mexico.* ○ *An ancient gigantic volcanic crater provides the perfectly shaped circle of Simpson Harbour.*

▸ COLLOCATIONS:
 a **volcanic/deep/shallow** crater
 gouge/blast/leave a crater

cred|ible /ˈkredɪbəl/

ADJECTIVE **Credible** means able to be trusted or believed. ○ [+ *to*] *Baroness Thatcher's claims seem credible to many.* ○ *But in order to maintain a credible threat of intervention, we have to maintain a credible alliance.*

→ see note at **conclusive**

▸ COLLOCATIONS:
 credible **to** *someone*
 appear/look/sound credible
 a credible **threat/claim/witness/theory**
 scarcely credible

▸ SYNONYM: plausible

cred|ibil|ity /ˌkredɪˈbɪlɪti/

UNCOUNTABLE NOUN If someone or something has **credibility**, people believe in them and trust them. ○ [+ *as*] *He cast doubt on Mr Zimet's credibility as a witness.* ○ *The president will have to work hard to restore his credibility.*

▸ COLLOCATIONS:
 the credibility **of** *something*
 someone's credibility **as** *something*

someone's credibility as a **witness/leader**
lose/gain/maintain credibility
enhance/damage someone's credibility

---

credi|tor /ˈkredɪtə/ (creditors) [BUSINESS] [ECONOMICS]

NOUN Your **creditors** are the people who you owe money to. ○ *The company said it would pay in full all its creditors.* ○ *a consortium of Korean creditor banks*

▶ COLLOCATIONS:
creditor **protection/banks**
owe/repay/persuade creditors
a creditor **approves/rejects/demands** something

▶ ANTONYM: debtor

---

cross-examine /ˌkrɒsɪɡˈzæmɪn, AM ˌkrɔːs/ [LAW]
(cross-examines, cross-examining, cross-examined)

VERB When a lawyer **cross-examines** someone during a trial or hearing, he or she questions them about the evidence that they have already given. ○ *The accused's lawyers will get a chance to cross-examine him.*
○ [+ *about*] *You know you are liable to be cross-examined mercilessly about the assault.*

▶ COLLOCATIONS:
cross-examine someone **about** something
cross-examined **by** someone
a **lawyer/defence counsel** cross-examines someone
cross-examine a **witness/victim/defendant**

cross-examination /ˌkrɒs ɪɡˌzæmɪˈneɪʃən, AM ˌkrɔːs/
(cross-examinations)

NOUN ○ [+ *of*] *during the cross-examination of a witness in a murder case*
○ *Under cross-examination, he admitted the state troopers used more destructive ammunition than usual.*

▶ COLLOCATIONS:
cross-examination **of/by** someone
under cross-examination
cross-examination of a **witness**
cross-examination by a **lawyer/prosecutor**
face cross-examination

▶ PHRASES:
testimony and cross-examination
evidence and cross-examination
cross-examination in court

C

---

cross-section /ˈkrɒsˌsekʃən/ **(cross-sections)** also **cross section**

1 NOUN If you refer to a **cross-section of** particular things or people, you mean a group of them that you think is typical or representative of all of them. ○ [+ of] *For most research projects it is necessary to talk to a cross-section of the public – people from all walks of life and all ages.* ○ [+ of] *He also said it was important that the study was done on a broad cross-section of children.*

▶ COLLOCATIONS:
  a cross-section **of** *people/things*
  a cross-section of **society/humanity**
  a cross-section of the **public/electorate/population**
  a **broad/wide** cross-section

2 NOUN A **cross-section** of an object is what you would see if you could cut straight through the middle of it. ○ [+ of] *a cross-section of an airplane* ○ *The hall is square in cross-section.*

▶ COLLOCATIONS:
  a cross-section **of** *something*
  in cross-section

---

cru|cial /ˈkruːʃəl/   `ACADEMIC WORD`

ADJECTIVE If you describe something as **crucial**, you mean it is extremely important. ○ *He had administrators under him but took the crucial decisions himself.* ○ *the most crucial election campaign for years* ○ [+ to] *Improved consumer confidence is crucial to an economic recovery.*

▶ COLLOCATIONS:
  crucial **to/for** *something*
  crucial for **survival/development**
  a crucial **decision/role/point/question**
  a crucial **difference/distinction/**
  a crucial **element/aspect/factor**

> **EXTEND YOUR VOCABULARY**
>
> You describe something as **crucial** or **critical** if the success of something depends on it. ○ *Intellectual-property law is crucial to economic success.* ○ *Interpersonal skills are critical for the successful personnel manager.*
>
> You say that something is **essential** or **vital** if it is necessary for something to exist or continue. ○ *Experience is an essential part of learning.* ○ *Calcium also plays a vital role in blood clotting.*

cru|cial|ly /ˈkruːʃəli/

ADVERB ○ *Chewing properly is crucially important.* ○ *Crucially, though, it failed to secure the backing of the banks.*

▶ **COLLOCATIONS:**
crucially **important**
crucially **affect** *something/someone*

---

crys|tal /ˈkrɪstəl/ (crystals) `ACADEMIC WORD` `CHEMISTRY`

NOUN A **crystal** is a small piece of a substance that has formed naturally into a regular symmetrical shape. ○ *salt crystals* ○ *ice crystals* ○ [+ *of*] *a single crystal of silicon*

▶ **COLLOCATIONS:**
a crystal **of** *something*
a **salt/ice/quartz** crystal
form/grow crystals

---

curb /kɜːb/ (curbs, curbing, curbed)

VERB If you **curb** something, you control it and keep it within limits. ○ *The president will now enact policies to curb greenhouse gas emissions.* ○ *Inflation needs to be curbed in Russia.*

▶ **COLLOCATION:** curb **inflation/violence/emissions**

▶ **SYNONYMS:** check, restrain

● **Curb** is also a noun. ○ [+ *on*] *He called for much stricter curbs on immigration.* ○ [+ *on*] *the government's plans to introduce tough curbs on dangerous dogs*

▶ **COLLOCATIONS:**
a curb **on** *something*
a curb on **immigration/advertising**
impose/propose/introduce a curb

---

cur|ricu|lum /kəˈrɪkjʊləm/ (curriculums or curricula) `EDUCATION`

NOUN A **curriculum** is all the different courses of study that are taught in a school, college, or university. ○ [+ *in*] *There should be a broader curriculum in schools for post-16-year-old pupils.* ○ *Russian is the one compulsory foreign language on the school curriculum.*

▶ **COLLOCATIONS:**
on the curriculum
a curriculum **in** *a school*
a **school/national/core** curriculum
a **broad/academic/balanced** curriculum
broaden/teach/implement a curriculum

cy|clone /ˈsaɪkləʊn/ (cyclones)　　　GEOGRAPHY

NOUN A **cyclone** is a violent tropical storm in which the air goes round and round. ○ [+ in] *A cyclone in the Bay of Bengal is threatening the eastern Indian states.* ○ *The Weather Bureau predicts more cyclones this season, after a relatively quiet five years.*

▶ COLLOCATIONS:
　a cyclone **in** *a place*
　a **tropical/powerful** cyclone
　a cyclone **hits/strikes** *somewhere*
　withstand/expect a cyclone

Dd

death pen|al|ty /ˈdeθ ˌpenəlti/ [LAW]

NOUN **The death penalty** is the punishment of death used in some countries for people who have committed very serious crimes.
○ *If convicted for murder, both youngsters could face the death penalty.*
○ *Prosecutors are seeking the death penalty against him.* ○ *a special circumstance of double homicide, which could carry the death penalty upon conviction*

▶ **COLLOCATIONS:**
 face/carry/seek/call for the death penalty
 oppose/abolish the death penalty

▶ **SYNONYMS:** capital punishment, execution

de|bris /ˈdeɪbri, AM deɪˈbriː/

UNCOUNTABLE NOUN **Debris** is pieces from something that has been destroyed or pieces of rubbish or unwanted material that are spread around. ○ [+ from] *Rescue workers routed traffic around the debris from the explosions.* ○ *A number of people were killed by flying debris.*

▶ **COLLOCATIONS:**
 debris **from** *something*
 debris from a **plane/shuttle/building/explosion**
 clear/remove debris
 floating/flying/volcanic debris
 debris is **scattered/strewn**
 debris **falls**

▶ **SYNONYMS:** waste, rubbish

de|cay /dɪˈkeɪ/ (decays, decaying, decayed) [BIOLOGY]

VERB When something such as a dead body, a dead plant, or a tooth **decays**, it is gradually destroyed by a natural process. ○ *The bodies buried in the fine ash slowly decayed.* ○ *Millipedes enjoy a diet which consists of rotting or partially decayed vegetation.*

▶ **COLLOCATIONS:**
 decaying **vegetation/flesh/teeth**
 a decaying **corpse**

a **body/tooth** decays
rapidly/slowly decay

▸ SYNONYMS: rot, deteriorate

▸ ANTONYM: improve

- **Decay** is also an uncountable noun. ○ *When not removed, plaque causes tooth decay and gum disease.* ○ *the problem of urban decay* ○ *[+ of] Radon is produced by the radioactive decay of uranium.*

  ▸ COLLOCATIONS:
  the decay **of** *something*
  tooth/dental decay
  urban/moral/physical/social decay
  radioactive decay
  gradual/rapid decay
  cause/prevent/reduce decay

  ▸ SYNONYMS: rot, destruction

  ▸ ANTONYM: improvement

---

de|duce /dɪˈdjuːs, AM -ˈduːs/ ACADEMIC WORD
(deduces, deducing, deduced)

VERB If you **deduce** something or **deduce** that something is true, you reach that conclusion because of other things that you know to be true. ○ *[+ that] The observations led the team to deduce that the two clusters approached one another from a different direction.* ○ *[+ from] The date of the document can be deduced from references to the Civil War.* ○ *The researchers have to analyse a huge amount of information in order to deduce any conclusions.*

  ▸ COLLOCATIONS:
  deduce *something* **from** *something*
  deduce *something* from a **fact/observation**
  deduce a **pattern/hypothesis/conclusion**
  deduce the **existence/presence** of *something*
  correctly/logically deduce

> **EXTEND YOUR VOCABULARY**
>
> You can use **deduce**, **infer** and **conclude** to talk about working something out from the evidence you have.
>
> If you **deduce** something, it is usually the result of a logical process based on evidence. ○ *The study of these patterns has been used to deduce the internal structure of the Earth.*

If you **infer** something, you think that it is probably correct based on the evidence you have and your own knowledge. ○ *The reader's left to infer the meaning.*

You use **conclude** to talk about your final analysis, based on all the evidence. ○ *The report concluded that transmission from bison to cattle in the wild was possible.*

de|duc|tion /dɪˈdʌkʃən/ (deductions)

1 NOUN A **deduction** is a conclusion that you have reached about something because of other things that you know to be true. ○ *It is a natural instinct rather than a logical deduction.* ○ [+ *about*] *Children can predict other people's behavior on the basis of deductions about their beliefs or feelings.*

▶ **COLLOCATIONS:**
a deduction **about** something
a **logical/rational** deduction

▶ **SYNONYMS:** conclusion, inference

2 UNCOUNTABLE NOUN Deduction is the process of reaching a conclusion about something because of other things that you know to be true. ○ *a case that tested his powers of deduction* ○ *The assessment was based on rational deduction, not hard evidence.*

▶ **COLLOCATIONS:**
powers of deduction
logical/rational deduction

▶ **SYNONYM:** reasoning

de|duc|tive /dɪˈdʌktɪv/

ADJECTIVE Deductive reasoning involves drawing conclusions logically from other things that are already known. [FORMAL] ○ *The force of deductive reasoning depends on the reliability of the premises.* ○ *The criteria for settling disputes in political theory are partly deductive and partly empirical.*

▶ **COLLOCATION:** deductive **reasoning/logic**

▶ **ANTONYM:** inductive

---

de|duct /dɪˈdʌkt/ (deducts, deducting, deducted)

VERB When you **deduct** an amount from a total, you subtract it from the total. ○ [+ *from*] *The company deducted this payment from his compensation.* ○ [+ *for*] *Up to 5% of marks in the exams will be deducted for spelling mistakes.*

▶ **COLLOCATIONS:**
deduct something **from/for** something

deduct *something* from a **salary/income/amount/account**
deduct a **cost/amount/fee/point**
deduct **expenses/payment/tax**
automatically/electronically deducted
▶ **SYNONYM:** subtract
▶ **ANTONYM:** add

de|duc|tion /dɪˈdʌkʃən/ (deductions)

NOUN A **deduction** is an amount that has been subtracted from a total.
○ *your gross income (before tax and National Insurance deductions)* ○ [+ *for*]
*After deductions for war reparations, the balance would be used to buy food and
humanitarian supplies.*

▶ **COLLOCATIONS:**
a deduction **for/from** *something*
a deduction for **expenses/costs/interest**
a deduction from *someone's* **salary/wages/income**
a **tax/payroll** deduction
a **corporate/charitable/standard** deduction
claim a deduction
▶ **ANTONYM:** addition

de|fault /dɪˈfɔːlt/   🆃

1 ADJECTIVE A **default** situation is what exists or happens unless someone
or something changes it. ○ *default passwords installed on commercial
machines* ○ *Death, not life, is the default state of cells.*

2 UNCOUNTABLE NOUN In computing, the **default** is a particular set of
instructions which the computer always uses unless the person using the
computer gives other instructions. ○ *The default is usually the setting that
most users would probably choose.* ○ *advising consumers to change default settings*

▶ **COLLOCATIONS:**
a default **password/rate/setting**
a default **mode/state/option**
▶ **SYNONYM:** standard

de|fer /dɪˈfɜː/ (defers, deferring, deferred)

VERB If you **defer** an event or action, you arrange for it to happen at a later
date, rather than immediately or at the previously planned time. ○ [+ *for*]
Customers often defer payment for as long as possible. ○ [+ *until*] *Sentence was
deferred until June 16 for background reports.* ○ [+ v-ing] *a system which will
allow approved companies to defer paying VAT on imports*

▶ COLLOCATIONS:
defer *something* **for** *a period of time*
defer *something* **until** *a time*
defer a **payment/decision**
defer **travel**
a **sentence** is deferred
defer *something* **indefinitely**

▶ SYNONYMS: postpone, delay

d

---

de|fi|cient /dɪˈfɪʃənt/

1 ADJECTIVE If someone or something is **deficient in** a particular thing, they do not have the full amount of it that they need in order to function normally or work properly. [FORMAL] ○ [+ *in*] *a diet deficient in vitamin B* ○ *The proposal was deficient in several respects.* ○ *a mentally deficient child*

• **Deficient** is also a combining form. ○ *Vegetarians can become iron-deficient.*

2 ADJECTIVE Someone or something that is **deficient** is not good enough for a particular purpose. [FORMAL] ○ *deficient landing systems* ○ *Slightly deficient rainfall could be catastrophic in rain-dependent areas.*

▶ COLLOCATIONS:
deficient **in** *something*
deficient in **nutrients/vitamins**
deficient in a **respect/area**
nutritionally/mentally/morally deficient
seriously/severely deficient
a deficient **diet**

▶ SYNONYMS: inadequate, lacking

▶ ANTONYM: sufficient

de|fi|cien|cy /dɪˈfɪʃənsi/ (deficiencies)

NOUN ○ *Diseases associated with protein and carbohydrate deficiency cause many deaths among young children.* ○ [+ *of*] *brain damage caused by a deficiency of vitamin B12* ○ [+ *in*] *a serious deficiency in our air defence*

▶ COLLOCATIONS:
a deficiency **in/of** *something*
a deficiency in/of **vitamins**
a deficiency in/of a **system/diet**
a **nutritional/dietary/structural** deficiency
a **vitamin/iron/zinc** deficiency
a **severe/serious/glaring/mild** deficiency
remedy/correct/identify a deficiency

▶ **SYNONYMS:** weakness, lack, inadequacy
▶ **ANTONYM:** sufficiency

---

defi|cit /'defəsɪt/ (deficits)   `ECONOMICS`

NOUN A **deficit** is the amount by which something is less than what is
required or expected, especially the amount by which the total money
received is less than the total money spent. ○ *They're ready to cut the federal
budget deficit for the next fiscal year.* ○ *[+ of] a deficit of 3.275 billion francs*
○ *The current account of the balance of payments is in deficit.*

▶ **COLLOCATIONS:**
  in deficit
  a deficit **of** £x
  cut/reduce/overcome a deficit
  a deficit **rises/grows/widens/narrows**
  a **fiscal/federal/budget** deficit
  a **trade/current-account** deficit
▶ **SYNONYM:** shortage
▶ **ANTONYM:** surplus

---

de|fini|tive /dɪ'fɪnɪtɪv/   `ACADEMIC WORD`

ADJECTIVE Something that is **definitive** provides a firm conclusion that
cannot be questioned. ○ *The study population was too small to reach any
definitive conclusions.* ○ *There is no definitive test as yet for the condition.*

→ see note at **conclusive**

▶ **COLLOCATIONS:**
  a definitive **answer/agreement/statement/conclusion**
  definitive **proof**
▶ **SYNONYMS:** conclusive, absolute, definite
▶ **ANTONYM:** inconclusive

de|fini|tive|ly /dɪ'fɪnɪtɪvli/

ADVERB ○ *The Constitution did not definitively rule out divorce.* ○ *The research
also definitively proves that second-hand smoke causes cancer.*

▶ **COLLOCATIONS:**
  definitively **identify/establish/prove** something
  say definitively
▶ **SYNONYMS:** conclusively, absolutely, definitely
▶ **ANTONYM:** inconclusively

---

de|hy|drate /ˌdiːhaɪˈdreɪt, -ˈhaɪdreɪt/ `SCIENCE` `MEDICINE`
(dehydrates, dehydrating, dehydrated)

1 VERB When something **is dehydrated**, all the water is removed from it, often in order to preserve it. ○ *Normally specimens have to be dehydrated.*

2 VERB If you **dehydrate** or if something **dehydrates** you, you lose too much water from your body so that you feel weak or ill. ○ *People can dehydrate in weather like this.* ○ *Alcohol quickly dehydrates your body.*

▶ **COLLOCATION:** dehydrate the **body**

▶ **SYNONYMS:** drain, dry

▶ **ANTONYM:** hydrate

de|hy|drat|ed /ˌdiːhaɪˈdreɪtɪd/

ADJECTIVE ○ *Dehydrated meals, soups and sauces contain a lot of salt.* ○ *During surgery, exposed tissue can become dehydrated.*

▶ **COLLOCATIONS:**
dehydrated **skin/food**
severely/badly dehydrated

▶ **ANTONYM:** hydrated

de|hy|dra|tion /ˌdiːhaɪˈdreɪʃən/

UNCOUNTABLE NOUN ○ *Cholera causes severe dehydration from vomiting and diarrhoea.*

▶ **COLLOCATIONS:**
avoid/prevent/cause/suffer from dehydration
severe/mild/extreme dehydration

de|mog|ra|phy /dɪˈmɒɡrəfi/ `SOCIAL SCIENCE` `SOCIOLOGY`

UNCOUNTABLE NOUN Demography is the study of the changes in numbers of births, deaths, marriages, and cases of disease in a community over a period of time. ○ [+ *of*] *a major work on the demography of preindustrial societies*

▶ **COLLOCATION:** the demography **of** *something/somewhere*

de|mo|graph|ic /ˌdeməˈɡræfɪk/ **(demographics)**

1 ADJECTIVE Demographic means relating to or concerning demography. ○ *The final impact of industrialization on the family was demographic.* ○ *the relationship between economic and demographic change*

▶ **COLLOCATIONS:**
a demographic **change/shift/trend/transition**
a demographic **profile**

2 PLURAL NOUN The **demographics** of a place or society are the statistics relating to the people who live there. ○ [+ of] *the changing demographics of the United States*

▶ **COLLOCATIONS:**
  the demographics **of** something/somewhere
  changing/shifting demographics

3 NOUN In business, a **demographic** is a group of people in a society, especially people in a particular age group. ○ *Most of our listeners are in the 25-39 demographic.* ○ *well-read individuals, the target demographic of this newspaper section*

▶ **COLLOCATIONS:**
  the **key/target/core** demographic
  the **consumer/audience/age** demographic

---

de|note /dɪ'nəʊt/ (denotes, denoting, denoted) ACADEMIC WORD

1 VERB If one thing **denotes** another, it is a sign or indication of it. [FORMAL] ○ *Red eyes denote strain and fatigue.* ○ [+ that] *a sound which denotes that a photograph has been taken*

2 VERB What a symbol **denotes** is what it represents. [FORMAL]
  ○ *In figure 24 'D' denotes quantity demanded and 'S' denotes quantity supplied.*
  ○ *We will denote the adjusted cost of capital by r^*.*

▶ **COLLOCATION:** a **number/symbol/sign** denotes *something*
▶ **SYNONYMS:** indicate, show, represent

---

dense /dens/ (denser, densest) SCIENCE

1 ADJECTIVE Something that is **dense** contains a lot of things or people in a small area. ○ *Where Bucharest now stands, there once was a large, dense forest.* ○ *an area of dense immigrant population*

▶ **COLLOCATIONS:**
  a dense **forest/jungle/thicket/rainforest**
  a dense **population/crowd/area/network**
  dense **foliage/undergrowth**

▶ **SYNONYM:** compressed
▶ **ANTONYM:** sparse

2 ADJECTIVE In science, a **dense** substance is very heavy in relation to its volume. ○ *a small dense star* ○ *The densest ocean water is the coldest and most saline.*

den|sity /'densɪti/ (densities)

1 NOUN Density is the extent to which something is filled or covered with people or things. ○ [+ of] *a law which restricts the density of housing* ○ *The region has a very high population density.*

2 NOUN In science, the **density** of a substance or object is the relation of its mass or weight to its volume. ○ *Jupiter's moon Io, whose density is 3.5 grams per cubic centimetre, is all rock.* ○ [+ of] *assessing the temperature, heat capacity, density and hardness of Mercury's surface*

▶ COLLOCATIONS:
the density **of** something
population/housing/traffic density
bone density
high/low/maximum density

▶ SYNONYMS: mass, hardness

---

de|pict /dɪ'pɪkt/ (depicts, depicting, depicted) `ARTS` `LITERATURE`

1 VERB To **depict** someone or something means to show or represent them in a work of art such as a drawing or painting. ○ *a gallery of pictures depicting Nelson's most famous battles* ○ [+ in] *St. Brigid is often depicted in art with a cow resting at her feet.*

2 VERB To **depict** someone or something means to describe them or give an impression of them in writing. ○ *Margaret Atwood's novel depicts a gloomy, futuristic America.* ○ [+ as] *The character was depicted as a compulsive shoplifter.*

▶ COLLOCATIONS:
depicted **as/in** something
a **painting/photograph** depicts something
a **mural/fresco/cartoon** depicts something
depict a **scene/landscape/character**
graphically/vividly/accurately depicted

▶ SYNONYMS: portray, represent

de|pic|tion /dɪ'pɪkʃən/ (depictions)

NOUN A **depiction** of something is a picture or a written description of it. ○ [+ of] *The lecture will trace the depiction of horses from earliest times to the present day.* ○ [+ of] *the depiction of socialists as Utopian dreamers*

▶ COLLOCATIONS:
the depiction **of** something
a **graphic/accurate/realistic/vivid** depiction

▶ SYNONYMS: portrayal, representation

d

de|plete /dɪ'pliːt/ (depletes, depleting, depleted)

VERB To **deplete** a stock or amount of something means to reduce it. [FORMAL] ○ *substances that deplete the ozone layer* ○ *Most native mammal species have been severely depleted.*

→ see note at **expend**

▶ COLLOCATIONS:
severely/seriously/rapidly depleted
deplete the **ozone layer**
deplete **reserves** of *something*

▶ SYNONYMS: reduce, diminish, augment

de|ple|tion /dɪ'pliːʃən/

UNCOUNTABLE NOUN ○ *the problem of ozone depletion* ○ [+ *of*] *the depletion of underground water supplies*

▶ COLLOCATIONS:
the depletion **of** *something*
the depletion of the **ozone layer**
the depletion of **resources**
oxygen/soil depletion

▶ SYNONYMS: reduction, augmentation

de|press /dɪ'pres/ `ACADEMIC WORD` `BUSINESS` `ECONOMICS`
(depresses, depressing, depressed)

VERB If something **depresses** prices, wages, or figures, it causes them to become less. ○ *The stronger U.S. dollar depressed sales.* ○ *The appreciation in the value of the euro is depressing import prices.*

▶ COLLOCATIONS:
depress **prices/earnings/wages/demand**
depress a **market**

▶ SYNONYMS: reduce, devalue

▶ ANTONYM: increase

de|pressed /dɪ'prest/

ADJECTIVE A **depressed** place or industry does not have enough business or employment to be successful. ○ *legislation to encourage investment in depressed areas* ○ *The construction industry is no longer as depressed as it was.*

▶ COLLOCATIONS:
economically depressed
a depressed **region/area**
a depressed **market/sector**

▶ ANTONYMS: thriving, booming

de|pres|sion /dɪ'preʃən/ (depressions)

NOUN A **depression** is a time when there is very little economic activity, which causes a lot of unemployment and poverty. ○ [+ of] He never forgot the hardships he witnessed during the Great Depression of the 1930s.

▶ **COLLOCATION:** the depression **of/in** a period

▶ **PHRASE:** the Great Depression

▶ **SYNONYMS:** slump, downturn, recession

▶ **ANTONYM:** recovery

---

de|prived /dɪ'praɪvd/   SOCIOLOGY

ADJECTIVE Deprived people or people from **deprived** areas do not have the things that people consider to be essential in life, for example acceptable living conditions or education. ○ probably the most severely deprived children in the country ○ the problems associated with life in a deprived inner city area

→ see note at **underprivileged**

▶ **COLLOCATIONS:**
a deprived **area/neighbourhood/community**
a deprived **child/citizen**
a deprived **childhood/background/upbringing**

▶ **SYNONYMS:** underprivileged, destitute

▶ **ANTONYM:** privileged

---

de|rive /dɪ'raɪv/ (derives, deriving, derived)   ACADEMIC WORD

VERB If you say that something **derives** or **is derived from** something else, you mean that it comes from that thing. ○ [ɪ from] Some modern drugs are derived from plant medicines. ○ [+ from] The word Easter derives from Eostre, the pagan goddess of spring.

▶ **COLLOCATIONS:**
derive **from** something
a **word/name/title** derives from something
empirically/logically/directly/ultimately derived

▶ **SYNONYM:** originate

de|riva|tive /dɪ'rɪvətɪv/ (derivatives)

NOUN A **derivative** is something which has been developed or obtained from something else. ○ a poppy-seed derivative similar to heroin ○ [+ of] synthetic derivatives of male hormones

▶ **COLLOCATIONS:**
a derivative **of** something

d

a **synthetic/complex/partial** derivative
▶ **SYNONYM:** by-product

---

de|ter /dɪˈtɜː/ (deters, deterring, deterred) `LAW`

VERB To **deter** someone **from** doing something means to make them not want to do it or continue doing it. ○ [+ *from*] *Supporters of the death penalty argue that it would deter criminals from carrying guns.* ○ *Arrests and jail sentences have done nothing to deter the protesters.* ○ *Far from being deterred by the regional financial crisis, the company plans to expand into Asia.*

▶ **COLLOCATIONS:**
deter someone **from** *something*
deterred **by** *something*
deter **terrorists/burglars/thieves**
deter **vandals/criminals**
deterred by **fear/weather/costs**

▶ **SYNONYM:** discourage

▶ **ANTONYM:** encourage

de|ter|rent /dɪˈterənt, AM -ˈtɜːr-/ (deterrents)

NOUN A **deterrent** is something that prevents people from doing something by making them afraid of what will happen to them if they do it. ○ *They seriously believe that capital punishment is a deterrent.* ○ *The tough new law should act as a deterrent.*

▶ **COLLOCATIONS:**
a **strong/significant/effective** deterrent
provide/prove/constitute/act as a deterrent

▶ **SYNONYM:** obstacle

▶ **ANTONYM:** incentive

---

de|terio|rate /dɪˈtɪəriəreɪt/ (deteriorates, deteriorating, deteriorated)

VERB If something **deteriorates**, it becomes worse in some way. ○ [+ *into*] *There are fears that the situation might deteriorate into full-scale war.* ○ [V-ing] *Surface transport has become less and less viable with deteriorating road conditions.* ○ *Relations between the two countries steadily deteriorated.*

▶ **COLLOCATIONS:**
deteriorate **into** *something*
a **condition/situation** deteriorates
someone's **health** deteriorates
a deteriorating **situation/condition**
deteriorating **relations**
quickly/rapidly/sharply/steadily deteriorate

▶ **SYNONYM:** worsen

▶ **ANTONYM:** improve

de|terio|ra|tion /dɪˌtɪəriəˈreɪʃən/

UNCOUNTABLE NOUN ○ [+ *in*] *concern about the rapid deterioration in relations between the two countries* ○ [+ *of*] *the slow steady deterioration of a patient with Alzheimer's disease*

▶ **COLLOCATIONS:**
   deterioration **in/of** *something/someone*
   rapid/gradual/marked/significant deterioration
   further/continued deterioration
   physical/mental/bone deterioration
   accelerate/reverse/prevent deterioration

▶ **SYNONYMS:** decline, decay, degeneration

▶ **ANTONYM:** improvement

---

de|vi|ate /ˈdiːvieɪt/ (deviates, deviating, deviated)   `ACADEMIC WORD`

VERB To **deviate from** something means to start doing something different or not planned, especially in a way that causes problems for others. ○ [+ *from*] *They stopped you as soon as you deviated from the script.* ○ [+ *from*] *wage levels that deviate significantly from international norms* ○ [+ *from*] *behaviour that deviates markedly from the expectations of the individual's culture*

▶ **COLLOCATIONS:**
   deviate **from** *something*
   deviate from a **norm/standard/path/script**
   deviate **markedly/significantly/slightly**

▶ **SYNONYM:** depart

▶ **ANTONYM:** adhere

de|via|tion /ˌdiːviˈeɪʃən/ (deviations)

NOUN Deviation means doing something that is different from what is considered to be normal or acceptable. ○ [+ *from*] *Deviation from the norm is not tolerated.* ○ [+ *in*] *radical deviations in blood sugar level*

▶ **COLLOCATIONS:**
   deviation **from/in** *something*
   deviation from a **norm/path/pattern/rule**
   slight/significant deviation

▶ **SYNONYM:** departure

▶ **ANTONYM:** adherence

de|vote /dɪ'vəʊt/ (devotes, devoting, devoted)　ACADEMIC WORD

1 VERB If you **devote** yourself, your time, or your energy **to** something, you spend all or most of your time or energy on it. ○ [+ to] *the increased time devoted to watching television* ○ [+ to] *Spanish manufacturers are devoting greater resources to advertising and promotion campaigns.* ○ [+ to] *She gave up her part-time job to devote herself entirely to her art.*

2 VERB If you **devote** a particular proportion of a piece of writing or a speech **to** a particular subject, you deal with the subject in that amount of space or time. ○ [+ to] *He devoted a major section of his massive report to an analysis of U.S. aircraft design.* ○ [+ to] *This chapter is devoted to clarifying the nature of risk.*

▶ **COLLOCATIONS:**
devote *something* **to** *something*
devote **time/space/energy/resources**
a **chapter/page/section** is devoted to *something*
a **museum/website/exhibition** is devoted to *something*
solely/exclusively/entirely devoted to *something*

▶ **SYNONYM:** dedicate

de|vo|tion /dɪ'vəʊʃən/

UNCOUNTABLE NOUN ○ [+ to] *devotion to the cause of the people and to socialism* ○ [+ to] *Darwin's devotion to his studies of plants and animals*

▶ **COLLOCATIONS:**
devotion **to** *something*
slavish/fanatical/utter/lifelong devotion

▶ **SYNONYM:** dedication

dia|lect /'daɪəlekt/ (dialects)　LANGUAGE

NOUN A **dialect** is a form of a language that is spoken in a particular area. ○ *In the fifties, many Italians spoke only local dialect.* ○ [+ of] *They spoke a dialect of Low German.* ○ *a selection of short stories written in dialect*

▶ **COLLOCATIONS:**
a dialect **of** *something*
in dialect
write in dialect
speak a dialect
a **local/regional** dialect

▶ **RELATED WORDS:** accent, language

dic|ta|tor /dɪk'teɪtə, AM 'dɪkteɪt-/ (dictators) `POLITICS`

NOUN A **dictator** is a ruler who has complete power in a country, especially power which was obtained by force and is used unfairly or cruelly. ○ *The country descended into anarchy when its dictator was overthrown.* ○ *a former dictator with innocent blood on his hands*

▶ **COLLOCATIONS:**
  a **deposed/toppled/former/brutal** dictator
  oust/overthrow a dictator

▶ **SYNONYMS:** despot, tyrant

dic|ta|tor|ship /dɪk'teɪtəʃɪp/ (dictatorships)

NOUN **Dictatorship** is government by a dictator. ○ *a new era of democracy after a long period of military dictatorship in the country* ○ *countries which are ruled by dictatorships*

▶ **COLLOCATION:** a **military/totalitarian/brutal** dictatorship

▶ **SYNONYM:** tyranny

dif|fer|en|ti|ate /ˌdɪfə'renʃieɪt/ `ACADEMIC WORD`
(differentiates, differentiating, differentiated)

1 VERB If you **differentiate between** things or if you **differentiate** one thing **from** another, you recognize or show the difference between them. ○ [+ *between*] *A child may not differentiate between his imagination and the real world.* ○ [+ *from*] *At this age your baby cannot differentiate one person from another.*

2 VERB A quality or feature that **differentiates** one thing **from** another makes the two things different. ○ [+ *from*] *distinctive policies that differentiate them from the other parties* ○ [+ *from*] *features which differentiate the pygmy elephant from the forest elephant* ○ [V-ing] *The brand did not have a differentiating factor.*

▶ **COLLOCATIONS:**
  differentiate **between** *things*
  differentiate *something* **from** *something*
  a differentiated **product/brand**
  a differentiating **factor**

▶ **SYNONYM:** distinguish

dif|fer|en|tia|tion /ˌdɪfərenʃi'eɪʃən/

UNCOUNTABLE NOUN ○ [+ *between*] *The differentiation between the two product ranges will increase.* ○ *increased product differentiation and customization to niche markets* ○ [+ *of*] *the differentiation of the social system*

d

▶ **COLLOCATIONS:**
differentiation **between** *things*
the differentiation **of** *something*
product/brand differentiation
achieve/increase/create differentiation

▶ **SYNONYM:** distinction

---

di|lute /daɪˈluːt/ (dilutes, diluting, diluted)   `SCIENCE`

1 VERB If a liquid **is diluted** or **dilutes**, it is added to or mixes with water or another liquid, and becomes weaker. ○ *The liquid is then diluted.* ○ [+ *with*] *a liquid concentrate of nicotine sulphate which is diluted with water and applied as a spray*

▶ **COLLOCATIONS:**
dilute *something* **with** *something*
highly/fully diluted

▶ **ANTONYM:** concentrate

2 ADJECTIVE A **dilute** liquid is very thin and weak, usually because it has had water added to it. ○ *a dilute solution of bleach*

di|lu|tion /daɪˈluːʃən/

1 UNCOUNTABLE NOUN **Dilution** is the process or action of diluting a liquid. ○ [+ *of*] *readings significantly lower owing to the dilution of the sample*

2 NOUN A **dilution** is a liquid that has been diluted with water or another liquid, so that it becomes weaker. ○ *The synthetic alcohol was mixed in graded dilutions.*

▶ **COLLOCATION:** dilution **of** *something*

▶ **ANTONYM:** concentration

---

di|min|ish /dɪˈmɪnɪʃ/   `ACADEMIC WORD`
(diminishes, diminishing, diminished)

VERB When something **diminishes**, or when something **diminishes** it, it becomes reduced in size, importance, or intensity. ○ *The threat of nuclear war has diminished.* ○ *Federalism is intended to diminish the power of the central state.* ○ [V-ing] *Universities are facing grave problems because of diminishing resources.* ○ *This could mean diminished public support for the war.*

▶ **COLLOCATIONS:**
diminish **in** *something*
diminish in **importance/size/number**
rapidly/gradually diminish
greatly/drastically/considerably diminished

▶ **SYNONYMS:** lessen, decrease
▶ **ANTONYM:** increase

---

dis|course /ˈdɪskɔːs/ LANGUAGE

UNCOUNTABLE NOUN Discourse is spoken or written communication between people, especially serious discussion of a particular subject. ○ *a tradition of political discourse* ○ [+ on] *public discourse on crime*

▶ **COLLOCATIONS:**
discourse **on** *something*
political/philosophical discourse
rational/feminist discourse

▶ **SYNONYMS:** communication, dialogue, debate, rhetoric

---

dis|crete /dɪsˈkriːt/ ACADEMIC WORD

ADJECTIVE Discrete ideas or things are separate and distinct from each other. [FORMAL] ○ *instruction manuals that break down jobs into scores of discrete steps* ○ *Herbal medicine does not treat mind and body as discrete entities, but holistically.*

▶ **COLLOCATION:** a discrete **entity/element/category**
▶ **SYNONYMS:** separate, distinct

> **USAGE: discrete** or **discreet**?
>
> Be careful not to confuse these two adjectives with the same pronunciation, but different spellings and different meanings.
>
> **Discrete** is a formal word to describe two things that are separate from each other.
>
> You use **discreet** to describe someone who is polite and avoids embarrassing or offending anyone, or something that is small, simple and not easily noticed. ○ *She was always very discreet about their relationship.* ○ *The hotel is discreet and stylish.*

---

dis|cre|tion /dɪsˈkreʃən/ ACADEMIC WORD

1 UNCOUNTABLE NOUN If someone in a position of authority uses their **discretion** or has **the discretion** to do something in a particular situation, they have the freedom and authority to decide what to do. [FORMAL] ○ *This committee may want to exercise its discretion to look into those charges.* ○ [+ to-inf] *School governors have the discretion to allow parents to withdraw pupils in exceptional circumstances.*

▶ **COLLOCATIONS:**
discretion **in** *something*
discretion in a **matter/case**
exercise discretion
judicial/parental/ministerial discretion

2 PHRASE If something happens **at** someone's **discretion**, it can happen only if they decide to do it or give their permission. [FORMAL] ○ *We may vary the limit at our discretion and will notify you of any change.* ○ *Visits are at the discretion of the owners.*

▶ **COLLOCATIONS:**
at *someone's* discretion
at the discretion of a **judge/court/authority**

dis|cre|tion|ary /dɪsˈkreʃənri, AM -neri/

ADJECTIVE ○ *Magistrates were given wider discretionary powers.* ○ *The committee decided to pay small discretionary bonuses to reflect the accomplishments of key directors.*

▶ **COLLOCATIONS:**
discretionary **authority/power**
a discretionary **bonus/grant/fund**

---

dis|crimi|nate /dɪsˈkrɪmɪneɪt/ `ACADEMIC WORD`
(discriminates, discriminating, discriminated)

VERB If you can **discriminate between** two things, you can recognize that they are different. ○ [+ *between*] *children who have difficulty discriminating between shapes* ○ [+ *between*] *The device can discriminate between the cancerous and the normal cells.*

▶ **COLLOCATION:** discriminate **between** *things*
▶ **SYNONYMS:** distinguish, differentiate, discern

dis|crimi|na|tion /dɪsˌkrɪmɪˈneɪʃən/

UNCOUNTABLE NOUN Discrimination is the ability to recognize and understand the differences between two things. ○ *colour discrimination* ○ [+ *between*] *the system that allows a mother to make the discrimination between her own and alien lambs*

▶ **COLLOCATION:** discrimination **between** *things*
▶ **SYNONYMS:** discernment, differentiation

---

dis|perse /dɪsˈpɜːs/ **(disperses, dispersing, dispersed)**

VERB When something **disperses** or when you **disperse** it, it spreads over a wide area. ○ [V-ing] *The oil appeared to be dispersing.* ○ *The intense currents disperse the sewage.* ○ *Because the town sits in a valley, air pollution is not easily dispersed.*

▶ COLLOCATION: **widely/quickly/slowly/easily** dispersed
▶ SYNONYMS: spread, scatter

dis|per|sal /dɪsˈpɜːsəl/

UNCOUNTABLE NOUN ○ *Plants have different mechanisms of dispersal for their spores.* ○ [+ of] *dispersal of ash during the hurricane season*

▶ COLLOCATION: dispersal **of** something
▶ SYNONYM: distribution

---

dis|place /dɪsˈpleɪs/ (displaces, displacing, displaced)   ACADEMIC WORD

1 VERB If one thing **displaces** another, it forces the other thing out of its place, position, or role, and then occupies that place, position, or role itself. ○ [+ as] *These factories have displaced tourism as the country's largest source of foreign exchange.* ○ *Coal is to be displaced by natural gas and nuclear power.*

▶ COLLOCATION: displaced **as/by** something

2 VERB If a person or group of people **is displaced**, they are forced to moved away from the area where they live. ○ *In Europe alone thirty million people were displaced.* ○ *Most of the civilians displaced by the war will be unable to return to their homes.* ○ *the task of resettling refugees and displaced persons*

▶ COLLOCATIONS:
displaced **by** something
displaced by **fighting/war/conflict/violence**
displaced by a **fire/flood/hurricane**
a displaced **person/refugee/worker**

dis|place|ment /dɪsˈpleɪsmənt/

UNCOUNTABLE NOUN [FORMAL] ○ [+ of] *too much resistance to the displacement of your reason by your emotions* ○ [+ of] *the gradual displacement of the American Indian* ○ *allegations of genocide, rape, and forced displacement*

▶ COLLOCATIONS:
displacement **of** people/things
forced/mass/massive displacement

---

dis|solve /dɪˈzɒlv/ (dissolves, dissolving, dissolved)   SCIENCE

VERB If a substance **dissolves** in liquid or if you **dissolve** it, it becomes mixed with the liquid and disappears. ○ [+ in] *More substances dissolve in water than in any other liquid.* ○ *Pumping water into an underground salt bed* *dissolves the salt to make a brine.* ○ *organic matter that consumes all dissolved oxygen in the water*

▶ **COLLOCATIONS:**
dissolve **in** *something*
gelatine/sugar dissolves
gradually/rapidly/completely dissolve

▶ **SYNONYM:** melt

---

dis|tort /dɪˈstɔːt/ **(distorts, distorting, distorted)**　　ACADEMIC WORD

1 VERB If you **distort** a statement, fact, or idea, you report or represent it in an untrue way. ○ *The media distorts reality; categorises people as all good or all bad.* ○ *allegations that the administration distorted scientific findings to justify political decisions*

2 VERB If something you can see or hear **is distorted** or **distorts**, its appearance or sound is changed so that it seems unclear. ○ *A painter may exaggerate or distort shapes and forms.* ○ [V-ing] *the distorting effects of Earth's atmosphere on light passing through it* ○ *This caused the sound to distort.*

▶ **COLLOCATIONS:**
distort the **truth**
distort **findings/facts/meaning/reality**
distort a **shape/image/pattern**
a distorting **mirror/lens/effect**
grossly/severely/deliberately distorted

▶ **SYNONYM:** misrepresent

dis|tor|tion /dɪˈstɔːʃən/ **(distortions)**

1 NOUN Distortion is the changing of something into something that is not true or not acceptable. ○ [+ of] *I think it would be a gross distortion of reality to say that they were motivated by self-interest.* ○ *He later accused reporters of wilful distortion and bias.*

2 NOUN Distortion is the changing of the appearance or sound of something in a way that makes it seem strange or unclear. ○ *Audio signals can be transmitted along cables without distortion.* ○ *symptoms including some perceptual distortions and hallucinations*

▶ **COLLOCATIONS:**
distortion **of** *something*
distortion of the **truth/history/facts**
distorition of **reality/history**
gross/deliberate distortion
visual/perceptual distortion

cause/introduce/create distortion
correct/eliminate/minimize/reduce distortion
▶ **SYNONYM:** misrepresentation

---

di|verse /daɪˈvɜːs, AM dɪ-/ `ACADEMIC WORD`

1 ADJECTIVE If a group or range of things is **diverse**, it is made up of a wide variety of things. ○ *a diverse range of habitats* ○ *Society is now much more diverse than ever before.*

2 ADJECTIVE Diverse people or things are very different from each other. ○ *Jones has a much more diverse and perhaps younger audience.* ○ *Studies of diverse populations have reached similar conclusions.*

▶ **COLLOCATIONS:**
  ethnically/culturally diverse
  geographically/linguistically diverse
  diverse **backgrounds**
  a diverse **group/range/population/society**
▶ **SYNONYM:** varied
▶ **ANTONYM:** uniform

di|ver|sity /daɪˈvɜːsɪti, AM dɪ-/

UNCOUNTABLE NOUN The **diversity** of something is the fact that it contains many very different elements. ○ [+ *of*] *the cultural diversity of British society* ○ *to introduce more choice and diversity into the education system*

▶ **COLLOCATIONS:**
  diversity **of** *things*
  diversity of **opinions/viewpoints**
  celebrate/promote diversity
  reflect/introduce/increase diversity
  ethnic/racial/cultural/linguistic diversity
  rich/wide/enormous diversity
▶ **SYNONYM:** variety
▶ **ANTONYM:** uniformity

di|ver|si|fy /daɪˈvɜːsɪfaɪ, AM dɪ-/ (diversifies, diversifying, diversified)

VERB When an organization or person **diversifies** into other things, or **diversifies** their range of something, they increase the variety of things that they do or make. ○ [+ *into*] *The company's troubles started only when it diversified into new products.* ○ *Manufacturers have been encouraged to diversify.* ○ *These firms have been given a tough lesson in the need to diversify their markets.*

► **COLLOCATIONS:**
diversify **into** something
diversify into a **field/area/sector**
diversify the **economy**
diversify a **company/market**
diversify **assets**

► **SYNONYM:** expand

di|ver|si|fi|ca|tion /daɪˌvɜːsɪfɪˈkeɪʃən, AM dɪ-/ (diversifications)

NOUN ○ [+ of] The seminar was to discuss diversification of agriculture.
○ These strange diversifications could have damaged or even sunk the entire company.

► **COLLOCATIONS:**
diversification **into/of** something
diversification into an **area**
promote/encourage/increase diversification
international/geographic/economic diversification

► **SYNONYM:** expansion

---

di|vert /daɪˈvɜːt, AM dɪ-/ (diverts, diverting, diverted)

1 VERB To **divert** something means to make it follow a different route or direction. ○ [+ from] a project intended to divert water from the north of the country to drought-prone southern and eastern states ○ [+ to] During the strike, ambulances will be diverted to private hospitals. ○ attempts to divert the lava flow ○ a diverted river

2 VERB To **divert** money or resources means to cause them to be used for a different purpose. ○ [+ from] The government is trying to divert more public funds from west to east. ○ [+ into] government departments involved in diverting resources into community care

► **COLLOCATIONS:**
divert something **to/from** somewhere
divert something **into** something
divert **water/traffic/cars**
divert a **river/plane**
divert the **flow** of something
divert **funds/aid/money/resources**
divert something **elsewhere**

DNA /ˌdiː en ˈeɪ/   SCIENCE MEDICINE

UNCOUNTABLE NOUN **DNA** is an acid in the chromosomes in the centre of

the cells of living things. DNA determines the particular structure
and functions of every cell and is responsible for characteristics being
passed on from parents to their children. DNA is an abbreviation for
'deoxyribonucleic acid'. ○ *DNA profiling matches samples of body fluids
left on a victim to the attackers.* ○ *techniques of extracting DNA from ancient
bones*

▶ COLLOCATIONS:
  extract/obtain/replicate/match DNA
  DNA **testing/fingerprinting/profiling/matching**
  a DNA **sample/test**
  mitochondrial DNA

---

docu|ment /'dɒkjəmənt/

ACADEMIC WORD

(documents, documenting, documented)

VERB If you **document** something, you make a detailed record of it in
writing or on film or tape. ○ *The book represents the first real attempt to
accurately document the history of the entire area.* ○ *The effects of smoking
have been well documented.*

▶ COLLOCATIONS:
  document the **history** of *something*
  document **instances** of *something*
  well/meticulously/extensively documented
  documented **cases/proof/evidence**

EXTEND YOUR VOCABULARY

In academic research, you often talk about writing down information
about something over a period of time.

Record is a general verb to describe keeping information about
something, either all the details or just particular information.
○ *Maharashtra State recorded the highest increase in accidental deaths.*

If you **document** something, you write down all the details.
○ *Colleagues documented 13 cases of unacceptable surgical outcomes.*

If you **catalogue** something, you make a list of things. ○ *Pollen
Botanists catalogued 66 different species of plant.*

If you **chart** something, you make a record that shows progress or a
trend over time, especially in the form of a graph. ○ *Progress is charted
through rigorous annual testing.*

dog|ma /ˈdɒgmə, AM ˈdɔːg-/ (dogmas)

NOUN If you refer to a belief or a system of beliefs as a **dogma**, you disapprove of it because people are expected to accept that it is true, without questioning it. ○ *Their political dogma has blinded them to the real needs of the country.* ○ *He stands for freeing the country from the grip of dogma.*

▶ **COLLOCATIONS:**
  accept/question/challenge dogma
  ideological/religious/outdated dogma
▶ **SYNONYMS:** ideology, doctrine

dog|mat|ic /dɒgˈmætɪk, AM dɔːg-/

ADJECTIVE If you say that someone is **dogmatic**, you are critical of them because they are convinced that they are right, and refuse to consider that other opinions might also be justified. ○ *Many writers at this time held rigidly dogmatic views.* ○ *The regime is dogmatic, and no one dares to express personal opinions.*

▶ **COLLOCATION:** a dogmatic **approach/belief/assertion**
▶ **SYNONYMS:** opinionated, intolerant
▶ **ANTONYM:** tolerant

dog|mati|cal|ly /dɒgˈmætɪkli, AM dɔːg-/

ADVERB ○ *He applies the Marxist world view dogmatically to all social phenomena.*

dog|ma|tism /ˈdɒgmətɪzəm, AM ˈdɔːg-/

UNCOUNTABLE NOUN ○ *We cannot allow dogmatism to stand in the way of progress.*

▶ **SYNONYM:** intolerance
▶ **ANTONYM:** tolerance

do|main /dəʊˈmeɪn/ (domains) `ACADEMIC WORD`

NOUN A **domain** is a particular field of thought, activity, or interest, especially one over which someone has control, influence, or rights. [FORMAL] ○ [+ of] *the great experimenters in the domain of art* ○ *This information should be in the public domain.*

▶ **COLLOCATIONS:**
  the domain **of** something
  the domain of **science/business/art**
  the **public** domain
  enter a domain
▶ **SYNONYM:** sphere

do|nate /dəʊˈneɪt/ (donates, donating, donated)   `MEDICINE`

VERB If you **donate** your blood or a part of your body, you allow doctors to use it to help someone who is ill. ○ *people who are willing to donate their organs for use after death* ○ *All donated blood is screened for HIV.*

▶ COLLOCATIONS:
donate **blood/sperm/eggs**
donate a **kidney/organ**
donate *something* **anonymously**

do|na|tion /dəʊˈneɪʃən/ (donations)

NOUN ○ *measures aimed at encouraging organ donation* ○ *routine screening of blood donations*

▶ COLLOCATION: **organ/blood** donation

do|nor /ˈdəʊnə/ (donors)

1 NOUN A **donor** is someone who gives a part of their body or some of their blood to be used by doctors to help a person who is ill. ○ *Doctors removed the healthy kidney from the donor.* ○ *trying to find a compatible bone marrow donor*

▶ COLLOCATIONS:
find/match/screen a donor
a **potential/suitable/compatible** donor
a **living/anonymous** donor
a **blood/kidney/organ** donor
a **bone marrow/sperm** donor

2 ADJECTIVE **Donor** organs or parts are organs or parts of the body which people allow doctors to use to help people who are ill. ○ *a shortage of donor eggs* ○ *Donor organs have to be matched to recipients.*

▶ COLLOCATION: donor **organs/eggs**

dor|mant /ˈdɔːmənt/   `SCIENCE`

ADJECTIVE Something that is **dormant** is not active, growing, or being used at the present time but is capable of becoming active later on. ○ *when the long dormant volcano of Mount St Helens erupted in 1980* ○ *The virus remains dormant in nerve tissue until activated.* ○ *[+ for] The United Nations is resuming a diplomatic effort that has lain dormant for almost two decades.*

▶ COLLOCATIONS:
dormant **for** *a period of time*
a dormant **volcano**
a dormant **period/season/state**
lie/remain dormant

▶ SYNONYM: inactive

▶ ANTONYM: active

---

dose /dəʊs/ (doses) `MEDICINE`

NOUN A **dose of** medicine or a drug is a measured amount of it which is intended to be taken at one time. ○ [+ of] *One dose of penicillin can wipe out the infection.* ○ [+ for] *The recommended dose for patients with cardiac arrest is 300 mg.*

▶ COLLOCATIONS:
  a dose **of** *something*
  the dose **for** *people*
  a dose of a **vaccine/vitamin/medication/hormone**
  a **daily/recommended/double/lethal** dose
  administer/repeat/prescribe a dose

dos|age /ˈdəʊsɪdʒ/ (dosages)

NOUN A **dosage** is the amount of a medicine or drug that someone takes or should take. ○ [+ of] *He was put on a high dosage of vitamin C.* ○ *Introduce one supplement at a time and increase the dosage gradually.*

▶ COLLOCATIONS:
  a dosage **of** *something*
  a **recommended/prescribed/high** dosage
  reduce/increase the dosage

---

dra|ma /ˈdrɑːmə/ (dramas) `ACADEMIC WORD` `LITERATURE`

NOUN A **drama** is a serious play for the theatre, television, or radio. **Drama** is the study of plays. ○ *He acted in radio dramas.* ○ *the study of Greek drama*

▶ COLLOCATIONS:
  a **TV/television/radio** drama
  Greek/Shakespearean drama
  a drama **teacher/student/department/school**
  study drama

▶ SYNONYMS: play, theatre

drama|tist /ˈdræmətɪst/ (dramatists)

NOUN A **dramatist** is someone who writes plays. ○ [+ who] *Tennessee Williams, the dramatist who wrote A Streetcar Named Desire* ○ *plays written jointly by several Elizabethan dramatists*

▶ COLLOCATIONS:
  a **Greek/Jacobean/Elizabethan** dramatist

a **modern/living** dramatist
▶ **SYNONYM:** playwright
▶ **RELATED WORDS:** novelist, poet

---

dual /'djuːəl, AM 'duː-/

ADJECTIVE Dual means having two parts, functions, or aspects. ○ *his dual role as head of the party and head of state* ○ *a law allowing dual nationality*

▶ **COLLOCATIONS:**
a dual **role/purpose**
a dual **carriageway**
dual **nationality/citizenship**

▶ **SYNONYMS:** twin, double
▶ **ANTONYM:** single

---

dwin|dle /'dwɪndəl/ (dwindles, dwindling, dwindled)

VERB If something **dwindles**, it becomes smaller, weaker, or less in number. ○ [+ from/to] *The factory's workforce has dwindled from over 4,000 to a few hundred.* ○ [V-ing] *a rapidly dwindling population* ○ [V-ing] *dwindling supplies of food and water*

▶ **COLLOCATIONS:**
dwindle **from/to** *something*
dwindling **supplies/resources/reserves**
a dwindling **number/population/stock**
dwindle **rapidly/steadily/alarmingly**

▶ **SYNONYM:** shrink
▶ **ANTONYMS:** expand, grow

---

dy|nam|ic /daɪ'næmɪk/ (dynamics)   ACADEMIC WORD PHYSICS

1 ADJECTIVE A **dynamic** process is one that constantly changes and progresses. ○ *a dynamic, evolving worldwide epidemic* ○ *Political debate is dynamic.*

▶ **COLLOCATIONS:**
a dynamic **economy/range**
economically dynamic

▶ **SYNONYMS:** active, progressive
▶ **ANTONYM:** static

2 NOUN The **dynamic** of a system or process is the force that causes it to change or progress. ○ [+ of] *The dynamic of the market demands constant change and adjustment.* ○ *Politics has its own dynamic.*

▶ COLLOCATIONS:
change/alter/create a dynamic
a **varied/internal/political** dynamic

3 PLURAL NOUN The **dynamics** of a situation or group of people are the opposing forces within it that cause it to change. ○ [+ *of*] *the dynamics of the social system* ○ *The interchange of ideas aids an understanding of family dynamics.*

4 UNCOUNTABLE NOUN Dynamics are forces which produce power or movement. ○ *Scientists observe the same dynamics in fluids.*

5 UNCOUNTABLE NOUN Dynamics is the scientific study of motion, energy, and forces. ○ *His idea was to apply geometry to dynamics.* ○ *the field of fluid dynamics*

▶ COLLOCATIONS:
the dynamics **of** *something*
the dynamics of a **situation/relationship/process**
family/market/group dynamics
changing/shifting/internal/underlying dynamics
understand/study the dynamics

Ee

ec|lec|tic /ɪˈklektɪk/

ADJECTIVE An **eclectic** collection of objects, ideas, or beliefs is wide-ranging and comes from many different sources. [FORMAL] ○ *an eclectic collection of paintings, drawings, and prints* ○ *These theories tend to be highly eclectic, drawing on several sociological theorists.* ○ *His musical tastes are eclectic.*

▶ **COLLOCATIONS:**
 eclectic **taste/style**
 an eclectic **crowd/mix/collection/assortment**
 fairly/highly/extremely eclectic

▶ **SYNONYMS:** diverse, wide-ranging

---

eco|sys|tem /ˈiːkəʊsɪstəm, AM ˈekə-/ `BIOLOGY` `GEOGRAPHY`
(ecosystems)

NOUN An **ecosystem** is all the plants and animals that live in a particular area together with the complex relationship that exists between them and their environment. ○ *Madagascar's ecosystems range from rainforest to semi-desert.* ○ *the forest ecosystem* ○ *Human over-fishing has destabilised marine ecosystems.*

▶ **COLLOCATIONS:**
 a **marine/forest/coastal** ecosystem
 a **balanced/fragile** ecosystem
 alter/damage/destroy an ecosystem
 preserve/protect/sustain an ecosystem

---

elec|trode /ɪˈlektrəʊd/ (electrodes) `PHYSICS`

NOUN An **electrode** is a small piece of metal or other substance that is used to take an electric current to or from a source of power, a piece of equipment, or a living body. ○ *The patient's brain activity is monitored via electrodes taped to the skull.* ○ *small electrodes attached to the scalp*

▶ **COLLOCATIONS:**
 implant/attach/tape electrodes
 fasten/place electrodes
 a **tiny** electrode

▶ **RELATED WORD:** anode

elec|tron /ɪˈlektrɒn/ (electrons)   `PHYSICS`

NOUN An **electron** is a tiny particle of matter that is smaller than an atom and has a negative electrical charge. ○ *a type of radiation that displaces electrons from atoms* ○ *an electron microscope capable of viewing single atoms* ○ *As these electrons are negatively charged they will attempt to repel each other.*

▶ **COLLOCATIONS:**
  a **single/unpaired/free** electron
  an electron **microscope/beam/micrograph**
  transfer electrons
  charged electrons

▶ **RELATED WORDS:** atom, proton, neutron

elite /ɪˈliːt, eɪ-/ (elites)   `SOCIOLOGY`

NOUN You can refer to the most powerful, rich, or talented people within a particular group, place, or society as the **elite**. ○ *a government comprised mainly of the elite* ○ [+ in] *We have a political elite in this country.* ○ [+ of] *the governing elite of the 18th-century Dutch republic*

▶ **COLLOCATIONS:**
  the elite **in** *somewhere*
  the elite **of** *something*
  a **political/intellectual/wealthy/governing** elite
  an elite **dominates/rules/governs**
  challenge/form/join an elite

elit|ist /ɪˈliːtɪst, eɪ-/

ADJECTIVE **Elitist** systems, practices, or ideas favour the most powerful, rich, or talented people within a group, place, or society. ○ *The party leadership denounced the Bill as elitist.* ○ *The legal profession is starting to be less elitist and more representative.*

▶ **COLLOCATIONS:**
  an elitist **attitude/view/institution**
  elitist **snobbery/nonsense**

elit|ism /ɪˈliːtɪzəm, eɪ-/

UNCOUNTABLE NOUN **Elitism** is the quality or practice of being elitist. ○ *a certain amount of cultural elitism* ○ *the stereotypes of snobbery and elitism associated with the institution* ○ *It became difficult to promote excellence without being accused of elitism.*

▶ **COLLOCATIONS:**
  societal/cultural/educational/academic elitism

condemn/oppose/end elitism
promote/foster/create elitism
▶ **PHRASE:** elitism and snobbery

---

el|lipse /ɪ'lɪps/ (ellipses)

NOUN An **ellipse** is an oval shape similar to a circle but longer and flatter. ○ *The Earth orbits in an ellipse.* ○ *Every known comet orbits the sun, although most of them move in extremely elongated ellipses.*

▶ **COLLOCATIONS:**
in an ellipse
a **distorted/irregular/elongated** ellipse

el|lip|ti|cal /ɪ'lɪptɪkəl/

ADJECTIVE [FORMAL] ○ *the moon's elliptical orbit* ○ [+ in] *The stadium is elliptical in plan.* ○ [+ in] *Spirals can seem to be elliptical in shape when viewed edge-on.*

▶ **COLLOCATIONS:**
elliptical **in** shape
an elliptical **orbit/trajectory/path**
an elliptical **shape/motion**

---

em|bryo /'embriəʊ/ (embryos)   BIOLOGY

NOUN An **embryo** is an unborn animal or human being in the very early stages of development. ○ *The embryo lives in the amniotic cavity.* ○ *the remarkable resilience of very young embryos* ○ *the cloning of human embryos for stem cell research*

▶ **COLLOCATIONS:**
an embryo **forms/grows/develops/survives**
clone/create an embryo
a **human/fertilized/discarded/frozen** embryo

em|bry|on|ic /,embri'ɒnɪk/

ADJECTIVE [FORMAL] ○ *embryonic stem-cell experiments* ○ *embryonic plant cells* ○ *How genes control this embryonic development is a central problem in biology.*

▶ **COLLOCATIONS:**
embryonic **development/tissue/biology**
an embryonic **cell/clone/gene/experiment**

em|pire /'empaɪə/ (empires) POLITICS HISTORY

NOUN An **empire** is a number of individual nations that are all controlled by the government or ruler of one particular country. ○ *the Roman Empire* ○ *The empire collapsed in 1918.* ○ *The French empire had expanded largely through military conquest.*

▶ **COLLOCATIONS:**
a **vast/colonial/mighty** empire
the **Russian/British/Turkish** empire
an empire **emerges/expands/extends**
an empire **collapses/crumbles/disintegrates**
build/rule an empire

em|per|or /'empərə/ (emperors)

NOUN An **emperor** is a man who rules an empire or is the head of state in an empire. ○ *An Indian emperor once proclaimed it a paradise on Earth.* ○ *the legendary Aztec emperor, Montezuma* ○ *The eighty-three-year-old emperor was deposed in September 1974.*

▶ **COLLOCATIONS:**
an emperor **abdicates/rules/dies**
an emperor **proclaims/builds/orders** *something*
crown/depose an emperor
a **Roman/Aztec/Chinese** emperor
a **divine/ailing/evil** emperor
Emperor **Nero/Augustus**

▶ **RELATED WORD:** empress

em|piri|cal /ɪmˈpɪrɪkəl/ ACADEMIC WORD

ADJECTIVE Empirical evidence or study relies on practical experience rather than theories. ○ *There is no empirical evidence to support his thesis.* ○ *a series of important empirical studies*

▶ **COLLOCATIONS:**
an empirical **observation/finding**
an empirical **study/investigation**
empirical **evidence/research/analysis/data**

▶ **ANTONYM:** theoretical

em|piri|cal|ly /ɪmˈpɪrɪkli/

ADVERB ○ *empirically based research* ○ *They approached this part of their task empirically.* ○ *the empirically confirmed relationship between high service levels and profitability*

▶ **COLLOCATIONS:**
  empirically **grounded/derived/based**
  empirically **confirm/verify/demonstrate** *something*
  empirically **supportable/verifiable/measurable**
▶ **ANTONYM:** theoretically

---

em|ploy /ɪmˈplɔɪ/ (employs, employing, employed)

VERB If you **employ** certain methods, materials, or expressions, you use them. ○ *The tactics the police are now to employ are definitely uncompromising.* ○ *[+ as] the language of vulgar speech employed as a political weapon* ○ *[+ in] the approaches and methods employed in the study*

▶ **COLLOCATIONS:**
  employ *something* **as/in** *something*
  employ *something* as a **weapon**
  employ **approaches/methods/techniques/tactics**
▶ **SYNONYM:** use

---

en|dorse /ɪnˈdɔːs/ (endorses, endorsing, endorsed) `BUSINESS`

1 VERB If you **endorse** someone or something, you say publicly that you support or approve of them. ○ *I can endorse their opinion wholeheartedly.* ○ *policies agreed by the Labour Party and endorsed by the electorate*

▶ **COLLOCATIONS:**
  endorsed **by** *someone*
  endorsed by the **electorate/parliament/state**
  endorse a **candidate/plan/idea/treaty**
  overwhelmingly/unanimously/heartily endorse *something*
▶ **SYNONYMS:** support, approve

2 VERB If you **endorse** a product or company, you appear in advertisements for it. ○ *The twins endorsed a line of household cleaning products.* ○ *The report also warned people to be wary of diets which are endorsed by celebrities.*

→ see note at **advocate**

▶ **COLLOCATIONS:**
  endorsed **by** *someone*
  endorsed by a **celebrity**
  endorse a **product/brand/company**
▶ **SYNONYMS:** promote, advertise

en|dorse|ment /ɪnˈdɔːsmənt/ (endorsements)

1 NOUN An **endorsement** is a statement or action which shows that you support or approve of something or someone. ○ *[+ of] That adds up to an* *endorsement of the status quo.* ○ [+ for] *This is a powerful endorsement for his softer style of government.*

▶ **COLLOCATIONS:**
an endorsement **by** *someone*
an endorsement **of/for** *something/someone*
a **ringing/resounding/glowing** endorsement

▶ **SYNONYM:** approval

2 NOUN An **endorsement for** a product or company involves appearing in advertisements for it or showing support for it. ○ *Fashion designers still value celebrity endorsements.* ○ *Bryant has earned millions of dollars in product endorsements.*

▶ **COLLOCATIONS:**
an endorsement **by** *someone*
an endorsement **of/for** *something*
an endorsement of/for a **product/brand/company**
a **celebrity/product/lucrative** endorsement
an endorsement **deal/contract/opportunity**

▶ **PHRASE:** a multi-million dollar endorsement

---

en|dure /ɪnˈdjʊə, AM -ˈdʊr/ **(endures, enduring, endured)**

1 VERB If you **endure** a painful or difficult situation, you experience it and do not avoid it or give up, usually because you cannot. ○ *The company endured heavy financial losses.* ○ *He endured physical pain and made many sacrifices for the benefit of others.*

▶ **COLLOCATIONS:**
endure **pain/discomfort/suffering**
endure **hardship/humiliation/ridicule**
endure a **taunt/ordeal/beating**
stoically/bravely/patiently endure *something*

▶ **SYNONYM:** undergo

2 VERB If something **endures**, it continues to exist without any loss in quality or importance. ○ *Somehow the language endures and continues to survive.* ○ *Whether this fragile marriage endures remains to be seen.*

▶ **COLLOCATION:** a **myth/legend/marriage/survivor** endures

▶ **SYNONYM:** persist

en|dur|ing /ɪnˈdjʊərɪŋ, AM -ˈdʊr/

ADJECTIVE ○ *the start of an enduring friendship* ○ *It remained one of his most enduring memories.* ○ *the enduring legacy of Christianity*

▶ **COLLOCATIONS:**
an enduring **friendship/legacy/myth**
an enduring **influence/memory**
▶ **SYNONYM:** lasting

---

en|force /ɪnˈfɔːs/ (enforces, enforcing, enforced) `ACADEMIC WORD` `LAW`

VERB If people in authority **enforce** a law or a rule, they make sure that it is obeyed, usually by punishing people who do not obey it. ○ *Until now, the government has only enforced the ban with regard to American ships.* ○ *The measures are being enforced by Interior Ministry troops.* ○ *A strict curfew was enforced.*

▶ **COLLOCATIONS:**
enforced **by** *someone*
strictly/aggressively/effectively enforce *something*
enforce a **law/regulation/ban/curfew**
a **court/regulator/law** enforces *something*
the **police/army/government** enforce *something*

en|force|ment /ɪnˈfɔːsmənt/

UNCOUNTABLE NOUN If someone carries out the **enforcement of** an act or rule, they enforce it. ○ [+ *of*] *The doctors want stricter enforcement of existing laws, such as those banning sales of cigarettes to children.* ○ *Interpol are liaising with all the major law enforcement agencies around the world.*

▶ **COLLOCATIONS:**
the enforcement **of** *something*
strict/tough/effective/lax/inadequate enforcement
enforcement of a **law/regulation/ban/agreement**
law/traffic/drug enforcement
an enforcement **agency/authority/official**
oversee/relax/tighten/strengthen enforcement

---

en|large /ɪnˈlɑːdʒ/ (enlarges, enlarging, enlarged)

VERB When you **enlarge** something or when it **enlarges**, it becomes bigger. ○ *the plan to enlarge Ewood Park into a 30,000 all-seater stadium* ○ *The glands in the neck may enlarge.* ○ *the use of silicone to enlarge the breasts*

▶ **COLLOCATIONS:**
enlarge the **breasts/penis**
enlarge a **hole/image**
an enlarged **heart/organ/prostate**
digitally/greatly/significantly enlarged

en|large|ment /ɪnˈlɑːdʒmənt/

UNCOUNTABLE NOUN ○ [+ of] *There is insufficient space for enlargement of the buildings.* ○ *EU enlargement is a process that is not yet complete.* ○ *millions of spam messages promoting penis enlargement pills*

▶ **COLLOCATIONS:**
the enlargement **of** something
enlargement of the **prostate/spleen/liver**
enlargement of the **heart/ovaries**
penis/breast/EU enlargement

---

en|ter|prise /ˈentəpraɪz/ (enterprises)   `BUSINESS`

NOUN An **enterprise** is a company or business, often a small one. ○ *There are plenty of small industrial enterprises.* ○ *Many small and relatively primitive enterprises flourish under laissez-faire.* ○ *one of Japan's most profitable enterprises*

▶ **COLLOCATIONS:**
a **commercial/industrial/state** enterprise
a **profitable/profit-making/loss-making** enterprise
an enterprise **flourishes/succeeds/collapses**
an enterprise **produces/supplies** something

▶ **PHRASE:** small-to-medium enterprises

▶ **SYNONYMS:** business, company

---

en|ti|tle /ɪnˈtaɪtəl/ (entitles, entitling, entitled)

1 VERB If you **are entitled to** something, you have the right to have it or do it. ○ [+ to] *If the warranty is limited, the terms may entitle you to a replacement or refund.* ○ [+ to-inf] *There is no document stating we are clearly entitled to vote in this election.* ○ [+ to-inf] *It is a democracy and people are entitled to express their views.*

▶ **COLLOCATIONS:**
entitle someone **to** something
entitled to **vote/protest/participate**
entitled to **receive/claim/express** something
legally/constitutionally/fully entitled

2 VERB If the title of something such as a book, film, or painting is, for example, 'Sunrise', you can say that it **is entitled** 'Sunrise'. ○ *Chomsky's review is entitled 'Psychology and Ideology'.* ○ *a 1953 article entitled 'A Cognitive Theory of Dreams'* ○ *an essay entitled 'The Great Terrorism Scare'*

▶ **COLLOCATIONS:**
a **book/article/essay** entitled something
a **lecture/thesis** entitled something
provisionally entitled

en|ti|tle|ment /ɪnˈtaɪtəlmənt/ (entitlements)

NOUN An **entitlement to** something is the right to have it or do it.
[FORMAL] ○ [+ *to*] *They lose their entitlement to benefit when they start work.*
○ [+ *to*] *All pupils share the same statutory entitlement to a broad and balanced curriculum.*

▶ COLLOCATIONS:
an entitlement **to** *something*
lose/receive/reduce/calculate an entitlement
a **contractual/statutory/automatic** entitlement
a **superannuation/pension/holiday** entitlement

---

en|tity /ˈentɪti/ (entities)   ACADEMIC WORD

NOUN An **entity** is something that exists separately from other things and has a clear identity of its own. [FORMAL] ○ *the earth as a living entity* ○ *the designation of Kurdistan as a separate federal entity with its own parliament*

▶ COLLOCATIONS:
merged/separate/combined entities
a **distinct/autonomous/independent** entity
form/create an entity

EXTEND YOUR VOCABULARY

In everyday English, **thing** is a very common general noun to describe almost anything that is not living. Where possible, it is better in academic writing to use more specific nouns. ○ *The first thing I want to discuss is ...* ○ *The first **point/idea/issue** I want to discuss is ...* ○ *The museum contains many historical things.* ○ *The museum contains many historical **artefacts/objects**.* ○ *the key thing that makes a good leader* ○ *the key **characteristic/feature/quality** that makes a good leader*

Sometimes, however, it is difficult to find a specific noun to describe the type of thing you are dealing with. The word **item** can be used to describe an individual example of many types of things. An **item** can be a physical object or a piece of written or spoken information. ○ *furniture and other household items* ○ *the main item on the agenda*

Entity is a more formal word often used to talk about something more abstract that is considered to be separate and to have its own identity. It is often used to describe a group of people, but can also describe other things that are abstract and difficult to define. ○ *Each subsidiary of the company is a separate legal entity.* ○ *Neanderthals are a distinct evolutionary entity from our own.*

en|tre|pre|neur /ˌɒntrəprəˈnɜː/ (entrepreneurs) `BUSINESS`

NOUN An **entrepreneur** is a person who sets up businesses and business deals. ○ *The two Sydney-based entrepreneurs founded the company in 1995.* ○ *the financial incentives for successful entrepreneurs to innovate and invest*

▶ **COLLOCATIONS:**
   an entrepreneur **founds/invents/launches** something
   a **budding/successful/visionary** entrepreneur
   an entrepreneur **owns/builds/founds/starts** something

en|tre|pre|neur|ial /ˌɒntrəprəˈnɜːriəl/

ADJECTIVE Entrepreneurial means having the qualities that are needed to succeed as an entrepreneur. ○ *her prodigious entrepreneurial flair* ○ *His initial entrepreneurial venture was setting up Britain's first computer-dating agency.* ○ *Germany's entrepreneurial culture is less vigorous than it was.*

▶ **COLLOCATIONS:**
   entrepreneurial **flair/spirit/skill**
   an entrepreneurial **culture/mind-set/venture**
   highly entrepreneurial

▶ **SYNONYM:** business

en|tre|pre|neur|ship /ˌɒntrəprəˈnɜːʃɪp/

UNCOUNTABLE NOUN Entrepreneurship is the state of being an entrepreneur, or the activities associated with being an entrepreneur. ○ *When we encourage entrepreneurship, we also encourage risk taking.* ○ *[+ among] measures to encourage innovation and entrepreneurship among small firms*

▶ **COLLOCATIONS:**
   entrepreneurship **among** people
   foster/encourage/promote/stifle entrepreneurship

▶ **PHRASE:** entrepreneurship and innovation

en|vis|age /ɪnˈvɪzɪdʒ/ (envisages, envisaging, envisaged)

VERB If you **envisage** something, you imagine that it is true, real, or likely to happen. ○ *He envisages the possibility of establishing direct diplomatic relations in the future.* ○ *[+ v-ing] He had never envisaged spending the whole of his working life in that particular job.* ○ *The plan envisaged the creation of an independent Palestinian state.*

▶ **COLLOCATIONS:**
   envisage the **creation/transformation/possibility** of something
   originally/initially/previously envisaged

▶ **SYNONYMS:** imagine, envision

epi|dem|ic /ˌɛpɪ'dɛmɪk/ (epidemics) `MEDICINE`

NOUN If there is an **epidemic of** a particular disease somewhere, it affects a very large number of people there and spreads quickly to other areas. ○ *A flu epidemic is sweeping through Moscow.* ○ [+ of] *a killer epidemic of yellow fever* ○ *A UN study warns the AIDs epidemic is nowhere near its peak.*

▶ **COLLOCATIONS:**
  an epidemic **of** *something*
  a **global/infectious/deadly** epidemic
  a **flu/cholera/malaria** epidemic
  the **AIDS/avian flu/swine flu** epidemic
  cause/prevent/fight an epidemic
  an epidemic **spreads/begins**
  an epidemic **hits/sweeps** *somewhere*

equa|tor /ɪ'kweɪtə/ `GEOGRAPHY`

NOUN The **equator** is an imaginary line around the middle of the Earth at an equal distance from the North Pole and the South Pole. ○ *an orbit 22,000 miles above the Earth's equator* ○ *Sarawak straddles the Equator and is hot and humid.* ○ *the vernal and autumnal equinox, when the sun crosses the equator travelling north and south*

▶ **COLLOCATION: straddle/cross/approach** the equator
▶ **RELATED WORDS:** tropic, hemisphere, dateline

eradi|cate /ɪ'rædɪkeɪt/ (eradicates, eradicating, eradicated)

VERB To **eradicate** something means to get rid of it completely. [FORMAL] ○ *They are already battling to eradicate illnesses such as malaria and tetanus.* ○ [+ in] *Vaccination has virtually eradicated anthrax in the developed world.* ○ *a campaign that genuinely sought to eradicate poverty*

▶ **COLLOCATIONS:**
  eradicate *something* **in/from** *a place*
  virtually/completely/almost eradicated
  eradicate **disease/poverty/illiteracy/racism**
▶ **SYNONYM:** eliminate

eradi|ca|tion /ˌrædɪ'keɪʃən/

UNCOUNTABLE NOUN ○ [+ of] *He is seen as having made a significant contribution towards the eradication of corruption.* ○ *the polio eradication programme* ○ [+ of] *the eradication of child poverty*

▶ **COLLOCATIONS:**
  the eradication **of** *something*

the eradication of **poverty/disease/corruption**
polio/smallpox/malaria eradication

▶ **SYNONYM:** elimination

---

erase /ɪˈreɪz, AM ɪˈreɪs/ (erases, erasing, erased)   IT

VERB If you **erase** information which has been stored in a computer, you
completely remove or destroy it. ○ [+ from] *It appears the names were*
accidentally erased from computer disks. ○ *software tools that permanently*
erase single files or entire disks ○ *The job included erasing all email records.*

▶ **COLLOCATIONS:**
erase something **from** something
digitally/accidentally/permanently erase something
erase a **file/disk/record**

▶ **SYNONYMS:** wipe, remove

---

erode /ɪˈrəʊd/ (erodes, eroding, eroded)   ACADEMIC WORD

1 VERB If someone's authority, right, or confidence **erodes** or **is eroded**, it
is gradually destroyed or removed. [FORMAL] ○ *His critics say his fumbling*
of the issue of reform has eroded his authority. ○ *America's belief in its own*
God-ordained uniqueness started to erode.

▶ **COLLOCATIONS:**
erode someone's **credibility/morale/confidence**
further erode something

2 VERB If the value of something **erodes** or **is eroded** by something such
as inflation or age, its value decreases. ○ *Competition in the financial*
marketplace has eroded profits. ○ *The value of the dollar began to erode rapidly*
just around this time.

▶ **COLLOCATIONS:**
eroded **by** something
steadily/gradually/quickly/rapidly erode
erode **profits**
inflation/competition erodes something
a **recession** erodes something

ero|sion /ɪˈrəʊʒən/

1 UNCOUNTABLE NOUN The **erosion of** a person's authority, rights, or
confidence is the gradual destruction or removal of them. ○ [+ of] *the*
erosion of confidence in world financial markets ○ [+ of] *the widespread erosion*
of civil liberties ○ [+ of] *the rapid erosion of privacy rights*

2 UNCOUNTABLE NOUN The **erosion of** support, values, or money is a gradual decrease in its level or standard. ○ [+ of] *the erosion of moral standards* ○ [+ of] *a dramatic erosion of support for the program*

▶ COLLOCATIONS:
the erosion **of** *something*
the erosion of **liberty/sovereignty/privacy**
the erosion of **standards/support/trust/confidence**
gradual/steady/rapid/widespread/dramatic erosion

---

et al. /ˌet ˈæl/ ACADEMIC STUDY

et al. is used after a name or a list of names to indicate that other people are also involved. It is used especially when referring to books or articles which were written by more than two people. ○ *Blough et al.* ○ *Second, the analyses of Bollini et al. (1994) suggest that increasing doses does not improve treatment response.*

→ see note at **cf.**

---

eth|ic /ˈeθɪk/ (ethics) ACADEMIC WORD

1 PLURAL NOUN **Ethics** are moral beliefs and rules about right and wrong. ○ *Its members are bound by a rigid code of ethics which includes confidentiality.* ○ *Refugee workers said such action was a violation of medical ethics.* ○ *the corporate ethics and social responsibility that society expects of business*

▶ COLLOCATIONS:
the ethics **of** *something*
the ethics of **journalism/genetics/war**
medical/professional/corporate/journalistic ethics
question/violate/embrace/instill ethics

2 UNCOUNTABLE NOUN **Ethics** is the study of questions about what is morally right and wrong. ○ *the teaching of ethics and moral philosophy* ○ *Lambert, an ethics professor at Wartburg College, concurs.*

▶ COLLOCATIONS:
study/teach ethics
an ethics **professor/faculty/seminar**

ethi|cal /ˈeθɪkəl/

1 ADJECTIVE **Ethical** means relating to beliefs about right and wrong. ○ *the moral and ethical standards in the school* ○ *the medical, nursing and ethical issues surrounding terminally-ill people* ○ *Indeed, the use of placebos raises a whole range of ethical dilemmas.*

2 ADJECTIVE If you describe something as **ethical**, you mean that it is morally right or morally acceptable. ○ *ethical investment schemes*

○ [+ to-inf] *Does the party think it is ethical to link tax policy with party fund-raising?* ○ *the ethical treatment of wild animals*

▶ **COLLOCATIONS:**
  ethical **standards/issues/implications**
  an ethical **dilemma/obligation/code/principle**
  ethical **behaviour/conduct/treatment**

▶ **PHRASE:** ethical and moral

USAGE: ethic, **ethics** or **ethical**?

A particular **ethic** is an idea or moral belief that influences the behaviour and attitudes of a group of people. ○ *He quickly embraced the American work ethic.*

When you use **ethics** to refer to moral beliefs and rules about what is right and wrong, it is a plural noun and you use it with a plural verb form. ○ *Journalistic ethics require reporters to conceal the identities of confidential sources.*

Ethic is never an adjective. The adjective meaning 'relating to ethics' is **ethical**. ○ *an ethical dilemma*

Ethical is often used to refer to the principles and standards in a particular profession or part of society. **Moral** is used more to talk about the beliefs and behaviour of an individual.

---

evapo|rate /ɪˈvæpəreɪt/   `SCIENCE` `GEOGRAPHY`
(evaporates, evaporating, evaporated)

VERB When a liquid **evaporates**, or **is evaporated**, it changes from a liquid state to a gas, because its temperature has increased. ○ *Moisture is drawn to the surface of the fabric so that it evaporates.* ○ *The water is evaporated by the sun.* ○ [+ into] *Hydrocarbons evaporate into the atmosphere.*

▶ **COLLOCATIONS:**
  evaporated **by/into** *something*
  water/moisture/sweat/liquid evaporates
  evaporate into the **air/atmosphere**
  quickly/completely evaporate

evapo|ra|tion /ɪˌvæpəˈreɪʃən/

UNCOUNTABLE NOUN ○ [+ from] *High temperatures also result in high evaporation from the plants.* ○ [+ of] *The soothing, cooling effect is caused by the evaporation of the sweat on the skin.*

▶ **COLLOCATIONS:**
the evaporation **of** *something*
evaporation **from** *something*
the evaporation of **water/moisture/sweat**
prevent/reduce evaporation

---

evoke /ɪˈvəʊk/ **(evokes, evoking, evoked)**　　**LITERATURE**

VERB To **evoke** a particular memory, idea, emotion, or response means to
cause it to occur. [FORMAL] ○ *the scene evoking memories of those old movies*
○ *Harriet Walter as Celia marvellously evokes the pathos of the middle-class
woman.* ○ *The entire piece evokes an atmosphere of comfort and quiescence.*

▶ **COLLOCATIONS:**
evoke **memories/emotions/feelings**
evoke a **response/reaction/atmosphere**
evoke **pathos/empathy/sympathy**
a **name/word/song** evokes *something*

---

ex|ac|er|bate /ɪɡˈzæsəbeɪt/ **(exacerbates, exacerbating, exacerbated)**

VERB If something **exacerbates** a problem or bad situation, it makes it
worse. [FORMAL] ○ *Mr Powell-Taylor says that depopulation exacerbates the
problem.* ○ *Longstanding poverty has been exacerbated by racial divisions.*
○ *Stress can also exacerbate the symptoms.*

▶ **COLLOCATIONS:**
exacerbated **by** *something*
exacerbate a **problem/situation/conflict/crisis**
exacerbate **tensions/symptoms**

▶ **SYNONYM:** aggravate

---

ex|ca|vate /ˈekskəveɪt/ **(excavates, excavating, excavated)**　　**HISTORY**

VERB When archaeologists or other people **excavate** a piece of land,
they remove earth carefully from it and look for things such as pots,
bones, or buildings which are buried there, in order to discover
information about the past. ○ *A new Danish expedition is again excavating
the site in annual summer digs.* ○ *Archaeologists excavated the skeletal remains
in Indonesia.*

▶ **COLLOCATIONS:**
excavate a **site/grave/crater**
excavate a **fossil/skeleton**
excavate **remains**

ex|ca|va|tion /ˌekskəˈveɪʃən/ (excavations)

NOUN ○ [+ of] the excavation of a bronze-age boat ○ In time these new excavations will require conservation. ○ Recent excavations have uncovered sensational evidence.

▶ **COLLOCATIONS:**
the excavation **of** something
an excavation **unearths/uncovers/reveals** something
undertake/conduct/lead an excavation
an **archaeological/extensive** excavation

ex|ecute /ˈeksɪkjuːt/ (executes, executing, executed)

VERB If you **execute** a plan, you carry it out. [FORMAL] ○ We are going to execute our campaign plan to the letter. ○ the expertly executed break-in in which three men overpowered and tied up a detective

▶ **COLLOCATION: brilliantly** executed

ex|ecu|tion /ˌeksɪˈkjuːʃən/

UNCOUNTABLE NOUN ○ [+ of] U.S. forces are fully prepared for the execution of any action once the order is given by the president. ○ the need for top-class customer care and flawless execution

▶ **COLLOCATIONS:**
the execution **of** something
the execution of a **plan/strategy/agreement**

ex|em|pli|fy /ɪgˈzemplɪfaɪ/ (exemplifies, exemplifying, exemplified)

VERB If a person or thing **exemplifies** something such as a situation, quality, or class of things, they are a typical example of it. [FORMAL] ○ The room's style exemplifies Conran's ideal of 'beauty and practicality'. ○ the emotional expressiveness of modern dance as exemplified by the work of Martha Graham

▶ **COLLOCATIONS:**
exemplified **by** something/someone
exemplify a **spirit/ideal/attitude/quality**
perfectly exemplify something

ex|empt /ɪgˈzempt/ (exempts, exempting, exempted)

1 ADJECTIVE If someone or something is **exempt from** a particular rule, duty, or obligation, they do not have to follow it or do it. ○ [+ from] Men in college were exempt from military service. ○ [+ from] Any income or capital gain received is exempt from tax.

▶ COLLOCATIONS:
exempt **from** *something*
exempt from **tax/conscription/VAT**
potentially/currently exempt

2 VERB To **exempt** a person or thing **from** a particular rule, duty, or obligation means to state officially that they are not bound or affected by it. ○ [+ *from*] *South Carolina claimed the power to exempt its citizens from the obligation to obey federal law.* ○ [+ *from*] *Companies with fifty-five or fewer employees would be exempted from the requirements.*

▶ COLLOCATIONS:
exempt *someone/something* **from** *something*
exempt *someone/something* from a **requirement/rule**
exempt a **business** from *something*

ex|emp|tion /ɪgˈzempʃən/ (exemptions)

NOUN ○ [+ *from*] *the exemption of employer-provided health insurance from taxation* ○ [+ *for*] *new exemptions for students and the low-paid*

▶ COLLOCATIONS:
exemption **from** *something*
an exemption **for** *someone*
the exemption **of** *something*
exemption from a **law/tax**
grant/seek an exemption

ex|ert /ɪgˈzɜːt/ (exerts, exerting, exerted)

VERB If someone or something **exerts** influence, authority, or pressure, they use it in a strong or determined way, especially in order to produce a particular effect. [FORMAL] ○ [+ *on*] *He exerted considerable influence on the thinking of the scientific community on these issues.* ○ [+ *on*] *The cyst was causing swelling and exerting pressure on her brain.*

▶ COLLOCATIONS:
exert *something* **on** *something*
exert **influence/pressure**
exert **authority/control/power**
a **community/group** exerts *something*

ex|hale /eksˈheɪl/ (exhales, exhaling, exhaled) `BIOLOGY`

VERB When you **exhale**, you breathe out the air that is in your lungs. [FORMAL] ○ [+ *through*] *The patient should inhale through the nose and exhale through the mouth.* ○ [+ *from*] *The carbon dioxide is exhaled from your lungs.* ○ *the process of inhaling and exhaling air*

► COLLOCATIONS:
exhale **through/from** *something*
exhale through the **nose/mouth**
exhale **slowly/gently/sharply/audibly**
exhale **smoke/air/gas/oxygen/carbon dioxide**

► SYNONYM: breathe out
► ANTONYM: inhale

ex|ha|la|tion /ˌekshəˈleɪʃən/ (exhalations)

NOUN ○ *Milton let out his breath in a long exhalation.* ○ *[+ of] the quick exhalation of breath through expanded nostrils*

► COLLOCATIONS:
exhalation **of** *something*
exhalation of **breath/smoke/air**
a **sharp/quick/long** exhalation

► ANTONYM: inhalation

---

ex|haust /ɪgˈzɔːst/ (exhausts, exhausting, exhausted)   SCIENCE

1 VERB If you **exhaust** something such as money or food, you use or finish it all. ○ *We have exhausted all our material resources.* ○ *They said that food supplies were almost exhausted.* ○ *Energy resources were virtually exhausted.*

► COLLOCATION: exhaust **resources/supplies/reserves**

2 UNCOUNTABLE NOUN Exhaust is the gas or steam that is produced when the engine of a vehicle is running. ○ *[+ from] the exhaust from a car engine* ○ *The city's streets are filthy and choked with exhaust fumes.* ○ *The particles in diesel exhaust can penetrate deeply into the lungs.*

► COLLOCATIONS:
the exhaust **from** *something*
the exhaust from an **engine**
exhaust **fumes/emissions/gas**
an exhaust **pipe/valve/vent/system**
diesel/dual exhaust

---

ex|hib|it /ɪgˈzɪbɪt/ (exhibits, exhibiting, exhibited)   ACADEMIC WORD

VERB If someone or something shows a particular quality, feeling, or type of behaviour, you can say that they **exhibit** it. [FORMAL] ○ *He has exhibited symptoms of anxiety and overwhelming worry.* ○ *Two cats or more in one house will also exhibit territorial behaviour.* ○ *The economy continued to exhibit signs of decline in September.*

▶ COLLOCATIONS:
exhibit **behaviour/signs/symptoms**
exhibit **characteristics/similarities/variation**
typically/commonly exhibit *something*
▶ SYNONYM: show

---

ex|pend /ɪkˈspend/ (expends, expending, expended)

VERB To **expend** something, especially energy, time, or money, means to use it or spend it. [FORMAL] ○ *Children expend a lot of energy and may need more high-energy food than adults.* ○ [+ in] *In fact, health experts have expended a great deal of effort in their search for an acceptable definition.*

▶ COLLOCATIONS:
expend *something* **in/on** *something*
expend a **lot/great deal** of *something*
expend a **huge amount/vast amount** of *something*
expend **energy/effort/money/resources**

> **EXTEND YOUR VOCABULARY**
>
> In everyday English, you often talk about **using** energy or resources. In more formal academic writing, you can use the verbs **expend** and **consume**. Usually, you say that people **expend** energy or resources, but a process or activity **consumes** energy, money or resources.
> ○ *Nowadays people expend less energy on everyday tasks.* ○ *Everyday tasks now consume less energy than in the past.*
>
> You can also say that something **depletes** resources, meaning that it uses the resources and so reduces the amount still available. ○ *a time of energy shortages and fears of depleting oil reserves*

---

ex|per|tise /ˌekspɜːˈtiːz/

UNCOUNTABLE NOUN Expertise is special skill or knowledge that is acquired by training, study, or practice. ○ [+ to-inf] *The problem is that most local authorities lack the expertise to deal sensibly in this market.* ○ [+ in] *students with expertise in forensics* ○ *a pooling and sharing of knowledge and expertise*

▶ COLLOCATIONS:
expertise **in** *something*
lack/possess/acquire/bring expertise
technical/managerial/scientific expertise
marketing/engineering/computer expertise

▶ **PHRASE:** knowledge and expertise

> **USAGE: expert** or **expertise**?
>
> An **expert** is a person with special knowledge or skills in a particular area. ○ *Experts are predicting that inflation will start to rise again next year.*
>
> **Expert** can also be used as an adjective. ○ *expert medical advice* ○ *They are accompanied by expert local guides.*
>
> **Expertise** is an uncountable noun that is used to talk about the specialized knowledge or skills that an **expert** has. ○ *employees with less technical expertise*

---

ex|plic|it /ɪkˈsplɪsɪt/ ACADEMIC WORD

ADJECTIVE Something that is **explicit** is expressed or shown clearly and openly, without any attempt to hide anything. ○ *sexually explicit scenes in films and books* ○ *explicit references to age in recruitment advertising* ○ *The FBI's instructions were explicit.*

▶ **COLLOCATIONS:**
an explicit **reference/instruction/photograph/scene**
explicit **material/content**
sexually/verbally explicit

▶ **SYNONYM:** overt

▶ **ANTONYM:** implicit

ex|plic|it|ly /ɪkˈsplɪsɪtli/

ADVERB ○ *The play was the first commercially successful work dealing explicitly with homosexuality.* ○ *Their intention is not to become involved in explicitly political activities.*

▶ **COLLOCATIONS:**
explicitly **political/sexual**
mention/state/express something explicitly
explicitly **authorize/forbid** something

▶ **SYNONYM:** overtly

▶ **ANTONYM:** implicitly

---

ex|plore /ɪkˈsplɔː/ (explores, exploring, explored)

VERB If you **explore** an idea or suggestion, you think about it or comment on it in detail, in order to assess it carefully. ○ *The secretary is expected to explore ideas for post-war reconstruction of the area.* ○ *The film explores the* *relationship between artist and instrument.*

▶ COLLOCATIONS:
explore a **topic/idea/subject/theme**
explore a **possibility/option/alternative**
a **book/film** explores *something*

ex|plo|ra|tion /ˌeksplə'reɪʃən/ (explorations)

NOUN ○ [+ *of*] *I looked forward to the exploration of their theories.*
  ○ [+ *of*] *an agonized exploration of the psychology of a criminal intellectual*

▶ COLLOCATIONS:
an exploration **of** *something*
an exploration of a **theme/possibility/myth**

---

ex|tract /ɪk'strækt/   `ACADEMIC WORD` `SCIENCE`
(extracts, extracting, extracted)

VERB To **extract** a substance means to obtain it from something else,
for example by using industrial or chemical processes. ○ *the traditional
method of pick and shovel to extract coal* ○ [+ *from*] *Citric acid can be extracted
from the juice of oranges, lemons, limes or grapefruit.* ○ *looking at the differences
in the extracted DNA*

▶ COLLOCATIONS:
extract *something* **from** *something*
extract *something* from a **plant/embryo**
extract **minerals/hydrogen/plutonium/DNA**

ex|trac|tion /ɪk'strækʃən/

UNCOUNTABLE NOUN ○ [+ *of*] *Petroleum engineers plan and manage the
extraction of oil.* ○ *Several mineral extraction companies operate on the lake.*

▶ COLLOCATIONS:
the extraction **of** *something*
the extraction of **oil**
peat/mineral/DNA extraction

---

ex|trapo|late /ɪk'stræpəleɪt/
(extrapolates, extrapolating, extrapolated)

VERB If you **extrapolate from** known facts, you use them as a basis for
general statements about a situation or about what is likely to happen
in the future. [FORMAL] ○ [+ *from*] *Extrapolating from his American findings,
he reckons about 80% of these deaths might be attributed to smoking.*
  ○ [+ *from*] *It is unhelpful to extrapolate general trends from one case.*

○ [+ *from*] *She concedes it will be difficult to extrapolate the data from studies of mice to humans.*

▶ **COLLOCATIONS:**
    extrapolate **from** *something*
    extrapolate *something* from a **study**
    extrapolate **trends/conclusions**
    extrapolate **projections/findings/data**

Ff

fa|cili|tate /fəˈsɪlɪteɪt/ ACADEMIC WORD
(facilitates, facilitating, facilitated)

VERB To **facilitate** an action or process, especially one that you would like to happen, means to make it easier or more likely to happen. ○ *The new airport will facilitate the development of tourism.* ○ *He argued that the economic recovery had been facilitated by his tough stance.* ○ *the facilitated diffusion of glucose in red blood cells*

▶ **COLLOCATIONS:**
  facilitated **by** *something*
  facilitate **communication/interaction/dialogue**
  facilitate **cooperation/integration/access**
  greatly facilitate

▶ **SYNONYMS:** assist, aid

fas|cism /ˈfæʃɪzəm/ POLITICS

UNCOUNTABLE NOUN Fascism is a set of right-wing political beliefs that includes strong control of society and the economy by the state, a powerful role for the armed forces, and the stopping of political opposition. ○ *the generation that defeated fascism in the 1940s* ○ *Our grandparents came together to fight fascism.* ○ *She was influenced more by Italian fascism than by Nazism.*

▶ **COLLOCATIONS:**
  defeat/fight/oppose fascism
  support/embrace fascism
  nascent/radical fascism
  Italian/German/Spanish fascism

fas|cist /ˈfæʃɪst/

ADJECTIVE ○ *an upsurge of support for extreme rightist, nationalist and fascist organisations* ○ *the threatening nature of fascist ideology*

▶ **COLLOCATIONS:**
  fascist **ideology/leanings/overtones**
  a fascist **organisation/dictator/sympathizer**

---

fau|na /ˈfɔːnə/ (faunas) BIOLOGY GEOGRAPHY

NOUN Animals, especially the animals in a particular area, can be referred to as **fauna**. ○ [+ *of*] *the flora and fauna of the African jungle* ○ *Brackish waters generally support only a small range of faunas.*

▶ **COLLOCATIONS:**
the fauna **of** *somewhere*
native/marine/terrestrial/diverse/local fauna
harbour/protect/study fauna

▶ **PHRASE:** flora and fauna

---

femi|nine /ˈfemɪnɪn/

ADJECTIVE Feminine qualities and things relate to or are considered typical of women, in contrast to men. ○ *male leaders worrying about their women abandoning traditional feminine roles* ○ *a manufactured ideal of feminine beauty*

▶ **COLLOCATIONS:**
stereotypically/traditionally feminine
a feminine **trait/attribute/ideal/role**
feminine **wiles/charm**

▶ **SYNONYM:** female

▶ **ANTONYM:** masculine

---

femi|nism /ˈfemɪnɪzəm/ SOCIOLOGY

UNCOUNTABLE NOUN Feminism is the belief and aim that women should have the same rights, power, and opportunities as men. ○ *Feminism may have liberated the feminists, but it has still to change the lives of the majority of women.* ○ *Barbara Johnson, that champion of radical feminism* ○ *Proponents of feminism have challenged the traditional views.*

▶ **COLLOCATIONS:**
radical/modern/Western/political feminism
feminism **influences/challenges/teaches** *something/someone*

femi|nist /ˈfemɪnɪst/ (feminists)

1 NOUN A **feminist** is a person who believes in and supports feminism.
○ *Only 16 per cent of young women in a 1990 survey considered themselves feminists.* ○ *radical feminists like Andrea Dworkin*

▶ **COLLOCATIONS:**
a feminist **asserts/argues/challenges/criticizes** *something*
a **radical/ardent/prominent** feminist

2 ADJECTIVE Feminist groups, ideas, and activities are involved in feminism. ○ *the concerns addressed by the feminist movement*

○ *the reconstruction of history from a feminist perspective*

▶ COLLOCATIONS:
a feminist **critique/discourse/analysis/perspective**
a feminist **academic/scholar/therapist**

▶ PHRASE: the feminist movement

---

fer|ti|lize /ˈfɜːtɪlaɪz/ (fertilizes, fertilizing, fertilized) BIOLOGY

VERB When an egg from the ovary of a woman or female animal **is fertilized**, a sperm from the male joins with the egg, causing a baby or young animal to begin forming. A female plant **is fertilized** when its reproductive parts come into contact with pollen from the male plant. [in BRIT, also use **fertilise**] ○ [+ *with*] *Certain varieties cannot be fertilised with their own pollen.* ○ *the normal sperm levels needed to fertilise the female egg* ○ *Pregnancy begins when the fertilized egg is implanted in the wall of the uterus.*

▶ COLLOCATIONS:
fertilize *something* **with** *something*
fertilize a **plant/flower/egg/ovum/embryo**
chemically/artificially/successfully fertilized

▶ SYNONYM: inseminate

fer|ti|li|za|tion /ˌfɜːtɪlaɪˈzeɪʃən/

UNCOUNTABLE NOUN [in BRIT, also use **fertilisation**] ○ *The average length of time from fertilization until birth is about 266 days.* ○ *emergency contraception that can prevent fertilization* ○ *an in vitro fertilization clinic*

▶ COLLOCATIONS:
undergo/prevent fertilization
chemical/artificial/in vitro fertilization

▶ SYNONYM: insemination

---

fi|bre /ˈfaɪbə/ (fibres)

NOUN A **fibre** is a thin thread of a natural or artificial substance, especially one that is used to make cloth or rope. [in AM, use **fiber**] ○ *If you look at the paper under a microscope you will see the fibres.* ○ *a variety of coloured fibres* ○ *But experts warn inhaling just one asbestos fibre could be enough to cause cancer.*

▶ COLLOCATIONS:
carbon/collagen/cellulose/asbestos fibres
nerve/muscle/dietary fibres
a **man-made/synthetic/natural** fibre
digest/contain/inhale fibres

f

field /fiːld/ (fields, fielding, fielded)

PHRASE Work or study that is done **in the field** is done in a real, natural environment rather than in a theoretical way or in controlled conditions. ○ *The zoo is doing major conservation work, both in captivity and in the field.* ○ *passing on the skills they had learned in the field* ○ *mutations when studied in the laboratory or in the field*

▶ **RELATED WORD:** field study

field|work /ˈfiːldwɜːk/ also **field work** `ACADEMIC STUDY`

UNCOUNTABLE NOUN Fieldwork is the gathering of information about something in a real, natural environment, rather than in a place of study such as a laboratory or classroom. ○ *anthropological fieldwork* ○ *fieldwork conducted among surviving hunting and gathering groups* ○ *This project, subject to funding, will include extensive fieldwork in both Pakistan and India.*

▶ **COLLOCATIONS:**
undertake/conduct fieldwork
anthropological/scientific/extensive fieldwork

fig|ura|tive /ˈfɪɡərətɪv, AM -ɡjər-/ `LANGUAGE` `LITERATURE`

ADJECTIVE If you use a word or expression in a **figurative** sense, you use it with a more abstract or imaginative meaning than its ordinary literal one. ○ *an event that will change your route – in both the literal and figurative sense* ○ *Most poems are written in figurative language.*

▶ **COLLOCATIONS:**
figurative **language**
a figurative **sense/description/image**

▶ **ANTONYM:** literal

fig|ura|tive|ly /ˈfɪɡərətɪvli, AM -ɡjər-/

ADVERB ○ *Europe, with Germany literally and figuratively at its centre, is still at the start of a remarkable transformation.* ○ *This is not an artist who, figuratively speaking, climbs into the picture.*

▶ **PHRASE:** figuratively speaking

fil|ter /ˈfɪltə/ (filters, filtering, filtered) `SCIENCE`

1 VERB To **filter** a substance means to pass it through a device which is designed to remove certain particles contained in it. ○ *The best prevention for cholera is to boil or filter water.* ○ *The liver filters toxins from the body.*

▶ **COLLOCATIONS:**
filter *something* **through** *something*

filter **water/liquid/fluid/toxins**

2 NOUN A **filter** is a device through which a substance is passed when it is being filtered. ○ *Sediment from the fuel filters had been stirred up.* ○ *a paper coffee filter* ○ *Most filters used in air conditioning systems are inefficient at removing many of these particles.*

▶ **COLLOCATIONS:**
   a **charcoal/fuel/cigarette/cartridge** filter
   a filter **removes/blocks/protects** *something*
   use/clean a filter

fis|cal /ˈfɪskəl/   ECONOMICS

ADJECTIVE Fiscal is used to describe something that relates to government money or public money, especially taxes. ○ *The government has tightened fiscal policy.* ○ *in a climate of increasing fiscal austerity*

▶ **COLLOCATIONS:**
   a fiscal **policy/deficit/year/crisis**
   fiscal **restraint/prudence/autonomy/austerity**

fis|cal|ly /ˈfɪskəli/

ADVERB ○ *The scheme would be fiscally dangerous.* ○ *Many members are determined to prove that they are fiscally responsible.*

▶ **COLLOCATION:** fiscally **responsible/prudent/conservative**

USAGE: economic, financial or **fiscal**?

You describe things to do with the whole economy of a country, its money, wealth, business, etc., as **economic**. ○ *a slowdown in economic growth* ○ *the world economic crisis*

You use **financial** particularly to describe things to do with money, finance and banking. You can describe things to do with the finances of an individual or a company as **financial**. ○ *financial markets in Asia* ○ *He was in deep financial trouble.*

Fiscal is a more specialized term used in Economics to describe policies to do with government money and taxes. ○ *a fiscal deficit of 7% of GDP*

---

flaw /flɔː/ (flaws)

NOUN A **flaw in** something such as a theory or argument is a mistake in it, which causes it to be less effective or valid. ○ [+ *in*] *There were, however, a number of crucial flaws in his monetary theory.* ○ *Almost all of these studies have serious flaws.*

▶ **COLLOCATIONS:**
a flaw **in** *something*
a **serious/critical/obvious/inherent/fatal** flaw
a **methodological/technical/structural/procedural** flaw
correct/fix/discover a flaw
overlook/exploit/expose a flaw

▶ **SYNONYM:** mistake

NOUN A **flaw in** something such as a pattern or material is a fault in it that should not be there. ○ *lenses containing flaws and imperfections* ○ *a special kind of glass that was treasured for its flaws rather than its perfection*

▶ **COLLOCATION:** a flaw **in** *something*

▶ **SYNONYM:** imperfection

flawed /flɔːd/

ADJECTIVE Something that is **flawed** has a mark, fault, or mistake in it. ○ *the unique beauty of a flawed object* ○ *These tests were so seriously flawed as to render the results meaningless.* ○ *The problem is the original forecast was based on flawed assumptions.*

▶ **COLLOCATIONS:**
a flawed **premise/assumption**
flawed **logic/reasoning**
fundamentally/seriously/fatally flawed

EXTEND YOUR VOCABULARY

In academic writing, you can criticize an argument, a method or evidence as **flawed** to mean that there are problems or mistakes that make it less strong or less valid. ○ *the original forecast was based on flawed assumptions*

You can also say that evidence, data or an argument is **inaccurate**, **incorrect** or **erroneous** to mean that it is wrong or contains mistakes. ○ *It has been demonstrated that his figures were inaccurate.* ○ *Nearly half of the files contained erroneous information.*

A longer piece of academic writing setting out an argument can be described as **incoherent** or **inconsistent** meaning that the ideas do not link together clearly and logically. ○ *A lot of the arguments have been incoherent and contradictory.*

You can also say that a piece of writing or research is **ambiguous**, meaning that the evidence is not completely clear and could be interpreted in different ways. ○ *guidelines which are both vague and ambiguous*

flo|ra /ˈflɔːrə/ `BIOLOGY` `GEOGRAPHY`

UNCOUNTABLE NOUN You can refer to plants as **flora**, especially the
plants growing in a particular area. [FORMAL] ○ *the variety of food crops
and flora which now exists in Dominica* ○ [+ of] *The purpose of the expedition
was to study the flora and fauna of the heavily wooded island.* ○ [+ in] *low levels
of normal intestinal flora in the small intestine*

▶ COLLOCATIONS:
  the flora **of** *somewhere*
  flora **in** *something/somewhere*
  native/alpine/tropical/aquatic flora
  bacterial/microbial/intestinal flora
  catalogue/protect/study/threaten flora

▶ PHRASE: flora and fauna

flour|ish /ˈflʌrɪʃ, AM ˈflɜːr-/ (flourishes, flourishing, flourished)

1 VERB If something **flourishes**, it is successful, active, or common,
and developing quickly and strongly. ○ *Business flourished and within six
months they were earning 18,000 roubles a day.* ○ *The Sumerian civilization
flourished between 3500 and 2000 B.C.* ○ *the sort of environment in which
corruption flourished*

▶ COLLOCATIONS:
  a **community/civilization/career** flourishes
  capitalism/corruption/creativity flourishes
  flourish **briefly/late/anew**

▶ SYNONYMS: thrive, prosper

▶ ANTONYMS: flounder, fail

2 VERB If a plant or animal **flourishes**, it grows well or is healthy
because the conditions are right for it. ○ [+ in] *The plant flourishes
particularly well in slightly harsher climes.* ○ [+ in] *bacteria that flourish
in damp conditions* ○ *a long-term management plan that will help wildlife
flourish*

▶ COLLOCATIONS:
  flourish **in** *something*
  flourish in a *particular* **climate/environment/region**
  flourish in *particular* **conditions/climes/regions**
  wildlife flourishes
  a **species** flourishes
  flowers/bacteria flourish

▶ SYNONYM: thrive

flour|ish|ing /ˈflʌrɪʃɪŋ, AM ˈflɜːr-/

ADJECTIVE ○ *Britain has the largest and most flourishing fox population in Europe.* ○ *London quickly became a flourishing port.* ○ *a flourishing career as a freelance writer*

▶ **COLLOCATIONS:**
a flourishing **business/career/civilization/colony**
flourishing **trade/commerce/industry**

▶ **SYNONYM:** thriving

---

food chain /ˈfuːd ˌtʃeɪn/ (food chains)　BIOLOGY

NOUN The **food chain** is a series of living things which are linked to each other because each thing feeds on the one next to it in the series. ○ *The whole food chain is affected by the over use of chemicals in agriculture.* ○ *Droppings from seabirds could be introducing radioactive isotopes into the food chain.* ○ *animals further up the food chain*

▶ **COLLOCATIONS:**
enter/pass through the food chain
introduce *something* into the food chain
the **human/ocean/global** food chain
the **top/bottom** of the food chain

▶ **PHRASE:** further up/down the food chain

---

foot|note /ˈfʊtnəʊt/ (footnotes)　ACADEMIC STUDY

NOUN A **footnote** is a note at the bottom of a page in a book which provides more detailed information about something that is mentioned on that page. ○ [+ *to*] *Chaumette then added a footnote to the document.* ○ [+ *in*] *a footnote in the Byzantine Book of Hours*

▶ **COLLOCATIONS:**
a footnote **to/in** *something*
a footnote in a **book/edition**
append/add/include a footnote
an **explanatory/accompanying/interesting** footnote

▶ **RELATED WORD:** endnote

---

force /fɔːs/ (forces)　PHYSICS

NOUN In physics, a **force** is the pulling or pushing effect that something has on something else. ○ *the earth's gravitational force* ○ *protons and electrons trapped by magnetic forces in the Van Allen belts* ○ [+ *of*] *interactions between the forces of gravity and electromagnetism*

▶ **COLLOCATIONS:**
the force **of** something
gravitational/magnetic/electromagnetic force
the force of **gravity/magnetism/electromagnetism**

---

fore|run|ner /ˈfɔːrʌnə/ (forerunners)   `HISTORY`

NOUN If you describe a person or thing as the **forerunner of** someone
or something similar, you mean they existed before them and either
influenced their development or were a sign of what was going to
happen. ○ [+ of] a machine which, in some respects, was the forerunner of the
modern helicopter ○ [+ of] The recent exhibition confirms the artist's reputation
as a pioneer of Impressionism and forerunner of Monet. ○ [+ of] the European
Economic Community, the forerunner of today's European Union

▶ **COLLOCATION:** the forerunner **of** something/someone
▶ **SYNONYMS:** precursor, predecessor

---

fore|see /fɔːˈsiː/ (foresees, foreseeing, foresaw, foreseen)

VERB If you **foresee** something, you expect and believe that it will happen.
○ Juveniles may find it harder than adults to foresee the consequences of their
actions. ○ a dangerous situation which could have been foreseen ○ He correctly
foresaw the importance of nuclear weapons.

▶ **COLLOCATIONS:**
foresee the **consequences/outcome** of something
foresee a **difficulty/danger**
accurately/correctly foresee something
▶ **SYNONYMS:** predict, forecast

---

for|mu|late /ˈfɔːmjʊleɪt/ (formulates, formulating, formulated)

VERB If you **formulate** something such as a plan or proposal, you invent it,
thinking about the details carefully. ○ Detectives tend to formulate one
hypothesis and then try to confirm it. ○ a scientifically formulated supplement
recommended for dogs and cats ○ Formulate a strategy for long term business
development.

▶ **COLLOCATIONS:**
formulate a **strategy/policy/proposal/plan/response**
formulate a **hypothesis/theory**
scientifically/specially/carefully formulated
▶ **SYNONYMS:** invent, devise

fos|sil /ˈfɒsəl/ (fossils)   `HISTORY` `BIOLOGY`

NOUN A **fossil** is the hard remains of a prehistoric animal or plant that are found inside a rock. ○ *a newly discovered 425 million-year-old fossil* ○ *Several enormous prehistoric fossils were found.* ○ [+ *of*] *fossils of dinosaurs and ammonites*

▶ **COLLOCATIONS:**
   a fossil **of** *something*
   a fossil of a **dinosaur/mammal/human**
   unearth/discover/find/excavate a fossil
   a **hominid/prehistoric/mammalian** fossil

fos|sil fuel /ˌfɒsəl ˈfjuːəl/ (fossil fuels) also **fossil-fuel**

NOUN **Fossil fuel** is fuel such as coal or oil that is formed from the decayed remains of plants or animals. ○ *By using less energy, she'll burn fewer fossil fuels and emit fewer greenhouse gases.* ○ *Gas – the world's cleanest fossil fuel – currently accounts for just over 2% of China's energy consumption.*

▶ **COLLOCATIONS:**
   burn/consume/use fossil fuels
   a **clean/dirty** fossil fuel

found /faʊnd/ (founds, founding, founded)   `ACADEMIC WORD`

VERB When an institution, company, or organization **is founded** by someone or by a group of people, they get it started, often by providing the necessary money. ○ *The Independent Labour Party was founded in 1893.* ○ *He founded the Centre for Journalism Studies at University College Cardiff.* ○ *The business, founded by Dawn and Nigel, suffered financial setbacks.*

▶ **COLLOCATIONS:**
   founded **by** *someone*
   founded **in** *a year*
   found a **company/charity/organization/institute**

▶ **SYNONYMS:** set up, establish

foun|da|tion /faʊnˈdeɪʃən/

NOUN ○ [+ *of*] *the 150th anniversary of the foundation of Kew Gardens* ○ [+ *of*] *With the foundation of the NHS there was a move away from traditional medicines towards synthetic ones.*

▶ **COLLOCATIONS:**
   the foundation **of** *something*
   the foundation of an **institution/organization**

found|er /ˈfaʊndə/ (founders)

NOUN The **founder** of an institution, organization, or building is the person who got it started or caused it to be built, often by providing the necessary money. ○ [+ of] *He was one of the founders of the university's medical faculty.* ○ [+ of] *the founder of the Zionist movement* ○ *Hsin Tao, the organization's founder and leader*

▶ **COLLOCATIONS:**
  the founder **of** *something*
  the founder of a **company/movement/museum/website/charity**
  the **original/joint** founder

fran|chise /ˈfræntʃaɪz/ (franchises, franchising, franchised) BUSINESS

1 NOUN A **franchise** is an authority that is given by an organization to someone, allowing them to sell its goods or services or to take part in an activity which the organization controls. ○ *fast-food franchises* ○ [+ to-inf] *the franchise to build and operate the tunnel* ○ *Talk to other franchise holders and ask them what they think of the parent company.*

▶ **COLLOCATIONS:**
  a **fast-food/pizza/banking/railway** franchise
  a franchise **holder/outlet/operator/chain/store**
  operate/own/secure/buy/run a franchise

2 VERB If a company **franchises** its business, it sells franchises to other companies, allowing them to sell its goods or services. ○ *She has recently franchised her business.* ○ *Though the service is available only in California, its founder Michael Cane says he plans to franchise it in other states.* ○ *It takes hundreds of thousands of dollars to get into the franchised pizza business.*

▶ **COLLOCATIONS:**
  franchise a **service/operation/business**
  franchise a **store/outlet**

fraud /frɔːd/ (frauds) LAW

NOUN **Fraud** is the crime of gaining money or financial benefits by a trick or by lying. ○ *He was jailed for two years for fraud and deception.* ○ *Tax frauds are dealt with by the Inland Revenue.* ○ *officials who are involved in security and fraud prevention*

▶ **COLLOCATIONS:**
  tax/benefit/insurance/passport/credit fraud
  alleged/suspected/attempted fraud
  perpetrate/orchestrate a fraud
  commit/combat/detect/prevent fraud

fraud **prevention/charges**
a fraud **investigation/inquiry**

▶ **PHRASES:**
the fraud squad
fraud and deception

fraudu|lent /ˈfrɔːdʒʊlənt/

ADJECTIVE A **fraudulent** activity is deliberately deceitful, dishonest, or untrue. ○ *fraudulent claims about being a nurse* ○ *He has brought an action for fraudulent misrepresentation against a businessman.* ○ *The claim should be met, provided the policyholder has not been fraudulent or deceitful.*

▶ **COLLOCATIONS:**
a fraudulent **claim/scheme/transaction/email**
fraudulent **activities/trading/conduct/misrepresentation**
allegedly/potentially fraudulent

---

ful|fil /fʊlˈfɪl/ (fulfils or fulfills, fulfilling, fulfilled) also **fulfill**

1 VERB If you **fulfil** something such as a promise, dream, or hope, you do what you said or hoped you would do. ○ *President Kaunda fulfilled his promise of announcing a date for the referendum.* ○ *the opportunity to fulfil a long-held ambition*

▶ **COLLOCATION:** fulfil a **promise/dream/ambition**
▶ **SYNONYM:** realize

2 VERB To **fulfil** a task, role, or requirement means to do or be what is required, necessary, or expected. ○ *Without them you will not be able to fulfil the tasks you have before you.* ○ *All the necessary conditions were fulfilled.* ○ *Buildings of this sort fulfil multiple functions.*

▶ **COLLOCATIONS:**
fulfil a **function/role/requirement**
fulfil a **need/expectation**
▶ **SYNONYMS:** perform, execute

ful|fil|ment /fʊlˈfɪlmənt/ also **fulfillment**

UNCOUNTABLE NOUN ○ [+ *of*] *Visiting Angkor was the fulfilment of a childhood dream.* ○ [+ *of*] *the fulfilment of a long-held ambition* ○ [+ *of*] *the fulfilment of an election promise*

▶ **COLLOCATIONS:**
the fulfilment **of** something
the fulfilment of a **promise/dream/ambition/wish**
the fulfilment of a **requirement/objective/obligation**
▶ **SYNONYM:** realization

Gg

gal|axy /ˈɡæləksi/ (galaxies) also **Galaxy**

1 NOUN A **galaxy** is an extremely large group of stars and planets that extends over many billions of light years. ○ *Astronomers have discovered a distant galaxy.* ○ [+ *of*] *At some later point, galaxies of stars started to form.*

▶ **COLLOCATIONS:**
a galaxy **of** *something*
a galaxy **of stars**
a **distant/nearby/entire** galaxy
discover/observe/form/study a galaxy

2 NOUN The **Galaxy** is the extremely large group of stars and planets to which the Earth and the Solar System belong. ○ *The Galaxy consists of 100 billion stars.* ○ *The more distant stars in the Galaxy crowd together in a hazy band called the Milky Way.*

---

gauge /ɡeɪdʒ/ (gauges, gauging, gauged)

1 VERB If you **gauge** the speed or strength of something, or if you gauge an amount, you measure or calculate it, often by using a device of some kind. ○ *He gauged the wind at over thirty knots.* ○ *Distance is gauged by journey time rather than miles.*

▶ **COLLOCATIONS:**
guaged **by** *something*
gauge the **strength/depth/pressure** of *something*
gauge a **distance**

▶ **SYNONYM:** measure

2 NOUN A **gauge** is a device that measures the amount or quantity of something and shows the amount measured. ○ *The unit keeps track of usage and, like a fuel gauge on a car, warns when the card is getting close to empty.* ○ *The pilot reads the altitude gauge, of course; but there are other people watching.*

▶ **COLLOCATIONS:**
read/mark/use a gauge
a **fuel/temperature/petrol/rain/depth** gauge

GDP /ˌdʒiː diː ˈpiː/ (GDPs)   `ECONOMICS`

NOUN In economics, a country's **GDP** is the total value of goods and
services produced within a country in a year, not including its income
from investments in other countries. **GDP** is an abbreviation for 'gross
domestic product'. ○ *That is 2.6 per cent of total UK GDP.* ○ *Per capita GDP has
increased, at today's rates, from 12,637 to 17,096.*

▶ **COLLOCATIONS:**
   annual/national/per capita GDP
   a **high/low** GDP

▶ **RELATED WORD:** GNP

gene /dʒiːn/ (genes)   `BIOLOGY` `MEDICINE`

NOUN A **gene** is the part of a cell in a living thing which controls its physical
characteristics, growth, and development. ○ *a change in a single DNA letter
that appears in 70 per cent of defective genes* ○ *Molecular genetics is enabling
scientists to identify individual genes involved in the control of sleep.*

▶ **COLLOCATIONS:**
   carry/inherit/identify/insert/discover a gene
   a **defective/recessive/human/faulty/mutant** gene
   a gene **encodes/controls/causes** *something*

ge|net|ics /dʒɪˈnetɪks/   `BIOLOGY` `MEDICINE`

UNCOUNTABLE NOUN Genetics is the study of heredity and how qualities
and characteristics are passed on from one generation to another by
means of genes. ○ *There is a plethora of government advisory committees
dealing with different aspects of human molecular genetics.* ○ *Psychology,
biology and genetics teach us that emotions should be broadly the same
worldwide in every period.*

▶ **COLLOCATIONS:**
   study/understand genetics
   molecular/human/behavioural/medical genetics
   genetics **research**

▶ **PHRASE:** biology and genetics

ge|net|ic /dʒɪˈnetɪk/

ADJECTIVE You use **genetic** to describe something that is concerned with
genetics or with genes. ○ *Cystic fibrosis is the most common fatal genetic
disease in the United States.* ○ *The causes of prostate cancer are unknown, but
environmental and genetic factors are suspected.*

▶ **COLLOCATIONS:**
genetic **engineering/modification/testing/material**
a genetic **mutation/predisposition/defect/code**
▶ **PHRASE:** genetic and environmental

ge|neti|cal|ly /dʒɪˈnetɪkli/

ADVERB ○ *Some people are genetically predisposed to diabetes.* ○ *foetuses that are genetically abnormal*

▶ **COLLOCATIONS:**
genetically **engineer/modify/alter** *something*
genetically **engineered/modified/identical/similar**

ge|neti|cist /dʒɪˈnetɪsɪst/ (geneticists)

NOUN A **geneticist** is a person who studies or specializes in genetics.
○ *In addition to cell biologists, some geneticists want to identify genes that encode for hearing.* ○ *She was the first molecular geneticist appointed at what was then the Poultry Research Centre.*

▶ **COLLOCATIONS:**
a **molecular/clinical/medical** geneticist
a **population/plant** geneticist

---

gen|re /ˈʒɒnrə/ (genres) ARTS LITERATURE

NOUN A **genre** is a particular type of literature, painting, music, film, or other art form which people consider as a class because it has special characteristics. [FORMAL] ○ *his love of films and novels in the horror genre* ○ *Genre films have a role in Scottish filmmaking whether or not it is to an individual's personal taste.*

▶ **COLLOCATIONS:**
invent/reinvent/spawn a genre
a **musical/literary/whole/popular** genre
the **horror/sci-fi/literary** genre
a genre **film/painting/piece**
genre **fiction**

---

ger|mi|nate /ˈdʒɜːmɪneɪt/ BIOLOGY
(germinates, germinating, germinated)

VERB If a seed **germinates** or if it **is germinated**, it starts to grow.
○ *Some seed varieties germinate fast, so check every day or so.* ○ *First, the researchers germinated the seeds.*

▶ **COLLOCATIONS:**
a **seed/spore** germinates
germinate a **seed**

ger|mi|na|tion /ˌdʒɜːmɪˈneɪʃən/

UNCOUNTABLE NOUN ○ [+ of] *The poor germination of your seed could be because the soil was too cold.* ○ *Some small seeds need light and alternating temperatures to trigger germination.*

▶ **COLLOCATIONS:**
germination **of** *something*
germination of **seedlings/seeds**
trigger/ensure/prevent germination

---

glaci|er /ˈglæsiə, AM ˈgleɪʃə/ (glaciers) ┆GEOGRAPHY┆

NOUN A **glacier** is an extremely large mass of ice which moves very slowly, often down a mountain valley. ○ *University of Alaska scientists report that the state's glaciers are melting faster than expected.* ○ *Twenty thousand years ago, the last great ice age buried the northern half of Europe under a massive glacier.*

▶ **COLLOCATIONS:**
an **Antarctic/Alaskan** glacier
a glacier **melts/retreats/moves**

---

grant /grɑːnt, grænt/ (grants, granting, granted) ┆ACADEMIC WORD┆

1 NOUN A **grant** is an amount of money that a government or other institution gives to an individual or to an organization for a particular purpose such as education or home improvements. ○ [+ to-inf] *They'd got a special grant to encourage research.* ○ *Unfortunately, my application for a grant was rejected.*

▶ **COLLOCATIONS:**
a grant **for** *something*
a grant **of** *x*
award/receive/obtain/provide a grant
a **federal/means-tested/annual/lottery/research** grant
a grant **application/recipient**
grant **money**

2 VERB If someone in authority **grants** you something, or if something **is granted to** you, you are allowed to have it. [FORMAL] ○ *France has agreed to grant him political asylum.* ○ [+ to] *It was a Labour government which granted independence to India and Pakistan.* ○ *Permission was granted a few weeks ago.*

▶ **COLLOCATIONS:**
be granted **to** *someone*
grant **permission/approval/asylum/access/bail**
grant a **request/licence/visa/pardon**
a **judge/court** grants *something*

▶ **SYNONYMS:** give, allow, award

▶ **ANTONYM:** refuse

---

gross /grəʊs/ (grosses, grossing, grossed) `BUSINESS` `ECONOMICS`

1 ADJECTIVE Gross means the total amount of something, especially money, before any has been taken away. ○ *a fixed rate account guaranteeing 10.4% gross interest or 7.8% net until October* ○ *a recorded gross profit before tax of £4.8 million*

▶ **COLLOCATIONS:**
a gross **profit/income/margin**
gross **interest/revenues**

• **Gross** is also an adverb. ○ *Interest is paid gross, rather than having tax deducted.* ○ *a father earning £20,000 gross a year*

▶ **COLLOCATION: paid** gross

▶ **RELATED WORD:** net

2 ADJECTIVE Gross means the total amount of something, after all the relevant amounts have been added together. ○ *National Savings gross sales in June totalled £709 million.* ○ *gross proceeds of about $20.4 million.*

▶ **COLLOCATION:** gross **sales/proceeds**

▶ **SYNONYM:** total

3 VERB If a person or a business **grosses** a particular amount of money, they earn that amount of money before tax has been taken away. ○ *a factory worker who grossed £9,900 last year* ○ *So far the films have grossed more than £590 million.*

▶ **COLLOCATION:** a **film/movie** grosses *x*

---

ground|break|ing /ˈɡraʊndbreɪkɪŋ/ also **ground-breaking**

ADJECTIVE You use **groundbreaking** to describe things which you think are significant because they provide new and positive ideas, and influence the way people think about things. ○ *his groundbreaking novel on homosexuality* ○ *It is clear their groundbreaking research has played a role in these outcomes.*

▶ COLLOCATIONS:
groundbreaking **research/work**
a groundbreaking **discovery/ceremony/study/series**
truly groundbreaking

▶ SYNONYMS: original, innovative

---

guid|ance /ˈgaɪdəns/

UNCOUNTABLE NOUN Guidance is help and advice. ○ [+ of] *an opportunity for young people to improve their performance under the guidance of professional coaches* ○ *The nation looks to them for guidance.*

▶ COLLOCATIONS:
the guidance **of** *someone*
under *someone's* guidance
give/issue/provide/seek/follow guidance
parental/spiritual/moral/official guidance

▶ SYNONYM: advice

Hh

---

har|ness /ˈhɑːnɪs/ **(harnesses, harnessing, harnessed)** `SCIENCE`

VERB If you **harness** something such as a natural source of energy, you bring it under your control and use it. ○ *Turkey plans to harness the waters of the Tigris and Euphrates rivers for big hydro-electric power projects.* ○ *chemical reactors that destroy dangerous chemicals by harnessing the power of the sun*

▶ **COLLOCATIONS:**
harness **power/energy/potential/technology**
successfully/properly harness *something*

▶ **SYNONYMS:** exploit, utilize

---

hemi|sphere /ˈhemɪsfɪə/ **(hemispheres)** `GEOGRAPHY` `BIOLOGY`

1 NOUN A **hemisphere** is one half of the earth. ○ *In the southern hemisphere with its reversed patterns of seasons, these festivals are usually held at different times.* ○ *In the northern hemisphere the sun rises in the east and sets in the west at the spring and autumn equinoxes.*

▶ **COLLOCATION:** the **southern/northern/western** hemisphere

2 NOUN A **hemisphere** is one half of the brain. ○ *In most people, the left hemisphere is bigger than the right.* ○ *the right hemisphere, which governs creativity, spatial perception, musical and visual appreciation, and intuition*

▶ **COLLOCATIONS:**
a hemisphere **of** *something*
a hemisphere of the **brain**
the **left/right** hemisphere

---

her|bi|vore /ˈhɜːbɪvɔː, AM ˈɜːb-/ **(herbivores)** `BIOLOGY`

NOUN A **herbivore** is an animal that only eats plants. ○ *They are found in both herbivores and omnivores but in carnivores they are replaced by carnassial teeth.* ○ *In herbivores the stomach has several chambers, for cellulose digestion.*

▶ **RELATED WORDS:** carnivore, omnivore

her|bi|vo|rous /hɜːˈbɪvərəs/

ADJECTIVE Herbivorous animals eat only plants. ○ *Mammoths were herbivorous mammals.* ○ *It comes from a group of long-necked herbivorous dinosaurs, the sauropods.*

▶ COLLOCATIONS:
a herbivorous **creature/dinosaur/fish**
a herbivorous **mammal/insect**

▶ RELATED WORDS: carnivorous, omnivorous

---

her|it|age /ˈherɪtɪdʒ/ (heritages) `HISTORY`

NOUN A country's **heritage** is all the qualities, traditions, or features of life there that have continued over many years and have been passed on from one generation to another. ○ *The historic building is as much part of our heritage as the paintings.* ○ *[+ of] the rich heritage of Russian folk music*

▶ COLLOCATIONS:
the heritage **of** *something*
preserve/protect/celebrate the heritage of *something*
a **cultural/natural/rich/musical** heritage
a heritage **site/building**

▶ PHRASES:
culture and heritage
history and heritage

---

hexa|gon /ˈheksəgən, AM -gɔːn/ (hexagons)

NOUN A **hexagon** is a shape that has six straight sides. ○ *The basic sixfold symmetry of the crystal is easily explained by the shape of water molecules, which link to form hexagons.* ○ *As a matter of fact there are twelve pentagons and twenty hexagons.*

▶ COLLOCATIONS:
a **regular** hexagon
a hexagon **shape**
form a hexagon

hex|ago|nal /hekˈsægənəl/

ADJECTIVE ○ *Each column was about half a metre in diameter, with a hexagonal or pentagonal outline.* ○ *With triangular, square, or hexagonal tiles, it is easy to cover a floor completely.*

▶ COLLOCATION: a hexagonal **tile/prism/snowflake**

---

hi|ber|nate /ˈhaɪbəneɪt/ (hibernates, hibernating, hibernated) `BIOLOGY`

VERB Animals that **hibernate** spend the winter in a state like a deep sleep. ○ *Dormice hibernate from October to May.* ○ *[V-ing] Hibernating insects begin to move.*

▶ COLLOCATIONS:
hibernate **for/in/during** a *time*
hibernate for/in/during **winter**
a **squirrel/animal/bear/insect/bat** hibernates

hibernation /ˌhaɪbəˈneɪʃən/

UNCOUNTABLE NOUN ○ *The animals consume three times more calories to prepare for hibernation.* ○ *A second litter is occasionally produced, but the young from this are less likely to survive the winter hibernation.*

▶ COLLOCATIONS:
winter hibernation
a **long/extended** hibernation

hi|er|ar|chy /ˈhaɪərɑːki/ (hierarchies) `ACADEMIC WORD`

NOUN A **hierarchy** is a system of organizing people into different ranks or levels of importance, for example in society or in a company. ○ *Like most other American companies with a rigid hierarchy, workers and managers had strictly defined duties.* ○ *She rose up the Tory hierarchy by the local government route.* ○ *Even in the desert there was a kind of social hierarchy.*

▶ COLLOCATIONS:
ascend/establish/create a hierarchy
a **social/Catholic/rigid/strict** hierarchy
a **church/party/corporate** hierarchy

hi|er|ar|chi|cal /haɪəˈrɑːkɪkəl/

ADJECTIVE A **hierarchical** system or organization is one in which people have different ranks or positions, depending on how important they are. ○ *the traditional hierarchical system of military organization* ○ *a rigidly hierarchical command structure*

▶ COLLOCATIONS:
a hierarchical **structure/organization/society/relationship**
rigidly/strictly hierarchical

hind|sight /ˈhaɪndsaɪt/

UNCOUNTABLE NOUN **Hindsight** is the ability to understand and realize something about an event after it has happened, although you did not understand or realize it at the time. ○ *With the benefit of hindsight, the benefits of Internet advertising were grossly exaggerated.* ○ *With hindsight it can be seen as an important first stage in the controlled evolution of democracy.*

▶ **COLLOCATIONS:**
with/in hindsight
historical/twenty-twenty hindsight
hindsight **suggests/prompts** *something*

▶ **PHRASE:** the benefit of hindsight

---

host /həʊst/ (hosts) `BIOLOGY`

NOUN The **host** of a parasite is the plant or animal which it lives on or inside and from which it gets its food. ○ *When the eggs hatch the larvae eat the living flesh of the host animal.* ○ [+ for] *Farmed fish are perfect hosts for parasites.*

▶ **COLLOCATIONS:**
a host **for** *something*
a host for a **parasite**
a host **organism/ant/species**
a **susceptible/intermediate** host

---

hos|tile /ˈhɒstaɪl, AM -təl/

ADJECTIVE Hostile situations and conditions make it difficult for you to achieve something. ○ *some of the most hostile climatic conditions in the world* ○ *If this round of talks fails, the world's trading environment is likely to become increasingly hostile.*

▶ **COLLOCATIONS:**
a hostile **environment/climate/atmosphere**
increasingly hostile

▶ **SYNONYMS:** unfavourable, difficult

▶ **ANTONYM:** favourable

---

hu|man|ity /hjuːˈmænɪti/

1 UNCOUNTABLE NOUN All the people in the world can be referred to as **humanity**. ○ *They face charges of committing crimes against humanity.* ○ *a young lawyer full of illusions and love of humanity*

▶ **COLLOCATIONS:**
benefit/save/unite humanity
humanity **progresses/evolves/survives**

▶ **PHRASE:** a crime against humanity

2 UNCOUNTABLE NOUN A person's **humanity** is their state of being a human being, rather than an animal or an object. [FORMAL] ○ *a man who's almost lost his humanity in his bitter hatred of his rivals* ○ *Only in dialogue* with those who are different from ourselves do we enrich understanding of our shared humanity.

▶ COLLOCATION: **shared/common/essential/basic** humanity

hu|mani|tar|ian /hjuːˌmænɪˈteəriən/

ADJECTIVE If a person or society has **humanitarian** ideas or behaviour, they try to avoid making people suffer or they help people who are suffering. ○ Air bombardment raised criticism on the humanitarian grounds that innocent civilians might suffer. ○ The UN also orchestrated humanitarian aid though there was much criticism at the lack of competence revealed that winter.

▶ COLLOCATIONS:
humanitarian **aid/assistance/relief**
a humanitarian **crisis/effort**

• A **humanitarian** is someone with humanitarian ideas. ○ Practitioners will arrive as sentinels rather than as kindly and concerned humanitarians. ○ Philanthropists and humanitarians head the list of Australia Day honours announced yesterday.

hur|ri|cane /ˈhʌrɪkən, AM ˈhɜːrɪkeɪn/ (hurricanes) `GEOLOGY`

NOUN A **hurricane** is an extremely violent wind or storm. ○ In September 1813, a major hurricane destroyed US gunboats and ships that were defending St Mary's, Georgia, from the British. ○ Around eight hurricanes are predicted to strike America this year.

▶ COLLOCATIONS:
a **devastating/deadly/major/powerful** hurricane
withstand/predict a hurricane
a hurricane **hits/destroys/damages** something

hy|brid /ˈhaɪbrɪd/ (hybrids) `BIOLOGY`

1 NOUN A **hybrid** is an animal or plant that has been bred from two different species of animal or plant. ○ All these brightly coloured hybrids are so lovely in the garden. ○ [+ between] a hybrid between water mint and spearmint

• **Hybrid** is also an adjective. ○ the hybrid maize seed ○ you can cheat by buying a disease-resistant hybrid tea

2 NOUN You can use **hybrid** to refer to anything that is a mixture of other things, especially two other things. ○ [+ of] a hybrid of solid and liquid fuel ○ [+ of] a hybrid of psychological thriller and sci-fi mystery

- **Hybrid** is also an adjective. ○ *a hybrid system* ○ *incredible, strange, hybrid nonfiction*

  ▶ **COLLOCATIONS:**
  a hybrid **between/of** *things*
  breed/produce/create a hybrid
  a hybrid **tea/rose/berry**
  a hybrid **vehicle/sedan**

---

hy|drau|lic /haɪˈdrɒlɪk, AM -ˈdrɔːl-/ `SCIENCE` `ENGINEERING`

ADJECTIVE Hydraulic equipment or machinery involves or is operated by a fluid that is under pressure, such as water or oil. ○ *The boat has no fewer than five hydraulic pumps.* ○ *Below 400-500 m, depth does not appear to be related to hydraulic conductivity.*

▶ **COLLOCATIONS:**
hydraulic **conductivity/fluid/steering**
a hydraulic **lift/pump/brake**

hy|drau|li|cal|ly /haɪˈdrɒlɪkli, AM -ˈdrɔːl-/

ADVERB ○ *hydraulically operated pistons for raising and lowering the blade* ○ *a giant hydraulically powered cargo lift*

▶ **COLLOCATION:** hydraulically **operated/powered/controlled**

hy|drau|lics /haɪˈdrɒlɪks, AM -ˈdrɔːl-/

UNCOUNTABLE NOUN Hydraulics is the study and use of systems that work using hydraulic pressure. ○ [+ on] *The impediments to exploration of hydraulics on boats include the very strong conservative bent of the marine industry.* ○ *So for simple propulsion situations, hydraulics clearly aren't cost effective.*

▶ **COLLOCATIONS:**
sophisticated/internal hydraulics
a hydraulics **failure/laboratory/engineer**

---

hydro|elec|tric /ˌhaɪdrəʊˈlektrɪk/ `ENGINEERING` `SCIENCE`
also **hydro-electric**

ADJECTIVE Hydroelectric means relating to or involving electricity made from the energy of running water. ○ *Engineers say the river has huge potential for developing hydroelectric power.* ○ *a vast impoverished region containing a hydroelectric dam and fertiliser factories*

▶ **COLLOCATIONS:**
a hydroelectric **dam/plant/project**
hydroelectric **power**

hydro|elec|tric|ity /ˌhaɪdrəʊɪlek'trɪsɪti/ also **hydro-electricity**

UNCOUNTABLE NOUN Hydroelectricity is electricity made from the energy of running water. ○ *The greater benefit in Manitoba is because renewable hydroelectricity is used to run ethanol plants.* ○ *Hydroelectricity is most efficiently generated in rugged topography.*

▶ **COLLOCATIONS:**
    abundant/affordable/reliable hydroelectricity
    generate hydroelectricity

---

hy|poth|esis /haɪ'pɒθɪsɪs/   `ACADEMIC STUDY` `ACADEMIC WORD`
(hypotheses)

NOUN A **hypothesis** is an idea which is suggested as a possible explanation for a particular situation or condition, but which has not yet been proved to be correct. [FORMAL] ○ *Work will now begin to test the hypothesis in rats.* ○ *Different hypotheses have been put forward to explain why these foods are more likely to cause problems.*

▶ **COLLOCATIONS:**
    test/support/confirm/propose a hypothesis
    a **null/testable/alternative** hypothesis
▶ **SYNONYM:** theory

hy|poth|esize /haɪ'pɒθɪsaɪz/ **(hypothesizes, hypothesizing, hypothesized)**

VERB If you **hypothesize that** something will happen, you say that you think that thing will happen because of various facts you have considered. [FORMAL; in BRIT, also use **hypothesise**] ○ [+ *that*] *To explain this, they hypothesize that galaxies must contain a great deal of missing matter which cannot be detected.* ○ *Hypothesizing other time dimensions does not in practice progress our understanding of precognition.*

▶ **COLLOCATION:** a **researcher/scientist** hypothesizes *something*

I i

---

ibid. /ˈɪbɪd/ `ACADEMIC STUDY`

CONVENTION **Ibid.** is used in books and journals to indicate that a piece of text taken from somewhere else is from the same source as the previous piece of text. ○ *Edwin A. Lane, Letter to the Editor, ibid., p. 950. 8.* ○ *'to be able to obliterate or rather to unite the names of federalists and republicans' (quoted ibid., p.155).*

→ see note at **cf.**

---

icon /ˈaɪkɒn/ (icons)

1 NOUN If you describe something or someone as an **icon**, you mean that they are important as a symbol of a particular thing. ○ *David Beckham is as much a fashion icon as a football deity.* ○ *Mondale's icon status was on display Wednesday night as nearly 1,000 Democrats nominated him for a return engagement in the Senate.*

▶ **COLLOCATIONS:**
a **national/international/global/cultural** icon
a **gay/feminist/fashion/style** icon
a **pop/rock/screen/film/sporting** icon
icon **status**

▶ **SYNONYM:** legend

2 NOUN An **icon** is a picture on a computer screen representing a particular computer function. If you want to use it, you move the cursor onto the icon using a mouse. ○ *If you write a person's name in a Word document you can click an icon to call up the person's address or e-mail, for example.* ○ [+ on] *By default, you have just three icons on the desktop.*

▶ **COLLOCATIONS:**
an icon **on** *something*
an icon on a **desktop/screen**
click (on)/drag/delete/select an icon

---

icon|ic /aɪˈkɒnɪk/

ADJECTIVE An **iconic** image or thing is important or impressive because it seems to be a symbol of something. [FORMAL] ○ *The Beatles achieved iconic status.* ○ *Doreen Lawrence is an iconic figure to many in the black community.*

▶ COLLOCATIONS:
iconic **status**
an iconic **figure/writer/star**
an iconic **building/brand**

---

ideol|ogy /ˌaɪdiˈɒlədʒi/ (ideologies) `ACADEMIC WORD` `POLITICS`

NOUN An **ideology** is a set of beliefs, especially the political beliefs on which people, parties, or countries base their actions. ○ [+ of] *Fifteen years after the president embraced the ideology of privatization, the people were worse off than ever.* ○ *North Carolina more than any other southern state, is the home of two disparate, yet equally powerful, political ideologies.*

▶ COLLOCATIONS:
the ideology **of** something
embrace/reject an ideology
an ideology **influences/motivates/drives** someone
the **dominant** ideology
a **political/religious/secular/economic** ideology
a **communist/liberal/conservative** ideology

▶ SYNONYMS: values, beliefs, doctrine

ideo|logi|cal /ˌaɪdiəˈlɒdʒɪkəl/

ADJECTIVE Ideological means relating to principles or beliefs. ○ *Others left the party for ideological reasons.* ○ *The ideological divisions between the parties aren't always obvious.* ○ *a world divided along ideological lines*

▶ COLLOCATIONS:
an ideological **difference/divide/division**
an ideological **commitment/battle/struggle/conflict/war**
ideological **reasons**

---

il|logi|cal /ɪˈlɒdʒɪkəl/ `ACADEMIC WORD`

ADJECTIVE If you describe an action, feeling, or belief as **illogical**, you are critical of it because you think that it does not result from a logical and ordered way of thinking. ○ [+ to -inf] *It is illogical to oppose the repatriation of economic migrants.* ○ *But, however hard it is, you have to accept that bombing is just the illogical conclusion of everyday prejudice.*

→ see note at **insufficient**

▶ COLLOCATIONS:
an illogical **conclusion/argument**
an illogical **fear/hatred**
totally/completely Illogical

▶ **SYNONYMS:** irrational, unreasonable
▶ **ANTONYMS:** logical, rational, reasonable

---

im|age|ry /ˈɪmɪdʒri/ `ACADEMIC WORD` `ARTS` `LITERATURE`

1 UNCOUNTABLE NOUN You can refer to the descriptions in something such as a poem or song, and the pictures they create in your mind, as its **imagery**. [FORMAL] ○ *Her prose was poetic and subtly energised by her use of visual imagery.* ○ [+ of] *the nature imagery of the ballad*

2 UNCOUNTABLE NOUN You can refer to pictures and representations of things as **imagery**, especially when they act as symbols. [FORMAL] ○ *This is an ambitious and intriguing movie, full of striking imagery.* ○ [+ in] *Sexual imagery in advertising is hardly anything new.*

▶ **COLLOCATIONS:**
imagery **in/of** *something*
vivid/powerful/striking/strong imagery
visual/mental/computer-generated/digital imagery
sexual/religious/erotic imagery

---

imi|tate /ˈɪmɪteɪt/ (imitates, imitating, imitated)

VERB If you **imitate** someone, you copy what they do or produce. ○ *It's a genuine German musical which does not try to imitate the American model.* ○ *an American style of architecture that has been widely imitated in Europe*

▶ **COLLOCATION: widely/much/often/slavishly** imitated
▶ **SYNONYMS:** copy, recreate

---

imi|ta|tion /ˌɪmɪˈteɪʃən/ (imitations)

NOUN An **imitation** of something is a copy of it. ○ [+ of] *the most accurate imitation of Chinese architecture in Europe* ○ [+ of] *Then the British invasion of Spanish beaches created the Euro-pub, albeit a pale imitation of the real thing.*

▶ **COLLOCATIONS:**
an imitation **of** *something*
a **poor/pale/cheap** imitation
a **passable/fair/good** imitation

▶ **SYNONYMS:** copy, replica

---

im|mi|nent /ˈɪmɪnənt/

ADJECTIVE If you say that something is **imminent**, especially something unpleasant, you mean it is almost certain to happen very soon. ○ *They warned that an attack is imminent.* ○ *He had no direct involvement in any alleged crimes and was not viewed as an imminent threat to security.*

▶ COLLOCATIONS:
an imminent **threat/danger/attack/war**
the imminent **demise/collapse/release** of *something*
an imminent **arrival/departure**

▶ SYNONYM: impending

---

im|mune /ɪˈmjuːn/   [MEDICINE] [BIOLOGY]

1 ADJECTIVE If you are **immune to** a particular disease, you cannot be affected by it. ○ [+ to] *This blood test will show whether or not you're immune to the disease.* ○ [+ to] *Most adults are immune to rubella.*

▶ COLLOCATIONS:
immune **to** *something*
immune to a **disease**
an immune **response/cell/function/reaction**

2 ADJECTIVE If you are **immune to** something that happens or is done, you are not affected by it. ○ [+ to] *Whilst Marc did gradually harden himself to the poverty, he did not become immune to the sight of death.* ○ [+ to] *Football is not immune to economic recession.*

▶ COLLOCATIONS:
immune **to** *something*
immune to **attack/fear/change**

▶ SYNONYM: unaffected

im|mun|ity /ɪˈmjuːnɪti/

UNCOUNTABLE NOUN ○ [+ to] *Birds in outside cages develop immunity to airborne bacteria.* ○ *The disease develops mostly in children since they have less natural immunity than adults.*

▶ COLLOCATIONS:
immunity **to** *something*
develop/boost/lower immunity
full/natural immunity
herd immunity

▶ SYNONYM: resistance

---

im|mune sys|tem /ɪˈmjuːn ˌsɪstəm/   [MEDICINE] [BIOLOGY]
(immune systems)

NOUN Your **immune system** consists of all the organs and processes in your body which protect you from illness and infection. ○ *People who exercise have stronger immune systems, so they're less likely to need time off due to illness.* ○ *Boost your immune system and prolong longevity.*

▶ **COLLOCATIONS:**
a **healthy/strong/weakened/weak** immune system
suppress/boost/stimulate/strengthen the immune system
the immune system **fights/attacks/suppresses** *something*
an immune system **response**

---

im|mun|ize /ˈɪmjʊnaɪz/ MEDICINE
(immunizes, immunizing, immunized)

VERB If people or animals **are immunized**, they are made immune to a particular disease, often by being given an injection. [in BRIT, also use **immunise**] ○ [+ *against*] *We should require that every student is immunized against hepatitis B.* ○ [+ *with*] *The monkeys had been immunized with a vaccine.* ○ *All parents should have their children immunized.*

▶ **COLLOCATIONS:**
immunize *someone* **against/with** *something*
immunize *someone* against a **disease**
immunize a **child/worker/patient** against *something*

▶ **SYNONYMS:** inoculate, vaccinate

im|mun|iza|tion /ˌɪmjʊnaɪˈzeɪʃən/ **(immunizations)**

NOUN [in BRIT, also use **immunisation**] ○ [+ *against*] *universal immunization against childhood diseases* ○ *Only half of America's children get the full range of immunisations.*

▶ **COLLOCATIONS:**
immunization **against** *something*
immunization against a **disease**
childhood/adult/polio/flu immunization
an immunization **programme/campaign**
the immunization **rate**

▶ **SYNONYMS:** inoculation, vaccination

---

im|plic|it /ɪmˈplɪsɪt/ ACADEMIC WORD

ADJECTIVE Something that is **implicit** is expressed in an indirect way.
○ *This is seen as an implicit warning not to continue with military action.*
○ *There has been an implicit assumption in much of the thinking that quality can only improve if productivity declines.*

▶ **COLLOCATIONS:**
an implicit **assumption/understanding/message**
an implicit **threat/criticism/warning**

▶ **SYNONYM:** indirect
▶ **ANTONYM:** explicit

im|plic|it|ly /ɪmˈplɪsɪtli/

ADVERB ○ *The jury implicitly criticised the government by their verdict.*
○ *The prime minister implicitly acknowledged the government's failure to enthuse the country.*

▶ **COLLOCATIONS:**
implicitly **acknowledge/accept/assume**
implicitly **criticize/threaten**

▶ **SYNONYM:** indirectly

▶ **ANTONYM:** explicitly

---

im|pris|on /ɪmˈprɪzən/ (imprisons, imprisoning, imprisoned) `LAW`

VERB If someone **is imprisoned**, they are locked up or kept somewhere, usually in prison as a punishment for a crime or for political opposition.
○ [+ *for*] *The local priest was imprisoned for 18 months on charges of anti-state agitation.* ○ [+ *for*] *Dutch colonial authorities imprisoned him for his part in the independence movement.* ○ *A Canadian civilian claims he was falsely imprisoned.*

▶ **COLLOCATIONS:**
imprison *someone* **for** *something*
be **falsely/wrongly/unjustly/wrongfully** imprisoned

▶ **SYNONYMS:** jail, detain, incarcerate

▶ **ANTONYMS:** free, release

im|pris|on|ment /ɪmˈprɪzənmənt/

UNCOUNTABLE NOUN ○ [+ *for*] *Brock was sentenced to life imprisonment for the murder of his wife.* ○ [+ *without*] *Many others face indefinite imprisonment without trial.*

▶ **COLLOCATIONS:**
imprisonment **for/without** *something*
sentenced to imprisonment
face/risk imprisonment
false/wrongful/unlawful/life imprisonment

▶ **SYNONYMS:** custody, detention, incarceration, captivity

---

in|cen|tive /ɪnˈsentɪv/ (incentives) `ACADEMIC WORD`

NOUN If something is an **incentive to** do something, it encourages you to do it. ○ [+ *to-inf*] *There is little or no incentive to adopt such measures.* ○ [+ *for*] *Many companies in Britain are keen on the idea of tax incentives for R&D.*

▶ **COLLOCATIONS:**
an incentive **for** *something/someone*
provide/offer/give/create an incentive
a **financial/economic/added/extra/additional** incentive
a **tax/cash/strong/powerful/perverse** incentive

▶ **SYNONYMS:** inducement, enticement

▶ **ANTONYM:** disincentive

---

in|ci|dent /ˈɪnsɪdənt/ (incidents) `ACADEMIC WORD`

NOUN An **incident** is something that happens, often something that is unpleasant. [FORMAL] ○ *These incidents were the latest in a series of disputes between the two nations.* ○ [+ in] *The attack on Liquica was the worst in a series of violent incidents in East Timor.* ○ *The voting went ahead without incident.*

▶ **COLLOCATIONS:**
an incident **in** *a place*
a **serious/unfortunate/tragic/alleged** incident
a **terrorist/friendly-fire/isolated** incident
investigate/witness an incident
an incident **happens/occurs/takes place**
an incident **involves** *someone/something*

in|ci|dence /ˈɪnsɪdəns/ (incidences)

NOUN The **incidence of** something bad, such as a disease, is the frequency with which it occurs, or the occasions when it occurs. ○ [+ of] *The incidence of breast cancer increases with age.* ○ [+ of] *Excess fat is thought to be responsible for the high incidence of heart disease in Western countries.* ○ [+ of] *It is time for action to prevent increasing incidences of HIV infection in prisons.*

▶ **COLLOCATIONS:**
the incidence **of** *something*
a **high/low** incidence
a **growing/rising/decreasing/increasing** incidence
the **overall** incidence
reduce/increase the incidence of *something*

EXTEND YOUR VOCABULARY

You can use **incidence** and **occurrence** to talk about something that happens repeatedly and how often it happens. Both words mainly refer to negative events, such as illness and violence. You can talk about **the incidence/occurence of** *something* to say how often or how much it happens generally. ○ *the occurrence/incidence of cancer in young women*

You can talk about **a common/rare/everyday occurrence** to say how frequent a type of event is. ○ *Earthquakes are a regular occurrence.*

You can also talk about the **frequency** of a type of event to say how often it happens. ○ *the frequency of the consumption of sugary food*

---

in|clined /ɪnˈklaɪnd/ ACADEMIC WORD

ADJECTIVE If you are **inclined to** behave in a particular way, you often behave in that way, or you want to do so. ○ [+ to-inf] *Nobody felt inclined to argue with Smith.* ○ *If you are so inclined, you can watch TV.*

▶ **COLLOCATIONS:**
  feel/seem inclined
  artistically/mathematically inclined

▶ **PHRASE:** be so inclined

▶ **SYNONYM:** disposed

in|cli|na|tion /ˌɪnklɪˈneɪʃən/ (inclinations)

NOUN An **inclination** is a feeling that makes you want to act in a particular way. ○ *He had neither the time nor the inclination to think of other things.* ○ *His natural inclination in such a dilemma was to do nothing and watch.*

▶ **COLLOCATIONS:**
  have/show an inclination
  a **slight/strong/natural** inclination

▶ **SYNONYM:** desire

---

in|co|her|ent /ˌɪnkəʊˈhɪərənt/

1 ADJECTIVE If someone is **incoherent**, they are talking in a confused and unclear way. ○ [+ with] *The man was almost incoherent with fear.*

▶ **COLLOCATIONS:**
  incoherent **with** *something*
  incoherent with **rage**
  incoherent **rambling/speech/sound**

▶ **SYNONYM:** unintelligible

▶ **ANTONYM:** coherent

2 ADJECTIVE If you say that something such as a policy is **incoherent**, you are criticizing it because the different parts of it do not fit together properly. ○ *an incoherent set of objectives* ○ *This is a vote against bad pension reform and a contradictory, incoherent pension policy.*

→ see note at **flaw**

▶ **PHRASE:** an incoherent mess
▶ **SYNONYM:** disjointed
▶ **ANTONYM:** coherent

in|co|her|ent|ly /ˌɪnkəʊ'hɪərəntli/

ADVERB ○ *He collapsed on the floor, mumbling incoherently.* ○ *Outside jail he lived on VP wine and babbled incoherently.*

▶ **COLLOCATION: mumble/babble/shout/ramble** incoherently
▶ **ANTONYM:** coherently

in|co|her|ence /ˌɪnkəʊ'hɪərəns/

UNCOUNTABLE NOUN ○ *Beth's incoherence told Amy that something was terribly wrong.* ○ *the general incoherence of government policy.*

▶ **ANTONYM:** coherence

in|com|pat|ible /ˌɪnkəm'pætɪbəl/ ACADEMIC WORD

ADJECTIVE If one thing or person is **incompatible with** another, they are very different in important ways, and do not suit each other or agree with each other. ○ [+ with] *They feel strongly that their religion is incompatible with the political system.* ○ [+ with] *His behavior has been incompatible with his role as head of state.* ○ *We were totally incompatible.*

▶ **COLLOCATIONS:**
  incompatible **with** *someone/something*
  totally/completely/mutually/seemingly incompatible
▶ **SYNONYMS:** mismatched, unsuited
▶ **ANTONYM:** compatible

in|com|pat|ibil|ity /ˌɪnkəmpætɪ'bɪlɪti/

UNCOUNTABLE NOUN ○ *Their sexual incompatibility eventually separated them.* ○ [+ between] *Incompatibility between the mother's and the baby's blood groups may cause jaundice.*

▶ **COLLOCATIONS:**
  incompatibility **between/of** *people/things*
  incompatibility of *something* **with** *something*
▶ **ANTONYM:** compatibility

in|con|clu|sive /ˌɪnkən'kluːsɪv/ ACADEMIC WORD

ADJECTIVE If research or evidence is **inconclusive**, it has not proved anything. ○ *Research has so far proved inconclusive.* ○ *The judge ruled that the medical evidence was inconclusive.*

▶ **COLLOCATIONS:**
prove inconclusive
an inconclusive **result/test**
inconclusive **evidence**

▶ **ANTONYM:** conclusive

EXTEND YOUR VOCABULARY

You can say that evidence or research findings that do not prove
something certainly are **inconclusive**, **tentative**, **provisional** or
preliminary. If results are **inconclusive**, they do not prove
something definitely one way or another, perhaps because there is
not enough evidence or data. ○ *The evidence is inconclusive that vitamin
C can prevent some cancers.*

If findings are **provisional**, the research has not yet been fully finished
or confirmed and you expect to have a final result later. ○ *These were
provisional findings pending the outcome of an autopsy.*

Preliminary findings are from a small study or the first part of a study
and you expect to have more complete, final data later. ○ *The enzyme
appears to be very promising from the preliminary research findings,
although it will need to undergo further tests.*

Tentative conclusions or suggestions are your first ideas, often based
on a relatively small amount of research or evidence, that you hope
to provide more support for later. ○ *By considering related results like
these, we can develop tentative conclusions that are likely, but not certain,
to be correct.*

---

in|cor|po|rate /ɪnˈkɔːpəreɪt/   ACADEMIC WORD
(incorporates, incorporating, incorporated)

1 VERB If one thing **incorporates** another thing, it includes the other
thing. [FORMAL] ○ *The new cars will incorporate a number of major
improvements.* ○ *Many sports garments now incorporate technology which
helps to carry any sweat away from the body.*

▶ **COLLOCATIONS:**
incorporate a **feature/element/idea**
incorporate **technology/information/material**

▶ **SYNONYMS:** include, contain

▶ **ANTONYM:** omit

2 VERB If someone or something **is incorporated into** a large group, system, or area, they become a part of it. [FORMAL] ○ [+ into] *The agreement would allow the rebels to be incorporated into a new national police force.* ○ [+ into] *The party vowed to incorporate environmental considerations into all its policies.*

▶ **COLLOCATION:** incorporate *something/someone* **into** *something*

▶ **ANTONYM:** exclude

In|cor|po|rated /ɪnˈkɔːpəreɪtɪd/   `ACADEMIC WORD` `BUSINESS`

ADJECTIVE Incorporated is used after a company's name to show that it is a legally established company in the United States. [AM] ○ *MCA Incorporated*

---

in|cur /ɪnˈkɜː/ (incurs, incurring, incurred)

VERB If you **incur** something unpleasant, it happens to you because of something you have done. [WRITTEN] ○ *The government had also incurred huge debts.* ○ *the terrible damage incurred during the past decade*

▶ **COLLOCATIONS:**
incur **costs/expenses/expenditure/damage**
incur a **charge/fee/loss/debt**
incur a **penalty/fine/liability**
incur *someone's* **wrath**

▶ **SYNONYM:** sustain

---

in|defi|nite /ɪnˈdefɪnɪt/   `ACADEMIC WORD`

ADJECTIVE If you describe a situation or period as **indefinite**, you mean that people have not decided when it will end. ○ *The trial was adjourned for an indefinite period.* ○ *an indefinite strike by government workers*

▶ **COLLOCATIONS:**
an indefinite **period/term/sentence/delay/postponement**
an indefinite **curfew/suspension/strike**
indefinite **detention/imprisonment/leave**

▶ **ANTONYM:** finite

in|defi|nite|ly /ɪnˈdefɪnɪtli/

ADVERB ○ *The visit has now been postponed indefinitely.* ○ *The school has been closed indefinitely.*

▶ **COLLOCATIONS:**
continue indefinitely
be **suspended/postponed/delayed/closed** indefinitely
be **held/detained** indefinitely

in|dig|enous /ɪnˈdɪdʒɪnəs/   BIOLOGY SOCIOLOGY

ADJECTIVE **Indigenous** people, animals, plants, or things belong to the country in which they are found, rather than coming there or being brought there from another country. [FORMAL] ○ *the country's indigenous population* ○ *[+ to] animals that are indigenous to Asia* ○ *It offers the opportunity of travel to places where Buddhism forms a part of the indigenous culture – Nepal, India, Japan, Thailand.*

▶ COLLOCATIONS:
  indigenous **to** *somewhere*
  the indigenous **community/population/people**
  indigenous **culture/language/art**
▶ SYNONYM: native
▶ ANTONYMS: non-indigenous, foreign

in|duce /ɪnˈdjuːs, AM -ˈduːs/   ACADEMIC WORD
(induces, inducing, induced)

VERB To **induce** a state or condition means to cause it. ○ *Doctors said surgery could induce a heart attack.* ○ *an economic crisis induced by high oil prices*

▶ COLLOCATIONS:
  induce a **state/feeling/sense/change**
  induce a **response/reaction/heart attack/coma**
  induce **sleep/vomiting/fear/panic/relaxation**
▶ SYNONYMS: cause, trigger, precipitate

in|equal|ity /ˌɪnɪˈkwɒlɪti/ (inequalities)   SOCIOLOGY

NOUN **Inequality** is the difference in social status, wealth, or opportunity between people or groups. ○ *People are concerned about social inequality.* ○ *[+ in] In addition to bearing down hard on unemployment, they would seek to reduce inequalities in wealth.* ○ *[+ between] inequality between the sexes*

▶ COLLOCATIONS:
  inequality **in/of** *something*
  inequality **between** *people/things*
  reduce/tackle/address inequality
  create/increase/reinforce/perpetuate inequality
  social/economic/racial/sexual inequality
  global/international/regional/gross inequality
▶ SYNONYMS: injustice, inequity
▶ ANTONYM: equality

in|exo|rable /ɪnˈeksərəbəl/

ADJECTIVE You use **inexorable** to describe a process which cannot be prevented from continuing or progressing. [FORMAL] ○ *the seemingly inexorable rise in unemployment* ○ *He is acutely aware of the inexorable march of time.*

▶ COLLOCATIONS:
   an inexorable **rise/decline/slide/force/pressure**
   inexorable **progress/growth/logic**
   seemingly inexorable

▶ PHRASE: the inexorable march of/towards sth
▶ SYNONYM: relentless

in|exo|rably /ɪnˈeksərəbli/

ADVERB ○ *Spending on health is growing inexorably.*

▶ COLLOCATIONS:
   move inexorably **to/towards** *something*
   move/lead/slide inexorably towards *something*
   inexorably **rise/grow/mount/slip**

▶ SYNONYM: relentlessly

in|fer /ɪnˈfɜː/ (infers, inferring, inferred)

VERB If you **infer** that something is the case, you decide that it is true on the basis of information that you already have. ○ [+ *that*] *I inferred from what she said that you have not been well.* ○ *By measuring the motion of the galaxies in a cluster, astronomers can infer the cluster's mass.*

→ see note at **deduce**

▶ COLLOCATIONS:
   infer the **meaning/existence** of *something*
   reasonably infer

▶ SYNONYM: deduce

in|fer|ence /ˈɪnfərəns/ (inferences)

1 NOUN An **inference** is a conclusion that you draw about something by using information that you already have about it. ○ *There were two inferences to be drawn from her letter.* ○ [+ *that*] *A more reasonable inference is that his evidence flows from a desire for self-preservation.*

▶ COLLOCATIONS:
   draw/make an inference
   a **reasonable/logical** inference

▶ SYNONYMS: conclusion, deduction

2 **UNCOUNTABLE NOUN Inference** is the act of drawing conclusions about something on the basis of information that you already have. ○ *It had an extremely tiny head and, by inference, a tiny brain.* ○ *The impression was conveyed to the jurymen, whether it was unsupported statement, hearsay or improper inference.*

▶ **COLLOCATION: by** inference
▶ **SYNONYM:** deduction

---

in|flate /ɪnˈfleɪt/ (inflates, inflating, inflated)

VERB If you **inflate** something such as a balloon or tyre, or if it **inflates**, it becomes bigger as it is filled with air or a gas. ○ *Stuart jumped into the sea and inflated the liferaft.* ○ *Don's life jacket had failed to inflate.*

▶ **COLLOCATIONS:**
  inflate a **balloon/tyre/airbag/raft/lung**
  a **balloon/airbag** inflates
▶ **ANTONYM:** deflate

---

in|hale /ɪnˈheɪl/ (inhales, inhaling, inhaled) `BIOLOGY`

VERB When you **inhale**, you breathe in. When you **inhale** something such as smoke, you take it into your lungs when you breathe in. ○ *He took a long slow breath, inhaling deeply.* ○ *He was treated for the effects of inhaling smoke.*

▶ **COLLOCATIONS:**
  inhale **deeply/sharply**
  inhale **smoke/fumes/gas/particles/dust**
  inhale a **scent/fragrance/aroma/drug**
▶ **SYNONYM:** breathe in
▶ **ANTONYM:** exhale

in|ha|la|tion /ɪnhəˈleɪʃən/ (inhalations)

UNCOUNTABLE NOUN [FORMAL] ○ *a complete cycle of inhalation and exhalation* ○ *They were taken to hospital suffering from smoke inhalation.*

▶ **COLLOCATION: smoke/steam** inhalation
▶ **ANTONYM:** exhalation

---

in|her|ent /ɪnˈherənt, -ˈhɪər-/ `ACADEMIC WORD`

ADJECTIVE The **inherent** qualities of something are the necessary and natural parts of it. ○ *There are inherent risks to operating any business, whether it is a franchise or not.* ○ *I doubt whether he realized the inherent contradiction in his own argument.* ○ [+ in] *the dangers inherent in an outbreak of war*

▸ **COLLOCATIONS:**
inherent **in** *something*
an inherent **risk/danger/problem/weakness/flaw**
an inherent **quality/characteristic/part/contradiction**
▸ **SYNONYMS:** intrinsic, integral

in|her|ent|ly /ɪnˈherəntli, -ˈhɪər-/

ADVERB ○ *Aeroplanes are not inherently dangerous.* ○ *There is nothing inherently wrong with pleasure.*

▸ **COLLOCATIONS:**
inherently **dangerous/unstable/risky**
inherently **wrong/evil/bad/unfair/unequal**
▸ **SYNONYM:** intrinsically

in|hib|it /ɪnˈhɪbɪt/ (inhibits, inhibiting, inhibited) `ACADEMIC WORD`

VERB If something **inhibits** an event or process, it prevents it or slows it down. ○ *Excessive trace elements, such as copper, in the soil will inhibit plant growth.* ○ *The high cost of borrowing is inhibiting investment by industry in new equipment.*

▸ **COLLOCATIONS:**
inhibit **growth/development**
inhibit **activity/production/formation**
▸ **SYNONYMS:** hamper, hinder, interfere with
▸ **ANTONYMS:** encourage, aid

in|hi|bi|tion /ˌɪnɪˈbɪʃən/

UNCOUNTABLE NOUN the fact or process of preventing something or slowing it down ○ [+ of] *Nicotine's many actions include both stimulation and inhibition of the nervous system, depending on dosage.* ○ *The study of enzyme inhibition has had practical benefits.*

▸ **COLLOCATIONS:**
the inhibition **of** *something*
the inhibition of **growth**

ini|ti|ate /ɪˈnɪʃieɪt/ (initiates, initiating, initiated) `ACADEMIC WORD`

VERB If you **initiate** something, you start it or cause it to happen. ○ *They wanted to initiate a discussion on economics.* ○ *A peace process was initiated by the Indian prime minister in April.*

▸ **COLLOCATIONS:**
initiate a **process/action/transaction/change/move**

initiate a **debate/discussion/conversation/investigation**
initiate **proceedings/contact/talks**
▶ SYNONYMS: instigate, set in motion

ini|tia|tion /ɪˌnɪʃiˈeɪʃən/

UNCOUNTABLE NOUN The **initiation** of something is the starting of it.
○ [+ *of*] *They announced the initiation of a rural development programme.*
○ [+ *of*] *Hypertension is perhaps the most common reason for initiation of lifelong drug treatment.*
▶ COLLOCATIONS:
the initiation **of** *something*
the initiation of **proceedings/negotiations/intercourse**
▶ SYNONYMS: instigation, launch

ini|tia|tive /ɪˈnɪʃətɪv/ (initiatives)   ACADEMIC WORD

NOUN An **initiative** is an important act or statement that is intended to solve a problem. ○ [+ *to-inf*] *Government initiatives to help young people have been inadequate.* ○ *There's talk of a new peace initiative.*
▶ COLLOCATIONS:
announce/launch/introduce an initiative
welcome/support/back an initiative
a **new/major/bold** initiative
a **diplomatic/strategic/private** initiative
a **peace/business/marketing** initiative
a **finance/policy/education** initiative

in|sol|uble /ɪnˈsɒljʊbəl/   SCIENCE

ADJECTIVE If a substance is **insoluble**, it does not dissolve in a liquid.
○ [+ *in*] *Carotenes are insoluble in water and soluble in oils and fats.* ○ *A mask of pure insoluble collagen fibre is placed over the skin.*
▶ COLLOCATION: insoluble **in** *something*
▶ ANTONYM: soluble

in|suf|fi|cient /ˌɪnsəˈfɪʃənt/   ACADEMIC WORD

ADJECTIVE Something that is **insufficient** is not large enough in amount or degree for a particular purpose. [FORMAL] ○ *He decided there was insufficient evidence to justify criminal proceedings.* ○ [+ *to-inf*] *These efforts were insufficient to contain the burgeoning crisis.* ○ [+ *to-inf*] *The income was proving insufficient to clear her debts.*

▶ **COLLOCATIONS:**
insufficient **for** *something*
prove insufficient
insufficient **evidence/information/data/time/attention**
insufficient **funds/funding/resources/money**
wholly/simply insufficient

▶ **SYNONYM:** inadequate

▶ **ANTONYMS:** sufficient, enough, adequate

in|suf|fi|cient|ly /ˌɪnsəˈfɪʃəntli/

ADVERB ○ *Food that is insufficiently cooked can lead to food poisoning.*
○ *The president has described the recovery as insufficiently robust.*

▶ **SYNONYM:** inadequately

▶ **ANTONYMS:** sufficiently, enough, adequately

in|suf|fi|cien|cy /ˌɪnsəˈfɪʃənsi/

UNCOUNTABLE NOUN ○ *Late miscarriages are usually not due to hormonal insufficiency.* ○ *Adrenal insufficiency has been documented in children with asthma.*

▶ **COLLOCATION: adrenal/renal/pancreatic** insufficiency

▶ **SYNONYM:** inadequacy

▶ **ANTONYM:** sufficiency

ACADEMIC WRITING: Avoiding negatives

In formal, academic writing, you need to be as clear and accurate as possible. It is better to avoid negative constructions by using words like **insufficient**, **illogical** and **unspecified** that have a negative meaning. For example, the sentence: *During exercise, the oxygen supply may be insufficient to meet the energy demand* is clearer than: *During exercise, there may not be a sufficient supply of oxygen to meet the energy demand.*

---

in|take /ˈɪnteɪk/ (intakes)   MEDICINE

NOUN Your **intake** of a particular kind of food, drink, or air is the amount that you eat, drink, or breathe in. ○ [+ *of*] *Your intake of alcohol should not exceed two units per day.* ○ *Reduce your salt intake.*

▶ **COLLOCATIONS:**
an intake **of** something
reduce/limit/restrict/increase *someone's* intake

a **daily/high/low/excessive** intake
the **recommended** intake
someone's **dietary/calorie/food/fluid** intake
someone's **fat/salt/alcohol/calcium** intake

▶ **SYNONYM:** consumption

---

in|te|ger /ˈɪntɪdʒə/ (integers) [MATHS]

NOUN In mathematics, an **integer** is an exact whole number such as 1, 7, or 24 as opposed to a number with fractions or decimals. ○ *Prime numbers are positive integers that can only be divided by themselves and one.* ○ *They asked patients to score the degree of discomfort or distress caused by their diagnostic test on an 0-6 integer scale.*

▶ **SYNONYM:** whole number

---

in|te|gral /ˈɪntɪgrəl/ [ACADEMIC WORD]

ADJECTIVE Something that is an **integral** part of something is an essential part of that thing. ○ *Rituals and festivals form an integral part of every human society.* ○ *The municipal park plays an integral role in urban Chinese life.* ○ [+ *to*] *Anxiety is integral to the human condition.*

▶ **COLLOCATIONS:**
integral **to** *something*
an integral **part/component/element/aspect/role**

▶ **SYNONYMS:** basic, fundamental, intrinsic

---

in|teg|rity /ɪnˈtegrɪti/ [ACADEMIC WORD]

1 UNCOUNTABLE NOUN If you have **integrity**, you are honest and firm in your moral principles. ○ *I have always regarded him as a man of integrity.* ○ [+ *of*] *The game relies on the integrity of the individual to show consideration for other players and to abide by the rules.*

▶ **COLLOCATIONS:**
the integrity **of** *someone*
question/maintain/protect/preserve *someone's* integrity
undermine/compromise/restore *someone's* integrity
personal/professional/moral integrity
artistic/intellectual/cultural/academic integrity

▶ **PHRASE:** honesty and integrity

2 UNCOUNTABLE NOUN The **integrity** of something such as a group of people or a text is its state of being a united whole. [FORMAL] ○ *Kerensky declared that he would maintain Russia's territorial integrity.* ○ [+ *of*] *Separatist movements are a threat to the integrity of the nation.*

▶ COLLOCATIONS:
the integrity **of** *something*
maintain/protect/preserve *something's* integrity
undermine/threaten *something's* integrity
territorial/structural integrity

▶ SYNONYM: unity

---

in|tense /ɪnˈtens/ `ACADEMIC WORD`

ADJECTIVE Intense is used to describe something that is very great or extreme in strength or degree. ○ *He was sweating from the intense heat.* ○ *His threats become more intense, agitated, and frequent.*

▶ COLLOCATIONS:
intense **heat/pain/pressure/scrutiny/fighting**
intense **debate/speculation/negotiations**
intense **competition/rivalry**

▶ SYNONYM: extreme

in|ten|sity /ɪnˈtensɪti/ (intensities)

NOUN ○ *The attack was anticipated but its intensity came as a shock.* ○ [+ *of*] *A detector measured the intensity of the light.*

▶ COLLOCATIONS:
the intensity **of** *something*
the intensity of a **feeling/emotion/flavour**
the intensity of **light/heat/pain**

in|ten|si|fy /ɪnˈtensɪfaɪ/ (intensifies, intensifying, intensified)

VERB If you **intensify** something or if it **intensifies**, it becomes greater in strength, amount, or degree. ○ *Britain is intensifying its efforts to secure the release of the hostages.* ○ *The conflict is almost bound to intensify.* ○ *Groups of refugees are on the move following intensified fighting in the region.*

▶ COLLOCATIONS:
intensify **pressure/competition/efforts/speculation**
intensify a **campaign/debate/attack/war/conflict**
intensify a **hunt** for *someone*
fighting/violence/competition/pressure intensifies
a **war/battle/attack/feeling** intensifies

▶ SYNONYM: increase
▶ ANTONYM: decrease

in|ten|si|fi|ca|tion /ɪnˌtensɪfɪˈkeɪʃən/

UNCOUNTABLE NOUN ○ [+ of] *The country was on the verge of collapse because of the intensification of violent rebel attacks.* ○ [+ of] *A further intensification of violence seems certain.*

▸ **COLLOCATIONS:**
   the intensification **of** *something*
   further intensification

▸ **SYNONYM:** increase

▸ **ANTONYM:** decrease

---

inter|act /ˌɪntəˈrækt/ (interacts, interacting, interacted)

1 VERB When people **interact with** each other or **interact**, they communicate as they work or spend time together. ○ *While the other children interacted and played together, Ted ignored them.* ○ [+ with] *rhymes and songs to help parents interact with their babies*

▸ **COLLOCATIONS:**
   interact **with** *someone*
   interact **directly/socially/easily**

▸ **SYNONYM:** communicate

2 VERB When people **interact with** computers, or when computers **interact with** other machines, information or instructions are exchanged. ○ [+ with] *Millions of people want new, simplified ways of interacting with a computer.* ○ *There will be a true global village in which telephones, computers and televisions interact.*

3 VERB When one thing **interacts with** another or two things **interact**, the two things affect each other's behaviour or condition. ○ *You have to understand how cells interact.* ○ [+ with] *Atoms within the fluid interact with the minerals that form the grains.*

▸ **COLLOCATIONS:**
   interact **with** *something*
   interact with a **protein/environment/object**

inter|ac|tion /ˌɪntəˈrækʃən/ (interactions)

1 NOUN ○ [+ with] *This can sometimes lead to somewhat superficial interactions with other people.* ○ [+ among] *our experience of informal social interaction among adults*

▸ **COLLOCATIONS:**
   interaction **with** *someone*
   interaction **between/among** *people*

social/human/personal interaction
face-to-face/interpersonal/direct interaction

▶ **SYNONYM:** communication

2 NOUN ○ *experts on human-computer interaction* ○ *Our children, tomorrow's consumers, are used to real-time interaction and a "point and click" environment*

3 NOUN ○ *[+ between] the interaction between physical and emotional illness* ○ *There is a slimmer body of research on drug interactions and correct dosages.*

▶ **COLLOCATIONS:**
interaction **between** *things*
interaction between **genes/proteins/cells**
a **complex** interaction

inter|ac|tive /ˌɪntəˈræktɪv/

ADJECTIVE An **interactive** computer program or television system is one which allows direct communication between the user and the machine. ○ *This will make video games more interactive than ever.* ○ *high speed Internet services and interactive television*

▶ **COLLOCATIONS:**
interactive **television**
an interactive **presentation/map/guide/display**

inter|con|nect /ˌɪntəkəˈnekt/
(interconnects, interconnecting, interconnected)

VERB Things that **interconnect** or **are interconnected** are connected to or with each other. You can also say that one thing **interconnects with** another. ○ *The causes are many and may interconnect.* ○ *[+ with] Their lives interconnect with those of celebrated figures of the late eighteenth-century.* ○ *a dense network of nerve fibres that interconnects neurons in the brain*

▶ **COLLOCATIONS:**
interconnect **with** *something*
an interconnected **system/network**

▶ **SYNONYMS:** link, interrelate

inter|con|nec|tion /ˌɪntəkəˈnekʃən/ **(interconnections)**

NOUN If you say that there is an **interconnection** between two or more things, you mean that they are very closely connected. [FORMAL] ○ *[+ between] the alarming interconnection between drug abuse and AIDS infection* ○ *Global population and industrial, urban, and environmental systems form complex interconnections.*

▶ **COLLOCATION:** the interconnection **between** *things*

▶ **SYNONYMS:** link, connection, interrelation

inter|de|pend|ent /ˌɪntədɪˈpendənt/

ADJECTIVE People or things that are **interdependent** all depend on each other. ○ *We live in an increasingly interdependent world.* ○ *the universe as a complex web of interdependent relationships*

▶ **COLLOCATIONS:**
an interdependent **world/economy**
interdependent **relationships**
highly/increasingly interdependent

inter|de|pend|ence /ˌɪntədɪˈpendəns/

UNCOUNTABLE NOUN ○ [+ *of*] *the interdependence of nations* ○ *economic interdependence*

▶ **COLLOCATIONS:**
the interdependence **of** *people/things*
economic/global/mutual interdependence

---

inter|face /ˈɪntəfeɪs/ (interfaces, interfacing, interfaced) `IT`

1 NOUN The **interface** between two subjects or systems is the area in which they affect each other or have links with each other. ○ [+ *between*] *a witty exploration of that interface between bureaucracy and the working world* ○ [+ *between*] *the new interface between capitalism and chaos in the old Soviet Union*

▶ **COLLOCATION:** the interface **between** *things*

2 NOUN If you refer to the user **interface** of a particular piece of computing software, you are talking about its presentation on screen and how easy it is to use. ○ *the development of better user interfaces* ○ *The software features a more user-friendly interface.*

▶ **COLLOCATIONS:**
a **user/computer/web/application/software** interface
a **graphical/simple/clean/user-friendly/intuitive** interface
use/provide/improve an interface

3 VERB If one thing **interfaces with** another, or if two things **interface**, they have connections with each other. If you **interface** one thing **with** another, you connect the two things. [FORMAL] ○ [+ *with*] *the way we interface with the environment* ○ *The different components all have to interface smoothly.* ○ [+ *with*] *He had interfaced all this machinery with a master computer.*

▶ **COLLOCATION:** interface **with** *something*

---

inter|fere /ˌɪntəˈfɪə/ (interferes, interfering, interfered)

1 VERB If you say that someone **interferes in** a situation, you mean they get involved in it although it does not concern them and their involvement is not wanted. ○ *Baldwin felt that the government had interfered enough.* ○ *[+ in/with] The U.N. cannot interfere in the internal affairs of any country.*

2 VERB Something that **interferes with** a situation, activity, or process has a damaging effect on it. ○ *[+ with] Smoking and drinking interfere with your body's ability to process oxygen.* ○ *[+ with] One hypothesis is that alcohol may interfere with the process of ovulation.*

▶ COLLOCATIONS:
interfere **in/with** *something*
interfere with the **metabolism/digestion**

▶ SYNONYMS: disrupt, affect

inter|fer|ence /ˌɪntəˈfɪərəns/

UNCOUNTABLE NOUN ○ *[+ in/with] The parliament described the decree as interference in the republic's internal affairs.* ○ *[+ from] Airlines will be able to set cheap fares without interference from the government.*

▶ COLLOCATIONS:
interference **in/with** *something*
interference **from** *someone*
government/state/political/bureaucratic interference
outside/foreign/unwarranted/undue interference

▶ SYNONYM: meddling

---

in|ter|im /ˈɪntərɪm/

1 ADJECTIVE Interim is used to describe something that is intended to be used until something permanent is done or established. ○ *She was sworn in as head of an interim government in March.* ○ *These interim reports provide an outline of the problem and a general idea of the work being carried out.*

▶ COLLOCATIONS:
an interim **government/constitution/administration/authority**
an interim **president/minister/coach/chairman/report**
interim **results**

2 PHRASE In the interim means until a particular thing happens or until a particular thing happened. [FORMAL] ○ *But, in the interim, we obviously have a duty to maintain law and order.* ○ *He was to remain in jail in the interim.*

▶ SYNONYMS: in the meantime, meanwhile

inter|mit|tent /ˌɪntəˈmɪtənt/

ADJECTIVE Something that is **intermittent** happens occasionally rather than continuously. ○ *After three hours of intermittent rain, the game was abandoned.* ○ *The constant movement of cables can easily damage the fragile wires inside, causing intermittent problems that are hard to detect.*

▶ **COLLOCATIONS:**
intermittent **rain/showers**
an intermittent **problem/fault**

▶ **SYNONYM:** sporadic

▶ **ANTONYMS:** constant, continuous

inter|mit|tent|ly /ˌɪntəˈmɪtəntli/

ADVERB ○ *The talks went on intermittently for three years.* ○ *He worked intermittently on building sites.*

▶ **SYNONYM:** sporadically

▶ **ANTONYMS:** constantly, continuously

inter|re|late /ˌɪntərɪˈleɪt/ (interrelates, interrelating, interrelated)

VERB If two or more things **interrelate**, there is a connection between them and they have an effect on each other. ○ *The body and the mind interrelate.* ○ [+ with] *Each of these cells have their specific jobs to do, but they also interrelate with each other.* ○ [+ with] *the way in which we communicate and interrelate with others* ○ *All things are interrelated.*

▶ **COLLOCATIONS:**
interrelate **with** something/someone
interrelate **closely**

▶ **SYNONYM:** interconnect

inter|sect /ˌɪntəˈsekt/ (intersects, intersecting, intersected)

1 VERB If two or more lines or roads **intersect**, they meet or cross each other. You can also say that one line or road **intersects** another. ○ *The orbit of this comet intersects the orbit of the Earth.* ○ *The circles will intersect in two places.*

▶ **COLLOCATIONS:**
a **curve/path/line/road/circle** intersects *something*
lines/roads intersect

▶ **SYNONYM:** cross

2 VERB If one thing **intersects with** another or if two things **intersect**, the two things have a connection at a particular point. ○ [+ *with*] *the ways in which historical events intersect with individual lives* ○ *Their histories intersect.*

▶ **COLLOCATIONS:**
intersect **with** *something*
lives intersect

▶ **SYNONYMS:** connect, overlap

inter|sec|tion /ˌɪntəˈsekʃən/ (intersections)

NOUN An **intersection** is a place where roads or other lines meet or cross. ○ [+ *of*] *at the intersection of two main canals* ○ *a busy highway intersection*

▶ **COLLOCATIONS:**
the intersection **of** *things*
a **busy/major** intersection
approach/reach an intersection
cross/enter/block an intersection

▶ **SYNONYM:** junction

inter|vene /ˌɪntəˈviːn/   `ACADEMIC WORD`
(intervenes, intervening, intervened)

VERB If you **intervene in** a situation, you become involved in it and try to change it. ○ *The situation calmed down when police intervened.* ○ [+ *in*] *The Government is doing nothing to intervene in the crisis.*

▶ **COLLOCATIONS:**
intervene **in** *something*
intervene **personally/directly**
intervene in a **dispute/conflict/war/row/crisis**
intervene in a **case/affair/matter/situation/process**

inter|ven|tion /ˌɪntəˈvenʃən/

UNCOUNTABLE NOUN ○ [+ *in*] *the role of the United States and its intervention in the internal affairs of many countries* ○ [+ *in*] *The impact of American military intervention in Europe was not felt for a year.*

▶ **COLLOCATIONS:**
intervention **in** *something/somewhere*
government/state/foreign/divine intervention
humanitarian/armed/military/medical intervention
direct/timely intervention

in|trin|sic /ɪnˈtrɪnsɪk/ `ACADEMIC WORD`

ADJECTIVE If something has **intrinsic** value or **intrinsic** interest, it is valuable or interesting because of its basic nature or character, and not because of its connection with other things. [FORMAL] ○ *The paintings have no intrinsic value except as curiosities.* ○ *The rate is determined by intrinsic qualities such as the land's slope.*

▶ **COLLOCATIONS:**
  intrinsic **value/worth/merit/importance**
  an intrinsic **part/quality/factor**

▶ **SYNONYMS:** basic, fundamental, inherent

in|trin|si|cal|ly /ɪnˈtrɪnsɪkli/

ADVERB ○ *There is nothing intrinsically wrong with a voluntary approach but there is a great concern that it will not work.* ○ *Soviet-style communism failed, not because it was intrinsically evil but because it was flawed.*

▶ **COLLOCATIONS:**
  intrinsically **wrong/evil**
  intrinsically **valuable/rewarding**

▶ **SYNONYMS:** basically, fundamentally, inherently

in|tui|tion /ˌɪntjʊˈɪʃən, AM -tu-/ **(intuitions)**

NOUN Your **intuition** or your **intuitions** are unexplained feelings you have that something is true even when you have no evidence or proof of it. ○ *Her intuition was telling her that something was wrong.* ○ *He'd have to rely on his own intuitions.*

▶ **COLLOCATIONS:**
  rely on/trust someone's intuition
  feminine/female intuition
  intuition **tells** someone something

▶ **SYNONYMS:** instinct

in|tui|tive /ɪnˈtjuːətɪv, AM -ˈtuː-/

ADJECTIVE If you have an **intuitive** idea or feeling about something, you feel that it is true although you have no evidence or proof of it. ○ *A positive pregnancy test soon confirmed her intuitive feelings.* ○ *He had a deep knowledge and intuitive understanding of cricket.*

▶ **COLLOCATION:** an intuitive **understanding/sense/grasp/feeling**

▶ **SYNONYM:** instinctive

in|tui|tive|ly /ɪnˈtjuːətɪvli, AM -ˈtuː-/

ADVERB ○ *Most children reading this sentence would probably fill in the blank with a noun, because they intuitively know how language works.* ○ *Today's children intuitively know more about technology by absorbing what has been called "click culture" from the cradle.*

▶ **COLLOCATION: know/understand** *something* intuitively
▶ **SYNONYM:** instinctively

in|voke /ɪnˈvəʊk/   ACADEMIC WORD   LAW   ARTS
(invokes, invoking, invoked)

1 VERB If you **invoke** a law, you state that you are taking a particular action because that law allows or tells you to. ○ *The judge invoked an international law that protects refugees.* ○ *The 18 Nato ambassadors invoked the mutual defence clause.*

▶ **COLLOCATIONS:**
invoke a **law/clause/rule**
invoke **legislation**

2 VERB If something such as a piece of music **invokes** a feeling or an image, it causes someone to have the feeling or to see the image. Many people consider this use to be incorrect. ○ *The music invoked the wide open spaces of the prairies.* ○ *The poem invokes the horrors of the Irish potato famine.*

▶ **COLLOCATIONS:**
invoke a **memory/image**
a **poem/poet** invokes *something*
▶ **SYNONYMS:** evoke, conjure up

ir|repa|rable /ɪˈreprəbəl/

ADJECTIVE Irreparable damage or harm is so bad that it cannot be repaired or put right. [FORMAL] ○ *The move would cause irreparable harm to the organization.* ○ *He had broken the trust between them and done irreparable damage.*

▶ **COLLOCATION:** irreparable **damage/harm/injury/loss**
▶ **SYNONYM:** irreversible
▶ **ANTONYM:** reversible

ir|repa|rably /ɪˈreprəbli/

ADVERB ○ *Her heart was irreparably damaged by a virus.* ○ *Commercial netting has already irreparably harmed many salmon stocks.*

▶ **COLLOCATION:** irreparably **damage/harm** *something*
▶ **SYNONYM:** irreversibly

Jj

ju|ris|dic|tion /ˌdʒʊərɪsˈdɪkʃən/ (jurisdictions)   `LAW`

UNCOUNTABLE NOUN Jurisdiction is the power that a court of law or an official has to carry out legal judgments or to enforce laws. [FORMAL]

○ [+ over] *The British police have no jurisdiction over foreign bank accounts.*
○ [+ to-inf] *U.S courts must assert jurisdiction to review detention of enemy combatants.*

▶ **COLLOCATIONS:**
  jurisdiction **over** *something*
  jurisdiction over a **crime/case/matter**
  the jurisdiction of a **court/tribunal/incorporation**
  assert/exercise/lack/confer jurisdiction
  provincial/exclusive/federal/territorial jurisdiction

▶ **SYNONYMS:** authority, power, influence

ki|net|ic /kɪˈnetɪk/

ADJECTIVE In physics, **kinetic** is used to describe something that is concerned with movement. ○ *Kinetic energy is shown in body movements including growth and physical activities.* ○ *Kinetic cues come from either your own motion or the motion of some object.*

▶ **COLLOCATION:** kinetic **energy**

k

Ll

land|fill /ˈlændfɪl/

UNCOUNTABLE NOUN Landfill is a method of getting rid of very large amounts of rubbish by burying it in a large deep hole. ○ *the environmental costs of landfill* ○ *There are serious scientific issues involved in the debate over landfill sites and global warming.*

▶ **COLLOCATIONS:**
landfill **gas/waste/rubbish/space**
a landfill **site/tax/operator**

land|mark /ˈlændmɑːk/ (landmarks)

1 NOUN A **landmark** is a building or feature which is easily noticed and can be used to judge your position or the position of other buildings or features. ○ *The Ambassador Hotel is a Los Angeles landmark.* ○ *The building, designated a historic landmark by the city, now houses apartments and a laundry business.*

▶ **COLLOCATIONS:**
a **historic/famous/architectural/local** landmark
a **city/tourist** landmark
a landmark **skyscraper/tower/hotel/building**

2 NOUN You can refer to an important stage in the development of something as a **landmark**. ○ *a landmark arms control treaty* ○ *In a landmark decision, the council of the Law Society voted to dismantle its present governing body.*

▶ **COLLOCATIONS:**
celebrate/reach/achieve a landmark
a landmark **decision/study/case/agreement/election**

▶ **SYNONYMS:** milestone, watershed

lar|va /ˈlɑːvə/ (larvae)   BIOLOGY

NOUN A **larva** is an insect at the stage of its life after it has developed from an egg and before it changes into its adult form. ○ *The eggs quickly hatch into larvae.* ○ *Moth larvae spin a thread and use wind currents to float from tree to tree.*

▶ **COLLOCATIONS:**
a **mosquito/beetle/butterfly/moth** larva
tiny/microscopic larvae
larvae **hatch/eat/grow**

la|ser /ˈleɪzə/ (lasers)

ENGINEERING SCIENCE

NOUN A **laser** is a narrow beam of concentrated light produced by a special machine. It is used for cutting very hard materials, and in many technical fields such as surgery and telecommunications. ○ *Therapies currently under investigation include laser surgery and bone-marrow transplants.* ○ *Researchers realized that a tunable laser beam might be useful in surgery.*

▶ **COLLOCATIONS:**
a laser **printer/beam/scanner**
laser **treatment/surgery/therapy**
shine/aim a laser
a **powerful/infrared/ultraviolet** laser

lati|tude /ˈlætɪtjuːd, AM -tuːd/ (latitudes)

GEOGRAPHY

NOUN The **latitude** of a place is its distance from the equator. ○ *In the middle to high latitudes rainfall has risen steadily over the last 20-30 years.* ○ *Vitamin D deficiency is widespread in the country, not just at northern latitudes.*

● **Latitude** is also an adjective. ○ *The army must cease military operations above 36 degrees latitude north.*

▶ **COLLOCATION:** a **high/low/northern/tropical** latitude
▶ **RELATED WORD:** longitude

law|suit /ˈlɔːsuːt/ (lawsuits)

LAW

NOUN A **lawsuit** is a case in a court of law which concerns a dispute between two people or organizations. [FORMAL] ○ [+ *against*] *The dispute culminated last week in a lawsuit against the government.* ○ *a lawsuit brought by Barclays Bank*

▶ **COLLOCATIONS:**
a lawsuit **against** *someone*
file/launch/bring/fight/settle a lawsuit
a **high-profile/ongoing/costly/pending** lawsuit
a **copyright/malpractice/patent/discrimination** lawsuit

▶ **SYNONYMS:** case, action, litigation

leg|is|la|ture /ˈledʒɪslətʃə, AM -leɪ-/ (legislatures)

ACADEMIC WORD LAW POLITICS

NOUN The **legislature** of a particular state or country is the group of people in it who have the power to make and pass laws. [FORMAL] ○ *The proposals before the legislature include the creation of two special courts to deal exclusively with violent crimes.* ○ *The legislature passed a bill that would permit referendums on constitutional and sovereignty issues.*

▶ COLLOCATIONS:
the legislature **approve/pass/authorize** something
elect/lobby/persuade the legislature
a legislature **building/member/committee**
▶ PHRASE: state legislature

---

le|giti|mate /lɪˈdʒɪtɪmət/   LAW

1 ADJECTIVE Something that is **legitimate** is acceptable according to the law. ○ *The French government has condemned the coup in Haiti and has demanded the restoration of the legitimate government.* ○ *The government will not seek to disrupt the legitimate business activities of the defendant.*

▶ COLLOCATIONS:
perfectly/wholly/democratically legitimate
a legitimate **heir/ruler/marriage**
▶ SYNONYMS: legal, authentic, valid
▶ ANTONYM: illegitimate

2 ADJECTIVE If you say that something such as a feeling or claim is **legitimate**, you think that it is reasonable and justified. ○ *That's a perfectly legitimate fear.* ○ *The New York Times has a legitimate claim to be a national newspaper.*

▶ COLLOCATION: a legitimate **claim/concern/excuse/expectation**
▶ SYNONYMS: reasonable, justified

le|giti|mate|ly /lɪˈdʒɪtɪmətli/

ADVERB ○ *The government has been legitimately elected by the people.* ○ *They could quarrel quite legitimately with some of my choices.*

▶ COLLOCATIONS:
legitimately **claim/acquire** something
legitimately **elect** someone
▶ SYNONYMS: legally, rightfully
▶ ANTONYM: illegitimately

le|giti|ma|cy /lɪˈdʒɪtɪmɪsi/

UNCOUNTABLE NOUN ○ [+ *of*] *The opposition parties do not recognise the political legitimacy of his government.* ○ [+ *of*] *As if to prove the legitimacy of these fears, the Cabinet of Franz von Papen collapsed on December 2.*

▶ COLLOCATIONS:
the legitimacy **of** something
political/democratic/international legitimacy
▶ SYNONYMS: authenticity, validity
▶ ANTONYM: illegitimacy

lens /lenz/ (lenses)

ENGINEERING   PHYSICS

NOUN A **lens** is a thin curved piece of glass or plastic used in things such as cameras, telescopes, and pairs of glasses. You look through a lens in order to make things look larger, smaller, or clearer. ○ *a seven-megapixel camera with an optical zoom lens* ○ *Hard contact lenses are more likely to give problems than the newer soft lenses.*

▶ **COLLOCATIONS:**
   a **contact/bifocal** lens
   a **telescopic/optical/camera** lens

levy /'levi/

ACADEMIC WORD   BUSINESS   ECONOMICS

(levies, levying, levied)

1 NOUN A **levy** is a sum of money that you have to pay, for example as a tax to the government. ○ [+ *on*] *an annual motorway levy on all drivers* ○ [+ *on*] *plans to impose a flat-rate levy on all businesses involved with the sale of food*

▶ **COLLOCATIONS:**
   a levy **on** *something/someone*
   impose/propose/introduce/pay a levy
   a **compulsory/annual/£100** levy
   a levy **surcharge/increase/payment**

▶ **SYNONYMS:** tax, charge

2 VERB If a government or organization **levies** a tax or other sum of money, it demands it from people or organizations. ○ [+ *on*] *They levied religious taxes on Christian commercial transactions.* ○ *Taxes should not be levied without the authority of Parliament.*

▶ **COLLOCATIONS:**
   levy *something* **on** *something/someone*
   levy a **fine/fee/tax/charge/penalty**

▶ **SYNONYMS:** tax, charge

lib|er|al /'lɪbərəl/ (liberals)

ACADEMIC WORD   POLITICS

ADJECTIVE A **liberal** system allows people or organizations a lot of political or economic freedom. ○ *a liberal democracy with a multiparty political system* ○ *They favour liberal free-market policies.*

● **Liberal** is also a noun. ○ *These kinds of price controls go against all the financial principles of the free market liberals.* ○ *Even the bleeding-heart liberals must surely realise that in a war zone occasionally innocents get killed.*

▶ **COLLOCATIONS:**
a liberal **government/party/leader/MP/candidate**
socially/relatively/politically liberal
a **bleeding-heart/tax-and-spend/free-market** liberal

▶ **RELATED WORD:** conservative

lib|er|al|ize /ˈlɪbrəlaɪz/ (liberalizes, liberalizing, liberalized)

VERB When a country or government **liberalizes**, or **liberalizes** its laws or its attitudes, it becomes less strict and allows people more freedom in their actions. [in BRIT, also use **liberalise**] ○ *authoritarian states that have only now begun to liberalise* ○ *the decision to liberalize travel restrictions*

▶ **COLLOCATIONS:**
liberalize **trade/laws/rules/society**
liberalize a **regime/economy**

▶ **SYNONYMS:** relax, ease, moderate

lib|er|ali|za|tion /ˌlɪbrəlaɪˈzeɪʃən/

UNCOUNTABLE NOUN [in BRIT, also use **liberalisation**] ○ [+ *of*] *the liberalization of divorce laws in the late 1960s*

▶ **COLLOCATIONS:**
the liberalization **of** *something*
the liberalization of **trade**
the liberalization of a **law/economy**

▶ **SYNONYMS:** relaxation, easing, moderation

POLITICS

lib|er|ty /ˈlɪbəti/ (liberties)

NOUN Liberty is the freedom to live your life in the way that you want, without interference from other people or the authorities. ○ *Wit Wolzek claimed the legislation could impinge on privacy, self determination and respect for religious liberty.* ○ [+ *of*] *Such a system would be a fundamental blow to the rights and liberties of the English people.*

▶ **COLLOCATIONS:**
the liberty **of** *someone/something*
liberty of the **press/individual**
liberty of **expression/thought/speech**
civil/personal/political/religious liberty
a liberty **group/campaigner/advocate**
protect/curtail/infringe liberty

▶ **PHRASE:** rights and liberties

▶ **SYNONYM:** freedom

lib|er|ate /ˈlɪbəreɪt/ (liberates, liberating, liberated)

1 VERB To **liberate** a place or the people in it means to free them from the political or military control of another country, area, or group of people. ○ *They planned to march on and liberate the city.* ○ *They made a triumphal march into their liberated city.*

▶ COLLOCATION: liberate a **land/territory/camp**

▶ SYNONYM: free

2 VERB To **liberate** someone **from** something means to help them escape from it or overcome it, and lead a better way of life. ○ *[+ from] He asked how committed the leadership was to liberating its people from poverty.* ○ *Knowledge can be both empowering, liberating and a source of economic well being.*

▶ COLLOCATION: liberate *someone* **from** *something*

▶ SYNONYM: free

lib|era|tion /ˌlɪbəˈreɪʃən/

UNCOUNTABLE NOUN ○ *Nelson Mandela became a symbol of the liberation struggle during his years in prison.* ○ *the women's liberation movement*

▶ COLLOCATIONS:
a liberation **movement/struggle/army/war**
sexual/women's/gay liberation

▶ SYNONYM: freedom

---

liq|ui|date /ˈlɪkwɪdeɪt/ (liquidates, liquidating, liquidated) `BUSINESS`

1 VERB To **liquidate** a company is to close it down and sell all its assets, usually because it is in debt. ○ *A unanimous vote was taken to liquidate the company.* ○ *The High Court has appointed an official receiver to liquidate a bankrupt travel company.*

▶ COLLOCATION: liquidate a **company**

▶ SYNONYMS: sell

2 VERB If a company **liquidates** its assets, its property such as buildings or machinery is sold in order to get money. ○ *The company closed down operations and began liquidating its assets in January.*

▶ COLLOCATIONS:
liquidate **assests/merchandise/securities**
gradually/periodically/systematically liquidate *something*

▶ SYNONYM: sell

liq|ui|da|tion /ˌlɪkwɪ'deɪʃən/ (liquidations)

NOUN ○ *The company went into liquidation.* ○ *The number of company liquidations rose 11 per cent.*

▶ **COLLOCATIONS:**
the liquidation **of** something
the liquidation of a **company/corporation**
the liquidation of **assets/shares**
voluntary/compulsory liquidation
avoid/force/face liquidation

---

lit|er|al /'lɪtərəl/ `LANGUAGE` `LITERATURE`

1 **ADJECTIVE** The **literal** sense of a word or phrase is its most basic sense.
○ *In many cases, the people there are fighting, in a literal sense, for their homes.*
○ *The concert ended with a bang in the most literal sense.* ○ *the literal definition of reaping what you sow*

▶ **COLLOCATION:** a literal **sense/meaning/interpretation/definition**

▶ **ANTONYMS:** metaphorical, figurative

2 **ADJECTIVE** A **literal** translation is one in which you translate each word of the original work rather than giving the meaning of each expression or sentence using words that sound natural. ○ *A literal translation of the name Tapies is 'walls'.* ○ *'Ethnic cleansing' is a literal translation of the Serbo-Croatian phrase etnicko ciscenje.*

▶ **PHRASE:** a literal translation

▶ **SYNONYM:** exact

lit|er|al|ly /'lɪtərəli/

ADVERB If a word or expression is translated **literally**, its most simple or basic meaning is translated. ○ *The word 'volk' translates literally as 'folk'.*
○ *A stanza is, literally, a room.*

▶ **COLLOCATIONS:**
translate/mean something literally
taken/meant literally

---

lit|er|ate /'lɪtərət/

1 **ADJECTIVE** Someone who is **literate** is able to read and write. ○ *Over one-quarter of the adult population are not fully literate.* ○ *Around one third of the prison population was literate and numerate.*

▶ **COLLOCATIONS:**
a literate **population/adult/citizen**
highly/functionally/fully/barely literate

▶ **RELATED WORD:** numerate

▶ **ANTONYM:** illiterate

2 ADJECTIVE If you describe someone as **literate** in a particular subject, especially one that many people do not know anything about, you mean that they have a good knowledge and understanding of that subject. ○ *Head teachers need to be financially literate.* ○ *We want to have more scientifically literate people running our television stations.*

▶ **COLLOCATION:** **financially/scientifically/politically** literate

lit|era|cy /ˈlɪtərəsi/

UNCOUNTABLE NOUN ○ *Many adults have some problems with literacy and numeracy.* ○ *Computer literacy may be essential to overcome social exclusion and improve employment prospects.*

▶ **COLLOCATIONS:**
adult/family literacy
computer/media literacy

▶ **PHRASE:** literacy and numeracy

liti|gate /ˈlɪtɪɡeɪt/ (litigates, litigating, litigated) `LAW`

VERB To **litigate** means to take legal action. ○ *the cost of litigating personal injury claims in the county court* ○ *The prospect of similar cases being successfully litigated in Britain seems unlikely.*

▶ **COLLOCATION:** litigate a **case/issue/matter/claim**

liti|ga|tion /ˌlɪtɪˈɡeɪʃən/

UNCOUNTABLE NOUN ○ *The settlement ends more than four years of litigation on behalf of the residents.* ○ *The company does not comment on pending litigation.*

▶ **COLLOCATIONS:**
civil/commercial/costly litigation
asbestos/patent/tobacco litigation
avoid/face litigation
pending litigation

lon|gi|tude /ˈlɒndʒɪtjuːd, AM -tuːd/ (longitudes) `GEOGRAPHY`

NOUN The **longitude** of a place is its distance to the west or east of a line passing through Greenwich. ○ *He noted the latitude and longitude, then made a mark on the admiralty chart.* ○ *determining longitude exactly was a problem of vital importance for the safety of commercial shipping*

- **Longitude** is also an adjective. ○ *A similar feature is found at 13 degrees North between 230 degrees and 250 degrees longitude.*

  ▶ **RELATED WORD:** latitude

lu|nar /ˈluːnə/ `GEOGRAPHY` `SCIENCE`

ADJECTIVE Lunar means relating to the moon. ○ *The vast volcanic slope was eerily reminiscent of a lunar landscape.* ○ *a magazine article celebrating the anniversary of man's first lunar landing*

  ▶ **COLLOCATIONS:**
  a lunar **eclipse/calendar/landing**
  the lunar **landscape/surface**

  ▶ **RELATED WORD:** solar

Mm

macro|eco|nom|ics /ˌmækroʊˌiːkəˈnɒmɪks, -ˌek-/
also **macro-economics**

UNCOUNTABLE NOUN Macroeconomics is the branch of economics that is
concerned with the major, general features of a country's economy, such
as the level of inflation, unemployment, or interest rates. ○ *Too many
politicians forget the importance of macroeconomics.* ○ *The UK macroeconomics
show that there will not be enough people to fulfil the work that needs to be done.*

▶ **RELATED WORD:** microeconomics

ma|cro|ec|o|nom|ic /ˌmækroʊˌiːkəˈnɒmɪk, -ˌek-/

ADJECTIVE ○ *the attempt to substitute low inflation for full employment as a goal
of macro-economic policy* ○ *Greater macroeconomic stability is a prize well
worth having.*

▶ **COLLOCATIONS:**
macroeconomic **stability/management/policy**
a macroeconomic **policy/condition/factor**

▶ **RELATED WORD:** microeconomic

mag|ni|tude /ˈmægnɪtjuːd, AM -tuːd/

UNCOUNTABLE NOUN If you talk about the **magnitude** of something, you
are talking about its great size, scale, or importance. ○ *An operation of this
magnitude is going to be difficult.* ○ *These are issues of great magnitude.* ○ [+ of]
No one seems to realise the magnitude of this problem.

▶ **COLLOCATIONS:**
the magnitude **of** *something*
the magnitude of the **problem/change/task/disaster**
the **sheer** magnitude
a **similar/preliminary/unprecedented** magnitude
measure/grasp/realize the magnitude of *something*

▶ **SYNONYMS:** immensity, extent, enormity

▶ **ANTONYM:** smallness

mam|mal /ˈmæməl/ (mammals)

BIOLOGY

NOUN **Mammals** are animals such as humans, dogs, lions, and whales. In general, female mammals give birth to babies rather than laying eggs, and feed their young with milk. ○ *This is the best place on the west coast of Scotland for seeing large marine mammals.*

▶ **COLLOCATIONS:**
 a **marine/endangered/wild** mammal
 a **sea/land** mammal
 hunt/protect/kill a mammal

▶ **RELATED WORDS:** bird, reptile

ma|nipu|late /məˈnɪpjʊleɪt/ (manipulates, manipulating, manipulated)

ACADEMIC WORD

1 VERB If you say that someone **manipulates** an event or situation, you disapprove of them because they use or control it for their own benefit, or cause it to develop in the way they want. ○ *He said that the state television was trying to manipulate the election outcome.* ○ *They felt he had been cowardly in manipulating the system to avoid the draft.*

▶ **COLLOCATIONS:**
 manipulate an **outcome/opinion**
 manipulate the **media**
 skilfully/easily/fraudulently/cynically manipulate *something*

2 VERB If you **manipulate** something that requires skill, such as a complicated piece of equipment or a difficult idea, you operate it or process it. ○ *The technology uses a pen to manipulate a computer.* ○ *The puppets are expertly manipulated by Liz Walker.* ○ *His mind moves in quantum leaps, manipulating ideas and jumping on to new ones as soon as he can.*

▶ **COLLOCATIONS:**
 manipulate a **puppet/gadget/object**
 deftly/skilfully manipulate *something*

▶ **SYNONYMS:** work, handle

ma|nipu|la|tion /məˌnɪpjʊˈleɪʃən/

NOUN ○ *science that requires only the simplest of mathematical manipulations* ○ *accusations of political manipulation*

▶ **COLLOCATIONS:**
 alleged/fraudulent manipulation
 genetic/statistical manipulation
 involve/avoid/require manipulation

m

---

manu|script /ˈmænjʊskrɪpt/ (manuscripts) `HISTORY` `LITERATURE`

NOUN A **manuscript** is a handwritten or typed document, especially a writer's first version of a book before it is published. ○ [+ *of*] *He had seen a manuscript of the book.* ○ [+ *of*] *discovering an original manuscript of the song in Paris*

▶ **COLLOCATIONS:**
a manuscript **of** *something*
a **handwritten/unpublished/unsolicited/original** manuscript
edit/submit/type/read a manuscript

---

mar|gin /ˈmɑːdʒɪn/ (margins) `ACADEMIC WORD`

1 NOUN A **margin** is the difference between two amounts, especially the difference in the number of votes or points between the winner and the loser in an election or other contest. ○ *They could end up with a 50-point winning margin.* ○ *The Sunday Times remains the brand leader by a huge margin.* ○ *The margin in favour was 280-to-153.*

▶ **COLLOCATIONS:**
a margin **of** *x*
a **gross/winning/narrow/slim/wide** margin
a **profit** margin

2 NOUN The **margin** of a written or printed page is the empty space at the side of the page. ○ *She added her comments in the margin.* ○ [+ *of*] *The wood-eating insects also don't like the taste of ink and prefer the binding and the margin of the pages.*

▶ **COLLOCATIONS:**
the margin **of** *something*
in the margin

3 NOUN The **margin** of a place or area is the extreme edge of it. ○ *the low coastal plain along the western margin* ○ [+ *of*] *These islands are on the margins of human habitation.*

▶ **COLLOCATIONS:**
the margin **of** *something*
on the margins

▶ **SYNONYMS:** edge, periphery

mar|gin|al /ˈmɑːdʒɪnəl/

1 ADJECTIVE If you describe something as **marginal**, you mean that it is small or not very important. ○ *This is a marginal improvement on October.* ○ *The role of the opposition party proved marginal.*

→ see note at **negligible**

▶ COLLOCATIONS:
   a marginal **rate/cost/increase**
   a marginal **seat/constituency**
▶ SYNONYM: slight

2 ADJECTIVE If you describe people as **marginal**, you mean that they are not involved in the main events or developments in society because they are poor or have no power. ○ *The tribunals were established for the well-integrated members of society and not for marginal individuals.* ○ *I don't want to call him marginal, but he's not a major character.*

▶ COLLOCATION: **socially** marginal
▶ ANTONYM: mainstream

mar|gin|al|ly /ˈmɑːdʒɪnəli/

ADVERB Marginally means to only a small extent. ○ *Sales last year were marginally higher than in 1991.* ○ *The Christian Democrats did marginally worse than expected.* ○ *These cameras have increased only marginally in value over the past decade.*

▶ COLLOCATIONS:
   marginally **profitable/low/high**
   increase/rise/decline/improve marginally
▶ SYNONYM: slightly

ma|rine /məˈriːn/ [GEOGRAPHY] [BIOLOGY]

ADJECTIVE Marine is used to describe things relating to the sea or to the animals and plants that live in the sea. ○ *breeding grounds for marine life* ○ *research in marine biology* ○ *By encouraging wider awareness of the marine environment, Sea Life Centres have a vital role to play in the conservation of our sea.*

▶ COLLOCATIONS:
   a marine **mammal/biologist/organism**
   a marine **environment/ecosystem**
   marine **biology**

mari|tal sta|tus /ˌmærɪtəl ˈsteɪtəs/ [SOCIOLOGY]

UNCOUNTABLE NOUN Your **marital status** is whether you are married, single, or divorced. [FORMAL] ○ *How well off you are in old age is largely determined by race, sex, and marital status.* ○ *It is possible that his marital status has hindered his rabbinic career, but he is not sure.*

mari|time /ˈmærɪtaɪm/

ADJECTIVE **Maritime** is used to describe things relating to the sea and to ships. ○ *the largest maritime museum of its kind* ○ *It was one of Africa's worst maritime disasters.*

▶ **COLLOCATIONS:**
maritime **heritage/surveillance**
a maritime **museum/border/aircraft/disaster**

marked /mɑːkt/

ADJECTIVE A **marked** change or difference is very obvious and easily noticed. ○ *There has been a marked increase in crimes against property.* ○ *He was a man of austere habits, in marked contrast to his more flamboyant wife.* ○ *The trends since the 1950s have become even more marked.*

▶ **COLLOCATIONS:**
a marked **contrast/improvement/increase/difference**
clearly marked

▶ **PHRASE:** in marked contrast

mark|ed|ly /ˈmɑːkɪdli/

ADVERB ○ *America's current economic downturn is markedly different from previous recessions.* ○ *The quality of their relationship improved markedly.*

▶ **COLLOCATIONS:**
markedly **different/high/low**
differ/improve/increase/change markedly

EXTEND YOUR VOCABULARY

If something is easily noticed, you can say it is **clear**, **obvious** or **noticeable**. However, these words all emphasize the perspective of the person looking at something, so are somewhat subjective.
○ *The guidelines would seem blatantly obvious to most people, yet still we witness examples of gross misconduct.*

In academic writing, you often want to talk about something that is clear and noticeable when measured in an objective way. You can say that a change or a difference is **marked**. ○ *This study does not indicate a marked increase in cancer risk.*

You can describe a noticeable feature or an effect as **pronounced**.
○ *The trend is more pronounced in the UK than in most other European countries.*

You can also describe a noticeable change or difference as **significant**, although in many academic contexts, this refers specifically to a statistical measurement. ○ *This difference was not statistically significant.*

---

m

---

mate /meɪt/ (mates, mating, mated)   `BIOLOGY`

1 NOUN An animal's **mate** is its sexual partner. ○ *The males guard their mates zealously.* ○ *Male nightingales sing to attract a mate and establish their territory.*

▶ **COLLOCATION: attract/seek/choose/find/kill** a mate

2 VERB When animals **mate**, a male and a female have sex in order to produce young. ○ *This allows the pair to mate properly and stops the hen staying in the nest-box.* ○ [+ with] *They want the males to mate with wild females.* ○ *It is easy to tell when a female is ready to mate.*

▶ **COLLOCATIONS:**
   mate **with** *something*
   a mating **ritual/pair**
   the mating **season**
   a **female/male/cat/dog/mouse** mates
   mate **successfully**

---

ma|terial /məˈtɪəriəl/

ADJECTIVE Material things are related to possessions or money, rather than to more abstract things such as ideas or values. ○ *Every room must have been stuffed with material things.* ○ *his descriptions of their poor material conditions*

▶ **COLLOCATIONS:**
   material **assistance/support**
   a material **possession/resource**
▶ **ANTONYM:** spiritual

ma|teri|al|ly /məˈtɪəriəli/

ADVERB ○ *He has tried to help this child materially and spiritually.* ○ *They believe that a tough, materially poor childhood is character-building.* ○ *The object has no real value, materially or emotionally.*

▶ **COLLOCATIONS:**
   differ/vary/increase materially
   affect *something/someone* materially
   materially **inadequate/deficient/poor/wealthy**

---

ma|ter|nal /məˈtɜːnəl/   `BIOLOGY` `SOCIOLOGY`

1 ADJECTIVE Maternal is used to describe feelings or actions which are typical of those of a kind mother towards her child. ○ *She had little maternal instinct.* ○ *Her feelings towards him were almost maternal.*

▶ COLLOCATIONS:
a maternal **urge/instinct**
maternal **affection/devotion**

▶ RELATED WORD: paternal

2 ADJECTIVE **Maternal** is used to describe things that relate to the mother of a baby. ○ *Maternal smoking can damage the unborn child.* ○ *Likewise the incidence of maternal morbidity is now so low that it makes the papers rather than popular novels.*

▶ COLLOCATION: maternal **morbidity/depression**

▶ RELATED WORD: paternal

3 ADJECTIVE A **maternal** relative is one who is related through a person's mother rather than their father. ○ *Her maternal grandfather was Mayor of Karachi.* ○ *If, for example, your mother, maternal aunt and sister had breast cancer, you would be in an extremely high-risk category.*

▶ COLLOCATION: a maternal **grandfather/grandmother/uncle/aunt**

▶ RELATED WORD: paternal

ma|ter|nity /məˈtɜːnɪti/

ADJECTIVE **Maternity** is used to describe things relating to the help and medical care given to a woman when she is pregnant and when she gives birth. ○ *Your job will be kept open for your return after maternity leave.* ○ *The boy was born at the city's maternity hospital.*

▶ COLLOCATIONS:
maternity **clothes/wear/leave/care**
a maternity **hospital/ward/nurse**

▶ RELATED WORD: paternity

---

max|im|ize /ˈmæksɪmaɪz/   `ACADEMIC WORD`
(maximizes, maximizing, maximized)

VERB If you **maximize** something, you make it as great in amount or importance as you can. [in BRIT, also use **maximise**] ○ *In order to maximize profit the firm would seek to maximize output.* ○ *They were looking for suitable ways of maximising their electoral support.*

▶ COLLOCATION: maximize **profit/revenue/appreciation/efficiency**

▶ ANTONYM: minimize

maxi|mi|za|tion /ˌmæksɪmaɪˈzeɪʃən/

UNCOUNTABLE NOUN [in BRIT, also use **maximisation**] ○ *a pricing policy that was aimed at profit maximisation* ○ *[+ of] Craftsmanship was conceived as*

m

a means of human fulfilment which could not survive where the maximization of profits was the primary end.
- ▶ **COLLOCATION:** the maximization **of** *something*
- ▶ **SYNONYM:** minimization

---

mean /miːn/   MATHS

NOUN The mean is a number that is the average of a set of numbers.
○ *Take a hundred and twenty values and calculate the mean.* ○ *the mean score for 26-year-olds*

> **EXTEND YOUR VOCABULARY**
>
> There are several ways to calculate the **average** of a set of numbers.
>
> If, for example, you have a class of 15 children with scores in a test, to calculate the **mean**, you add together all the scores and then divide the total by fifteen.
>
> To calculate the **median** score, you arrange the scores in order, from lowest to highest, and take the middle one, in this example, the eighth.

---

me|dian /ˈmiːdiən/   MATHS

ADJECTIVE The median value of a set of values is the middle one when they are arranged in order. For example, if a group of five students take a test and their marks are 5, 7, 7, 8, and 10, the median mark is 7. ○ *The median sentence for hard drugs offences increased by 60 per cent from 150 in 1982 to 240 days in 1986.* ○ *Pessimists point out that the median price for new homes has slipped.*
- → see note at **mean**
- ▶ **COLLOCATION:** a median **income/age/price/estimate**

---

me|di|ate /ˈmiːdieɪt/ (mediates, mediating, mediated)   ACADEMIC WORD

1 VERB If someone **mediates between** two groups of people, or **mediates** an agreement **between** them, they try to settle an argument between them by talking to both groups and trying to find things that they can both agree to. ○ [+ between] *My mom was the one who mediated between Zelda and her mom.* ○ [+ between] *United Nations officials have mediated a series of peace meetings between the two sides.* ○ [+ in] *The Vatican successfully mediated in a territorial dispute between Argentina and Chile in 1984.* ○ *U.N. peacekeepers mediated a new cease-fire.*

► COLLOCATIONS:
mediate **between** *people*
mediate **in** *something*
mediate a **dispute/crisis**
mediate **talks**

► SYNONYM: arbitrate

2 VERB If something **mediates** a particular process or event, it allows that process or event to happen and influences the way in which it happens. [FORMAL] ○ *the thymus, the organ which mediates the response of the white blood cells* ○ *People's responses to us have been mediated by their past experience of life.*

► COLLOCATIONS:
mediated **by** *something*
a **cell/organism/mechanism** mediates *something*
mediate a **response/allergy**
mediate **behaviour**

► SYNONYM: influence

me|dia|tion /ˌmiːdiˈeɪʃən/

UNCOUNTABLE NOUN ○ [+ *between*] *The agreement provides for United Nations mediation between the two sides.* ○ [+ *of*] *There is still a possibility the two sides could reach a compromise through the mediation of a third party.* ○ [+ *of*] *This works through the mediation of the central nervous system.*

► COLLOCATIONS:
mediation **between** *people*
the mediation **of** *someone/something*
try/accept/attempt/require mediation
international/third-party/federal mediation
a mediation **effort/process/session**

► SYNONYM: arbitration

---

me|di|eval /ˌmediˈiːvəl, AM ˌmiːd-/ `HISTORY`

ADJECTIVE Something that is **medieval** relates to or was made in the period of European history between the end of the Roman Empire in 476 AD and about 1500 AD. [in BRIT, also use **mediaeval**] ○ *In the English medieval castle the whole household ate and slept together in the great hall.* ○ *It goes back to a medieval knight's sense of personal honour.*

► COLLOCATION: a medieval **castle/fortress/village/church/knight**

me|dium /'miːdiəm/ (mediums, media) `ACADEMIC WORD`

1 NOUN A **medium** is a way or means of expressing your ideas or of communicating with people. ○ [+ of] *In Sierra Leone, English is used as the medium of instruction for all primary education.* ○ *But Artaud was increasingly dissatisfied with film as a medium.*

▶ **COLLOCATIONS:**
   a medium **of** *something*
   a medium of **instruction/exchange/communication**
   the medium of **television/film/radio**

▶ **SYNONYM:** means

2 NOUN A **medium** is a substance or material which is used for a particular purpose or in order to produce a particular effect. ○ *Blood is the medium in which oxygen is carried to all parts of the body.* ○ [+ of] *Hyatt has found a way of creating these qualities using the more permanent medium of oil paint.*

▶ **COLLOCATION:** the medium **of** *something*

▶ **SYNONYMS:** material, substance

> **USAGE:** Plural forms
>
> In everyday language, we often talk about **the media** to refer to television, radio, newspapers, etc. together. This is actually the plural form of the noun **medium**, meaning a means of communication. ○ *Franklin Roosevelt mastered the new medium of radio during the Great Depression.*
>
> The plural of the noun **medium** can be **media** or **mediums**. ○ *McKean uses mixed media of photographs, paint and the computer to create a surreal setting.* ○ *More and more companies are turning to technological mediums such as the internet.*

merge /mɜːdʒ/ (merges, merging, merged) `BUSINESS`

VERB If one thing **merges with** another, or **is merged with** another, they combine or come together to make one whole thing. You can also say that two things **merge**, or **are merged**. ○ [+ with] *Bank of America merged with a rival bank.* ○ *The rivers merge just north of a vital irrigation system.* ○ [+ into] *The two countries merged into one.*

▶ **COLLOCATIONS:**
   merge **with/into** *something*
   merge with a **rival/bank/company**
   a **bank/firm/company** merges with *something*

merge into the **traffic/background/crowd**
merge **together/successfully**

▶ **SYNONYM:** join

▶ **ANTONYMS:** separate, split

mer|ger /'mɜːdʒə/ (mergers)

NOUN A **merger** is the joining together of two separate companies or organizations so that they become one. ○ [+ between] *a merger between two of Britain's biggest trades unions* ○ [+ of] *the proposed merger of two Japanese banks*

▶ **COLLOCATIONS:**
a merger **between/of** things
a merger between/of **companies/banks/parties**
propose/approve/complete/announce a merger
a merger **forms/fails/succeeds**
a **planned/three-way/friendly/bank** merger
a merger **talk/proposal/agreement**

▶ **SYNONYMS:** union, amalgamation

---

meta|phor /'metəfɔːr/ (metaphors) `LANGUAGE` `LITERATURE`

NOUN A **metaphor** is an imaginative way of describing something by referring to something else which is the same in a particular way. For example, if you want to say that someone is very shy and frightened of things, you might say that they are a mouse. ○ *the avoidance of 'violent expressions and metaphors' like 'kill two birds with one stone'* ○ *the writer's use of metaphor*

▶ **COLLOCATIONS:**
a metaphor **for** something
a metaphor for **life/something/everything**
become/provide a metaphor
a **visual/apt/mixed/fitting/perfect** metaphor

▶ **PHRASE:** metaphor and simile

meta|phori|cal /ˌmetə'fɒrɪkəl, AM -'fɔːr-/

ADJECTIVE You use the word **metaphorical** to indicate that you are not using words with their ordinary meaning, but are describing something by means of an image or symbol. ○ *It turns out Levy is talking in metaphorical terms.* ○ *The ship may be heading for the metaphorical rocks unless a buyer can be found.*

▶ COLLOCATIONS:
metaphorical **language/significance**
a metaphorical **meaning/narrative/approach**
▶ ANTONYM: literal

meta|phori|cal|ly /ˌmetəˈfɒrɪkli, AM -ˈfɔːr-/

ADVERB ○ *Her camel journey across the Western Australian desert was one of shedding burdens both literally and metaphorically.* ○ *If, metaphorically speaking, Derrida is reason, there was no choice about the matter.*

▶ PHRASES:
literally and metaphorically
metaphorically speaking
▶ ANTONYM: literally

---

me|teor|ol|ogy /ˌmiːtiəˈrɒlədʒi/   `GEOGRAPHY`

UNCOUNTABLE NOUN **Meteorology** is the study of the processes in the Earth's atmosphere that cause particular weather conditions, especially in order to predict the weather. ○ *Meteorology is science in action, and it happens in close to real time.* ○ *some interesting and important research in meteorology and evolutionary biology*

▶ COLLOCATIONS:
dynamic/comparative meteorology
a meteorology **forecaster/department**

me|teoro|logi|cal /ˌmiːtiərəˈlɒdʒɪkəl/

ADJECTIVE ○ *adverse meteorological conditions* ○ *The science of this meteorological phenomenon is well explained.*

▶ COLLOCATIONS:
a meteorological **phenomenon/office/department**
meteorological **conditions/data**

me|teor|olo|gist /ˌmiːtiəˈrɒlədʒɪst/ (meteorologists)

NOUN ○ *Meteorologists have predicted mild rains for the next few days.* ○ *A senior meteorologist with the National Climate Centre said the weather was linked to a major shift of climate.*

▶ COLLOCATIONS:
meteorologists **predict/forecast** *something*
meteorologists **warn** *people*

micro|bi|ol|ogy /ˌmaɪkrəʊbaɪˈɒlədʒi/ `BIOLOGY`

UNCOUNTABLE NOUN **Microbiology** is the branch of biology which is concerned with very small living things such as bacteria and their effects on people. ○ *a professor of microbiology and immunology* ○ *[+ of] The Center provides a valuable base for research into the immunology and microbiology of marine mammals.*

▶ **COLLOCATIONS:**
the microbiology **of** something
a microbiology **laboratory/professor/department**
medical microbiology

micro|bio|logi|cal /ˌmaɪkrəʊbaɪəˈlɒdʒɪkəl/

ADJECTIVE ○ *There is also regular in-house microbiological testing, to guard against eight different types of bacteria.* ○ *There was no evidence of a public health risk and to date there have been no adverse microbiological or chemical results.*

▶ **COLLOCATIONS:**
microbiological **testing/safety**
a microbiological **parameter/sample**

micro|bi|olo|gist /ˌmaɪkrəʊbaɪˈɒlədʒɪst/ (microbiologists)

NOUN ○ *a microbiologist at Liverpool University*

▶ **COLLOCATION:** a **medical/clinical** microbiologist

micro|ec|o|nom|ics /ˌmaɪkrəʊˌiːkəˈnɒmɪks, -ˌek-/ `ECONOMICS`
also **micro-economics**

UNCOUNTABLE NOUN **Microeconomics** is the branch of economics that is concerned with individual areas of economic activity, such as those within a particular company or relating to a particular market. ○ *He has 250 students in his microeconomics module.* ○ *Microeconomics is concerned with the efficient supply of particular products.*

▶ **RELATED WORD:** macroeconomics

micro|ec|o|nom|ic /ˌmaɪkrəʊˌiːkəˈnɒmɪk, -ˌek-/

ADJECTIVE ○ *a textbook on microeconomic theory* ○ *The integration of markets for manufactures has also changed the microeconomic environment.*

▶ **COLLOCATION:** microeconomic **theory/reform**
▶ **RELATED WORD:** macroeconomic

Mid|dle Ages /ˌmɪdəl ˈeɪdʒɪz/ HISTORY

PLURAL NOUN In European history, **the Middle Ages** was the period between the end of the Roman Empire in 476 AD and about 1500 AD, especially the later part of this period. ○ *In the Middle Ages theories about madness were concerned with possession by the Devil and damnation by God.* ○ *Up until the Middle Ages, however, the low-lying lands surrounding the Tor were indeed regularly flooded.*

---

mi|grate /maɪˈgreɪt, ACADEMIC WORD BIOLOGY SOCIAL SCIENCE
AM ˈmaɪgreɪt/ **(migrates, migrating, migrated)**

1 VERB If people **migrate**, they move from one place to another, especially in order to find work or to live somewhere for a short time. ○ [+ *to*] *People migrate to cities like Jakarta in search of work.* ○ *Farmers have learned that they have to migrate if they want to survive.*

▶ **COLLOCATIONS:**
  migrate **from/to** *somewhere*
  migrate from the **countryside**
  a **family/ancestor/peasant** migrates

▶ **SYNONYM:** move

2 VERB When birds, fish, or animals **migrate**, they move at a particular season from one part of the world or from one part of a country to another, usually in order to breed or to find new feeding grounds. ○ *Most birds have to fly long distances to migrate.* ○ *a dam system that kills the fish as they migrate from streams to the ocean*

▶ **COLLOCATIONS:**
  migrate **from/to** *somewhere*
  a **whale/bird/fish/animal** migrates
  migrate **north/south/inland**

▶ **PHRASE:** migrate for winter

mi|gra|tion /maɪˈgreɪʃən/ **(migrations)**

NOUN ○ [+ *of*] *the migration of Soviet Jews to Israel* ○ [+ *of*] *the migration of animals in the Serengeti*

▶ **COLLOCATIONS:**
  the migration **of** *someone/something*
  the migration of **birds/workers/jobs**
  ease/force/prevent/encourage migration
  bird/labour/mass/large-scale/illegal migration
  annual/seasonal/winter/spring migration
  a migration **pattern/route/issue/policy**

▶ **SYNONYMS:** movement, shift

m

mile|stone /ˈmaɪlstəʊn/ (milestones) `HISTORY`

NOUN A **milestone** is an important event in the history or development of something or someone. ○ [+ in] *He said the launch of the party represented a milestone in Zambian history.* ○ [+ for] *Starting school is a milestone for both children and parents.*

▶ **COLLOCATIONS:**
a milestone **in** *something*
a milestone **for** *someone*
mark/reach/celebrate/achieve a milestone
a **key/significant/major/important** milestone

▶ **PHRASE:** a milestone in history

mil|len|nium /mɪˈleniəm/ (millenniums or millennia) `HISTORY`

NOUN A **millennium** is a period of one thousand years, especially one which begins and ends with a year ending in 'ooo', for example the period from the year 1000 to the year 2000. [FORMAL] ○ *But then many Japanese companies are unsure whether they will survive until the new millennium at all.* ○ *France begins celebrating the millennium an hour before Britain, and Eurotunnel wants to make sure supplies are maintained.*

▶ **COLLOCATIONS:**
celebrate/approach/reach the millennium
a **new/next/second/third** millennium

mini|mize /ˈmɪnɪmaɪz/ `ACADEMIC WORD`
(minimizes, minimizing, minimized)

VERB If you **minimize** a risk, problem, or unpleasant situation, you reduce it to the lowest possible level, or prevent it increasing beyond that level. [in BRIT, also use **minimise**] ○ *Concerned people want to minimize the risk of developing cancer.* ○ *Many of these problems can be minimised by sensible planning.*

▶ **COLLOCATIONS:**
minimize a **risk/impact/effect**
minimize **damage**

▶ **ANTONYM:** maximize

mir|ror /ˈmɪrə/ (mirrors, mirroring, mirrored)

VERB If something **mirrors** something else, it has similar features to it, and therefore seems like a copy or representation of it. ○ *The book inevitably mirrors my own interests and experiences.* ○ *It touched off a row which mirrored exactly the ideological struggles taking place over diversity.*

▶ COLLOCATIONS: **closely/exactly/perfectly** mirror *something*

▶ SYNONYM: reflect

mis|in|ter|pret /ˌmɪsɪnˈtɜːprɪt/ ACADEMIC WORD
(misinterprets, misinterpreting, misinterpreted)

VERB If you **misinterpret** something, you understand it wrongly. ○ *The Prince's words had been misinterpreted.* ○ *people who deliberately misinterpret behaviour in order to sell papers*

▶ COLLOCATIONS:
deliberately/grossly/widely misinterpret *something*
misinterpret a **comment/remark/meaning**

▶ SYNONYM: misread

mis|in|ter|pre|ta|tion /ˌmɪsɪnˌtɜːprɪˈteɪʃən/ (misinterpretations)

NOUN ○ *The message left no room for misinterpretation.* ○ [+ *of*] *a misinterpretation of the aims and ends of socialism*

▶ COLLOCATIONS:
misinterpretation **of** *something*
a **deliberate/gross/serious** misinterpretation

m

mode /məʊd/ (modes) ACADEMIC WORD

1 NOUN A **mode** of life or behaviour is a particular way of living or behaving. [FORMAL] ○ [+ *of*] *the capitalist mode of production* ○ *He switched automatically into interview mode.*

▶ COLLOCATIONS:
a mode **of** *something*
a mode of **transport/production/transmission/expression/dress**

2 NOUN On some cameras or electronic devices, the different **modes** available are the different programs or settings that you can choose when you use them. ○ *when the camera is in manual mode* ○ *In automatic mode, shutter priority and aperture priority are selected by the mere touch of a button next to the control dial.*

▶ COLLOCATION: **manual/automatic** mode

mol|ecule /ˈmɒlɪkjuːl/ (molecules) CHEMISTRY

NOUN A **molecule** is the smallest amount of a chemical substance which can exist by itself. ○ *the hydrogen bonds between water molecules* ○ *At high temperatures, the two strands of the famous double helix that constitutes a DNA molecule come apart.*

▶ **COLLOCATIONS:**
a molecule **of** *something*
a molecule of **water**
a **biological/organic/circular** molecule
a **DNA/protein/oxygen** molecule
signal/bind/detect a molecule

mo|lecu|lar /məˈlekjʊlə/

ADJECTIVE ○ *the molecular structure of fuel* ○ *This coincided with the rise of molecular biology.*

▶ **COLLOCATIONS:**
molecular **biology/genetics**
a molecular **biologist/structure**

---

mo|men|tum /məʊˈmentəm/　[PHYSICS]

1 UNCOUNTABLE NOUN If a process or movement gains **momentum**, it keeps developing or happening more quickly and keeps becoming less likely to stop. ○ *This campaign is really gaining momentum.* ○ *[+ of] They are each anxious to maintain the momentum of the search for a solution.*

▶ **COLLOCATIONS:**
the momentum **of** *something*
gain/gather/maintain/keep/lose momentum

▶ **SYNONYM:** impetus

2 UNCOUNTABLE NOUN In physics, **momentum** is the mass of a moving object multiplied by its speed in a particular direction. ○ *[+ of] The position, energy, and momentum of particles vary over time in an unpredictable manner.* ○ *The planet's gravity can rob the comet of some of its orbital momentum.*

▶ **COLLOCATIONS:**
the momentum **of** *something*
angular/orbital momentum

---

mon|arch /ˈmɒnək/ (monarchs)　[POLITICS] [HISTORY]

NOUN The **monarch** of a country is the king, queen, emperor, or empress. ○ *His attempts to act as an absolute monarch eventually provoked a successful rebellion.* ○ *Australia is an effectively independent member of the Commonwealth, with the British monarch as Head of State.*

▶ **COLLOCATIONS:**
a monarch **reigns/rules**
a **crowned/exiled** monarch
a **constitutional/absolute** monarch

mon|ar|chy /ˈmɒnəki/ (monarchies)

1 NOUN A **monarchy** is a system in which a country has a monarch. ○ *In a few years we may no longer have a monarchy.* ○ *a serious debate on the future of the monarchy*

▶ **COLLOCATIONS:**
  abolish/overthrow/restore the monarchy
  a **constitutional/absolute** monarchy
  the **British/Danish/Saudi** monarchy

▶ **ANTONYM:** republic

2 NOUN A **monarchy** is a country that has a monarch. ○ *Until a few years ago the place had actually been a monarchy.* ○ *The country was a monarchy until 1973.*

▶ **ANTONYM:** republic

3 NOUN The **monarchy** is used to refer to the monarch and his or her family. ○ *The monarchy has to create a balance between its public and private lives.* ○ *the tendency for the monarchy and aristocracy to ally for their own purposes against the people*

▶ **SYNONYM:** royal family

---

mono|logue /ˈmɒnəlɒg, AM -lɔːg/   LANGUAGE   LITERATURE
(monologues)

1 NOUN In linguistics, a **monologue** is a long period of speech by one person. ○ *the communication characteristics of both monologue and dialogue*

2 NOUN A **monologue** is a long speech which is spoken by one person as an entertainment, or as part of an entertainment such as a play. ○ *a monologue based on the writing of Quentin Crisp* ○ *her brilliant series of dramatic monologues*

▶ **COLLOCATIONS:**
  a **comic/dramatic/opening** monologue
  deliver/perform/write a monologue

▶ **SYNONYM:** speech

▶ **RELATED WORD:** dialogue

---

mo|nopo|ly /məˈnɒpəli/ (monopolies)   BUSINESS

1 NOUN If a company, person, or state has a **monopoly on** something such as an industry, they have complete control over it, so that it is impossible for others to become involved in it. ○ [+ on] *Russian moves to end a state monopoly on land ownership.* ○ [+ over] *the governing party's monopoly over the media* ○ *an inquiry by the Monopolies Commission*

m

▶ COLLOCATIONS:
a monopoly **on/over** something
a monopoly on **power/trade**
enjoy/hold/grant/create/break a monopoly
a **virtual/near** monopoly

2 NOUN A **monopoly** is a company which is the only one providing a particular product or service. ○ *a state-owned monopoly* ○ *The television industry continues to rake in the profits as a protected, regulated monopoly.*

▶ COLLOCATION: a **state-owned/regulated/privatized** monopoly

mo|nopo|lize /məˈnɒpəlaɪz/
(monopolizes, monopolizing, monopolized)

VERB If you say that someone **monopolizes** something, you mean that they have a very large share of it and prevent other people from having a share. [in BRIT, also use **monopolise**] ○ *They are controlling so much cocoa that they are virtually monopolizing the market.* ○ *He himself is pushing quite aggressively to try to monopolize power in the government.*

▶ COLLOCATIONS:
monopolize a **conversation/market**
monopolize **power/trade**

▶ SYNONYMS: control, dominate

---

mo|noto|nous /məˈnɒtənəs/

ADJECTIVE Something that is **monotonous** is very boring because it has a regular, repeated pattern which never changes. ○ *It's monotonous work, like most factory jobs.* ○ *The food may get a bit monotonous, but there'll be enough of it.*

▶ COLLOCATIONS:
monotonous **regularity**
a monotonous **voice/task/diet**

▶ SYNONYM: repetitive
▶ ANTONYM: varied

mo|noto|nous|ly /məˈnɒtənəsli/

ADVERB ○ *The rain dripped monotonously from the trees.* ○ *It's almost impossible to say such sentences monotonously.*

mo|noto|ny /məˈnɒtəni/

UNCOUNTABLE NOUN The **monotony** of something is the fact that it never changes and is boring. ○ *[+ of] A night on the town may help to break the monotony of the week.* ○ *a life of secure monotony*

▶ **COLLOCATIONS:**
the monotony **of** *something*
the monotony of **life**
break/relieve/avoid the monotony of *something*

---

mon|soon /mɒn'suːn/ (monsoons) `GEOGRAPHY`

NOUN The **monsoon** is the season in Southern Asia when there is a lot of very heavy rain. ○ *the end of the monsoon* ○ *Light monsoon rain falls from June to September.*

▶ **COLLOCATIONS:**
monsoon **rain/conditions/floods**
the monsoon **season**
a **heavy/summer/annual/Asian/southwest** monsoon

---

moth|er tongue /ˈmʌðə ˌtʌŋ/ (mother tongues) `LANGUAGE`
also **mother-tongue**

NOUN Your **mother tongue** is the language that you learn from your parents when you are a baby. ○ *The islanders speak English, but their mother tongue is Gaelic.* ○ *A truly bilingual person has not one mother tongue, but two.*

▶ **SYNONYMS:** native tongue, first language

---

mo|tion /ˈməʊʃən/ (motions) `ACADEMIC WORD` `SCIENCE`

1 UNCOUNTABLE NOUN Motion is the activity or process of continually changing position or moving from one place to another. ○ *the laws governing light, sound, and motion* ○ *One group of muscles sets the next group in motion.*

▶ **COLLOCATIONS:**
planetary/slow/perpetual/constant motion
motion **sickness/detection**
a motion **detector/sensor**

▶ **SYNONYM:** movement

2 PHRASE If you say that someone **is going through the motions**, you think they are only saying or doing something because it is expected of them without being interested, enthusiastic, or sympathetic. ○ *The startled players went through the motions of the rest of the script.* ○ *The Home Office is "merely going through the motions so that they can come back with a compulsory scheme," he said.*

m

mo|tive /ˈməʊtɪv/ (motives)

`ACADEMIC WORD` `LAW`

NOUN Your **motive** for doing something is your reason for doing it. ○ [+ *for*] *Police have ruled out robbery as a motive for the killing.* ○ [+ *of*] *the motives and objectives of British foreign policy* ○ *The doctor's motive was to bring an end to his patient's suffering.*

▶ **COLLOCATIONS:**
a motive **for** something
a motive **of** someone/something
a motive for a **crime/attack/killing/shooting/murder**
question/establish/suggest/understand a motive
a **possible/apparent/clear/ulterior** motive

▶ **SYNONYMS:** reason, grounds, motivation

multi|cul|tur|al /ˌmʌltiˈkʌltʃərəl/
also **multi-cultural**

`SOCIOLOGY`

ADJECTIVE Multicultural means consisting of or relating to people of many different nationalities and cultures. ○ *children growing up in a multicultural society* ○ *The school has been attempting to bring a multicultural perspective to its curriculum.*

▶ **COLLOCATION:** a multicultural **society/community/approach**

multi|cul|tur|al|ism /ˌmʌltiˈkʌltʃərəlɪzəm/

UNCOUNTABLE NOUN Multiculturalism is a situation in which all the different cultural or racial groups in a society have equal rights and opportunities, and none is ignored or regarded as unimportant. ○ *Malik's attempt to start a debate about multiculturalism is commendable.* ○ *the latest troubled liberal to criticize multiculturalism*

▶ **COLLOCATION:** **embrace/celebrate** multiculturalism

Nn

nar|ra|tive /ˈnærətɪv/ (narratives)

1 NOUN A **narrative** is a story or an account of a series of events.
○ *a fast-moving narrative* ○ *Sloan began his narrative with the day of the murder.*

▶ **COLLOCATIONS:**
interrupt/write/create/construct a narrative
a **chronological/linear/autobiographical** narrative

▶ **SYNONYMS:** account, story

2 UNCOUNTABLE NOUN **Narrative** is the description of a series of events, usually in a novel. ○ *Neither author was very strong on narrative.* ○ *Nye's simple narrative style*

▶ **COLLOCATION: gripping/compelling/metaphorical** narrative

▶ **SYNONYM:** description

nar|rate /nəˈreɪt, AM ˈnæreɪt/ (narrates, narrating, narrated)

VERB If you **narrate** a story, you tell it from your own point of view. [FORMAL] ○ *The three of them narrate the same events from three perspectives.* ○ *The book is narrated by Richard Papen, a Californian boy.*

▶ **COLLOCATIONS:**
narrate a **tale/documentary/story**
a **character/voice/actor/writer** narrates

▶ **SYNONYMS:** tell, recount, relate

nar|ra|tor /nəˈreɪtə, AM ˈnæreɪt-/ (narrators)

NOUN ○ *Jules, the story's narrator, is an actress in her late thirties.* ○ [+ of] *Jay, the narrator of this depressing novella* ○ *the omniscient narrator's manipulation and control of the various voices within the text*

▶ **COLLOCATIONS:**
a narrator **of** something
a narrator of a **story/novel/documentary**
the **novel's/book's/film's** narrator
an **omniscient/unnamed/female/unreliable** narrator
the narrator **explains/describes/tells** something

NB /ˌen 'biː/ You write **NB** to draw someone's ACADEMIC STUDY
attention to what you are about to say or write. ○ *NB The opinions stated in this essay do not necessarily represent those of the Church of God Missionary Society.* ○ *NB The above course is subject to approval.*

→ see note at **cf.**

need|less /'niːdləs/

1 ADJECTIVE Something that is **needless** is completely unnecessary. ○ *But his death was so needless.* ○ *It has taken many centuries of needless suffering to close the gap of medical ignorance.*

▶ **COLLOCATIONS:**
needless **suffering/waste/expense/pain**
entirely/totally/almost needless

▶ **SYNONYMS:** unnecessary, useless

▶ **ANTONYMS:** essential, necessary

2 PHRASE You use **needless to say** when you want to emphasize that what you are about to say is obvious and to be expected in the circumstances. ○ *Soon the story was in all the papers, and the book, needless to say, became a best-seller.* ○ *Needless to say, the differences in diet between these two populations goes far beyond the amount of fat in it.* ○ *Our budgie got out of its cage while our cat was in the room. Needless to say, the cat moved quicker than me and caught it.*

▶ **SYNONYMS:** of course, obviously

need|less|ly /'niːdləsli/

ADVERB ○ *Half a million women die needlessly each year during childbirth.* ○ *The argument has been needlessly complicated by futile disagreements over the body count.*

▶ **COLLOCATIONS:**
needlessly **complex/cruel/prolonged**
needlessly **complicate/risk/waste** *something*
needlessly **alarm** *someone*

▶ **SYNONYM:** unnecessarily

ne|gate /nɪ'geɪt/ (negates, negating, negated)

VERB If one thing **negates** another, it causes that other thing to lose the effect or value that it had. [FORMAL] ○ *These weaknesses negated his otherwise progressive attitude towards the staff.* ○ *An amendment to the bill effectively negated federal regulations that require organic feed for farm animals.*

> ▶ **COLLOCATIONS:**
> negate a **benefit/need/advantage/effect**
> **completely/largely/effectively** negate *something*
> ▶ **SYNONYMS:** nullify, invalidate, cancel, neutralize
> ▶ **ANTONYMS:** confirm, affirm

ne|ga|tion /nɪˈgeɪʃən/

NOUN [FORMAL] ○ [+ of] *Unintelligible legislation is the negation of the rule of law and of parliamentary democracy.* ○ *The very foundation of this agency is a complete negation of the Quebec identity.*

> ▶ **COLLOCATIONS:**
> the negation **of** *something*
> the negation of **democracy**
> ▶ **SYNONYMS:** opposite, denial, contradiction
> ▶ **ANTONYMS:** confirmation, affirmation

---

ne|glect /nɪˈglekt/ (neglects, neglecting, neglected)

VERB If you **neglect** someone or something, you fail to look after them properly. ○ *The woman denied that she had neglected her child.* ○ *an ancient and neglected church*

> ▶ **COLLOCATIONS:**
> **unjustly/sadly/largely/shamefully** neglected
> neglect a **child/issue/need/area**
> a **parent/government/authority** neglects *something*
> ▶ **SYNONYM:** disregard
> ▶ **ANTONYM:** look after

● **Neglect** is also an uncountable noun. ○ *The town's old quayside is collapsing after years of neglect.* ○ *Niwano's business began to suffer from neglect.*

> ▶ **COLLOCATIONS:**
> neglect **of** *something*
> neglect of a **child**
> **willful/parental/gross** neglect
> ▶ **PHRASE:** neglect and abuse
> ▶ **SYNONYM:** disregard
> ▶ **ANTONYM:** care

neg|li|gent /ˈneglɪdʒənt/   `LAW`

ADJECTIVE If someone in a position of responsibility is **negligent**, they do not do something which they ought to do. ○ [+ in] *The jury determined that the airline was negligent in training and supervising the crew.* ○ *The Council had acted in a negligent manner.* ○ *claims against a negligent third party for personal injury*

▸ **COLLOCATIONS:**
negligent **in** *something*
a negligent **driver/act/employer**
negligent **homicide/driving/conduct**
criminally/grossly negligent

▸ **SYNONYMS:** neglectful, careless, remiss

▸ **ANTONYMS:** careful, attentive

neg|li|gence /ˈneglɪdʒəns/

UNCOUNTABLE NOUN If someone is guilty of **negligence**, they have failed to do something which they ought to do. [FORMAL] ○ *The soldiers were ordered to appear before a disciplinary council on charges of negligence.* ○ *He now stands accused of treating classified secrets with gross negligence.*

▸ **COLLOCATIONS:**
allege/prove/deny negligence
negligence **causes** *something*
gross/criminal/medical/professional negligence
a negligence **claim/case**

▸ **SYNONYMS:** carelessness, failure, dereliction, omission, oversight

neg|li|gible /ˈneglɪdʒɪbəl/

ADJECTIVE An amount or effect that is **negligible** is so small that it is not worth considering or worrying about. ○ *The pay that the soldiers received was negligible.* ○ *Senior managers are convinced that the strike will have a negligible impact.* ○ *cut down to negligible proportions*

▸ **COLLOCATIONS:**
a negligible **impact/effect/contribution**
a negligible **amount/level/risk/cost**
almost/essentially negligible

▸ **ANTONYM:** significant

EXTEND YOUR VOCABULARY

In everyday English, you often say that an amount or an effect is **small** or **slight**.

In more formal writing, you can describe a very small amount or effect as **marginal** or **minimal**. Both adjectives can be used with a positive or a negative meaning, depending on the context. ○ *The audit found only marginal improvements in services.* ○ *Necessary work was completed causing minimal disruption.*

You use **negligible** to say that something is so small that it is not worth considering. ○ *The radioactive iodine decays to negligible levels within a year.*

You use **trivial** or **insignificant** to say that something is so small and unimportant that it is not worth serious attention. **Trivial** especially expresses disapproval. ○ *unwarranted requests for reports on insignificant matters* ○ *Fierce debates erupt over the most trivial issues.*

---

nerv|ous sys|tem /ˈnɜːvəs ˌsɪstəm/ `BIOLOGY` `MEDICINE`
(nervous systems)

NOUN Your **nervous system** consists of all the nerves in your body together with your brain and spinal cord. ○ *It is oxygen that powers the nervous system and feeds the brain.* ○ *diseases of the brain and nervous system*

---

net /net/ `BUSINESS` `ECONOMICS`

1 ADJECTIVE A **net** amount is one which remains when everything that should be subtracted from it has been subtracted. [in BRIT, also use **nett**] ○ *a rise in sales and net profit* ○ *At the year end, net assets were £18 million.* ○ [+ *of*] *What you actually receive is net of deductions for the airfare and administration.*

● **Net** is also an adverb. ○ *Balances of £5,000 and above will earn 11 per cent gross, 8.25 per cent net.* ○ *a first year profit of around £50,000 net.* ○ *All bank and building society interest is paid net.*

2 ADJECTIVE The **net** weight of something is its weight without its container or the material that has been used to wrap it. [in BRIT, also use **nett**] ○ *350 mg net weight* ○ *the net weight of snacks packed*

3 ADJECTIVE A **net** result is a final result after all the details have been considered or included. [in BRIT, also use **nett**] ○ *We have a net gain of nearly 50 seats, the biggest for any party in Scotland.*

▶ COLLOCATIONS:
net **of** *something*
net **profit/income/value/assets**
net **weight**
a net **gain/loss/result**
▶ SYNONYMS: eventual, final, remaining
▶ RELATED WORD: gross

---

neu|ral /'njʊərəl, AM 'nʊr-/ `BIOLOGY` `MEDICINE`

ADJECTIVE **Neural** means relating to a nerve or to the nervous system.
○ *neural pathways in the brain* ○ *Brains consist of multiple neural networks.*
○ *Folic acid is important for helping to prevent neural tube defects such as spina bifida.*

▶ COLLOCATIONS:
a neural **network/pathway/defect/impulse**
neural **tissue**

neu|rol|ogy /njʊə'rɒlədʒi, AM nʊr-/

UNCOUNTABLE NOUN **Neurology** is the study of the structure, function, and diseases of the nervous system. ○ *He trained in neurology at the National Hospital for Nervous Diseases.* ○ *the university's department of clinical neurology*

▶ COLLOCATION: **clinical/paediatric/restorative** neurology

neu|rolo|gist /njʊə'rɒlədʒist, AM nʊr-/ (neurologists)

NOUN ○ *Dr Simon Shorvon, consultant neurologist of the Chalfont Centre for Epilepsy* ○ *Neurologists examine the nerves of the head and neck, muscle movement, balance, and other cognitive abilities.*

▶ COLLOCATIONS:
a **consultant/paediatric/clinical** neurologist
a neurologist **examines/treats/diagnoses** *someone/something*

---

neu|tron /'njuːtrɒn, AM 'nuːt-/ (neutrons) `PHYSICS`

NOUN A **neutron** is an atomic particle that has no electrical charge.
○ *Each atomic cluster is made up of neutrons and protons.* ○ *A typical neutron star is a mere 20 km in diameter, but contains as much mass as one or two Suns.*

▶ COLLOCATION: a neutron **star/bomb**
▶ RELATED WORD: proton

niche /niːʃ, AM nɪtʃ/ (niches)   `BUSINESS`

1 NOUN A **niche** in the market is a specific area of marketing which has its own particular requirements, customers, and products. ○ [+ *in*] *a niche in the toy market* ○ *Small companies can do extremely well if they can fill a specific market niche.*

▶ **COLLOCATIONS:**
   a niche **in** *something*
   find/carve/fill a niche
   a **lucrative/profitable/particular** niche
   a **market** niche

▶ **PHRASE:** a niche in the market

2 ADJECTIVE **Niche** marketing is the practice of dividing the market into specialized areas for which particular products are made. A **niche** market is one of these specialized areas. ○ *Many media experts see such all-news channels as part of a general move towards niche marketing.* ○ *The Japanese are able to supply niche markets because of their flexible production methods.*

▶ **COLLOCATIONS:**
   niche **marketing**
   a niche **market/brand/product**

none|the|less /ˌnʌnðəˈles/   `ACADEMIC WORD`

ADVERB **Nonetheless** means the same as **nevertheless**. [FORMAL] ○ *There was still a long way to go. Nonetheless, some progress had been made.* ○ *Many a country awash in violence has nonetheless managed the transition to democracy.* ○ *a second-hand gift, but nonetheless pleasurable for its recipient*

▶ **SYNONYMS:** nevertheless, however

no|tion|al /ˈnəʊʃənəl/

ADJECTIVE Something that is **notional** exists only in theory or as a suggestion or idea, but not in reality. [FORMAL] ○ *the notional value of state assets* ○ *He made around two hundred thousand pounds notional profit last year.* ○ *a notional concept of what makes a good parents*

▶ **COLLOCATION:** a notional **amount/value/profit/margin**

▶ **SYNONYM:** theoretical

▶ **ANTONYMS:** actual, real

no|tion|al|ly /ˈnəʊʃənəli/

ADVERB ○ *those who notionally supported the republic but did nothing in terms of action* ○ *That meant that he, notionally at least, outranked them all.*

▶ **SYNONYM:** theoretically

▶ **ANTONYM:** actually

not|with|stand|ing /ˌnɒtwɪðˈstændɪŋ/ `ACADEMIC WORD`

PREPOSITION If something is true **notwithstanding** something else, it is true in spite of that other thing. [FORMAL] ○ *He despised William Pitt, notwithstanding the similar views they both held.* ○ *Millen expected they would take action notwithstanding his absence.*

• **Notwithstanding** is also an adverb. ○ *His relations with colleagues, differences of opinion notwithstanding, were unfailingly friendly.*

▶ **SYNONYMS:** in spite of, despite

nu|ance /ˈnjuːɑːns, AM ˈnuː-/ **(nuances)** `LANGUAGE`

NOUN A **nuance** is a small difference in sound, feeling, appearance, or meaning. ○ [+ *of*] *We can use our eyes and facial expressions to communicate virtually every subtle nuance of emotion there is.* ○ *If you read the Koran or the Torah simply in translation, you miss the nuances of the original language.*

▶ **COLLOCATIONS:**
a nuance **of** *something*
a nuance of **language/expression/culture**
a **subtle/fine/emotional/social** nuance
understand/explain/appreciate/learn nuances

▶ **SYNONYM:** subtlety

nur|ture /ˈnɜːtʃə/ **(nurtures, nurturing, nurtured)** `BIOLOGY`

1 VERB If you **nurture** something such as a young child or a young plant, you care for it while it is growing and developing. [FORMAL] ○ *Parents want to know the best way to nurture and raise their child to adulthood.* ○ *The modern conservatory is not an environment for nurturing plants.*

▶ **COLLOCATIONS:**
nurture a **child/infant/youngster**
nurture a **seedling/plant**
a **mother/father/parent/teacher** nurtures *someone*
carefully/lovingly/actively nurture *something/someone*

▶ **SYNONYM:** care for

▶ **ANTONYM:** neglect

2 UNCOUNTABLE NOUN Nurture is care that is given to someone while they are growing and developing. ○ *The human organism learns partly by nature, partly by nurture.* ○ *Young men were living without maternal nurture.* ○ *Visiting the doctor can be a way of getting the nurture and attention you feel unable to ask for any other way.*

▶ **SYNONYMS:** care, rearing
▶ **RELATED WORD:** nature

---

nu|tri|ent /ˈnjuːtriənt, AM ˈnuː-/ (nutrients)   BIOLOGY

NOUN Nutrients are substances that help plants and animals to grow. ○ *the role of vegetable fibres, vitamins, minerals and other essential nutrients* ○ *Studies show that a depressed person often lacks several key nutrients.* ○ *daily nutrient intakes*

▶ **COLLOCATIONS:**
 absorb/supply/contain/lack nutrients
 essential/vital/basic/important nutrients
▶ **RELATED WORDS:** vitamin, mineral

---

n

Oo

obese /əʊˈbiːs/

MEDICINE

ADJECTIVE If someone is **obese**, they are extremely fat. ○ *The tendency to become obese is at least in part hereditary.* ○ *Obese people tend to have higher blood pressure than lean people.* ○ *More than 300 million people globally were considered obese in 2000.*

▶ COLLOCATIONS:
grossly/severely/extremely obese
morbidly/clinically obese
an obese **patient/child/man/woman**
become obese
deemed/considered obese

▶ SYNONYM: overweight

obesity /əʊˈbiːsɪti/

UNCOUNTABLE NOUN ○ *the excessive consumption of sugar that leads to problems of obesity* ○ *There is a real obesity epidemic in Eastern Europe, where they have 35 % obesity in some regions.* ○ *some facts about obesity*

▶ COLLOCATIONS:
tackle/prevent/fight/reduce/cause obesity
the obesity **epidemic/rate/problem**
childhood/child/adult obesity
morbid/extreme/severe obesity

ob|sta|cle /ˈɒbstəkəl/ (obstacles)

1 NOUN An **obstacle** is an object that makes it difficult for you to go where you want to go, because it is in your way. ○ *Most competition cars will only roll over if they hit an obstacle.* ○ *He left her to navigate her own way round the trolleys and other obstacles.*

▶ COLLOCATIONS:
an obstacle **blocks/prevents** *something/someone*
encounter/place/clear an obstacle

2 NOUN You can refer to anything that makes it difficult for you to do something as an **obstacle**. ○ *[+ to] Overcrowding remains a large obstacle to improving conditions.* ○ *To succeed, you must learn to overcome obstacles.*

▶ **COLLOCATIONS:**
an obstacle **to** *something*
face/overcome/tackle an obstacle
a **major/insurmountable/formidable** obstacle
an obstacle **stands/remains/exists**

▶ **SYNONYM:** hindrance

---

ob|struct /ɒbˈstrʌkt/ (obstructs, obstructing, obstructed)

1 VERB To **obstruct** someone or something means to make it difficult for them to move forward by blocking their path. ○ *A number of local people have been arrested for trying to obstruct lorries loaded with logs.* ○ *Drivers who park their cars illegally, particularly obstructing traffic flow, deserve to be punished.*

▶ **COLLOCATIONS:**
obstruct **traffic**
obstruct a **highway/footpath/artery/airway**
obstruct the **flow/passage** of *something*

▶ **SYNONYM:** block

2 VERB To **obstruct** progress or a process means to prevent it from happening properly. ○ *The authorities are obstructing a United Nations investigation.* ○ *He was convicted of obstructing justice for trying to evade a DNA test.*

▶ **COLLOCATIONS:**
obstruct **justice/progress**
obstruct an **investigation**
deliberately/willfully obstruct *something*

▶ **SYNONYMS:** prevent, hinder

ob|struc|tion /ɒbˈstrʌkʃən/ (obstructions)

NOUN ○ *parked drivers causing an obstruction* ○ *Mr Guest refused to let them in and now faces a criminal charge of obstruction.*

▶ **COLLOCATIONS:**
obstruction **of** *something*
obstruction of **justice**
obstruction of a **trial/charge**
remove/clear/cause an obstruction
deliberate/criminal obstruction

▶ **SYNONYMS:** blockage, prevention, hindrance

off|set /ˈɒfˌset, AM ˌɔːf-/ (offsets, offsetting)

The form **offset** is used in the present tense and is also the past tense and past participle of the verb.

VERB If one thing **is offset** by another, the effect of the first thing is reduced by the second, so that any advantage or disadvantage is cancelled out. ○ [+ by] *The increase in pay costs was more than offset by higher productivity.* ○ *The move is designed to help offset the shortfall in world oil supplies caused by the U.N. embargo.*

▶ COLLOCATIONS:
offset **by** *something*
partially/partly/largely/somewhat offset *something*
offset the **loss/cost/impact/effect** of *something*

▶ SYNONYMS: balance, counteract

omit /əʊˈmɪt/ (omits, omitting, omitted)

VERB If you **omit** something, you do not include it in an activity or piece of work, deliberately or accidentally. ○ [+ from] *Some details of the initial investment were inadvertently omitted from the financial statements.* ○ [+ from] *Our apologies to David Pannick for omitting his name from last week's article.*

▶ COLLOCATIONS:
omit *something* **from** *something*
omit **information**
omit a **word/fact/name/reference**
inadvertently/deliberately/carefully omit *something*

▶ SYNONYM: leave out
▶ ANTONYM: include

omis|sion /əʊˈmɪʃən/ (omissions)

1 **NOUN** An **omission** is something that has not been included or has not been done, either deliberately or accidentally. ○ [+ from] *The duke was surprised by his wife's omission from the guest list.* ○ *Williams is the most notable omission from the 33-strong party announced yesterday.*

2 **UNCOUNTABLE NOUN Omission** is the act of not including a particular person or thing or of not doing something. ○ [+ of] *the prosecution's seemingly malicious omission of recorded evidence* ○ *This scrupulous omission of certain facts is not unusual.*

▶ COLLOCATIONS:
the omission **of/from** *something*
the omission of a **fact/reference/detail**

a **glaring/notable/surprising** omission
deliberate/intentional omission
rectify/correct/contain an omission

▶ **SYNONYM:** exclusion
▶ **ANTONYM:** inclusion

---

om|niv|or|ous /ɒmˈnɪvərəs/ `BIOLOGY`

ADJECTIVE An **omnivorous** person or animal eats all kinds of food, including both meat and plants. [FORMAL] ○ *Brown bears are omnivorous, eating anything that they can get their paws on.* ○ *Like other starlings this species is omnivorous.*

▶ **RELATED WORDS:** carnivorous, herbivorous

omnivore /ˈɒmnɪˌvɔː/

NOUN An **omnivore** is an animal that eats both meat and plants. ○ *It is a tree-dwelling omnivore with a body resembling a cat's and the face of a weasel.* ○ *These teeth replace the premolars and molars found in herbivores and omnivores.*

▶ **RELATED WORDS:** carnivore, herbivore

---

opin|ion poll /əˈpɪnjən ˌpəʊl/ (opinion polls) `POLITICS` `SOCIOLOGY`

NOUN An **opinion poll** involves asking people's opinions on a particular subject, especially one concerning politics. ○ *Nearly three-quarters of people questioned in an opinion poll agreed with the government's decision.* ○ *So, though the opinion polls suggested otherwise, Major won, taking power with a majority of twenty-one.*

▶ **COLLOCATIONS:**
carry out an opinion poll
an opinion poll **suggests/shows/indicates** *something*

▶ **SYNONYM:** poll

---

opt /ɒpt/ (opts, opting, opted)

VERB If you **opt for** something, or **opt to** do something, you choose it or decide to do it in preference to anything else. ○ [+ *for*] *Depending on your circumstances you may wish to opt for one method or the other.* ○ [+ *to-inf*] *Our students can also opt to stay in residence.*

▶ **COLLOCATION:** opt **for** *something*

> **EXTEND YOUR VOCABULARY**
>
> In everyday English, you often use the verb **choose** to talk about making **choices**. ○ *She chose just two paint colours for the house.*
>
> In more formal writing, you can use **select** especially to talk about the action of choosing as part of a process. ○ *They surveyed a thousand randomly selected Americans.*
>
> You use **opt** or **decide** especially to talk about the outcome of your choice, your **decision**. ○ *An executive meeting last week opted for a more long-term approach.*

---

op|ti|cal /ˈɒptɪkəl/ `ENGINEERING` `PHYSICS`

ADJECTIVE **Optical** devices, processes, and effects involve or relate to vision, light, or images. ○ *optical telescopes* ○ *the optical effects of volcanic dust in the stratosphere* ○ *An optical zoom physically adjusts the lens to magnify a distant object.*

▶ **COLLOCATION:** an optical **illusion/fibre/telescope/zoom**

---

op|ti|mum /ˈɒptɪməm/ or **optimal**

ADJECTIVE The **optimum** or **optimal** level or state of something is the best level or state that it could achieve. [FORMAL] ○ *Aim to do some physical activity three times a week for optimum health.* ○ *regions in which optimal conditions for farming can be created*

▶ **COLLOCATION:** an optimum **level/size/condition**
▶ **SYNONYM:** ideal
▶ **ANTONYM:** worst

op|ti|mize /ˈɒptɪmaɪz/ (optimizes, optimizing, optimized)

VERB To **optimize** a plan, system, or machine means to arrange or design it so that it operates as smoothly and efficiently as possible. [FORMAL; in BRIT, also use **optimise**] ○ *Doctors are concentrating on understanding the disease better, and on optimizing the treatment.* ○ [+ for] *The new systems have been optimised for running Microsoft Windows.*

▶ **COLLOCATIONS:**
optimize *something* **for** *something*
optimize a **process/system/setting**

oral /ˈɔːrəl/   `LANGUAGE` `MEDICINE`

1 ADJECTIVE Oral communication is spoken rather than written. ○ *the written and oral traditions of ancient cultures* ○ *an oral agreement* ○ *our reliance upon oral records*

▶ **COLLOCATION:** an oral **argument/agreement/tradition/exam**

▶ **SYNONYM:** spoken

▶ **RELATED WORD:** written

2 ADJECTIVE You use **oral** to indicate that something is done with a person's mouth or relates to a person's mouth. ○ *good oral hygiene* ○ *Standard treatment is oral antibiotics.*

▶ **COLLOCATIONS:**
oral **hygiene**
an oral **contraceptive/cavity/vaccine/pill**

oral|ly /ˈɔːrəli/

ADVERB ○ *tablets taken orally* ○ *their ability to present ideas orally and in writing*

▶ **COLLOCATIONS:**
communicate/deliver orally
administer/take/give orally

---

or|bit /ˈɔːbɪt/ (orbits, orbiting, orbited)   `GEOGRAPHY` `SCIENCE`

1 NOUN An **orbit** is the curved path in space that is followed by an object going round and round a planet, moon, or star. ○ *Mars and Earth have orbits which change with time.* ○ *The planet is probably in orbit around a small star.* ○ *the radius of the orbit of the planet Jupiter round the sun*

▶ **COLLOCATIONS:**
the orbit **of** *something*
in/into orbit
enter/reach the orbit of *something*
the **Earth's/planet's/moon's** orbit

2 VERB If something such as a satellite **orbits** a planet, moon, or sun, it moves around it in a continuous, curving path. ○ *In 1957 the Soviet Union launched the first satellite to orbit the Earth.* ○ *About 120 planets have been discovered orbiting other stars.*

▶ **COLLOCATION:** orbit the **Earth/planet/moon/sun**

▶ **SYNONYM:** circle

ori|ent /ˈɔːrient/

ACADEMIC WORD

(orients, orienting, oriented) or **orientate**

VERB When you **orient yourself to** a new situation or course of action, you learn about it and prepare to deal with it. [FORMAL] ○ [+ towards/to] *You will need the time to orient yourself to your new way of eating.* ○ [+ towards/ to] *orienting students to new ways of thinking about their participation in classroom learning* ○ [+ in] *Anxiety comes from not being able to orient yourself in your own existence.*

▶ **COLLOCATIONS:**
orient someone **to/towards/in** something
orient **yourself**

▶ **SYNONYMS:** accustom, familiarize

ori|ent|ed /ˈɔːrientɪd/ or **orientated**

ADJECTIVE If someone **is oriented towards** or **oriented to** a particular thing or person, they are mainly concerned with that thing or person. ○ [+ towards] *It seems almost inevitable that North African economies will still be primarily oriented towards Europe.* ○ [+ to] *Most students here are oriented to computers.*

▶ **COLLOCATION:** oriented **to/towards** something

ori|en|ta|tion /ˌɔːriənˈteɪʃən/ (orientations)

NOUN If you talk about the **orientation** of an organization or country, you are talking about the kinds of aims and interests it has. ○ *a marketing orientation* ○ *To a society which has lost its orientation he has much to offer.* ○ *The movement is liberal and social democratic in orientation.*

▶ **COLLOCATION:** orientation **towards** something

▶ **SYNONYM:** inclination

ortho|dox /ˈɔːθədɒks/

ADJECTIVE **Orthodox** beliefs, methods, or systems are ones which are accepted or used by most people. ○ *Payne gained a reputation for sound, if orthodox, views.* ○ *Many of these ideas are now being incorporated into orthodox medical treatment.* ○ *orthodox police methods*

▶ **COLLOCATIONS:**
strictly/fairly/religiously orthodox
orthodox **medicine/theology/religion/economics**

▶ **SYNONYM:** conventional

▶ **ANTONYM:** unorthodox

over|popu|la|tion /ˌəʊvəˌpɒpjʊˈleɪʃən/ SOCIAL SCIENCE

UNCOUNTABLE NOUN If there is a problem of **overpopulation** in an area, there are more people living there than can be supported properly. ○ [+ *in*] *young persons who are concerned about overpopulation in the world* ○ *Bavaria, like all the German lands, was by 1600 suffering from alarming overpopulation, causing food shortages.*

▶ **COLLOCATION:** overpopulation **in** *a place*

▶ **SYNONYM:** overcrowding

over|weight /ˌəʊvəˈweɪt/ MEDICINE

ADJECTIVE Someone who is **overweight** weighs more than is considered healthy. ○ *Being even moderately overweight increases your risk of developing high blood pressure.* ○ *Studies show that overweight children are generally teased more on average than their peers.*

▶ **COLLOCATIONS:**
an overweight **adult/teenager/patient/child/person**
grossly/slightly/seriously overweight

▶ **SYNONYM:** obese

▶ **ANTONYMS:** slim, underweight

o

Pp

pa|per /ˈpeɪpə/ (papers)

ACADEMIC STUDY

NOUN A **paper** is a long, formal piece of writing about an academic subject.
- ○ [+ *in*] *He just published a paper in the journal Nature analysing the fires.*
- ○ *a controversial paper suggesting that many SIDS cases are caused by a rare inherited condition*

▶ **COLLOCATIONS:**
a paper **in/on** *something*
a paper in a **journal**
a paper on a **topic/subject**
publish/write/present a paper
a paper **says/reports/reveals/argues** *something*
a **scientific/academic/unpublished/research** paper

ACADEMIC WRITING: Academic texts

University students often write **essays** or **assignments**.
A **dissertation** is a longer piece of writing, usually at the end of
a degree course and a **thesis** is a long research project written by
a PhD student.

A **paper** is a formal piece of academic writing usually to be presented
at a conference or published in a **journal** or **periodical**. ○ *Albert
Einstein published three seminal research papers which changed scientific
thinking about the universe.*

In American English, a **paper** can also be a piece of writing by
a student at high school or univeristy.

You can also describe a piece of writing in an **academic journal** as an
article. ○ *She has published several journal articles on these areas.*

---

para|digm /ˈpærədaɪm/ (paradigms)

ACADEMIC WORD

NOUN A **paradigm** is a model for something which explains it or shows
how it can be produced. [FORMAL] ○ [+ *of*] *a new paradigm of production*
○ *a course that challenges the traditional paradigm adopted in conventional
faculties*

▶ **COLLOCATIONS:**
a paradigm **of** something
a **new/dominant/scientific** paradigm
shift/change/adopt/challenge a paradigm

▶ **SYNONYMS:** model, pattern

---

pa|ram|eter /pəˈræmɪtə/ (parameters) `ACADEMIC WORD`

NOUN Parameters are factors or limits which affect the way that something can be done or made. [FORMAL] ○ [+ of] *That would be enough to make sure we fell within the parameters of our loan agreement.* ○ *some of the parameters that determine the taste of a wine*

▶ **COLLOCATIONS:**
the parameters **of** something
within the parameters of something
define/set/establish parameters
broad/certain/various/acceptable parameters

▶ **SYNONYM:** limits

---

para|phrase /ˈpærəfreɪz/ `ACADEMIC STUDY` `LANGUAGE`
(paraphrases, paraphrasing, paraphrased)

1 VERB If you **paraphrase** someone or **paraphrase** something that they have said or written, you express what they have said or written in a different way. ○ *Parents, to paraphrase Philip Larkin, can seriously damage your health.* ○ *Baxter paraphrased the contents of the press release.*

▶ **COLLOCATIONS:**
paraphrase *someone/something*
paraphrase a **cliché/quotation/passage**

▶ **SYNONYM:** summarize

2 NOUN A **paraphrase** of something written or spoken is the same thing expressed in a different way. ○ [+ from] *In addition, quotations and paraphrases from an interview can give your paper immediacy and authority.* ○ [+ of] *You must remember to cite all your paraphrases and summaries of other writers' ideas.*

▶ **COLLOCATION:** a paraphrase **from/of** something

▶ **SYNONYMS:** summary, rewording

---

para|site /ˈpærəsaɪt/ (parasites) `BIOLOGY`

NOUN A **parasite** is a small animal or plant that lives on or inside a larger animal or plant, and gets its food from it. ○ *Victims have tested positive for intestinal parasites, bacterial infection and viruses which cause fever and* *diarrhoea.* ○ *The infection is caused by a tiny parasite which can affect humans and pets.*

▶ COLLOCATIONS:
a **malarial/intestinal/microscopic** parasite
a parasite **causes** *something*
a parasite **infects/inhabits** *someone/something*
kill/attack/transmit/spread/carry a parasite

para|sit|ic /ˌpærəˈsɪtɪk/ also **parasitical**

ADJECTIVE ○ *Will global warming mean the spread of tropical parasitic diseases?*
○ *tiny parasitic insects*

▶ COLLOCATIONS:
a parasitic **wasp/worm/organism**
a parasitic **infection/disease/illness**

---

par|ti|cle /ˈpɑːtɪkəl/ (particles)   PHYSICS

1 NOUN A **particle of** something is a very small piece or amount of it.
○ *a particle of hot metal* ○ [+ *of*] *There is a particle of truth in his statement.*
○ *food particles*

▶ COLLOCATIONS:
a particle **of** *something*
a particle of **dust/food**
a **tiny/small** particle
a **dust/soil/soot** particle

2 NOUN In physics, a **particle** is a piece of matter smaller than an atom, for example an electron or a proton ○ [+ *from*] *Fewer cosmic rays reach the Earth when the Sun is very active, because the charged particles from the Sun deflect them.* ○ *Molecules, atoms, and even elementary particles all fall to bits at high temperatures.*

▶ COLLOCATIONS:
a particle **from/of** *something*
a particle of **matter/light/energy**
a **subatomic/elementary/radioactive/charged** particle

---

pas|sive /ˈpæsɪv/   ACADEMIC WORD

1 ADJECTIVE If you describe someone as **passive**, you mean that they do not take action but instead let things happen to them. ○ *His passive attitude made things easier for me.* ○ *Even passive acceptance of the regime was a kind of collaboration.*

▶ **COLLOCATIONS:**
passive **acceptance/obedience**
a passive **attitude**

▶ **ANTONYM:** active

2 ADJECTIVE Passive resistance involves showing opposition to the people
in power in your country by not co-operating with them and protesting
in non-violent ways. ○ *They made it clear that they would only exercise passive
resistance in the event of a military takeover.* ○ *a policy of passive resistance or
peaceful demonstration for political purposes*

▶ **SYNONYM:** peaceful

▶ **ANTONYM:** active

---

pa|tent /ˈpeɪtənt, ʌm ˈpæt-/   SCIENCE BUSINESS
(patents, patenting, patented)

1 NOUN A **patent** is an official right to be the only person or company
allowed to make or sell a new product for a certain period of time. ○ [+ *on*]
P&G applied for a patent on its cookies. ○ [+ *for*] *He held a number of patents for
his many innovations.* ○ *It sued Centrocorp for patent infringement.*

▶ **COLLOCATIONS:**
a patent **on/for** *something*
grant/issue/own/infringe a patent
a patent **pends/expires**
a **questionable/exclusive/worldwide/existing** patent
a **drug/product/software** patent
patent **infringement/protection**
a patent **application/dispute/attorney**

▶ **RELATED WORD:** copyright

2 VERB If you **patent** something, you obtain a patent for it. ○ *He patented
the idea that the atom could be split.* ○ *The invention has been patented by the
university.* ○ *a patented machine called the VCR II*

▶ **COLLOCATIONS:**
patent a **method/technique/design**
patent a **device/invention**

▶ **PHRASE:** invent and patent something

---

pa|ter|nal /pəˈtɜːnəl/   BIOLOGY SOCIOLOGY

1 ADJECTIVE Paternal is used to describe feelings or actions which are
typical of those of a kind father towards his child. ○ *paternal love for his
children* ○ *Maternal and paternal instincts are those behaviours which a mother
or father performs without conscious thought.*

▶ **COLLOCATIONS:**
paternal **pride/affection/devotion**
a paternal **instinct**

▶ **RELATED WORD:** maternal

▶ **SYNONYM:** fatherly

2 ADJECTIVE A **paternal** relative is one that is related through a person's father rather than their mother. ○ *my paternal grandparents* ○ *His paternal uncle had been diagnosed as manic depressive.*

▶ **COLLOCATION:** a paternal **grandfather/grandmother/uncle/aunt**

▶ **RELATED WORD:** maternal

---

pa|thol|ogy /pəˈθɒlədʒi/   MEDICINE BIOLOGY

UNCOUNTABLE NOUN Pathology is the study of the way diseases and illnesses develop. ○ *Anatomy, physiology, and pathology are studied to a similar level.* ○ *One part was sent to a pathology laboratory for viewing under a microscope.*

▶ **COLLOCATIONS:**
forensic/social/molecular pathology
a pathology **department/report/laboratory**

pa|tholo|gist /pəˈθɒlədʒɪst/ (pathologists)

NOUN A **pathologist** is someone who studies or investigates diseases and illnesses, and examines dead bodies in order to find out the cause of death. ○ *But a pathologist found that a 6cm cut on her head was consistent with a blow, possibly from a hammer.* ○ *Most forensic pathologists have little experience in examining infant deaths.*

▶ **COLLOCATIONS:**
a **forensic/paediatric/veterinary** pathologist
a pathologist **finds/confirms/examines** *something*

---

peer /pɪə/ (peers)   SOCIOLOGY

NOUN Your **peers** are the people who are the same age as you or who have the same status as you. ○ *children who are much cleverer than their peers* ○ *His engaging personality made him popular with his peers.*

▶ **COLLOCATIONS:**
working/fellow/industry peers
a peer **group**
peer **pressure**

▶ **SYNONYMS:** associate, colleague

peer review /ˈpɪə rɪvjuː/ ACADEMIC STUDY

UNCOUNTABLE NOUN Peer review is the evaluation by fellow specialists of
research that someone has done in order to assess its suitability for
publication or further development. ○ *Future funding is influenced by the
process of peer review.* ○ *At the research end most decisions are made by some
form of peer review.*

▶ **COLLOCATION:** a peer review **process**

pen|ta|gon /ˈpentəgən, AM -gɑːn/ **(pentagons)**

NOUN A **pentagon** is a shape with five sides. ○ *Workspace for each module of
the spacecraft is physically arranged as a pentagon seating five persons.* ○ *One
thinks of the common soccer ball which is actually composed of a pattern of
hexagons and pentagons.*

pe|nul|ti|mate /peˈnʌltɪmət/

ADJECTIVE The **penultimate** thing in a series of things is the last but one.
[FORMAL] ○ *on the penultimate day of the Asian Games* ○ *in the penultimate
chapter*

▶ **COLLOCATIONS:**
  the penultimate **round/stage/phase**
  the penultimate **chapter/paragraph**

▶ **RELATED WORD:** last

per capi|ta /pə ˈkæpɪtə/

ADJECTIVE The **per capita** amount of something is the total amount of it in
a country or area divided by the number of people in that country or area.
○ *They have the world's largest per capita income.* ○ *The per capita consumption
of alcohol has dropped over the past two years.*

▶ **COLLOCATION:** the per capita **income/output/GDP/consumption**

● **Per capita** is also an adverb. ○ *Ethiopia has almost the lowest oil
consumption per capita in the world.* ○ *This year Americans will eat about 40%
more fresh apples per capita than the Japanese.*

▶ **SYNONYM:** per head

pe|ri|od|ic /ˌpɪəriˈɒdɪk/ ACADEMIC WORD

ADJECTIVE Periodic events or situations happen occasionally, at fairly
regular intervals. ○ *Periodic checks are taken to ensure that high standards are
maintained.* ○ *periodic bouts of illness*

▶ **COLLOCATIONS:**
a periodic **update/inspection/review**
periodic **payments**
▶ **SYNONYMS:** regular, periodical

pe|ri|odi|cal /ˌpɪəriˈɒdɪkəl/　ACADEMIC STUDY

ADJECTIVE Periodical events or situations happen occasionally, at fairly regular intervals. ○ *She made periodical visits to her dentist.* ○ *periodical screening for cancer*

▶ **COLLOCATION:** a periodical **payment/bout/review**
▶ **SYNONYMS:** regular, periodic

pe|ri|odi|cal|ly /ˌpɪəriˈɒdɪkli/

ADVERB ○ *Meetings are held periodically to monitor progress on the case.* ○ *Police were periodically patrolling the area.*

▶ **COLLOCATION:** **review/revise/check/evaluate** something periodically
▶ **SYNONYM:** regularly

---

pe|ri|odi|cal /ˌpɪəriˈɒdɪkəl/ (periodicals)

NOUN Periodicals are magazines, especially serious or academic ones, that are published at regular intervals. ○ *The walls would be lined with books and periodicals.* ○ *This important periodical is published six times annually and analyses all aspects of workers' compensation insurance.*

→ see note at **paper**

▶ **COLLOCATIONS:**
a **literary/popular/educational** periodical
a **weekly/monthly** periodical
publish/read/edit a periodical

---

pe|ri|od|ic ta|ble /ˌpɪəriɒdɪk ˈteɪbəl/　CHEMISTRY

NOUN In chemistry, **the periodic table** is a table showing the chemical elements arranged according to their atomic numbers. ○ *The periodic table once predicted the existence of elements that had yet to be discovered.* ○ *Some textbooks even state that quantum theory predicts the structure of the periodic table.*

---

perk /pɜːk/ (perks, perking, perked)　BUSINESS

NOUN Perks are special benefits that are given to people who have a particular job or belong to a particular group. ○ *a company car, private medical insurance and other perks* ○ *[+ of] One of the perks of being a student is cheap travel.*

▶ **COLLOCATIONS:**
a perk **of** *something*
a perk of a **job**
enjoy/offer/receive a perk
a **generous/executive/additional** perk
travel/tax/economy perks

▶ **SYNONYMS:** advantage, benefit

perk up

1 **PHRASAL VERB** If something **perks** you **up** or if you **perk up**, you become cheerful and lively, after feeling tired, bored, or depressed. ○ *The barman and the reps had perked up considerably.* ○ *suggestions to make you smile and perk you up*

▶ **SYNONYM:** cheer up

2 **PHRASAL VERB** If you **perk** something **up**, you make it more interesting. ○ *To make the bland taste more interesting, the locals began perking it up with local produce.* ○ *Psychological twists perk up an otherwise predictable storyline.*

3 **PHRASAL VERB** If sales, prices, or economies **perk up**, or if something **perks** them **up**, they begin to increase or improve. ○ *House prices could perk up during the autumn.* ○ *Anything that could save the company money and perk up its cash flow was examined.*

▶ **SYNONYM:** increase

per|me|ate /ˈpɜːmieɪt/ (permeates, permeating, permeated)

VERB If an idea, feeling, or attitude **permeates** a system or **permeates** society, it affects every part of it or is present throughout it. ○ *Bias against women permeates every level of the judicial system.* ○ [+ *through*] *An obvious change of attitude at the top will permeate through the system.*

▶ **COLLOCATIONS:**
permeate **through** *something*
permeate **society/consciousness/everything**
permeate a **culture/organization**
a **mood/attitude/influence/atmosphere** permeates *something*

per|me|able /ˈpɜːmiəbəl/

ADJECTIVE If a substance is **permeable**, something such as water or gas can pass through it or soak into it. ○ [+ *to*] *A number of products have been developed which are permeable to air and water.* ○ *Selectively permeable membranes are thought to have tiny pores which allow the rapid passage of small water molecules.*

▶ COLLOCATIONS:
permeable **to** *something*
permeable to **water/oxygen/molecules**
a permeable **membrane/material/boundary**
▶ ANTONYM: impermeable

---

per|pe|trate /ˈpɜːpɪtreɪt/ (perpetrates, perpetrating, perpetrated) LAW

VERB If someone **perpetrates** a crime or any other immoral or harmful act, they do it. [FORMAL] ○ *A high proportion of crime in any country is perpetrated by young males in their teens and twenties.* ○ [+ on] *Tremendous wrongs were being perpetrated on the poorest and least privileged human beings.*

▶ COLLOCATIONS:
perpetrate *something* **on** *someone*
perpetrate **fraud/genocide/violence**
perpetrate a crime/massacre/atrocity
intentionally/allegedly perpetrate *something*
▶ SYNONYM: commit

per|pe|tra|tor /ˈpɜːpɪtreɪtə/ (perpetrators)

NOUN ○ [+ of] *The perpetrator of this crime must be traced.* ○ *At some point the perpetrator shot him twice in the torso.*

▶ COLLOCATIONS:
a perpetrator **of** *something*
a perpetrator of a **crime/atrocity/attack**
a perpetrator of **violence/genocide/abuse**
prosecute/identify/punish a perpetrator
▶ SYNONYM: culprit

---

per|sist /pəˈsɪst/ (persists, persisting, persisted) ACADEMIC WORD

VERB If something undesirable **persists**, it continues to exist. ○ *Contact your doctor if the cough persists.* ○ [+ for] *These problems persisted for much of the decade.* ○ [+ in] *The ceremony still persists in some parishes.*

▶ COLLOCATIONS:
persist **for** *a time*
persist **in** *a place*
a **rumour/symptom/doubt** persists
fighting/speculation/suspicion persists
still/obstinately/stubbornly persist
▶ SYNONYMS: continue, exist, endure

per|sis|tent /pəˈsɪstənt/

ADJECTIVE Something that is **persistent** continues to exist or happen for a long time; used especially about bad or undesirable states or situations. ○ Her position as national leader has been weakened by persistent fears of another coup attempt. ○ The public has to be reassured that children are safe from persistent predatory offenders.

▶ **COLLOCATIONS:**
a persistent **rumour/offender**
a persistent **infection/cough/headache**
persistent **speculation/refusal/rain**
more/increasingly/stubbornly persistent

▶ **SYNONYMS:** continuous, constant, relentless, perpetual, incessant

per|sis|tent|ly /pəˈsɪstəntli/

ADVERB ○ The allegations have been persistently denied by ministers. ○ People with rail season tickets will get refunds if trains are persistently late.

▶ **COLLOCATIONS:**
persistently **refuse/fail/deny** something
persistently **high/low/dangerous/weak**

per|va|sive /pəˈveɪsɪv/

ADJECTIVE Something, especially something bad, that is **pervasive** is present or felt throughout a place or thing. [FORMAL] ○ the pervasive influence of the army in national life ○ So pervasive is this propaganda it has become part of the fabric of women's lives and isn't even recognised as propaganda. ○ No individual company is poised to dominate the era of pervasive computing.

▶ **COLLOCATIONS:**
a pervasive **influence/fear/presence/smell**
pervasive **corruption/disorder/computing**
increasingly/dangerously pervasive

pes|ti|cide /ˈpestɪsaɪd/ (pesticides) `BIOLOGY`

NOUN **Pesticides** are chemicals which farmers put on their crops to kill harmful insects. ○ Many environmental activists and food experts are keen to ban pesticides from British farming. ○ In agricultural settings, poisonings can occur when agricultural workers misuse pesticides.

▶ **COLLOCATIONS:**
use/spray/apply/contain pesticides
ban/avoid pesticides
natural/synthetic/toxic/harmful/agricultural pesticides

Pet|ri dish /ˈpetrɪ ˌdɪʃ/ (Petri dishes) `SCIENCE`

NOUN A **Petri dish** is a flat dish with a lid, used in laboratories for producing cultures of microorganisms. ○ *The embryos are placed in Petri dishes which have tags attached to the bottom.* ○ *Other exhibits allowed visitors to watch bacteria grow in petri dishes.*

phar|ma|ceu|ti|cal /ˌfɑːməˈsuːtɪkəl/ `MEDICINE` `BUSINESS`
(pharmaceuticals)

1 ADJECTIVE Pharmaceutical means connected with the industrial production of medicine. ○ *a Swiss pharmaceutical company* ○ *The pharmaceutical industry is the second-largest industry in the world, the largest being the armaments industry.*

▶ **COLLOCATIONS:**
  a pharmaceutical **company/firm/manufacturer/product**
  the pharmaceutical **industry/sector**

2 PLURAL NOUN Pharmaceuticals are medicines. ○ *Antibiotics were of no use; neither were other pharmaceuticals.* ○ *The family firm had for decades supplied its pharmaceuticals to the third world.*

phar|ma|col|ogy /ˌfɑːməˈkɒlədʒi/ `MEDICINE`

UNCOUNTABLE NOUN Pharmacology is the branch of science relating to drugs and medicines. ○ *Their eldest daughter studied pharmacology and English at London University before becoming a fashion journalist.* ○ *He was appointed professor of clinical pharmacology in Aberdeen in 1985.*

▶ **COLLOCATION: clinical/molecular** pharmacology

phar|ma|co|logi|cal /ˌfɑːməkəˈlɒdʒɪkəl/

ADJECTIVE ○ *As little as 50mg of caffeine can produce pharmacological effects.* ○ *Pharmacological treatment of schizophrenia and related psychoses is usually for the long-term.*

▶ **COLLOCATIONS:**
  pharmacological **intervention/therapy/treatment**
  a pharmacological **effect/property**

phar|ma|colo|gist /ˌfɑːməˈkɒlədʒist/ (pharmacologists)

NOUN ○ *a pharmacologist from the University of California* ○ *This clinical pharmacologist says there's no biological reason why antibiotics should cause cancer.*

▶ **COLLOCATION: a clinical** pharmacologist

p

283 | **pilot study**

photo|syn|the|sis /ˌfəʊtəʊˈsɪnθəsɪs/ BIOLOGY

UNCOUNTABLE NOUN **Photosynthesis** is the way that green plants make their food using sunlight. ○ *Chloroplasts contain the green pigment chlorophyll and photosynthesis occurs in them.* ○ *It is sunlight that provides the energy for the process of photosynthesis so that plants may grow.*

▶ COLLOCATIONS:
   stimulate/perform photosynthesis
   photosynthesis **occurs**
   oxygenic/artificial photosynthesis

physio|thera|py /ˌfɪziəʊˈθerəpi/ MEDICINE

UNCOUNTABLE NOUN **Physiotherapy** is medical treatment for problems of the joints, muscles, or nerves, which involves doing exercises or having part of your body massaged or warmed. ○ *He'll need intensive physiotherapy.* ○ *An alternative is to visit an osteopathy or physiotherapy clinic at an NHS health centre.*

▶ COLLOCATIONS:
   undergo/receive/need physiotherapy
   intensive/extensive/daily physiotherapy
   physiotherapy **treatment**
   a physiotherapy **clinic/department/student**

physio|thera|pist /ˌfɪziəʊˈθerəpɪst/ (physiotherapists)

NOUN ○ *Chartered physiotherapists are trained to degree level which is followed by two years experience in an NHS hospital.* ○ *Disabling conditions such as cerebral palsy and Parkinson's Disease are treated by physiotherapists.*

▶ COLLOCATIONS:
   a **chartered/qualified/personal** physiotherapist
   a physiotherapist **treats/assesses** *something/someone*

pilot study /ˈpaɪlət stʌdi/ ACADEMIC STUDY

NOUN A **pilot study** is a small-scale experiment or set of observations undertaken to decide how and whether to launch a full-scale project. ○ *The trials follow the success of a pilot study, revealed by New Scientist in 1999.* ○ [+ of] *This child is one of a number who are taking part in a pilot study of children exposed to drugs in the womb.*

▶ COLLOCATION: a pilot study **of** *something*

pin|point /'pɪnpɔɪnt/ (pinpoints, pinpointing, pinpointed)

VERB If you **pinpoint** the cause of something, you discover or explain the cause exactly. ○ *It was almost impossible to pinpoint the cause of death.* ○ [+ as] *The commission pinpoints inadequate housing as a basic problem threatening village life.*

▶ **COLLOCATIONS:**
pinpoint something **as** something
pinpoint the **location/cause/origin** of something
accurately/exactly/precisely pinpoint something

▶ **SYNONYM:** identify

piv|ot|al /'pɪvətəl/

ADJECTIVE A **pivotal** role, point, or figure in something is one that is very important and affects the success of that thing. ○ *The Court of Appeal has a pivotal role in the English legal system.* ○ *The elections may prove to be pivotal in Colombia's political history.*

▶ **COLLOCATIONS:**
pivotal **in** something
a pivotal **role/moment/figure/point/position**
potentially/absolutely pivotal
prove/become pivotal

▶ **SYNONYMS:** critical, crucial

▶ **ANTONYM:** peripheral

pla|gia|rism /'pleɪdʒərɪzəm/ ACADEMIC STUDY

UNCOUNTABLE NOUN **Plagiarism** is the practice of using or copying someone else's idea or work and pretending that you thought of it or created it. ○ *The punishment depends largely on the extent of the plagiarism committed.* ○ *"It's almost impossible to control or contain plagiarism now,"* he said.

▶ **COLLOCATIONS:**
detect/commit/avoid plagiarism
deliberate/accidental/blatant/academic plagiarism
a plagiarism **allegation/scandal**

pla|gia|rize /'pleɪdʒəraɪz/ (plagiarizes, plagiarizing, plagiarized)

VERB If someone **plagiarizes** another person's idea or work, they use it or copy it and pretend that they thought of it or created it. [in BRIT, also use **plagiarise**] ○ *Moderates are plagiarizing his ideas in hopes of wooing voters.* ○ [+ from] *The poem employs as its first lines a verse plagiarized from a billboard.*

▶ COLLOCATIONS:
  plagiarize **from** *something*
  plagiarize a **story/site/speech/passage/essay**
▶ SYNONYMS: copy, steal

---

plead /pliːd/ (pleads, pleading, pleaded) `LAW`

VERB When someone charged with a crime **pleads guilty** or **not guilty** in a court of law, they officially state that they are guilty or not guilty of the crime. ○ *Morris had pleaded guilty to robbery.* ○ *They consistently pleaded innocent and were finally cleared at a hearing in Cartagena yesterday.*

▶ COLLOCATION: plead **guilty/innocent/not guilty**

plea /pliː/ (pleas)

1 NOUN In a court of law, a person's **plea** is the answer that they give when they have been charged with a crime, saying whether or not they are guilty of that crime. ○ *The judge questioned him about his guilty plea.* ○ *[+ of]* *We will enter a plea of not guilty.* ○ *[+ of]* *Her plea of guilty to manslaughter through provocation was rejected.*

▶ COLLOCATIONS:
  a plea **of** *something*
  a plea of **guilty/not guilty/innocence**
  a **guilty/not guilty** plea

2 NOUN A **plea** is a reason which is given, to a court of law or to other people, as an excuse for doing something or for not doing something. ○ *[+ of]* *Phillips murdered his wife, but got off on a plea of insanity.* ○ *[+ of]* *Mr Dunn's pleas of poverty are only partly justified.*

▶ COLLOCATIONS:
  a plea **of** *something*
  a plea of **manslaughter/insanity/self-defence**

---

point out /pɔɪnt ˈaʊt/ (points out, pointing out, pointed out)

PHRASAL VERB If you **point out** a fact or mistake, you tell someone about it or draw their attention to it. ○ *[+ that]* *Critics point out that the prince, on his income, should be paying tax.* ○ *[+ that]* *Dr Newlinds also pointed out that in 1960 doctors had not known of any drugs causing major defects in the newborn.*

---

pol‖len /ˈpɒlən/ (pollens) `BIOLOGY`

NOUN Pollen is a fine powder produced by flowers. It fertilizes other flowers of the same species so that they produce seeds. ○ *Your susceptibility to pollen*

allergy or other sensitivities can be increased by emotional stresses.
○ *The flowers produce no new pollen after they have been cut.*

▶ **COLLOCATIONS:**
   a pollen **grain/count/allergy/tube**
   carry/produce/transfer/spread pollen

pol|li|nate /ˈpɒlɪneɪt/ (pollinates, pollinating, pollinated)

VERB To **pollinate** a plant or tree means to fertilize it with pollen. This is often done by insects. ○ *Many of the indigenous insects are needed to pollinate the local plants.* ○ *So for the first time bees can be brought into glasshouses to pollinate crops by natural means.*

▶ **COLLOCATIONS:**
   a **bee/insect/bird** pollinates *something*
   pollinate a **flower/crop/plant**

pol|li|na|tion /ˌpɒlɪˈneɪʃən/

UNCOUNTABLE NOUN ○ *Without sufficient pollination, the growth of the corn is stunted.* ○ *The blossom of your chosen varieties must be produced at the same time to ensure successful pollination.*

▶ **COLLOCATIONS:**
   pollination **of/by** *something*
   pollination of **crops/flowers**
   pollination by **bees/insects**
   ensure/require pollination

po|rous /ˈpɔːrəs/ SCIENCE GEOGRAPHY

ADJECTIVE Something that is **porous** has many small holes in it, which water and air can pass through. ○ *The local limestone is very porous.* ○ *Rough porous surfaces will soak up paint more quickly than smooth sealed surfaces.*

▶ **COLLOCATIONS:**
   a porous **rock/surface/material**
   highly porous

por|trait /ˈpɔːtreɪt/ (portraits) ARTS

NOUN A **portrait** is a painting, drawing, or photograph of a particular person. ○ [+ *of*] *Lucian Freud has been asked to paint a portrait of the Queen.* ○ *the English portrait painter Augustus John*

▶ **COLLOCATIONS:**
   a portrait **of** *someone*
   hang/paint/unveil/draw/commission a portrait

a portrait **hangs**
a **photographic/intimate/nude/vivid/full-length** portrait
a portrait **gallery/painter/photographer**

---

pose /pəʊz/ (poses, posing, posed)　　　ACADEMIC WORD

1 VERB If something **poses** a problem or a danger, it is the cause of that problem or danger. ○ *This could pose a threat to jobs in the coal industry.* ○ *His ill health poses serious problems for the future.*

▶ **COLLOCATIONS:**
pose something **to** something/someone
pose a **threat/risk/challenge/problem** to something/someone

▶ **SYNONYM:** present

2 VERB If you **pose** a question, you ask it. If you **pose** an issue that needs considering, you mention the issue. [FORMAL] ○ *the moral issues posed by new technologies* ○ *Islam poses the ultimate question: 'what is intelligence and what does it really mean to be intelligent?'*

▶ **COLLOCATION:** pose a **question/issue**

▶ **SYNONYM:** put forward

---

pos|ture /ˈpɒstʃə/ (postures)　　　MEDICINE

NOUN Your **posture** is the position in which you stand or sit. ○ *You can make your stomach look flatter instantly by improving your posture.* ○ *Exercise, fresh air, and good posture are all helpful.* ○ *Sit in a relaxed upright posture.*

▶ **COLLOCATIONS:**
upright/correct/good/bad posture
improve/correct posture
adopt/assume/maintain a posture

pos|tur|al /ˈpɒstʃərəl/

ADJECTIVE [FORMAL] ○ *Children can develop bad postural habits from quite an early age.* ○ *With her back held in the correct postural alignment she rose from the sofa.*

▶ **COLLOCATIONS:**
a postural **muscle/habit**
postural **imbalance/alignment**

pow|er /paʊə/ (powers) [MATHS]

NOUN In mathematics, **power** is used in expressions such as **2 to the power of 4** or **2 to the 4th power** to indicate that 2 must be multiplied by itself 4 times. This is written in numbers as 2^4, or $2 \times 2 \times 2 \times 2$, which equals 16. ○ [+ *of*] *Any number to the power of nought is equal to one.* ○ *A trillion is 10 raised to the 12th power.*

▸ COLLOCATIONS:
the power **of** x
the **10th/12th/100th** power

▸ PHRASE: to the power of x

prac|ti|tion|er /præk'tɪʃənə/ [ACADEMIC WORD] [MEDICINE]
(practitioners)

NOUN Doctors are sometimes referred to as **practitioners** or **medical practitioners**. [FORMAL] ○ *Some orthodox medical practitioners claim that a balanced diet will provide all the necessary vitamins.* ○ *If in doubt consult a qualified practitioner.*

▸ COLLOCATIONS:
a **general/qualified/medical/alternative** practitioner
consult/visit a practitioner
a practitioner **prescribes/treats** something

prag|mat|ic /præg'mætɪk/

ADJECTIVE A **pragmatic** way of dealing with something is based on practical considerations, rather than theoretical ones. A **pragmatic** person deals with things in a practical way. ○ *a pragmatic approach to the problems faced by Latin America* ○ *a thoroughly pragmatic politician with an acute instinct for the popular mood*

▸ COLLOCATIONS:
a pragmatic **approach/attitude/view/politician/reason**
very/purely/fairly pragmatic

▸ SYNONYMS: realistic, practical

prag|mati|cal|ly /præg'mætɪkli/

ADVERB ○ *'I can't ever see us doing anything else,' states Brian pragmatically.* ○ *Pragmatically, MTV's survival depends on selling the youth market to advertisers.*

▸ COLLOCATION: **act/behave/respond** pragmatically
▸ SYNONYMS: realistically, practically

prag|ma|tism /ˈprægmətɪzəm/

UNCOUNTABLE NOUN [FORMAL] ○ *She had a reputation for clear thinking and pragmatism.* ○ *The search for a middle road is not just political pragmatism.*

▸ **COLLOCATIONS:**
political/ruthless/hardheaded/levelheaded pragmatism
pragmatism **dictates** *something*
display pragmatism

pre|cau|tion /prɪˈkɔːʃən/ (precautions)

NOUN A **precaution** is an action that is intended to prevent something dangerous or unpleasant from happening. ○ [+ to-inf] *He took elaborate precautions to conceal his true persona.* ○ *Extra safety precautions are essential in homes where older people live.*

▸ **COLLOCATIONS:**
a precaution **against** *something*
sensible/extra/necessary/proper/simple precautions
take/recommend/follow/use precautions
safety/security/fire/health precautions
▸ **PHRASE:** as a precaution

pre|cau|tion|ary /prɪˈkɔːʃənri, AM -neri/

ADJECTIVE [FORMAL] ○ *The local administration says the curfew is a precautionary measure.* ○ *the process of taking precautionary steps to ensure that no blame will attach if something goes wrong*

▸ **COLLOCATIONS:**
a precautionary **measure/principle/approach/step**
purely precautionary

pre|cede /prɪˈsiːd/ (precedes, preceding, preceded) `ACADEMIC WORD`

VERB If one event or period of time **precedes** another, it happens before it. [FORMAL] ○ *Intensive negotiations between the main parties preceded the vote.* ○ [+ by] *The earthquake was preceded by a loud roar and lasted 20 seconds.* ○ [V-ing] *Industrial orders had already fallen in the preceding months.*

▸ **COLLOCATIONS:**
immediately/usually/always/often precede *something*
precede a **date/chapter/arrival**
a **period/month/warning** precedes *something*

prec|edent /ˈpresɪdənt/ **(precedents)**

NOUN If there is a **precedent for** an action or event, it has happened before, and this can be regarded as an argument for doing it again. [FORMAL] ○ [+ for] *The trial could set an important precedent for dealing with large numbers of similar cases.* ○ *There are plenty of precedents in Hollywood for letting people out of contracts.*

▶ **COLLOCATIONS:**
 a precedent **for** something
 set/establish/create/follow a precedent
 a **dangerous/historical/legal** precedent

prec|edence /ˈpresɪdəns/

UNCOUNTABLE NOUN If one thing takes **precedence over** another, it is regarded as more important than the other thing. ○ [+ over] *The shocking, glamorous, or the extreme is always given precedence over the true and the mundane.* ○ [+ over] *As the King's representative he took precedence over everyone else on the island.*

▶ **COLLOCATIONS:**
 precedence **over** something
 precedence over **law**
 a **historical** precedence
 take/give precedence

▶ **SYNONYM:** priority

---

pré|cis /ˈpreɪsi, AM preɪˈsiː/　　　[ACADEMIC STUDY]

> The form **précis** is both the singular and the plural form. It is pronounced /ˈpreɪsiz/ when it is the plural.

NOUN A **précis** is a short written or spoken account of something, which gives the important points but not the details. [FORMAL] ○ [+ of] *A précis of the manuscript was sent to the magazine New Idea.* ○ [+ of] *The power of this book cannot be judged from a précis of its plot.*

→ see note at **abstract**

▶ **COLLOCATIONS:**
 a précis **of** something
 a **brief/inaccurate** précis

▶ **SYNONYM:** summary

pre|date /ˌpriːˈdeɪt/ (predates, predating, predated) `HISTORY`

VERB If you say that one thing **predated** another, you mean that the first thing happened or existed some time before the second thing. ○ *His troubles predated the recession.* ○ *The monument predates the arrival of the druids in Britain.*

▶ COLLOCATIONS:
  actually/long predate *something*
  predate the **arrival/rise/discovery/creation** of *something*
  predate **the internet/Christianity**

preda|tor /ˈpredətə/ (predators) `BIOLOGY`

NOUN A **predator** is an animal that kills and eats other animals. ○ *The mites in turn were eaten by other arachnid predators.* ○ *Tomato growers are using natural predators to control the pests which could otherwise destroy the crop.*

▶ COLLOCATIONS:
  a **natural/violent/marine/feral/nocturnal** predator
  a predator **attacks/hunts/eats** *something*
  attract/escape/avoid a predator

preda|tory /ˈpredətri, AM -tɔːri/

ADJECTIVE ○ *predatory birds like the eagle* ○ *the predatory instincts of foxes* ○ *non-lethal solutions for controlling predatory marine mammals*

▶ COLLOCATIONS:
  a predatory **instinct/mite/dinosaur/mammal**
  predatory **behaviour**

pre|domi|nant /prɪˈdɒmɪnənt/ `ACADEMIC WORD`

ADJECTIVE If something is **predominant**, it is more important or noticeable than anything else in a set of people or things. ○ *The third survivor is Hope, who manifests the predominant symptoms of multiple personality disorder.* ○ *The predominant theme of this book is the idea of the sacred or god.*

▶ COLLOCATIONS:
  a predominant **symptom/characteristic**
  a predominant **theme/role**

▶ SYNONYM: main

pre|domi|nant|ly /prɪˈdɒmɪnəntli/

ADVERB ○ *The landscape has remained predominantly rural in appearance.* ○ *a predominantly female profession* ○ *Although it is predominantly a teenage problem, acne can occur in early childhood.*

▶ **COLLOCATIONS:**
rely/focus predominantly on *something*
consist/compose predominantly of *something*
predominantly **Muslim/white/black/male/Christian**

▶ **SYNONYMS:** mainly, largely

---

press|ing /ˈpresɪŋ/

ADJECTIVE A **pressing** problem, need, or issue has to be dealt with immediately. ○ *It is one of the most pressing problems facing this country.* ○ *There is a pressing need for more funds.*

▶ **COLLOCATIONS:**
a pressing **issue/need/concern/problem/question**
equally/increasingly pressing

▶ **SYNONYM:** urgent

---

prey /preɪ/ (preys, preying, preyed)   `BIOLOGY`

1 UNCOUNTABLE NOUN A creature's **prey** are the creatures that it hunts and eats in order to live. ○ *Electric rays stun their prey with huge electrical discharges.* ○ *[+ of] These animals were the prey of hyenas.*

▶ **COLLOCATIONS:**
the prey **of** *something*
easy/natural/potential prey
hunt/capture/kill/become prey
a prey **species/animal**

2 VERB A creature that **preys on** other creatures lives by catching and eating them. ○ *[+ on/upon] The effect was to disrupt the food chain, starving many animals and those that preyed on them.* ○ *[+ on/upon] The larvae prey upon small aphids.*

▶ **COLLOCATIONS:**
prey **on/upon** *something*
prey on a **creature/insect**

▶ **SYNONYMS:** feed, hunt

---

prime num|ber /ˈpraɪm ˌnʌmbə/ (prime numbers)   `MATHS`

NOUN In mathematics, a **prime number** is a whole number greater than 1 that cannot be divided exactly by any whole number except itself and the number 1, for example 17. ○ *The progress takes the project tantalisingly close to finding the first 10 million-digit prime number.* ○ *his work on prime numbers, the building blocks of arithmetic*

primi|tive /'prɪmɪtɪv/ `HISTORY`

ADJECTIVE **Primitive** means belonging to a society in which people live in a very simple way, usually without industries or a writing system. ○ *studies of primitive societies* ○ *Weston A. Price, who studied the health of many primitive tribes in Central and Southern America*

▶ **COLLOCATION:** a primitive **tribe/tribesman/society**

---

privi|lege /'prɪvɪlɪdʒ/ (privileges) `SOCIOLOGY`

1 NOUN A **privilege** is a special right or advantage that only one person or group has. ○ *[+ for] The Russian Federation has issued a decree abolishing special privileges for government officials.* ○ *[+ of] the ancient powers and privileges of the House of Commons*

▶ **COLLOCATIONS:**
a privilege **for/of** *someone*
grant/enjoy/suspend/extend/abuse privileges
special/parliamentary/legal privileges
trading/class privileges

▶ **PHRASE:** rights and privileges

2 UNCOUNTABLE NOUN If you talk about **privilege**, you are talking about the power and advantage that only a small group of people have, usually because of their wealth or their high social class. ○ *Pironi was the son of privilege and wealth, and it showed.* ○ *Having been born to privilege in old Hollywood, she was carrying on a family tradition by acting.*

▶ **PHRASES:**
be born to privilege
a child of privilege
privilege and wealth

privi|leged /'prɪvɪlɪdʒd/

1 ADJECTIVE Someone who is **privileged** has an advantage or opportunity that most other people do not have, often because of their wealth or high social class. ○ *They were, by and large, a very wealthy, privileged elite.* ○ *She was born in Croydon to Scottish parents and had a fairly privileged upbringing.*

▶ **COLLOCATIONS:**
a privileged **background/upbringing/position/class**
economically privileged

• **The privileged** are people who are privileged. ○ *They are only interested in preserving the power of the privileged.* ○ *Family problems are found in every class, he said, but were more common among the less privileged.*

2 **ADJECTIVE** **Privileged** information is known by only a small group of people, who are not legally required to give it to anyone else. ○ *The data is privileged information, not to be shared with the general public.* ○ *Mr Nixon argued the tapes were privileged.*

▶ **COLLOCATIONS:**
  privileged **access/information**
  a privileged **document**

▶ **SYNONYM:** confidential

---

pro|ceed /prəˈsiːd/ **(proceeds, proceeding, proceeded)** `ACADEMIC WORD`

VERB If you **proceed with** a course of action, you continue with it.
[FORMAL] ○ [+ with] *The group proceeded with a march they knew would lead to bloodshed.* ○ *The trial has been delayed until November because the defence is not ready to proceed.*

▶ **COLLOCATIONS:**
  proceed **with** something
  proceed with **caution**
  proceed with a **prosecution/plan/negotiation**

▶ **SYNONYM:** continue

▶ **ANTONYMS:** stop, discontinue

---

pro|ceed|ings /prəˈsiːdɪŋz/ `ACADEMIC WORD` `LAW`

1 **NOUN** Legal **proceedings** are legal action taken against someone.
[FORMAL] ○ [+ against] *criminal proceedings against the former prime minister* ○ [+ to-inf] *The Council had brought proceedings to stop the store from trading on Sundays.*

▶ **COLLOCATIONS:**
  proceedings **against** someone
  legal/criminal/judicial proceedings
  court/divorce/libel/defamation proceedings
  institute/initiate/commence proceedings

▶ **SYNONYM:** action

2 **NOUN** The **proceedings** are an organized series of events that take place in a particular place. [FORMAL] ○ [+ of] *The proceedings of the enquiry will take place in private.* ○ *He viewed the proceedings with doubt and alarm.*

▶ **COLLOCATIONS:**
  the proceedings **of** something
  watch/dominate the proceedings

prod|uct /ˈprɒdʌkt/ (products)

NOUN If you say that someone or something is a **product of** a situation or process, you mean that the situation or process has had a significant effect in making them what they are. ○ [+ of] *We are all products of our time.* ○ [+ of] *The bank is the product of a 1971 merger of two Japanese banks.*

▸ COLLOCATIONS:
   a product **of** something
   a product of a **culture/upbringing/era**

pro|found /prəˈfaʊnd/ (profounder, profoundest)

ADJECTIVE You use **profound** to emphasize that something is very great or intense. ○ *discoveries which had a profound effect on many areas of medicine* ○ *The overwhelming feeling is just deep, profound shock and anger.* ○ *Anna's patriotism was profound.*

▸ COLLOCATIONS:
   a profound **sense** of something
   a profound **change/impact/effect/influence/implication**
   profound **shock/sadness**

▸ SYNONYMS: deep, intense, extreme

pro|found|ly /prəˈfaʊndli/

ADVERB ○ *This has profoundly affected my life.* ○ *In politics, as in other areas, he is profoundly conservative.*

▸ COLLOCATIONS:
   profoundly **influence/affect/alter** something
   profoundly **unsatisfactory/undemocratic**
   profoundly **different/disturbing/depressed**

▸ SYNONYMS: deeply, intensely

pro|long /prəˈlɒŋ, AM -lɔːŋ/ (prolongs, prolonging, prolonged)

VERB To **prolong** something means to make it last longer. ○ *Mr Chesler said foreign military aid was prolonging the war.* ○ *The actual action of the drug can be prolonged significantly.*

▸ COLLOCATIONS:
   prolong **life/suffering/agony/conflict**
   only/actually prolong something

▸ SYNONYMS: lengthen, extend

▸ ANTONYM: shorten

pro|longed /prəˈlɒŋd, AM -lɔːŋd/

ADJECTIVE A **prolonged** event or situation continues for a long time, or for longer than expected. ○ *a prolonged period of low interest rates* ○ *a prolonged drought*

▶ **COLLOCATIONS:**
a prolonged **period/drought/absence/recession**
merely/unnecessarily prolonged

▶ **SYNONYM:** lasting

▶ **ANTONYM:** brief

promi|nent /ˈprɒmɪnənt/

1 ADJECTIVE Someone who is **prominent** is important. ○ *a prominent member of the Law Society* ○ *the children of very prominent or successful parents*

▶ **COLLOCATIONS:**
a prominent **role/figure/member/politician/businessman**
especially/increasingly/socially/nationally prominent

▶ **SYNONYM:** well-known

2 ADJECTIVE Something that is **prominent** is very noticeable or is an important part of something else. ○ *Here the window plays a prominent part in the design.* ○ *Romania's most prominent independent newspaper*

▶ **COLLOCATIONS:**
a prominent **feature/landmark**
prominent **cheekbones**

promi|nent|ly /ˈprɒmɪnəntli/

ADVERB ○ *Trade will figure prominently in the second day of talks in Washington.* ○ *Entries will be prominently displayed in the exhibition hall.*

▶ **COLLOCATION:** **figure/feature/display** prominently

promi|nence /ˈprɒmɪnəns/

UNCOUNTABLE NOUN If someone or something is in a position of **prominence**, they are well-known and important. ○ *He came to prominence during the World Cup in Italy.* ○ *Crime prevention had to be given more prominence.*

▶ **COLLOCATIONS:**
come/rise to prominence
gain/achieve/give prominence
national/international/great/political prominence

prompt /prɒmpt/ (prompts, prompting, prompted)

VERB To **prompt** someone **to** do something means to make them decide to do it. ○ [+ to-inf] *Japan's recession has prompted consumers to cut back on buying cars.* ○ *The need for villagers to control their own destinies has prompted a new plan.*

▶ **COLLOCATIONS:**
  prompt *someone* to **write/ask** *something*
  prompt *someone* to **act**

▶ **SYNONYM:** encourage

prone /prəʊn/

ADJECTIVE To be **prone to** something, usually something bad, means to have a tendency to be affected by it or to do it. ○ [+ to] *For all her experience, she was still prone to nerves.* ○ [+ to] *People with fair skin who sunburn easily are very prone to skin cancer.*

● **-prone** combines with nouns to make adjectives that describe people who are frequently affected by something bad. ○ *the most injury-prone rider on the circuit*

▶ **COLLOCATIONS:**
  prone **to** *something*
  prone to **damage/attack/stress/panic/worry**
  injury-/accident- prone

pro|nounced /prə'naʊnst/

ADJECTIVE Something that is **pronounced** is very noticeable. ○ *Most of the art exhibitions have a pronounced Scottish theme.* ○ *a pronounced Australian accent* ○ *Since then, the contrast between his two careers has become even more pronounced.*

→ see note at **marked**

▶ **COLLOCATIONS:**
  a pronounced **limp/accent/flavor/taste/tendency**
  pronounced **differences**
  more/less/particularly pronounced

▶ **SYNONYMS:** noticeable, marked, distinct, conspicuous

▶ **ANTONYM:** imperceptible

propa|gan|da /ˌprɒpə'gændə/ POLITICS

UNCOUNTABLE NOUN Propaganda is information, often inaccurate information, which a political organization publishes or broadcasts in order to influence people. ○ *The Front adopted an aggressive propaganda campaign against its rivals.* ○ *anti-European propaganda movies*

▶ COLLOCATIONS:
Nazi/racist/anti-American propaganda
war/government/party/election propaganda
a propaganda **machine/campaign/war/film**
spread/broadcast/disseminate/believe/counter propaganda

---

pro|pel /prəˈpel/ (propels, propelling, propelled) `SCIENCE`

VERB To **propel** something in a particular direction means to cause it to move in that direction. ○ *The tiny rocket is attached to the spacecraft and is designed to propel it toward Mars.* ○ *the club propels the ball forward rather than up*

• **-propelled** combines with nouns to form adjectives which indicate how something, especially a weapon, is propelled. ○ *rocket-propelled grenades* ○ *the first jet-propelled aeroplane*

▶ COLLOCATIONS:
rocket-/jet-/wind-/engine- propelled
propel a **grenade/rocket/vehicle/ball**
propel *something* **forward/onwards**

▶ SYNONYMS: drive, launch, thrust

---

pro|por|tion|al /prəˈpɔːʃənəl/ `ACADEMIC WORD`

ADJECTIVE If one amount is **proportional to** another, the two amounts increase and decrease at the same rate so there is always the same relationship between them. [FORMAL] ○ [+ to] *Loss of weight is directly proportional to the rate at which the disease is progressing.* ○ *a proportional fee based on the final sale price*

▶ COLLOCATIONS:
proportional **to** *something*
directly/inversely proportional
proportional **representation**
a proportional **system/increase/model**

pro|por|tion|al|ly /prəˈpɔːʃənəli/

ADVERB ○ *You have proportionally more fat on your thighs and hips than anywhere else on your body.* ○ *Candidates would be elected proportionally.*

▶ COLLOCATIONS:
increase/represent/allocate/divide proportionally
elect/vote proportionally

pros|ecute /ˈprɒsɪkjuːt/ (prosecutes, prosecuting, prosecuted) LAW

VERB If the authorities **prosecute** someone, they charge them with a crime and put them on trial. ○ *The police have decided not to prosecute because the evidence is not strong enough.* ○ [+ for] *Photographs taken by roadside cameras will soon be enough to prosecute drivers for speeding.* ○ [+ for] *He is being prosecuted for two criminal offences.*

▶ COLLOCATIONS:
   prosecute *someone* **for** *something*
   prosecute a **criminal/offender/perpetrator**
   a **government/lawyer/authority** prosecutes *someone*
   successfully/criminally/unsuccessfully prosecute *someone*

pros|ecu|tion /ˌprɒsɪˈkjuːʃən/ (prosecutions)

1 NOUN Prosecution is the action of charging someone with a crime and putting them on trial. ○ [+ of] *Yesterday the head of government called for the prosecution of those responsible for the deaths.* ○ [+ for] *He had fled when facing prosecution for libel.*

▶ COLLOCATIONS:
   the prosecution **of** *someone*
   prosecution **for** *something*
   avoid/escape/face prosecution
   successful/criminal/malicious prosecution

2 NOUN The lawyers who try to prove that a person on trial is guilty are called **the prosecution**. ○ *Colonel Pugh, for the prosecution, said that the offences occurred over a six-year period.* ○ *During his trial the prosecution claimed he lay in wait for the burglars before firing his pump action shotgun three times.*

▶ COLLOCATIONS:
   counsel for the prosecution
   a **witness/lawyer** for the prosecution
   the prosecution **alleges/argues/claims/proves** *something*
▶ ANTONYM: the defence

pros|ecu|tor /ˈprɒsɪkjuːtə/ (prosecutors)

NOUN In some countries, a **prosecutor** is a lawyer or official who brings charges against someone or tries to prove in a trial that they are guilty. ○ [+ in] *For the last quarter of a century she has been a state prosecutor in the Parquet at Nantes.* ○ *Prosecutors allege that cars and trucks were stored at privately-owned depots at government expense.*

P

▶ **COLLOCATIONS:**
a prosecutor **in/at** *somewhere/something*
a prosecutor in/at a **case/trial/court**
appoint/assign a prosecutor
a prosecutor **says/argues/alleges/asks/seeks** *something*

---

pros|per|ous /ˈprɒspərəs/

ADJECTIVE Prosperous people, places, and economies are rich and successful. [FORMAL] ○ *the youngest son of a relatively prosperous British family* ○ *The place looks more prosperous than ever.*

▶ **COLLOCATIONS:**
relatively/moderately/economically prosperous
a prosperous **nation/economy/town/businessman/farmer**

EXTEND YOUR VOCABULARY

You often describe people or countries with a lot of money as being **rich** or **wealthy**. ○ *There are rich countries where most people have enough and some have untold wealth, while in the poor countries desperate poverty is widespread.*

Both of these words often suggest a judgement about whether the wealth is positive, unfair, or unequal. In more formal writing, you can use the words **prosperous** and **affluent** to describe areas where people have a relatively high income and a good standard of living. ○ *Australia's economy is prosperous and stable.* ○ *This occurs twice as much in the inner city area as compared with the more affluent suburbs.*

---

pros|per|ity /prɒˈsperɪti/

UNCOUNTABLE NOUN Prosperity is a condition in which a person or community is doing well financially. ○ *a new era of peace and prosperity* ○ *Japan's economic prosperity*

▶ **COLLOCATIONS:**
future/economic/long-term/relative prosperity
bring/increase/achieve/enjoy prosperity

▶ **PHRASE:** peace and prosperity

▶ **SYNONYM:** wealth

P

---

pro|tein /ˈprəʊtiːn/ **(proteins)**   SCIENCE   MEDICINE

NOUN **Protein** is a substance found in food and drink such as meat, eggs, and milk. You need protein in order to grow and be healthy. ○ *Fish was a major source of protein for the working man.* ○ *a high protein diet*

▶ COLLOCATIONS:
  a **viral/animal/abnormal** protein
  produce/contain/digest protein

▶ RELATED WORDS: carbohydrate, fat

---

proto|col /ˈprəʊtəkɒl, AM -kɔːl/   ACADEMIC WORD   IT   POLITICS
(protocols)

1 NOUN A **protocol** is a set of rules for exchanging information between computers. ○ *an open source email encryption protocol* ○ *A serious problem with the most commonly used internet communications protocol has been revealed by computer experts.*

▶ COLLOCATION: a **wireless/internet/encryption/network** protocol

2 NOUN A **protocol** is a written record of a treaty or agreement that has been made by two or more countries. [FORMAL] ○ *the Montreal Protocol to phase out use and production of CFCs.* ○ [+ on] *There are also protocols on the testing of nuclear weapons.*

▶ COLLOCATIONS:
  a protocol **on** *something*
  sign/ratify/breach/develop a protocol

▶ SYNONYM: accord

3 NOUN A **protocol** is a plan for a course of medical treatment, or a plan for a scientific experiment. [AM, FORMAL] ○ *the detoxification protocol* ○ *Their purification protocol yielded only degraded polymerase, according to Cetus.*

▶ COLLOCATION: **treatment/testing** protocol

---

proto|type /ˈprəʊtətaɪp/ **(prototypes)**   ENGINEERING   SCIENCE

NOUN A **prototype** is a new type of machine or device which is not yet ready to be made in large numbers and sold. ○ [+ of] *Chris Retzler has built a prototype of a machine called the wave rotor.* ○ *the first prototype aircraft*

▶ COLLOCATIONS:
  a prototype **of** *something*
  a prototype of a **device/vehicle/robot**
  build/develop/test/design a prototype
  a **first/early/original/working/full-scale** prototype

pro|vi|sion|al /prəˈvɪʒənəl/

ADJECTIVE You use **provisional** to describe something that has been arranged or appointed for the present, but may be changed in the future. ○ *the possibility of setting up a provisional coalition government* ○ *If you have never held a driving licence before, you should apply for a provisional licence.* ○ *It was announced that the times were provisional and subject to confirmation.*

→ see note at **inconclusive**

▶ **COLLOCATIONS:**
   a provisional **ballot/pole/licence**
   a provisional **government/authority**

pro|vi|sion|al|ly /prəˈvɪʒənəli/

ADVERB ○ *The seven republics had provisionally agreed to the new relationship on November 14th.* ○ *A meeting is provisionally scheduled for early next week.*

▶ **COLLOCATIONS:**
   provisionally **agreed/accepted/scheduled**
   provisionally **entitled/titled**

pro|voke /prəˈvəʊk/ (provokes, provoking, provoked)

VERB If something **provokes** a reaction, it causes it. ○ *His election success has provoked a shocked reaction.* ○ *The destruction of the mosque has provoked anger throughout the Muslim world.*

▶ **COLLOCATIONS:**
   provoke **outrage/fury/controversy/fury/anger**
   provoke a **reaction/response/backlash/outcry/debate**

▶ **SYNONYMS:** cause, excite, generate

prox|im|ity /prɒkˈsɪmɪti/

UNCOUNTABLE NOUN Proximity to a place or person is nearness to that place or person. [FORMAL] ○ [+ to] *Part of the attraction is Darwin's proximity to Asia.* ○ [+ of] *He became aware of the proximity of the Afghans.* ○ [+ to] *Families are no longer in close proximity to each other.*

▶ **COLLOCATIONS:**
   proximity **to/of** *something/someone*
   close/geographical/physical proximity

psy|chia|try /saɪˈkaɪətri, AM sɪ-/

UNCOUNTABLE NOUN **Psychiatry** is the branch of medicine concerned with the treatment of mental illness. ○ *The new professions of psychology and psychiatry welcomed the opportunity to extend their work.* ○ *a consultant and senior lecturer in child and adolescent psychiatry*

▶ **COLLOCATIONS:**
  study/teach/practise psychiatry
  forensic/adolescent/child/clinical psychiatry

▶ **PHRASE:** psychiatry and psychology

psy|chi|at|ric /ˌsaɪkiˈætrɪk/

ADJECTIVE ○ *We finally insisted that he seek psychiatric help.* ○ *About 4% of the prison population have chronic psychiatric illnesses.*

▶ **COLLOCATIONS:**
  a psychiatric **ward/hospital/patient/disorder/illness**
  psychiatric **help/treatment/care**

psy|chia|trist /saɪˈkaɪətrɪst, AM sɪ-/ **(psychiatrists)**

NOUN A **psychiatrist** is a doctor who treats people suffering from mental illness. ○ *Alex will probably be seeing a psychiatrist for many months or even years.* ○ *Having seen most forms of human perversion and violence, the average forensic psychiatrist doesn't shock easily.*

▶ **COLLOCATIONS:**
  consult/see/visit/tell a psychiatrist
  a **forensic/eminent/adolescent/clinical** psychiatrist
  a psychiatrist **examines/treats/ diagnoses** *someone/something*
  a psychiatrist **testifies**

pyra|mid /ˈpɪrəmɪd/ **(pyramids)**

NOUN A **pyramid** is a shape, object, or pile of things with a flat base and sloping triangular sides that meet at a point. ○ [+ *of*] *On a plate in front of him was piled a pyramid of flat white biscuits.* ○ *Pei's solitary glass pyramid in the courtyard of the Louvre*

▶ **COLLOCATIONS:**
  a pyramid **of** *something*
  build/form/construct a pyramid
  a **human/inverted/tall/glass** pyramid

Qq

qual|ity /ˈkwɒlɪti/

ACADEMIC WORD

UNCOUNTABLE NOUN The **quality** of something is how good or bad it is. ○ [+ of] OCD sufferers who undergo treatment report a substantial improvement in their quality of life. ○ Other services vary dramatically in quality. ○ Employees whose work is of a consistently high quality should not fear unemployment.

▶ **COLLOCATIONS:**
the quality **of** something
the quality of **life/service/teaching**
poor/high/low/excellent/superior quality
improve/enhance/ensure/assess the quality of something
vary in quality
a **variation/improvement** in quality

▶ **PHRASE:** quality and quantity

▶ **RELATED WORD:** quantity

quali|ta|tive /ˈkwɒlɪtətɪv, AM -teɪt-/

ADJECTIVE Qualitative means relating to the nature or standard of something, rather than to its quantity. [FORMAL] ○ There are qualitative differences in the way children and adults think. ○ That's the whole difference between quantitative and qualitative research.

▶ **COLLOCATIONS:**
a qualitative **difference/distinction**
a qualitative **assessment/evaluation/study**
qualitative **research/analysis**

▶ **PHRASE:** qualitative and quantitative

▶ **RELATED WORD:** quantitative

quali|ta|tive|ly /ˈkwɒlɪtətɪvli, AM -teɪt-/

ADVERB ○ The new media are unlikely to prove qualitatively different from the old. ○ a group with minimal demands for housing, both quantitatively and qualitatively

▶ COLLOCATIONS:
qualitatively **different/distinct/superior/inferior**
assess/evaluate *something* qualitatively
▶ PHRASE: qualitatively and quantitatively
▶ RELATED WORD: quantitatively

> **USAGE: qualitative or quantitative?**
>
> It is easy to confuse these two key terms to describe academic research.
>
> Remember that **quantitative** research methods involve looking at the **quantity** of something; counting numbers, measuring, statistics, etc. ○ *Quantitative studies in cities where the non-smoking bylaw already exists have shown no measurable negative impact on the economic fortunes of bars and restaurants.*
>
> **Qualitative** research methods involve making judgements about the **quality** of something; how good or effective something is, people's opinions, experiences, etc. ○ *We carried out a qualitative study to obtain insight into people's thoughts on stroke.*

---

quan|tity /ˈkwɒntɪti/ (quantities)   `ACADEMIC WORD`

NOUN A **quantity** is an amount that you can measure or count. ○ [+ *of*] *a small quantity of water* ○ [+ *of*] *huge quantities of narcotics* ○ *Cheap goods are available, but not in sufficient quantities to satisfy demand.*

▶ COLLOCATIONS:
a quantity **of** *something*
a **vast/uknown/large/small** quantity
▶ PHRASE: quality and quantity
▶ RELATED WORD: quality

quan|ti|ta|tive /ˈkwɒntɪtətɪv, AM -teɪt-/

ADJECTIVE **Quantitative** means relating to different sizes or amounts of things. [FORMAL] ○ *An important distinction must be made between quantitative and qualitative similarities.* ○ *the quantitative analysis of migration*

→ see note at **qualitative**
▶ COLLOCATION: quantitative **research/analysis/restrictions**
▶ PHRASE: quantitative and qualitative
▶ RELATED WORD: qualitative

quan|ti|ta|tive|ly /ˈkwɒntɪtətɪvli, AM -teɪt-/

ADVERB ○ *We cannot predict quantitatively the value or the cost of a new technology.* ○ *The response was tremendous, quantitatively and qualitatively.*

▶ **COLLOCATION: analyse/assess/interpret** *something* quantitatively

▶ **PHRASE:** quantitatively and qualitatively

▶ **RELATED WORD:** qualitatively

---

quar|ter /ˈkwɔːtə/   `BUSINESS` `ECONOMICS`

NOUN A **quarter** is a fixed period of three months. Companies often divide their financial year into four quarters. ○ *The group said results for the third quarter are due on October 29.* ○ *PeopleSoft announced yesterday that it had performed better than expected in its current financial quarter.*

▶ **COLLOCATIONS:**
the **first/second/third/fourth** quarter
the **previous/final/consecutive/current** quarter
a **fiscal/financial** quarter

quar|ter|ly /ˈkwɔːtəli/

ADJECTIVE A **quarterly** event happens four times a year, at intervals of three months. ○ *the latest Bank of Japan quarterly survey of 5,000 companies* ○ *the software group, last night announced record quarterly profits of $1.98 billion*

● **Quarterly** is also an adverb. ○ *It makes no difference whether dividends are paid quarterly or annually.* ○ *The list will be updated quarterly by the nonprofit Direct Marketing Association.*

▶ **COLLOCATIONS:**
a quarterly **survey/report/loss**
quarterly **profits/earnings/revenue/results**
update/measure/sample *something* quarterly

---

que|ry /ˈkwɪəri/ (queries, querying, queried)

1 NOUN A **query** is a question, especially one that you ask an organization, publication, or expert. ○ [+ *on*] *The major queries on this subject were from Dr Guy Jansen.* ○ *The Ministry of Defence is considering the appointment of an official spokesman to answer media queries.*

▶ COLLOCATIONS:
a query **about/on** *something*
a **specific/technical** query
a **customer/health** query
have/answer/resolve/handle/submit a query

▶ SYNONYM: question

2 VERB If you **query** something, you check it by asking about it because you are not sure if it is correct. ○ *Dr Grout had not queried the payments when they were debited from his credit-card account in 1999.* ○ *Some councillors who are in arrears are querying the amounts reflected in their accounts.*

▶ COLLOCATIONS:
query a **payment/bill/amount**
a **customer** queries *something*

▶ SYNONYMS: question, verify, check

---

quo|ta /ˈkwəʊtə/ (quotas)　　BUSINESS

1 NOUN A **quota** is the limited number or quantity of something which is officially allowed. ○ [+ *of*] *The quota of four tickets per person had been reduced to two.* ○ [+ *on*] *South Korea now imposes quotas on beef imports to protect its weak farm industry.*

▶ COLLOCATIONS:
a quota **of/on** *something*
a quota of *x* **barrels/tonnes**
a quota on **imports**
impose/allocate/assign a quota

2 NOUN A **quota** is a fixed maximum or minimum proportion of people from a particular group who are allowed to do something, such as come and live in a country or work for the government. ○ *The bill would force employers to adopt a quota system when recruiting workers.* ○ *The court, on a 5-4 vote, outlawed racial quotas in university admissions.*

▶ COLLOCATIONS:
racial/race-based/gender quotas
a quota **system**

q

Rr

radio|ac|tive /ˌreɪdiəʊˈæktɪv/ SCIENCE

ADJECTIVE Something that is **radioactive** contains a substance that produces energy in the form of powerful and harmful rays.
○ *The government has been storing radioactive waste at Fernald for 50 years.*
○ *24.7 tonnes of highly radioactive fuel*

▶ **COLLOCATIONS:**
radioactive **waste/material**
highly/dangerously radioactive

ra|dia|tion /ˌreɪdiˈeɪʃən/

1 UNCOUNTABLE NOUN Radiation consists of very small particles of a radioactive substance. Large amounts of radiation can cause illness and death. ○ *They suffer from health problems and fear the long term effects of radiation.* ○ *If the cancer returns, radiation therapy is successful in 90 per cent of cases.*

▶ **COLLOCATIONS:**
solar/ultraviolet/harmful radiation
radiation **sickness/exposure/therapy/poisoning**
emit/absorb/detect/produce/measure radiation

▶ **PHRASE:** radiation and chemotherapy

2 UNCOUNTABLE NOUN Radiation is energy, especially heat, that comes from a particular source. ○ *[+ from] The satellite will study energy radiation from stars.* ○ *To measure cosmic radiation in the early 1930s he sent up balloons of rubber.*

▶ **COLLOCATIONS:**
solar/thermal/cosmic/high-energy radiation
radiation **from** *something*

rati|fy /ˈrætɪfaɪ/ (ratifies, ratifying, ratified) POLITICS LAW

VERB When national leaders or organizations **ratify** a treaty or written agreement, they make it official by giving their formal approval to it, usually by signing it or voting for it. ○ *The parliaments of Australia and Indonesia have yet to ratify the treaty.* ○ *Russia formally ratified the Kyoto Protocol on Thursday.*

▶ **COLLOCATIONS:**
officially/formally/unanimously ratify *something*
ratify a **treaty/agreement/contract/deal**
a **parliament/committee** ratifies *something*
a **nation/country/state** ratifies *something*

▶ **SYNONYMS:** approve, affirm

▶ **ANTONYM:** annul

rati|fi|ca|tion /ˌrætɪfɪˈkeɪʃən/

UNCOUNTABLE NOUN ○ [+ *of*] *The E.U. will now complete ratification of the treaty by June 1.* ○ *The agreement next required ratification by the parliaments of the provinces.*

▶ **COLLOCATIONS:**
ratification **of** *something*
ratification of a **treaty/constitution/agreement/deal**
require/support/oppose/need ratification

▶ **SYNONYM:** approval

---

ra|tion|ale /ˌræʃəˈnɑːl, -ˈnæl/ (rationales)

NOUN The **rationale** for a course of action, practice, or belief is the set of reasons on which it is based. [FORMAL] ○ [+ *for*] *However, the rationale for such initiatives is not, of course, solely economic.* ○ [+ *behind*] *The best managers explain the rationale behind their decisions.*

▶ **COLLOCATIONS:**
the rationale **for/behind** *something*
explain/provide/understand/offer a rationale
a **moral/economic/strategic/convincing** rationale

▶ **SYNONYMS:** basis, reasons, justification

ACADEMIC WRITING: Explaining your reasons for research

When you undertake a piece of academic work, you need to make clear why you are doing it and what you hope to achieve.

You often start a piece of academic work with a **thesis**; an argument, a position, or a theory that you want to prove by providing arguments and evidence to support it.

If you are carrying out academic research, you often give a **rationale**, explaining your reasons for what you are doing, which research methods you choose, etc. ○ *Overall, we find this paper lacking in a coherent scientific rationale.*

You also talk about your **aims**; what you want to do, such as to find out more about a topic, to collect data, etc. and your **objectives**; what you want to achieve at the end, such as answering a research question, proving your thesis or developing a new method or system.

---

raw /rɔː/ (rawer, rawest)

1 ADJECTIVE Raw materials or substances are in their natural state before being processed or used in manufacturing. ○ *We import raw materials and energy, and export mainly industrial products.* ○ *two ships carrying raw sugar from Cuba*

▶ COLLOCATION: raw **material/sewage/sugar/cotton**

▶ SYNONYM: untreated

▶ ANTONYM: processed

2 ADJECTIVE Raw data is facts or information that has not yet been sorted, analysed, or prepared for use. ○ *Analyses were conducted on the raw data.* ○ *a statistical model that fully adjusts the census's raw figures*

▶ COLLOCATION: raw **data/figures**

▶ ANTONYM: analysed

---

re|as|sess /ˌriːəˈses/ ACADEMIC WORD
(reassesses, reassessing, reassessed)

VERB If you **reassess** something, you think about it and decide whether you need to change your opinion about it. ○ *But yesterday they admitted that it might be time to reassess the situation.* ○ *Security in the area will have to be reassessed.*

▶ COLLOCATIONS:
   continually/constantly/regularly reassess *something*
   reassess the **situation/risk/value**

▶ SYNONYMS: reappraise, review

re|as|sess|ment /ˌriːəˈsesmənt/ (reassessments)

NOUN ○ *a major reassessment of the impact of nuclear weapons on military doctrine* ○ *There are three questions in particular which should concern the Prime Minister and prompt a reassessment of policy.*

▶ COLLOCATIONS:
   a reassessment **of** *something*
   a **critical/complete/major** reassessment
   trigger/prompt/require a reassessment

▶ SYNONYM: reappraisal

re|bel /'rebəl/ (rebels) `POLITICS`

NOUN **Rebels** are people who are fighting against their own country's army in order to change the political system there. ○ *fighting between rebels and government forces* ○ *Before any instructions could be given, the rebels attacked again, with a much larger force.*

▶ **COLLOCATIONS:**
  seize/attack/capture/fight a rebel
  a rebel **group/leader/movement/force/faction**
  a **leftist/anti-government/suspected** rebel

▶ **SYNONYMS:** revolutionary, insurgent

re|bel|lion /rɪˈbeliən/ (rebellions)

NOUN A **rebellion** is a violent organized action by a large group of people who are trying to change their country's political system. ○ *The British soon put down the rebellion.* ○ *the ruthless and brutal suppression of rebellion*

▶ **COLLOCATIONS:**
  crush/lead/suppress/quell a rebellion
  a **failed/armed/slave/separatist** rebellion

▶ **SYNONYMS:** revolt, uprising, insurgency

---

re|call (recalls, recalling, recalled)

> The verb is pronounced /rɪˈkɔːl/. The noun is pronounced /ˈriːkɔːl/.

1 VERB When you **recall** something, you remember it and tell others about it. ○ *Henderson recalled that he first met Pollard during a business trip to Washington.* ○ *[+ with] Colleagues today recall with humor how meetings would crawl into the early morning hours.*

▶ **COLLOCATIONS:**
  recall something **with** something
  recall something with **fondness/pride/amusement**
  recall a **conversation/incident/occasion/moment**
  fondly/correctly/proudly/wistfully recall something

▶ **SYNONYMS:** remember, relate

2 UNCOUNTABLE NOUN **Recall** is the ability to remember something that has happened in the past or the act of remembering it. ○ *[+ of] He had a good memory, and total recall of her spoken words.* ○ *He was impressed by her effortless recall of detail.* ○ *his encyclopaedic recall*

▶ **COLLOCATIONS:**
  recall **of** something
  total/instant/photographic/vivid recall

r

re|ces|sion /rɪˈseʃən/ (recessions) BUSINESS ECONOMICS

NOUN A **recession** is a period when the economy of a country is doing badly, for example because industry is producing less and more people are becoming unemployed. ○ *The recession caused sales to drop off.* ○ *We should concentrate on sharply reducing interest rates to pull the economy out of recession.* ○ *The oil price increases sent Europe into deep recession.*

▶ **COLLOCATIONS:**
  avoid/survive/escape/enter a recession
  a **global/deep/severe/economic/mild** recession
▶ **PHRASE:** recession and unemployment
▶ **SYNONYMS:** depression, slump
▶ **ANTONYM:** boom

re|de|fine /ˌriːdɪˈfaɪn/ (redefines, redefining, redefined) ACADEMIC WORD

VERB If you **redefine** something, you cause people to consider it in a new way. ○ *We will finally have to redefine our relationship with neighbouring states in north Africa.* ○ *Feminists have redefined the role of women.*

▶ **COLLOCATION:** redefine a **role/stereotype/relationship**
▶ **SYNONYM:** reinvent

re|dis|trib|ute SOCIOLOGY ACADEMIC WORD POLITICS
/ˌriːdɪˈstrɪbjuːt/ (redistributes, redistributing, redistributed)

VERB If something such as money or property **is redistributed**, it is shared among people or organizations in a different way from the way that it was previously shared. ○ *Wealth was redistributed more equitably among society.* ○ *Taxes could be used to redistribute income.*

▶ **COLLOCATION:** redistribute **wealth/income/land/money**

re|dis|tri|bu|tion /ˌriːdɪstrɪˈbjuːʃən/

UNCOUNTABLE NOUN ○ [+ *of*] *some redistribution of income so that the better off can help to keep the worse off out of poverty* ○ *Others also believe that Labour has now abandoned support for the redistribution of power and wealth.*

▶ **COLLOCATIONS:**
  the redistribution **of** something
  redistribution of **wealth/land/income/power**

re|dun|dant /rɪˈdʌndənt/ BUSINESS

1 ADJECTIVE If you are made **redundant**, your employer tells you to leave because your job is no longer necessary or because your employer cannot afford to keep paying you. [BRIT, in AM, use **be dismissed**] ○ *My husband was made redundant late last year.* ○ *a redundant miner*

▶ COLLOCATIONS:
  redundant **staff**
  a redundant **employee/worker/workforce**
  make *someone* redundant

2 ADJECTIVE Something that is **redundant** is no longer needed because its job is being done by something else or because its job is no longer necessary or useful. ○ *Changes in technology may mean that once-valued skills are now redundant.* ○ *the conversion of redundant buildings to residential use*

▶ COLLOCATIONS:
  increasingly/effectively/largely redundant
  a redundant **building/factory/church**
  redundant **equipment**

re|dun|dan|cy /rɪˈdʌndənsi/ (redundancies)

NOUN [BRIT, in AM, use **dismissals**, **layoffs**] ○ *The ministry has said it hopes to avoid compulsory redundancies.* ○ *Thousands of bank employees are facing redundancy as their employers cut costs.* ○ *The company has had to make redundancy payments of £472 million.*

▶ COLLOCATIONS:
  face redundancy
  announce/expect/avoid redundancies
  compulsory/voluntary redundancy
  a redundancy **payment/package/programme**

---

re|fine /rɪˈfaɪn/ (refines, refining, refined) `ACADEMIC WORD`

1 VERB When a substance **is refined**, it is made pure by having all other substances removed from it. ○ *Oil is refined to remove naturally occurring impurities.* ○ *All white sugar is refined, however, this refined sugar may then be ground or coloured.*

▶ COLLOCATION: refine **oil/uranium/gasoline/sugar**
▶ SYNONYM: process

2 VERB If something such as a process, theory, or machine **is refined**, it is improved by having small changes made to it. ○ *Surgical techniques are constantly being refined.* ○ *Twentieth century botanists have continually refined these classifications.*

▶ COLLOCATIONS:
  refine a **technique/procedure/skill**
  continually/constantly/greatly refine *something*
▶ SYNONYM: improve

re|fine|ment /rɪˈfaɪnmənt/ (refinements)

NOUN ○ *Older cars inevitably lack the latest safety refinements.* ○ *development and refinement of the game*

▶ **COLLOCATIONS:**
refinement **of** something
refinement of a **technique/model/concept**
further/continual/technical refinement

▶ **SYNONYM:** improvement

re|flect /rɪˈflekt/ (reflects, reflecting, reflected)   PHYSICS

VERB When light, heat, or other rays **reflect** off a surface or when a surface **reflects** them, they are sent back from the surface and do not pass through it. ○ *The sun reflected off the snow-covered mountains.* ○ *The glass appears to reflect light naturally.*

▶ **COLLOCATIONS:**
reflect **off** something
reflect off a **surface/window**
reflect off **water**
reflect **light/sunlight/heat**
reflect an **image**

re|flec|tion /rɪˈflekʃən/

UNCOUNTABLE NOUN ○ [+ *of*] *the reflection of a beam of light off a mirror*

▶ **COLLOCATIONS:**
the reflection **of** something
the reflection of **light/sunlight/heat**

refu|gee /ˌrefjuːˈdʒiː/ (refugees)

NOUN Refugees are people who have been forced to leave their homes or their country, either because there is a war there or because of their political or religious beliefs. ○ *About one hundred Vietnamese refugees have escaped from a detention camp in Hong Kong.* ○ *Thousands of Hungarian refugees fled to the West, and armed resistance in Hungary was soon crushed.*

▶ **COLLOCATIONS:**
return/repatriate/house/resettle refugees
refugees **live/return/flee/arrive** somewhere
a refugee **camp**
refugee **status**

ref|use /ˈrefjuːs/

UNCOUNTABLE NOUN Refuse consists of the rubbish and all the things that are not wanted in a house, shop, or factory, and that are regularly thrown away; used mainly in official language. ○ *The District Council made a weekly collection of refuse.* ○ *Vast amounts of unwanted domestic refuse including TVs and washing machines have been dumped on the path.*

▶ COLLOCATIONS:
   collect/dump/discard refuse
   domestic/industrial refuse
   refuse **disposal/collection**
   a refuse **collector/bin/truck**

▶ SYNONYMS: waste, rubbish

re|gard|less /rɪˈɡɑːdləs/

PHRASE If something happens **regardless of** something else, it is not affected or influenced at all by that other thing. ○ *It takes in anybody regardless of religion, colour, or creed.* ○ *Regardless of whether he is right or wrong, we have to abide by his decisions.*

re|gime /reɪˈʒiːm/ (regimes)   ACADEMIC WORD POLITICS

NOUN If you refer to a government or system of running a country as a **regime**, you are critical of it because you think it is not democratic and uses unacceptable methods. ○ *the collapse of the Fascist regime at the end of the war* ○ *Pujol was imprisoned and tortured under the Franco regime.*

▶ COLLOCATIONS:
   a **Communist/authoritarian/strict/dictatorial/brutal** regime
   overthrow/impose a regime
   a regime **collapses/falls/crumbles**

▶ SYNONYMS: government, system, administration

re|im|burse /ˌriːɪmˈbɜːs/   BUSINESS
(reimburses, reimbursing, reimbursed)

VERB If you **reimburse** someone **for** something, you pay them back the money that they have spent or lost because of it. [FORMAL] ○ [+ *for*] *Participants will be reimbursed for any out-of-pocket expenses such as travel.* ○ *The funds are supposed to reimburse policyholders in the event of insurer failure.*

▶ **COLLOCATIONS:**
reimburse *someone* **for** *something*
reimburse a **fund/cost/expense/customer/taxpayer**
partly/fully reimburse *someone*

▶ **SYNONYM:** refund

re|im|burse|ment /ˌriːɪmˈbɜːsmənt/ (reimbursements)

NOUN ○ [+ for] *She is demanding reimbursement for medical and other expenses.*
○ *It can take up to six months before reimbursements are paid.*

▶ **COLLOCATIONS:**
reimbursement **for** *something*
seek/receive/claim reimbursement

▶ **SYNONYMS:** compensation, refund

---

re|inforce /ˌriːɪnˈfɔːs/   `ACADEMIC WORD`
(reinforces, reinforcing, reinforced)

1 VERB If something **reinforces** a feeling, situation, or process, it makes it
stronger or more intense. ○ *A stronger European Parliament would, they fear,
only reinforce the power of the larger countries.* ○ *This sense of privilege tends to
be reinforced by the outside world.*

▶ **COLLOCATIONS:**
reinforce a **perception/view/impression/belief**
mutually/powerfully/constantly/further reinforce *something*

▶ **SYNONYM:** strengthen

▶ **ANTONYM:** weaken

2 VERB If something **reinforces** an idea or point of view, it provides more
evidence or support for it. ○ *The delegation hopes to reinforce the idea that
human rights are not purely internal matters.*

▶ **COLLOCATIONS:**
reinforce a **notion/message/stereotype**
powerfully/further reinforce *something*

▶ **SYNONYM:** support

▶ **ANTONYM:** undermine

re|inforce|ment /ˌriːɪnˈfɔːsmənt/

UNCOUNTABLE NOUN ○ [+ of] *I am sure that this meeting will contribute to the
reinforcement of peace and security all over the world.* ○ [+ for] *What the teacher
now has to do is remove the reinforcement for this bad behaviour.*

▶ **COLLOCATIONS:**
the reinforcement **of/for** *something*
need/provide reinforcement
positive/negative/constant reinforcement
▶ **SYNONYM:** support

---

re|lax /rɪˈlæks/ (relaxes, relaxing, relaxed)　ACADEMIC WORD

VERB If you **relax** a rule or your control over something, or if it **relaxes**, it becomes less firm or strong. ○ *Rules governing student conduct relaxed somewhat in recent years.* ○ *How much can the President relax his grip over the nation?* ○ *Some analysts believe that the government soon will begin relaxing economic controls.*

▶ **COLLOCATIONS:**
relax a **rule/regulation/approach**
relax **control**

▶ **SYNONYM:** loosen
▶ **ANTONYM:** tighten

re|laxa|tion /ˌriːlæˈkseɪʃən/

UNCOUNTABLE NOUN ○ [+ *of/in*] *the relaxation of travel restrictions* ○ *This year's pork price crash was directly related to the relaxation of laws prohibiting pig meat imports.*

▶ **COLLOCATIONS:**
relaxation **of/in** *something*
relaxation of a **rule/restriction/regulation/law**

▶ **SYNONYM:** easing
▶ **ANTONYM:** tightening

---

rem|edy /ˈremədi/ (remedies)　MEDICINE

1 NOUN A **remedy** is a successful way of dealing with a problem. ○ *The remedy lies in the hands of the government.* ○ [+ *for*] *a remedy for economic ills*

▶ **COLLOCATIONS:**
a remedy **for** *something*
propose/suggest/devise a remedy

▶ **SYNONYM:** solution

2 NOUN A **remedy** is something that is intended to cure you when you are ill or in pain. ○ [+ *to-inf*] *natural remedies to help overcome winter infections* ○ [+ *for*] *St John's wort is a popular herbal remedy for depression.*

▶ **COLLOCATIONS:**
a remedy **for** something
a remedy for **depression/disease/illness/pain**
a **herbal/homeopathic/natural** remedy
an **alternative/effective** remedy
a **cough/cold/indigestion** remedy

▶ **SYNONYMS:** cure, treatment

Re|nais|sance /rɪˈneɪsɒns, AM ˌrenɪˈsɑːns/ `HISTORY`

NOUN The **Renaissance** was the period in Europe, especially Italy, in the 14th, 15th, and 16th centuries, when there was a new interest in art, literature, science, and learning. ○ the Renaissance masterpieces in London's galleries ○ Science took a new and different turn in the Renaissance.

▶ **COLLOCATION:** Renaissance **art/architecture/studies**

---

re|per|cus|sion /ˌriːpəˈkʌʃən/ (repercussions)

NOUN If an action or event has **repercussions**, it causes unpleasant things to happen some time after the original action or event. [FORMAL] ○ It was an effort which was to have painful repercussions. ○ Members of congress were warned of possible repercussions if their vote went through.

▶ **COLLOCATIONS:**
serious/possible/potential/negative repercussions
have/suffer/fear repercussions

▶ **SYNONYM:** consequence

---

rep|li|cate /ˈreplɪkeɪt/ (replicates, replicating, replicated)

VERB If you **replicate** someone's experiment, work, or research, you do it yourself in exactly the same way. [FORMAL] ○ He invited her to his laboratory to see if she could replicate the experiment. ○ Tests elsewhere have not replicated the findings.

▶ **COLLOCATIONS:**
replicate a **finding/experiment/experience**
successfully/exactly replicate something

▶ **SYNONYMS:** duplicate, reproduce, repeat

---

re|port|ed|ly /rɪˈpɔːtɪdli/

ADVERB If you say that something is **reportedly** true, you mean that someone has said that it is true, but you have no direct evidence of it. [FORMAL] ○ More than two hundred people have reportedly been killed in the past

week's fighting. ○ *Now Moscow has reportedly agreed that the sale can go ahead.*
○ *General Breymann had been shot dead, reportedly by one of his own men.*

ACADEMIC WRITING: Careful language

In academic writing, you try not to present as facts things you do not
have clear evidence for. You often use adverbs to show how certain
(or not) you are about an idea or a piece of information.

Reportedly, **allegedly** and **ostensibly** show that something is
based on what other people or sources have said, but that you do not
have direct evidence for and may have doubts about. ○ *France is
reportedly planning to boost military spending by 1 billion Euro.* ○ *The
scheme was ostensibly designed to promote exports.*

Apparently, **seemingly** and **supposedly** show that you are
describing what seems to be true, based on your impression of the
situation, but without clear evidence.

---

re|pro|duce /ˌriːprəˈdjuːs, AM -ˈduːs/ `BIOLOGY`
(reproduces, reproducing, reproduced)

1 VERB If you try to **reproduce** something, you try to copy it. ○ *I shall not try
to reproduce the policemen's English.* ○ *The effect has proved hard to reproduce.*

▶ **COLLOCATION:** reproduce a **sound/image/form**

▶ **SYNONYMS:** imitate, copy

2 VERB When people, animals, or plants **reproduce**, they produce young.
○ *a society where women are defined by their ability to reproduce* ○ *We are reproducing
ourselves at such a rate that our numbers threaten the ecology of the planet.*

▶ **COLLOCATIONS:**
animals/humans reproduce
reproduce a **species**

▶ **SYNONYM:** breed

re|pro|duc|tion /ˌriːprəˈdʌkʃən/

UNCOUNTABLE NOUN ○ *Genes are those tiny bits of biological information
swapped in sexual reproduction.* ○ *the acids which are vital for normal cell
reproduction* ○ *the low marginal cost of reproduction of film and television
programmes*

▶ **COLLOCATIONS:**
the reproduction **of** *something*
the reproduction of a **species/photograph/painting**
sexual/sound/photographic reproduction

rep|tile /ˈreptaɪl, AM -tɪl/ (reptiles)

`BIOLOGY`

NOUN **Reptiles** are a group of cold-blooded animals which have skins covered with small hard plates called scales, and lay eggs. Snakes, lizards, and crocodiles are reptiles.

▶ **COLLOCATION:** a **marine/giant/venomous** reptile

▶ **RELATED WORDS:** amphibian, mammal

re|sem|ble /rɪˈzembəl/ (resembles, resembling, resembled)

VERB If one thing or person **resembles** another, they are similar to each other. ○ *Some of the commercially produced venison resembles beef in flavour.* ○ *It is true that both therapies do closely resemble each other.*

▶ **COLLOCATION:** **closely/somewhat/strongly** resemble *something*

re|sem|blance /rɪˈzembləns/ (resemblances)

NOUN ○ [+ *between*] *There was a remarkable resemblance between him and Pete.* ○ [+ *to*] *Our tour prices bore little resemblance to those in the holiday brochures.*

▶ **COLLOCATIONS:**
  a resemblance **between** *things/people*
  a resemblance **to** *something/someone*
  a **remarkable/uncanny** resemblance
  see/show/bear a resemblance

▶ **SYNONYM:** similarity

re|sist /rɪˈzɪst/ (resists, resisting, resisted)

1 VERB If you **resist** something such as a change, you refuse to accept it and try to prevent it. ○ *She says she will resist a single European currency being imposed.* ○ *They resisted our attempts to modernize the distribution of books.*

▶ **COLLOCATION:** **fiercely/strongly** resist *something*

▶ **SYNONYM:** oppose

2 VERB If someone or something **resists** damage of some kind, they are not damaged. ○ *bodies trained and toughened to resist the cold* ○ *Chemicals form a protective layer that resists both oil and water-based stains.*

▶ **COLLOCATION:** resist **cold/damage/illness**

▶ **SYNONYM:** withstand

re|sist|ance /rɪˈzɪstəns/

UNCOUNTABLE NOUN **Resistance** to something such as a change or a new idea is a refusal to accept it. ○ *The U.S. wants big cuts in European agricultural export subsidies, but this is meeting resistance.* ○ [+ *to*] *stubborn resistance to social reform*

▶ COLLOCATIONS:
resistance **to** *something*
armed/stubborn/fierce/stiff resistance
meet/face/encounter/overcome resistance

▶ SYNONYM: opposition

re|sist|ant /rɪˈzɪstənt/

1 ADJECTIVE Someone who is **resistant to** something is opposed to it and wants to prevent it. ○ [+ to] *Some people are very resistant to the idea of exercise.*

▶ COLLOCATIONS:
resistant **to** *something*
stubbornly/highly/fiercely resistant

▶ SYNONYM: opposed

2 ADJECTIVE If something is **resistant to** a particular thing, it is not harmed by it. ○ [+ to] *how to improve plants to make them more resistant to disease* ○ *The body may be less resistant if it is cold.*

▶ COLLOCATIONS:
resistant **to** *something*
resistant to **disease/cold/illness**

---

re|solve /rɪˈzɒlv/ (resolves, resolving, resolved)   `ACADEMIC WORD`

1 VERB To **resolve** a problem, argument, or difficulty means to find a solution to it. [FORMAL] ○ *We must find a way to resolve these problems before it's too late.* ○ *They hoped the crisis could be resolved peacefully.*

▶ COLLOCATIONS:
quickly/peacefully/amicably resolve *something*
resolve a **dispute/conflict/crisis/issue/problem**

▶ PHRASE: a way to resolve something

2 VERB If you **resolve to** do something, you make a firm decision to do it. [FORMAL] ○ [+ to-inf] *She resolved to report the matter to the hospital's nursing manager.* ○ *The PM had finally resolved to retire.*

▶ SYNONYM: decide

reso|lu|tion /ˌrezəˈluːʃən/ (resolutions)

1 NOUN A **resolution** is a formal decision taken at a meeting by means of a vote. ○ *He replied that the U.N. had passed two major resolutions calling for a complete withdrawal.* ○ [+ on] *a draft resolution on the occupied territories*

▶ **COLLOCATIONS:**
pass/approve/propose a resolution
a resolution **on** *something*

▶ **SYNONYM:** decision

2 NOUN The **resolution** of a problem or difficulty is the final solving of it. [FORMAL] ○ [+ *to/of*] *the successful resolution of a dispute involving U.N. inspectors in Baghdad* ○ *in order to find a peaceful resolution to the crisis* ○ *Most problems don't require instant resolution.*

▶ **COLLOCATIONS:**
a resolution **to/of** *something*
a **peaceful/acceptable/speedy/alternative** resolution
conflict resolution
a resolution to/of a **dispute/crisis/issue/problem**

▶ **SYNONYMS:** solution, settlement

---

res|pi|ra|tion /ˌrespɪˈreɪʃən/ BIOLOGY MEDICINE

UNCOUNTABLE NOUN Your **respiration** is your breathing. ○ *His respiration grew fainter throughout the day.*

▶ **COLLOCATIONS:**
anaerobic/artificial/slow/rapid respiration
assist/stimulate respiration

▶ **SYNONYM:** breathing

res|pira|tory /ˈrespərətri, AM -tɔːri/

ADJECTIVE **Respiratory** means relating to breathing. ○ *people with severe respiratory problems* ○ *If you smoke then the whole respiratory system is constantly under attack.* ○ *complete respiratory failure*

▶ **COLLOCATIONS:**
a respiratory **disease/infection/illness**
the respiratory **system/tract**
respiratory **failure**

▶ **SYNONYM:** breathing

---

re|spond /rɪˈspɒnd/ (responds, responding, responded) ACADEMIC WORD

VERB When you **respond** to something that is done or said, you react to it by doing or saying something yourself. ○ [+ *to*] *They are likely to respond positively to the President's request for aid.* ○ [+ *with*] *The army responded with gunfire and tear gas.*

▶ **COLLOCATIONS:**
respond **to/with** *something*
respond **positively/appropriately/immediately**
a **government/patient/audience** responds
a **paramedic/officer** responds

▶ **SYNONYM:** react

re|sponse /rɪ'spɒns/ (responses)

NOUN ○ [+ *to/from*] *There has been no response to his remarks from the government.* ○ *Your positive response will reinforce her actions.* ○ *The meeting was called in response to a request from Venezuela.*

▶ **COLLOCATIONS:**
a response **to/from** *something*
a **positive/immediate/initial/overwhelming** response
provoke/receive/trigger a response

▶ **PHRASE:** in response to sth

▶ **SYNONYM:** reaction

re|spond|ent /rɪ'spɒndənt/ (respondents)

NOUN A **respondent** is a person who replies to something such as a survey or set of questions. ○ *60 percent of the respondents said they disapproved of the president's performance.* ○ *Three hundred and fifty questionnaire respondents were asked four questions.* ○ *the medical background of the respondents*

▶ **COLLOCATIONS:**
ask a respondent
survey/poll/questionnaire respondents
a respondent **believes/reports/admits/says** *something*
respondents' **answers/perceptions/attitudes/preferences/views**

---

re|store /rɪ'stɔː/ (restores, restoring, restored)   `ACADEMIC WORD`

1 VERB To **restore** a situation or practice means to cause it to exist again. ○ *The army has recently been brought in to restore order.* ○ *restore the status quo* ○ *The death penalty was never restored.*

▶ **COLLOCATION:** restore **confidence/order/peace/democracy**

▶ **SYNONYMS:** bring back, reinstate, re-establish

▶ **ANTONYM:** abolish

2 VERB To **restore** someone or something **to** a previous condition means to cause them to be in that condition once again. ○ [+ *to*] *We will restore her to health but it may take time.* ○ *He said the ousted president must be* *restored to power.* ○ *His country desperately needs Western aid to restore its ailing economy.*

▶ **COLLOCATION:** restore *something/someone* **to** *something*

▶ **SYNONYMS:** reinstate, return

res|to|ra|tion /ˌrestəˈreɪʃən/

UNCOUNTABLE NOUN ○ [+ *of*] *His visit is expected to lead to the restoration of diplomatic relations.* ○ *They were committed to the eventual restoration of a traditional monarchy.*

▶ **COLLOCATIONS:**
the restoration **of** *something*
the restoration of a **monarchy/sovereignty/democracy**
oppose/support/demand/facilitate the restoration of *something*

---

re|strain /rɪˈstreɪn/ (restrains, restraining, restrained) `ACADEMIC WORD`

1 VERB If you **restrain** someone, you stop them from doing what they intended or wanted to do, usually by using your physical strength. ○ *One onlooker had to be restrained by police.* ○ *One Labour MP was physically restrained during an argument with a minister.* ○ *the bare minimum of force necessary to restrain the attackers*

▶ **COLLOCATION:** **forcibly/physically** restrain *someone*

2 VERB To **restrain** something that is growing or increasing means to prevent it from getting too large. ○ *The radical 500-day plan was very clear on how it intended to try to restrain inflation.* ○ *In the 1970s, the government tried to restrain corruption.* ○ *to restrain the growth in state spending*

▶ **COLLOCATION:** restrain **spending/growth/inflation/costs**

▶ **SYNONYMS:** limit, check

▶ **ANTONYM:** encourage

re|straint /rɪˈstreɪnt/ (restraints)

NOUN **Restraints** are rules or conditions that limit or restrict someone or something. ○ [+ *on*] *The Prime Minister is calling for new restraints on trade unions.* ○ *With open frontiers and lax visa controls, criminals could cross into the country without restraint.* ○ *free of any restraints which social convention might impose*

▶ **COLLOCATIONS:**
restraints **on** *something*
restraints on **expenditure/freedom**
impose restraints

▶ **SYNONYMS:** limitation, check, constraint

▶ **ANTONYM:** freedom

re|struc|ture /ˌriːˈstrʌktʃə/ ACADEMIC WORD BUSINESS
(restructures, restructuring, restructured)

VERB To **restructure** an organization or system means to change the way it is organized, usually in order to make it work more effectively. ○ *The President called on educators and politicians to help him restructure American education.* ○ *At the same time as firms were restructuring, popular attitudes toward saving and investing were changing.* ○ *an effort to restructure or re-engineer their businesses*

▶ **COLLOCATIONS:**
restructure a **company/industry/operation/economy**
radically/successfully/drastically/financially restructure *something*

▶ **SYNONYM:** reorganize

re|struc|tur|ing /ˌriːˈstrʌktʃərɪŋ/ (restructurings)

NOUN ○ *1,520 workers were laid off as part of a restructuring.* ○ *In an effort to increase profitability, it announced a broad restructuring aimed at lowering expenses.*

▶ **COLLOCATIONS:**
a **corporate/radical/massive** restructuring
debt/industry/capital restructuring
announce/propose a restructuring

▶ **SYNONYM:** reorganization

retro|spect /ˈretrəspekt/

PHRASE When you consider something **in retrospect**, you think about it afterwards, and often have a different opinion about it from the one that you had at the time. ○ *In retrospect, I wish that I had thought about alternative courses of action.* ○ *In retrospect, it was a role he should have avoided, but fatigue and a lack of direction played their part in the choice.*

▶ **SYNONYM:** with hindsight
▶ **ANTONYM:** with foresight

retro|spec|tive /ˌretrəˈspektɪv/

ADJECTIVE **Retrospective** feelings or opinions concern things that happened in the past. ○ *Afterwards, retrospective fear of the responsibility would make her feel almost faint.* ○ *The examples I have cited have been based on retrospective accounts.*

▶ **COLLOCATION:** retrospective **fear/insight/knowledge**
▶ **ANTONYM:** prospective

retro|spec|tive|ly /ˌretrəˈspektɪvli/

ADVERB ○ *Retrospectively, it seems as if they probably were negligent.* ○ *To ascribe opinions retrospectively is of course very dangerous.*

▶ **COLLOCATION: apply/act** retrospectively

▶ **SYNONYMS:** in retrospect, with hindsight

---

re|turn /rɪˈtɜːn/ (returns) BUSINESS ECONOMICS

NOUN The **return on** an investment is the profit that you get from it. ○ *Profits have picked up this year but the return on capital remains tiny.* ○ *Higher returns and higher risk usually go hand in hand.*

▶ **COLLOCATIONS:**
generate/expect/earn/achieve a return
diminish/maximize a return
a **high/average/annual/total** return

▶ **SYNONYM:** profit

▶ **ANTONYM:** loss

---

rev|enue /ˈrevənjuː/ ACADEMIC WORD BUSINESS ECONOMICS

UNCOUNTABLE NOUN Revenue is money that a company, organization, or government receives from people. ○ *a boom year at the cinema, with record advertising revenue and the highest ticket sales since 1980* ○ *The government would gain about $12 billion in tax revenues over five years.* ○ *Fishing is the main industry, with seal-hunting in season an additional source of revenue.*

▶ **COLLOCATIONS:**
generate/expect/increase/raise/boost revenue
revenue **declines/grows/increases/falls**
annual/total/net/average/additional revenue
advertising/tax/oil/tourism revenue

▶ **SYNONYMS:** profit, income, proceeds

▶ **ANTONYM:** expenditure

---

rheto|ric /ˈretərɪk/ LANGUAGE

1 UNCOUNTABLE NOUN If you refer to speech or writing as **rhetoric**, you disapprove of it because it is intended to convince and impress people but may not be sincere or honest. ○ *What is required is immediate action, not rhetoric.* ○ *The harsh rhetoric had so soured officials that the two sides were barely speaking.*

▶ **COLLOCATIONS:**
empty/harsh rhetoric
spout rhetoric

2 UNCOUNTABLE NOUN Rhetoric is the skill or art of using language effectively. [FORMAL] ○ *the noble institutions of political life, such as political rhetoric, public office and public service* ○ *the absence of rhetoric and symbol, which poets and other writers may redress*

rhe|tori|cal /rɪ'tɒrɪkəl, AM -'tɔːr-/

1 ADJECTIVE A **rhetorical** question is one which is asked in order to make a statement rather than to get an answer. ○ *He grimaced slightly, obviously expecting no answer to his rhetorical question.* ○ *He made no answer to the Commandante's question, which had been rhetorical in any case.*

▶ **COLLOCATION:** a rhetorical **question/situation/consideration**

2 ADJECTIVE Rhetorical language is intended to be grand and impressive. [FORMAL] ○ *These arguments may have been used as a rhetorical device to argue for a perpetuation of a United Nations role.* ○ *Some of Larkin's poetry denies itself the traditional rhetorical flourishes of poetry.*

▶ **COLLOCATION:** a rhetorical **device/flourish**

---

rig|id /'rɪdʒɪd/   ACADEMIC WORD

1 ADJECTIVE Laws, rules, or systems that are **rigid** cannot be changed or varied, and are therefore considered to be rather severe. ○ *Several colleges in our study have rigid rules about student conduct.* ○ *Hospital routines for nurses are very rigid.*

▶ **COLLOCATIONS:**
  a rigid **structure/hierarchy/timetable**
  rigid **discipline**

▶ **SYNONYMS:** strict, inflexible

▶ **ANTONYM:** flexible

2 ADJECTIVE A **rigid** substance or object is stiff and does not bend, stretch, or twist easily. ○ *rigid plastic containers* ○ *These plates are fairly rigid.*

▶ **ANTONYM:** flexible

rig|id|ly /'rɪdʒɪdli/

ADVERB ○ *The caste system was rigidly enforced.* ○ *The soldiers stood rigidly, awaiting orders.*

▶ **COLLOCATIONS:**
  rigidly **hierarchical/segregated/conservative**
  adhere/enforce/control rigidly
  stand/sit/stare rigidly

▶ **SYNONYMS:** strictly, stiffly

ri|gid|ity /rɪˈdʒɪdɪti/

UNCOUNTABLE NOUN ○ [+ of] *the rigidity of government policy* ○ [+ of] *the strength and rigidity of glass.*

▸ **COLLOCATIONS:**
the rigidity **of** something
ideological/structural rigidity
▸ **SYNONYM:** inflexibility
▸ **ANTONYM:** flexibility

rig|our /ˈrɪɡə/

UNCOUNTABLE NOUN If something is done with **rigour**, it is done in a strict, thorough way. [in AM, use **rigor**] ○ *The new current affairs series promises to address challenging issues with freshness and rigour.* ○ *They must believe you will pursue injustice with rigour and not be nudged off course.*

▸ **COLLOCATION:** do something **with** rigour
▸ **SYNONYMS:** strictness, thoroughness

rig|or|ous /ˈrɪɡərəs/

ADJECTIVE A test, system, or procedure that is **rigorous** is very thorough and strict. ○ *The selection process is based on rigorous tests of competence and experience.* ○ *a rigorous system of blood analysis* ○ *rigorous military training*

▸ **COLLOCATION:** rigorous **testing/scrutiny/analysis/examination**
▸ **SYNONYMS:** thorough, strict, tough
▸ **ANTONYMS:** soft, careless

rig|or|ous|ly /ˈrɪɡərəsli/

ADVERB ○ *rigorously conducted research* ○ *A car must be very rigorously tested before the company making it is allowed to sell it to the public.*

▸ **COLLOCATION:** **enforce/test/assess/examine** rigorously
▸ **SYNONYM:** thoroughly

ritu|al /ˈrɪtʃʊəl/ (rituals) SOCIOLOGY HISTORY

NOUN A **ritual** is a religious service or other ceremony which involves a series of actions performed in a fixed order. ○ *This is the most ancient, and holiest of the Shinto rituals.* ○ *These ceremonies were already part of pre-Christian ritual in Mexico.*

▸ **COLLOCATIONS:**
a **religious/ancient/tribal** ritual
a **courtship/healing/cleansing/Buddhist** ritual
▸ **SYNONYMS:** ceremony, custom, rite

329 | **Roman numeral**

---

ri|val /ˈraɪvəl/ (rivals)　　　　　　　　　　BUSINESS

NOUN Your **rival** is a person, business, or organization who you are
competing or fighting against in the same area or for the same things.
○ *The world champion finished more than two seconds ahead of his nearest rival.*
○ *[+ in] He eliminated his rivals in a brutal struggle for power.* ○ *The police believe
the fight was due to a dispute between rival teenage gangs.* ○ *[+ for] The two are
rivals for the leadership of the party.*

▶ **COLLOCATIONS:**
　a rival **in/for** something
　rivals for the **nomination/presidency/leadership**
　rivals in a **race/market/election**
　a **main/fierce/close/arch/political** rival
　beat/defeat/eliminate a rival

▶ **SYNONYMS:** opponent, contender, adversary

ri|val|ry /ˈraɪvəlri/ (rivalries)

NOUN ○ *[+ between] the rivalry between the Inkatha and the ANC* ○ *[+ among]*
The rivalry among her peers was intense. ○ *a city torn by deep ethnic rivalries*

▶ **COLLOCATIONS:**
　rivalry **between/among** people
　rivalry **exists/grows/begins/continues/develops**
　intensify/fuel/spark/overcome rivalry
　intense/fierce/bitter/ethnic rivalry
　friendly/sporting/sibling/clan rivalry

▶ **SYNONYMS:** competition, competitiveness

Ro|man nu|mer|al /ˌrəʊmən ˈnjuːmərəl, AM ˈnuː-/
(Roman numerals)

NOUN **Roman numerals** are the letters used by the ancient Romans to
represent numbers, for example I, IV, VIII, and XL, which represent 1, 4, 8,
and 40. Roman numerals are still sometimes used today. ○ *'VII', the Roman
numeral for seven* ○ *The date was written in Roman numerals as MIIM for 1998.*
○ *a Roman numeral indicating the order in which the enzyme was discovered*

▶ **COLLOCATION: in** Roman numerals
▶ **RELATED WORD:** Arabic numeral

Ss

safe|guard /ˈseɪfɡɑːd/ (safeguards, safeguarding, safeguarded)

1 VERB To **safeguard** something or someone means to protect them from being harmed, lost, or badly treated. [FORMAL] ○ *They will press for international action to safeguard the ozone layer.* ○ *The interests of minorities will have to be safeguarded under a new constitution.* ○ [+ from/against] *They are taking precautionary measures to safeguard their forces from the effects of chemical weapons.*

▶ **COLLOCATIONS:**
safeguard something **from/against** something
safeguard against **attack/failure/abuse**
safeguard someone's **integrity/privacy/rights/interests/liberty**
safeguard the **future**
adequately/carefully/properly safeguard something

▶ **SYNONYMS:** protect, defend

2 NOUN A **safeguard** is a law, rule, or measure intended to prevent someone or something from being harmed. ○ [+ against] *Many people took second jobs as a safeguard against unemployment.* ○ [+ for] *A system like ours lacks adequate safeguards for civil liberties.*

▶ **COLLOCATIONS:**
a safeguard **against** something
a safeguard **for** someone/something
a safeguard against **abuse/misuse/fraud/disease**
provide/implement/introduce a safeguard
adequate/appropriate/sufficient safeguards
a **legal/environmental** safeguard

▶ **SYNONYMS:** protection, defence

---

sanc|tion /ˈsæŋkʃən/

POLITICS LAW

(sanctions, sanctioning, sanctioned)

1 VERB If someone in authority **sanctions** an action or practice, they officially approve of it and allow it to be done. ○ *He may now be ready to sanction the use of force.* ○ *He seemed to be preparing to sanction an increase in public borrowing.*

▶ COLLOCATIONS:
sanction a **marriage/law/loan**
sanction the **use** of *something*
officially/legally/religiously sanction *something*

▶ SYNONYM: approve

● **Sanction** is also an uncountable noun. ○ [+ *of*] *The king could not enact laws without the sanction of Parliament.* ○ [+ *of*] *Protestors argued that the military campaign should only happen with the sanction of the UN Security Council.*

▶ COLLOCATIONS:
the sanction **of** *something*
the sanction of **law**
the sanction of the **government**

▶ SYNONYM: approval

2 PLURAL NOUN **Sanctions** are measures taken by countries to restrict trade and official contact with a country that has broken international law. ○ [+ *against/on*] *The continued abuse of human rights has now led the United States to impose sanctions against the regime.* ○ *He expressed his opposition to the lifting of sanctions.*

▶ COLLOCATIONS:
sanctions **against** *something*
sanctions **against** a **country/regime/government**
impose/lift/tighten/apply sanctions
economic/international/punitive/trade sanctions

3 NOUN A **sanction** is a severe course of action which is intended to make people obey instructions, customs, or laws. ○ *As an ultimate sanction, they can sell their shares.* ○ *The authority concluded that Mr Paddick had not behaved in a way that justified the imposition of a sanction.*

▶ COLLOCATIONS:
a **criminal/ultimate** sanction
impose a sanction

---

scarce /skeəs/ (scarcer, scarcest)

ADJECTIVE If something is **scarce**, there is not enough of it. ○ *Food was scarce and expensive.* ○ *Jobs are becoming increasingly scarce.* ○ *the allocation of scarce resources*

▶ COLLOCATIONS:
increasingly/relatively/extremely scarce
scarce **resources/commodities/supplies**
scarce **food/money/employment/jobs**

▶ ANTONYM: plentiful

sce|nario /sɪˈnɑːriəʊ, AM -ˈner-/ (scenarios) `ACADEMIC WORD`

NOUN If you talk about a likely or possible **scenario**, you are talking about the way in which a situation may develop. ○ [+ of] *the nightmare scenario of a divided and irrelevant Royal Family* ○ *Try to imagine all the possible scenarios and what action you would take.*

▸ **COLLOCATIONS:**
a scenario **of** something
envision/imagine/outline/present a scenario
a **typical/likely/unlikely/possible** scenario
a **worst-case/nightmare/best-case** scenario

▸ **SYNONYM:** situation

scep|tic /ˈskeptɪk/ (sceptics)

NOUN A **sceptic** is a person who has doubts about things that other people believe. [in AM, use **skeptic**] ○ *He was a born sceptic.* ○ *But he now has to convince sceptics that he has a serious plan.*

▸ **COLLOCATIONS:**
confound/silence sceptics
convince/defy/persuade sceptics

▸ **ANTONYM:** believer

scep|ti|cal /ˈskeptɪkəl/

ADJECTIVE If you are **sceptical about** something, you have doubts about it. [in AM, use **skeptical**] ○ [+ about] *Other archaeologists are sceptical about his findings.* ○ [+ of] *scientists who are sceptical of global warming and its alleged consequences*

▸ **COLLOCATIONS:**
sceptical **about/of** something
a sceptical **analyst/observer/expert/view/attitude**
deeply/increasingly/understandably sceptical

▸ **SYNONYM:** doubtful
▸ **ANTONYM:** convinced

scep|ti|cism /ˈskeptɪsɪzəm/

UNCOUNTABLE NOUN [in AM, use **skepticism**] ○ [+ about] *There was considerable scepticism about the Chancellor's forecast of a booming economy.* ○ *The report has inevitably been greeted with scepticism.*

▸ **COLLOCATIONS:**
scepticism **about** something
widespread/considerable/deep scepticism
express/overcome/voice scepticism

▶ **SYNONYMS:** disbelief, doubt
▶ **ANTONYM:** belief

---

sche|mat|ic /skiːˈmætɪk/ `ACADEMIC WORD`

ADJECTIVE A **schematic** diagram or picture shows something in a simple way. ○ *This is represented in the schematic diagram below.* ○ *a schematic picture of the solar system*

▶ **COLLOCATION:** a schematic **diagram/representation/drawing**

---

schol|ar /ˈskɒlə/ (scholars) `EDUCATION`

NOUN A **scholar** is a person who studies an academic subject and knows a lot about it. [FORMAL] ○ *The library attracts thousands of scholars and researchers.* ○ *an influential Islamic scholar*

▶ **COLLOCATIONS:**
   a **visiting/leading/Islamic/legal/literary** scholar
   scholars **argue/study/believe** *something*

> **EXTEND YOUR VOCABULARY**
>
> To talk very generally about people who study an academic subject, you can refer to **scholars** or **academics**. ○ *Medieval historians and literary scholars have pulled together a considerable body of information about the anchoritic life.* ○ *According to academics who've studied the economics of digital music distribution ...*
>
> You can talk about people who carry out academic research as **researchers**. ○ *The researchers found that there were marked changes.*
>
> You can refer to people who know a lot about a subject as **experts** or **specialists**. ○ *The world's most senior medical specialists remain uncertain of its cause or treatment.*
>
> You can also, of course, use the relevant term for people studying a particular subject; **economists**, **physicists**, **sociologists**, etc.

---

scru|ti|nize /ˈskruːtɪnaɪz/ (scrutinizes, scrutinizing, scrutinized)

VERB If you **scrutinize** something, you examine it very carefully, often to find out some information from it or about it. [in BRIT, also use **scrutinise**] ○ *The events that are scrutinized range from large data series on insurance company accident claims to single cases.* ○ *Lloyds' results were carefully scrutinised as a guide to what to expect from the other banks.*

▶ COLLOCATIONS:
closely/carefully/heavily scrutinize *something*
scrutinize **spending/legislation/expenditure**
scrutinize a **decision/application/bill/proposal**
a **committee/investigator/authority** scrutinizes *something*

▶ SYNONYM: examine

scru|ti|ny /'skru:tɪni/

UNCOUNTABLE NOUN If a person or thing is under **scrutiny**, they are being studied or observed very carefully. ○ *His private life came under media scrutiny.* ○ *The President promised a government open to public scrutiny.*

▶ COLLOCATIONS:
under/open to scrutiny
increase/face/avoid/undergo scrutiny
intense/close/public/parliamentary scrutiny

▶ SYNONYM: examination

---

sculp|ture /'skʌlptʃə/ (sculptures)   `ARTS`

1 NOUN A **sculpture** is a work of art that is produced by carving or shaping stone, wood, clay, or other materials. ○ [+ *of*] *stone sculptures of figures and animals* ○ *a collection of 20th-century art and sculpture*

▶ COLLOCATIONS:
carve/create/unveil/exhibit a sculpture
a **bronze/ice/metal/stone** sculpture
a sculpture **garden/gallery/exhibition**

▶ PHRASE: paintings and sculptures

2 UNCOUNTABLE NOUN **Sculpture** is the art of creating sculptures. ○ *Both studied sculpture.* ○ *The Arts Academy offers courses in sculpture and painting.* ○ *He studied sculpture at the Royal College of Art.*

sculp|tor /'skʌlptə/ (sculptors)

NOUN A **sculptor** is someone who creates sculptures. ○ *The critic at the Washington Post called him the most innovative sculptor of the decade.* ○ *He is a glass sculptor, so his true skill lies with glass itself.*

▶ COLLOCATIONS:
a **glass/ice/sand** sculptor
a **renowned/innovative/Italian/talented** sculptor

▶ PHRASES:
painter and sculptor
artist and sculptor

secu|lar /ˈsekjʊlə/

SOCIOLOGY

ADJECTIVE You use **secular** to describe things that have no connection with religion. ○ *He spoke about preserving the country as a secular state.* ○ *secular and religious education*

▶ **COLLOCATIONS:**
a secular **democracy/society/regime**
a secular **ruler/saint/ideology**
increasingly/largely/completely secular

▶ **ANTONYM:** religious

secu|lar|ized /ˈsekjʊləraɪzd/

ADJECTIVE **Secularized** societies are no longer under the control or influence of religion. [in BRIT, also use **secularised**] ○ *The Pope had no great sympathy for the secularized West.* ○ *the changes brought about by an increasingly secularized society*

▶ **COLLOCATION:** a secularized *society*

▶ **ANTONYM:** religious

se|cure /sɪˈkjʊə/ (secures, securing, secured)

ACADEMIC WORD

VERB If you **secure** something that you want or need, you obtain it, often after a lot of effort. [FORMAL] ○ *Federal leaders continued their efforts to secure a ceasefire.* ○ *Graham's achievements helped secure him the job.*

▶ **COLLOCATIONS:**
secure a **victory/conviction/place/win/deal**
secure the **approval/support/backing** of *someone*
secure **funding/peace**

▶ **SYNONYM:** obtain

semi|nal /ˈsemɪnəl/

ADJECTIVE **Seminal** is used to describe things such as books, works, events, and experiences that have a great influence in a particular field. [FORMAL] ○ *author of the seminal book 'Animal Liberation'* ○ *The reforms have been a seminal event in the history of the NHS.*

▶ **COLLOCATIONS:**
a seminal **moment/event**
a seminal **paper/essay/work/thinker/influence**

▶ **SYNONYMS:** significant, ground-breaking, influential

sex|ism /ˈseksɪzəm/

UNCOUNTABLE NOUN **Sexism** is the belief that the members of one sex, usually women, are less intelligent or less capable than those of the other sex and need not be treated equally. It is also the behaviour which is the result of this belief. ○ *Groups like ours are committed to eradicating homophobia, racism and sexism.* ○ *A small number of women have reached senior positions only to find a glass ceiling or even blatant sexism.*

▶ **COLLOCATION: blatant/reverse/institutional** sexism

▶ **PHRASE:** racism and sexism

sex|ist /ˈseksɪst/ (sexists)

ADJECTIVE If you describe people or their behaviour as **sexist**, you mean that they are influenced by the belief that the members of one sex, usually women, are less intelligent or less capable than those of the other sex and need not be treated equally. ○ *Old-fashioned sexist attitudes are still common.* ○ *There is a continued reluctance to recognize the racist, sexist and ageist biases in our social system as a whole.*

● A **sexist** is someone with sexist views or behaviour. ○ *The judges are, however inadvertently, adopting the logic of generalization, of racists and sexists.* ○ *she seems to have had a soft spot for old-fashioned sexists*

▶ **COLLOCATIONS:**
a sexist **remark/attitude/joke/comment**
sexist **behaviour/language**

▶ **PHRASE:** racist and sexist

share /ʃeə/ (shares) `BUSINESS` `ECONOMICS`

NOUN A company's **shares** are the many equal parts into which its ownership is divided. Shares can be bought by people as an investment. ○ [+ in] *This is why Sir Colin Marshall, British Airways' chairman, has been so keen to buy shares in U.S.-AIR.* ○ *For some months the share price remained fairly static.*

▶ **COLLOCATIONS:**
shares **in** *something*
buy/purchase/trade/sell/redeem shares
shares **rise/fall/soar/drop**
a share **price/scheme/profit**

▶ **PHRASE:** stocks and shares

---

short|coming /ˈʃɔːtkʌmɪŋ/ (shortcomings)

NOUN Someone's or something's **shortcomings** are the faults or weaknesses which they have. ○ [+ of] *Marriages usually break down as a result of the shortcomings of both partners.* ○ *His book has its shortcomings.*

▶ **COLLOCATIONS:**
   the shortcomings **of** *someone/something*
   perceive/highlight/expose/address shortcomings
   marked/serious/glaring shortcomings

▶ **SYNONYMS:** failing, weakness

▶ **ANTONYM:** strength

---

shrink /ʃrɪŋk/ (shrinks, shrinking, shrank, shrunk)

VERB If something **shrinks** or something else **shrinks** it, it becomes smaller. ○ *The vast forests of West Africa have shrunk.* ○ *Hungary may have to lower its hopes of shrinking its state sector.*

▶ **COLLOCATIONS:**
   a **workforce/economy/deficit** shrinks
   drastically/dramatically/steadily shrink

▶ **SYNONYM:** decrease

▶ **ANTONYM:** grow

---

sig|ni|fy /ˈsɪɡnɪfaɪ/ (signifies, signifying, signified)   `ACADEMIC WORD`

VERB If an event, a sign, or a symbol **signifies** something, it is a sign of that thing or represents that thing. ○ *The contrasting approaches to Europe signified a sharp difference between the major parties.* ○ [+ that] *The symbol displayed outside a restaurant signifies there's excellent cuisine inside.*

▶ **COLLOCATIONS:**
   signify a **shift** in *something*
   signify the **beginning/end** of *something*

▶ **SYNONYM:** indicate

---

sign lan|guage /ˈsaɪn ˌlæŋɡwɪdʒ/ (sign languages)

NOUN **Sign language** is movements of your hands and arms used to communicate. There are several official systems of sign language, used for example by deaf people. Movements are also sometimes invented by people when they want to communicate with someone who does not speak the same language. ○ *Her son used sign language to tell her what happened.* ○ *He indicated with sign language that he too would like to go there.*

▶ **COLLOCATION:** **use/know/speak/learn** sign language

sili|con chip /ˈsɪlɪkən ˌtʃɪp/ (silicon chips)

NOUN A **silicon chip** is a very small piece of silicon inside a computer. It has electronic circuits on it and can hold large quantities of information or perform mathematical or logical operations. ○ *This silicon chip implant will perform the same processes as the damaged part of the brain it is replacing.* ○ *RFID tags are tiny silicon chips that broadcast a unique identification code when prompted by a reader device.*

▶ **SYNONYM:** microchip

skull /skʌl/ (skulls) BIOLOGY

NOUN Your **skull** is the bony part of your head which encloses your brain. ○ *Her husband was later treated for a fractured skull.* ○ *I discovered two human skulls, obviously very old and half disintegrated*

▶ **COLLOCATIONS:**
   fracture/crack a skull
   a **fossil/fractured/human** skull
   a skull **bone/fracture/cap**

so-called /ˈsəʊkɔːld/ also so called ACADEMIC WORD

1 ADJECTIVE You use **so-called** to indicate that you think a word or expression used to describe someone or something is in fact wrong. ○ *These are the facts that explode their so-called economic miracle.* ○ *More and more companies have gone 'green' and started producing so-called environmentally-friendly products.*

▶ **COLLOCATION:** a so-called **expert**

2 ADJECTIVE You use **so-called** to indicate that something is generally referred to by the name that you are about to use. ○ *a summit of the world's seven leading market economies, the so-called G-7* ○ *She was one of the so-called Gang of Four.*

> **ACADEMIC WRITING: Careful language**
>
> In academic writing, it is important to choose your language carefully. In an academic context particular terms often have very specific meanings, that may be slightly different from their everyday usage.
>
> Sometimes you want to include a term that you know is not completely accurate or appropriate, but is commonly used, for example, in the media. You can use **so-called** to show that you

understand the usage of the term or you can use expressions such as **commonly/popularly known as**. ○ *The virus was found on farms outside a so-called hot zone.* ○ *the International Bank for Reconstruction and Development (IBRD), commonly known as the World Bank*

so|lar sys|tem /ˈsəʊlə ˌsɪstəm/ (solar systems) `GEOGRAPHY` `SCIENCE`

NOUN The **solar system** is the sun and all the planets that go round it. ○ *Saturn is the second biggest planet in the solar system.* ○ *All the objects in the solar system shine by reflecting the light coming from the Sun.*

sole /səʊl/ `ACADEMIC WORD`

1 ADJECTIVE The **sole** thing or person of a particular type is the only one of that type. ○ *Their sole aim is to destabilize the Indian government.* ○ *It's the sole survivor of an ancient family of plants.*

▶ COLLOCATIONS:
   the sole **purpose/aim/responsibility**
   a sole **survivor**
▶ SYNONYM: only

2 ADJECTIVE If you have **sole** charge or ownership of something, you are the only person in charge of it or who owns it. ○ *Many women are left as the sole providers in families after their husband has died.* ○ *Chief Hart had sole control over that fund.*

▶ COLLOCATIONS:
   sole **possession/responsibility/custody**
   a sole **proprietor/representative/breadwinner**

sole|ly /ˈsəʊlli/

ADVERB If something involves **solely** one thing, it involves only this thing and no others. ○ *Too often we make decisions based solely upon what we see in the magazines.* ○ *This program is a production of NPR, which is solely responsible for its content.*

▶ COLLOCATIONS:
   rely/concentrate/focus solely on *something*
   based solely on *something*
   solely **responsible**
▶ SYNONYM: only

son|ic /'sɒnɪk/ `PHYSICS`

ADJECTIVE **Sonic** is used to describe things related to sound. ○ *He activated the door with the miniature sonic transmitter.* ○ *It was shown that the noise of sonic booms could be reduced by modifying an aircraft's shape.*

▶ **COLLOCATION:** a sonic **boom/transmitter**

▶ **RELATED WORD:** visual

sov|er|eign /'sɒvrɪn/ `POLITICS`

ADJECTIVE A **sovereign** state or country is independent and not under the authority of any other country. ○ *Lithuania and Armenia signed a treaty in Vilnius recognising each other as independent sovereign states.* ○ *The Russian Federation declared itself to be a sovereign republic.*

▶ **COLLOCATION:** a sovereign **nation/state/government**

▶ **SYNONYM:** autonomous

span /spæn/ (spans)

1 NOUN A **span** is the period of time between two dates or events during which something exists, functions, or happens. ○ [+ *of*] *The batteries had a life span of six hours.* ○ [+ *between*] *Gradually the time span between sessions will increase.*

▶ **COLLOCATIONS:**
a span **of** *something*
the span **between** *things*
a **life/time** span
a **short/four-year/five-minute** span

2 NOUN Your concentration **span** or your attention **span** is the length of time you are able to concentrate on something or be interested in it. ○ *His ability to absorb information was astonishing, but his concentration span was short.* ○ *Young children have a limited attention span and can't concentrate on one activity for very long.*

▶ **COLLOCATION:** a **concentration/attention** span

speci|fy /'spesɪfaɪ/ (specifies, specifying, specified) `ACADEMIC WORD`

1 VERB If you **specify** something, you give information about what is required or should happen in a certain situation. ○ *They specified a spacious entrance hall.* ○ [+ *what*] *He has not specified what action he would like them to take.*

2 VERB If you **specify** what should happen or be done, you explain it in an exact and detailed way. ○ *Each recipe specifies the size of egg to be used.*

○ [+ that] *One rule specifies that learner drivers must be supervised by adults.*
○ *Patients eat together at a specified time.*

▶ COLLOCATIONS:
specify a **date/size/time/period**
exactly/explicitly specify *something*

speci|fi|ca|tion /ˌspesɪfɪˈkeɪʃən/ (specifications)

NOUN A **specification** is a requirement which is clearly stated, for example about the necessary features in the design of something. ○ [+ *for*] *Legislation will require U.K. petrol companies to meet an E.U. specification for petrol.* ○ *officials constrained by rigid job specifications*

▶ COLLOCATIONS:
a specification **for** *something*
exacting/detailed/technical specifications
meet/check/alter specifications

▶ SYNONYM: requirement

---

spec|trum /ˈspektrəm/ (spectra or spectrums)   PHYSICS

1 NOUN **The spectrum** is the range of different colours which is produced when light passes through a glass prism or through a drop of water. A rainbow shows the colours in the spectrum. ○ *lights known as ultraviolet because on the colour spectrum they lie above violet* ○ *Yellow is the most luminous of the colour spectrum.*

▶ PHRASE: the colour spectrum

2 NOUN A **spectrum** is a range of a particular type of thing. ○ *She'd seen his moods range across the emotional spectrum.* ○ *Politicians across the political spectrum have denounced the act.* ○ [+ *of*] *The term 'special needs' covers a wide spectrum of problems.*

▶ COLLOCATIONS:
a spectrum **of** *things*
a **broad/wide/entire** spectrum
the **political/emotional** spectrum

▶ SYNONYM: range

3 NOUN A **spectrum** is a range of light waves or radio waves within particular frequencies. ○ *Vast amounts of energy, from X-rays right through the spectrum down to radio waves, are escaping into space.* ○ *The individual colours within the light spectrum are believed to have an effect on health.* ○ *the ultraviolet spectra of hot stars*

▶ COLLOCATION: the **light/ultraviolet/radio** spectrum

specu|late /ˈspekjʊleɪt/ **(speculates, speculating, speculated)**

VERB If you **speculate** about something, you make guesses about its nature or identity, or about what might happen. ○[+ *about*] *Critics of the project speculate about how many hospitals could be built instead.* ○ [+ *that*] *The doctors speculate that he died of a cerebral haemorrhage caused by a blow on the head.*

▶ **COLLOCATIONS:**
speculate **about** *something*
analysts/observers/researchers/experts speculate

specu|la|tion /ˌspekjʊˈleɪʃən/ **(speculations)**

NOUN ○ [+ *over*] *The President has gone out of his way to dismiss speculation over the future of the economy minister.* ○ [+ *about*] *I had published my speculations about the future of the universe in the Review of Modern Physics.*

▶ **COLLOCATIONS:**
speculation **about/over** *something*
fuel/prompt/spark/dismiss speculation
intense/widespread/pure speculation
media/press speculation
speculation **mounts/continues/grows**

EXTEND YOUR VOCABULARY

You use **speculate/speculation** and **conjecture** to talk about ideas that are guesses, often based on evidence or facts that are not complete. So an academic, for example, uses their knowledge of the subject together with limited evidence to draw conclusions or make predictions. ○ *The researchers speculate that this weather spreads the disease.* ○ *We have more basis for conjecture about the Polynesians, for we can study their descendants today.*

You also use **assume/assumption** to refer to a guess you have made about something, based on your knowledge of it. You then use this assumption as the basis for further ideas. If you **assume** something, you believe it is true, but if you **speculate** about something, you think it may be true. ○ *Each approach springs from a particular set of assumptions about the nature of learning.*

sphere /sfɪə/ (spheres) ACADEMIC WORD

NOUN A **sphere of** activity or interest is a particular area of activity or interest. ○ [+ of] *the sphere of international politics* ○ [+ of] *nurses, working in all spheres of the health service*

▶ **COLLOCATIONS:**
  a sphere **of** something
  a sphere of **activity/influence/life**

▶ **SYNONYM:** field

spine /spaɪn/ (spines) BIOLOGY MEDICINE

NOUN Your **spine** is the row of bones down your back. ○ *Her spine was severed, but within eight months, she already was back in the saddle, riding again.* ○ *a degenerative bone disease of the upper spine and neck*

▶ **COLLOCATIONS:**
  sever/straighten/damage/fracture someone's spine
  a spine **deformity/injury/surgeon**

spi|nal /ˈspaɪnəl/

ADJECTIVE **Spinal** means relating to your spine. ○ *The spinal cord is a cylindrical mass of nerve cells which connect with the brain and also with other parts of the body.* ○ *The boy had been taken into a hospital in Sheffield well known for its work in spinal injuries.*

▶ **COLLOCATIONS:**
  a spinal **cord/injury/fracture**
  the spinal **column**
  spinal **surgery**

stake /steɪk/ (stakes) BUSINESS

NOUN If you have a **stake in** something such as a business, it matters to you, for example because you own part of it or because its success or failure will affect you. ○ [+ in] *He was eager to return to a more entrepreneurial role in which he had a big financial stake in his own efforts.* ○ [+ in] *Detectives now believe the Mafia also had a stake in the plot and killed him when it went wrong.*

▶ **COLLOCATIONS:**
  a stake **in** something
  a stake in a **company/firm/venture**
  have/hold/buy/sell/acquire a stake in something
  a **controlling/substantial/50 percent** stake

stake|hold|er /ˈsteɪkhəʊldə/ (stakeholders) `BUSINESS`

NOUN **Stakeholders** are people who have an interest in a company's or organization's affairs. ○ *The assessment resulted in major stakeholders receiving different percentages of the available equity.* ○ *In future, key stakeholders should be part of any plan for fighting the disease, should it ever return.*

▶ **COLLOCATIONS:**
 a **key/minority/majority/major** stakeholder
 a stakeholder **pension/scheme/plan**

stance /stæns/ (stances)

NOUN Your **stance** on a particular matter is your attitude to it. ○ [+ *on*] *The Congress had agreed to reconsider its stance on the armed struggle.* ○ *They have maintained a consistently neutral stance.* ○ [+ *towards*] *His stance towards the story is quite similar to ours.*

▶ **COLLOCATIONS:**
 someone's stance **towards/on** *something*
 adopt/maintain/take/assume a stance
 a **neutral/tough/aggressive/moral** stance
▶ **SYNONYM:** position

sta|ple /ˈsteɪpəl/ (staples)

ADJECTIVE A **staple** food, product, or activity is one that is basic and important in people's everyday lives. ○ *Rice is the staple food of more than half the world's population.* ○ *The Chinese also eat a type of pasta as part of their staple diet.* ○ *Staple goods are disappearing from the shops.*

• **Staple** is also a noun. ○ [+ *in*] *Fish is a staple in the diet of many Africans.* ○ *boutiques selling staples such as jeans and T-shirts*

▶ **COLLOCATIONS:**
 a staple **in** *something*
 a staple **diet/food/ingredient/crop**
▶ **SYNONYM:** basic

state /steɪt/ (states)

NOUN When you talk about the **state of** someone or something, you are referring to the condition they are in or what they are like at a particular time. ○ [+ *of*] *He will be in a state of great emotional shock due to his wife's death.* ○ [+ *of*] *the president declared a state of emergency*

▶ COLLOCATIONS:
a state **of** something
a state of **emergency/affairs**
a state of **shock/consciousness**
someone's state of **mind**

▶ SYNONYM: condition

state-of-the-art /ˌsteɪt əv ði 'ɑːt/

ADJECTIVE If you describe something as **state-of-the-art**, you mean that it is the best available because it has been made using the most modern techniques and technology. ○ *the production of state-of-the-art military equipment* ○ *state-of-the-art technology*

▶ COLLOCATIONS:
state-of-the-art **equipment/technology**
a state-of-the-art **facility/stadium/kitchen**

sta|tus quo /ˌsteɪtəs 'kwəʊ/

NOUN **The status quo** is the state of affairs that exists at a particular time, especially in contrast to a different possible state of affairs. ○ *By 492 votes to 391, the federation voted to maintain the status quo.* ○ *They have no wish for any change in the status quo.* ○ *We must not return to the status quo.*

▶ COLLOCATIONS:
maintain/support/change/threaten the status quo
return to the status quo

statu|tory /'stætʃʊtəri, AM -tɔːri/   LAW

ADJECTIVE **Statutory** means relating to rules or laws which have been formally written down. [FORMAL] ○ *We had a statutory duty to report to Parliament.* ○ *Compliance with the statutory requirements is necessary to secure the monies.*

▶ COLLOCATIONS:
a statutory **declaration/duty/requirement**
a statutory **obligation/provision**

stem /stem/ (stems, stemming, stemmed)

1 VERB If a condition or problem **stems from** something, it was caused originally by that thing. ○ [+ from] *Much of the instability stems from the economic effects of the war.* ○ [+ from] *Much of London's energy and resilience stems from the fact that London has always been a city that relied on migrants.*

▶ **COLLOCATIONS:**
stem **from** *something*
a **problem** stems from *something*
stem from a **fact/incident/belief/misconception**

▶ **SYNONYM:** originate

2 VERB If you **stem** something, you stop it spreading, increasing, or continuing. [FORMAL] ○ *Austria has sent three army battalions to its border with Hungary to stem the flow of illegal immigrants.* ○ *He was still conscious, trying to stem the bleeding with his right hand.*

▶ **COLLOCATION:** stem the **tide/flow/spread** of *something*

▶ **SYNONYM:** stop

---

strik|ing /ˈstraɪkɪŋ/

ADJECTIVE Something that is **striking** is very noticeable or unusual.
○ *The most striking feature of those statistics is the high proportion of suicides.*
○ *He bears a striking resemblance to Lenin.*

▶ **COLLOCATIONS:**
a striking **similarity/resemblance/contrast/feature/example**
visually/particularly/especially striking

strik|ing|ly /ˈstraɪkɪŋli/

ADVERB ○ *In one respect, however, the men really were strikingly similar.* ○ *Most strikingly, the amount consumers spent in the shops grew much more quickly than anyone expected.*

▶ **COLLOCATION:** strikingly **similar/different/beautiful/handsome**

---

strive /straɪv/ (strives, striving)

The past tense is either **strove** or **strived**, and the past participle is either **striven** or **strived**.

VERB If you **strive to** do something or **strive for** something, you make a great effort to do it or get it. ○ [+ to-inf] *He strives hard to keep himself very fit.* ○ [+ for] *Mr Annan said the region must now strive for economic development as well as peace.*

▶ **COLLOCATIONS:**
strive **for** *something*
strive for **perfection/excellence/consistency**
strive to **achieve/overcome/maintain** *something*
continually/constantly strive

---

stroke /strəʊk/ (strokes) MEDICINE

NOUN If someone has a **stroke**, a blood vessel in their brain bursts or becomes blocked, which may kill them or make them unable to move one side of their body. ○ *He had a minor stroke in 1987, which left him partly paralysed.* ○ *He suffered a stroke in 1919 which made it very difficult for him to cope in the last years of his presidency.*

▶ **COLLOCATIONS:**
  a **suspected/minor/severe/fatal/mini** stroke
  a stroke **victim/patient/unit**
  suffer/have/prevent a stroke

---

sub|or|di|nate /sə'bɔːdɪnət/ ACADEMIC WORD

ADJECTIVE Something that is **subordinate to** something else is less important than the other thing. ○ [+ to] *It was an art in which words were subordinate to images.* ○ [+ to] *However, this critique of conspiracy or integrationist theory is subordinate to Connell's main contention.*

▶ **COLLOCATIONS:**
  subordinate **to** *something*
  a subordinate **role/position**
  a subordinate **group/class**

▶ **SYNONYM:** inferior

▶ **ANTONYM:** superior

---

sub|sidi|ary /səb'sɪdiəri, AM -dieri/ ACADEMIC WORD BUSINESS
(subsidiaries)

1 NOUN A **subsidiary** or a **subsidiary** company is a company which is part of a larger and more important company. ○ [+ of] *British Asia Airways, a subsidiary of British Airways* ○ *It's one of ten companies that are subsidiaries of Cossack Holdings.*

▶ **COLLOCATIONS:**
  a subsidiary **of** *something*
  a subsidiary of a **company/firm/conglomerate/bank**
  a subsidiary **company/corporation/bank**
  a **fully-owned/majority-owned** subsidiary

2 ADJECTIVE If something is **subsidiary**, it is less important than something else with which it is connected. ○ *The economics ministry has increasingly played a subsidiary role to the finance ministry.* ○ *This character may be pushed into a subsidiary position or even abandoned altogether.*

▶ **COLLOCATION:** a subsidiary **role/position**

▶ **SYNONYM:** secondary

suc|ces|sive /sək'sesɪv/

ADJECTIVE **Successive** means happening or existing one after another without a break. ○ *Jackson was the winner for a second successive year.* ○ *Britain was suffering from the failure of successive governments to co-ordinate a national transport policy.*

▶ COLLOCATIONS:
the **second/third/fourth** successive *something*
successive **governments/defeats/wins/generations**

suc|cinct /sək'sɪŋkt/

ADJECTIVE Something that is **succinct** expresses facts or ideas clearly and in few words. ○ *The book gives an admirably succinct account of the technology and its history.* ○ *If you have something to say make sure that it is accurate, succinct and to the point.*

▶ COLLOCATIONS:
a succinct **summary/description/statement**
a succinct **account/verdict**

suc|cinct|ly /sək'sɪŋktli/

ADVERB ○ *He succinctly summed up his manifesto as 'Work hard, train hard and play hard'.* ○ *Succinctly, the Commission explored real social and legal problems, while developing a theoretical approach.*

▶ COLLOCATION: succinctly **put/summed up/summarized/stated**

EXTEND YOUR VOCABULARY

When someone expresses something in few words, you can say that the piece of speech or writing is **short** or **brief**.

▶ a short **answer/speech/essay/report/version**
▶ a brief **description/summary/overview/statement**

You can also say that someone explains or describes something **briefly** (but not 'shortly'). ○ *Briefly describe the steps in the risk management process.*

You use **succinct/succinctly** or **concise/concisely** to talk about a piece of speech or writing that expresses the important facts or ideas clearly in a few words, without unnecessary details. ○ *Weston's essay provides a succinct overview of the historical development of human rights ideas.* ○ *You must state clearly and concisely exactly what your goals are.*

sum|mit /ˈsʌmɪt/ (summits)   `POLITICS` `GEOGRAPHY`

1 NOUN A **summit** is a meeting at which the leaders of two or more countries discuss important matters. ○ *next week's Washington summit* ○ *the NATO summit meeting in Rome* ○ *The Palestinian leader would then be able to attend the Arab summit on March 27th in Beirut.*

▶ COLLOCATIONS:
   attend/host/hold a summit
   a **peace/emergency/annual/economic/Arab** summit
   a summit **meeting**

2 NOUN The **summit** of a mountain is the top of it. ○ *[+ of] the first man to reach the summit of Mount Everest* ○ *[+ of] He reached the summit of the mountain at about noon.*

▶ COLLOCATIONS:
   the summit **of** *something*
   reach the summit
   the summit of a **hill/mountain/volcano**
   the summit of **Everest/Mount Ararat**

---

sup|press /səˈpres/   `POLITICS` `MEDICINE`
(suppresses, suppressing, suppressed)

1 VERB If someone in authority **suppresses** an activity, they prevent it from continuing, by using force or making it illegal. ○ *drug traffickers, who continue to flourish despite international attempts to suppress them* ○ *nationwide demonstrations for democracy, suppressed after 7 weeks by the army*

▶ COLLOCATIONS:
   suppress a **rebellion/uprising/revolt**
   a **government/authority/regime** suppresses *something*
   brutally/violently/ruthlessly suppress *something*

2 VERB If a natural function or reaction of your body **is suppressed**, it is stopped, for example by drugs or illness. ○ *The reproduction and growth of the cancerous cells can be suppressed by bombarding them with radiation.* ○ *the strongest evidence so far that ultraviolet light can suppress human immune responses*

▶ COLLOCATIONS:
   suppress the **appetite**
   suppress **ovulation/menstruation**
   a **pill/drug/treatment** suppresses *something*

▶ SYNONYM: inhibit

S

sup|pres|sion /sə'preʃən/

UNCOUNTABLE NOUN ○ [+ of] *Eye problems can indicate an unhealthy lifestyle with subsequent suppression of the immune system.* ○ [+ of] *people who were imprisoned after the violent suppression of the pro-democracy movement protests*

▶ **COLLOCATIONS:**
suppression **of** *something*
suppression of a **symptom/emotion**
suppression of a **movement/demonstration/uprising/rebellion**
brutal/violent/bloody/ruthless suppression

▶ **SYNONYM:** subdue

sur|pass /sə'pɑːs, -'pæs/ (surpasses, surpassing, surpassed)

VERB If one person or thing **surpasses** another, the first is better than, or has more of a particular quality than, the second. ○ *He was determined to surpass the achievements of his older brothers.* ○ *Warwick Arts Centre is the second largest Arts Centre in Britain, surpassed in size only by London's Barbican.*

▶ **COLLOCATIONS:**
surpass **expectations**
surpass a **mark/record/achievement**
even/far/easily surpass *something*

EXTEND YOUR VOCABULARY

You can use **surpass** and **exceed** to say that one thing is greater than another. Usually, **exceed** is used to say that something is simply greater in number or size than another amount or a limit. **Surpass** often suggests a judgement about quality, that something is bigger, but also better than something else. ○ *They are consuming toxic pollutants at levels exceeding international safety limits.* ○ *The Helios reached 85,100 feet, surpassing the all-time record for a non-rocket craft of 85,068.*

You can say that something **exceeds** or **surpasses expectations** to mean that it is better than expected. ○ *Sales in the first quarter exceeded/surpassed all expectations.*

---

sus|pend /sə'spend/ (suspends, suspending, suspended) ACADEMIC WORD

1 VERB If you **suspend** something, you delay it or stop it from happening for a while or until a decision is made about it. ○ *The union suspended strike action this week.* ○ [+ until] *A U.N. official said aid programs will be suspended until there's adequate protection for relief convoys.*

▶ COLLOCATIONS:
suspend *something* **until** *a time*
immediately/temporarily/indefinitely suspend *something*
suspend **aid/trading/operations**
suspend a **flight/shipment/sentence**

▶ PHRASE: suspend disbelief

▶ SYNONYM: delay

2 VERB If something **is suspended** from a high place, it is hanging from
that place. ○ *a mobile of birds or nursery rhyme characters which could be
suspended over the cot* ○ *chandeliers suspended on heavy chains from the ceiling*

▶ COLLOCATIONS:
suspended **from/by/over/above** *something*
suspended from a **ceiling/rafter/hook**
suspended by **wire/rope**
suspended above the **floor/ground**

▶ SYNONYM: hang

sus|pen|sion /sə'spenʃən/

UNCOUNTABLE NOUN ○ [+ *of*] *A strike by British Airways ground staff has led to
the suspension of flights between London and Manchester.* ○ [+ *of*] *Art experts
have appealed for the suspension of plans to restore one of Leonardo da Vinci's
most celebrated paintings.*

▶ COLLOCATIONS:
the suspension **of** *something*
the suspension of **trading/aid/activity**

▶ PHRASE: the suspension of disbelief

---

syl|la|bus /'sɪləbəs/ (syllabuses)   EDUCATION

NOUN You can refer to the subjects that are studied in a particular course
as the **syllabus**. [mainly BRIT] ○ *the GCSE history syllabus* ○ *The instructor
will follow the syllabus outlined in the students' workbooks.*

▶ COLLOCATIONS:
teach/follow a syllabus
the **maths/science/education/school** syllabus

---

syn|drome /'sɪndrəʊm/ (syndromes)   MEDICINE

NOUN A **syndrome** is a medical condition that is characterized by a
particular group of signs and symptoms. ○ *Irritable bowel syndrome seems
to affect more women than men.* ○ *The syndrome is more likely to strike those
whose immune systems are already below par.*

▸ **COLLOCATIONS:**
  cause/acquire/diagnose/have a syndrome
  a **bowel/respiratory/acute/chronic/infant** syndrome

syn|ony|mous /sɪˈnɒnɪməs/

ADJECTIVE If you say that one thing is **synonymous with** another, you mean that the two things are very closely associated with each other so that one suggests the other, or one cannot exist without the other.
  ○ [+ with] *Paris has always been synonymous with elegance, luxury and style.*
  ○ *In politics, power and popularity are not synonymous.*

▸ **COLLOCATIONS:**
  synonymous **with** *something*
  a **name** synonymous with *something*
  synonymous with **quality/excellence/wealth**
  almost/practically/once synonymous
  become/be synonymous

syn|the|size /ˈsɪnθɪsaɪz/   `SCIENCE`
(synthesizes, synthesizing, synthesized)

VERB To **synthesize** a substance means to produce it by means of chemical or biological reactions. [in BRIT, also use **synthesise**] ○ *After extensive research, Albert Hoffman first succeeded in synthesizing the acid in 1938.* ○ *A vitamin is a chemical compound that cannot be synthesized by the human body.*

▸ **COLLOCATIONS:**
  synthesize a **protein/compound/molecule**
  synthesize **DNA**

syn|thet|ic /sɪnˈθetɪk/

ADJECTIVE **Synthetic** products are made from chemicals or artificial substances rather than from natural ones. ○ *Boots made from synthetic materials can usually be washed in a machine.* ○ *progestogen, the synthetic hormone contained in the pill*

▸ **COLLOCATIONS:**
  a synthetic **hormone/chemical**
  a synthetic **fibre/fabric/material**
▸ **SYNONYMS:** man-made, artificial
▸ **ANTONYM:** natural

syn|theti|cal|ly /sɪnˈθetɪkli/

ADVERB ○ *the therapeutic use of natural and synthetically produced hormones*
○ *Although some vitamins are made from foods, the majority are manufactured synthetically.*

▶ **COLLOCATIONS:**
prepare/produce/manufacture *something* synthetically
synthetically **reproduced/derived**

▶ **SYNONYM:** artificially

▶ **ANTONYM:** naturally

Tt

tail off /teɪl 'ɒf/ (tails off, tailing off, tailed off)

PHRASAL VERB When something **tails off**, it gradually becomes less in amount or value, often before coming to an end completely. ○ [+ to] *Last year, economic growth tailed off to below four percent.* ○ *The drug's effect does not tail off after it has been used repeatedly.*

▶ **COLLOCATION:** tail off **to** *an amount*

▶ **SYNONYMS:** wear off, abate

▶ **ANTONYM:** increase

take|over /'teɪkəʊvə/ (takeovers) `BUSINESS`

NOUN A **takeover** is the act of gaining control of a company by buying more of its shares than anyone else. ○ [+ of] *the government's takeover of the Bank of New England Corporation* ○ *a hostile takeover bid for NCR, America's fifth-biggest computer-maker*

▶ **COLLOCATIONS:**
a takeover **of** *something*
propose/complete/finance a takeover
a **£x** takeover
a **corporate/hostile/friendly** takeover
a takeover **bid/offer**

▶ **SYNONYM:** buyout

▶ **RELATED WORD:** merger

tal|ly /'tæli/ (tallies, tallying, tallied)

VERB If one number or statement **tallies with** another, they agree with each other or are exactly the same. You can also say that two numbers or statements **tally**. ○ [+ with] *Its own estimate of three hundred tallies with that of another survey.* ○ *The figures didn't seem to tally.*

▶ **COLLOCATIONS:**
tally **with** *something*
votes/results tally

▶ **SYNONYMS:** correspond, agree, match

▶ **ANTONYMS:** differ, contradict

tar|iff /ˈtærɪf/ (tariffs) `BUSINESS`

NOUN A **tariff** is a tax that a government collects on goods coming into a country. ○ [+ on] *America wants to eliminate tariffs on items such as electronics.* ○ *a rise in import tariffs*

▶ **COLLOCATIONS:**
a tariff **on** *something*
a tariff on **imports/goods/products**
a **trade/import/lumber/steel** tariff
a **punitive/protective** tariff
impose/levy/reduce/raise a tariff
tariff **reduction/cuts**

▶ **SYNONYMS:** tax, duty

tele|scope /ˈtelɪskəʊp/ (telescopes) `SCIENCE`

NOUN A **telescope** is a long instrument shaped like a tube. It has lenses inside it that make distant things seem larger and nearer when you look through it. ○ *It's hoped that the telescope will enable scientists to see deeper into the universe than ever before.* ○ *light or heat detected by telescopes*

▶ **COLLOCATIONS:**
a **radio/optical** telescope
a **space/ground-based** telescope

▶ **RELATED WORD:** microscope

tem|per|ate /ˈtempərɪt/ `GEOGRAPHY`

ADJECTIVE Temperate is used to describe a climate or a place which is never extremely hot or extremely cold. ○ *The Nile Valley keeps a temperate climate throughout the year.* ○ *crops grown mainly in temperate zones*

▶ **COLLOCATIONS:**
a temperate **climate/area/region/zone**
a temperate **rainforest**

▶ **RELATED WORD:** tropical

ten|ta|tive /ˈtentətɪv/

ADJECTIVE Tentative agreements, plans, or arrangements are not definite or certain, but have been made as a first step. ○ *Political leaders have reached a tentative agreement to hold a preparatory conference next month.* ○ *Such theories are still very tentative.* ○ *The study was adequate to permit at least tentative conclusions.*

→ see note at **inconclusive**

t

▶ **COLLOCATIONS:**
a tentative **step/agreement/settlement/deal**
a tentative **conclusion/thesis/theory**

▶ **SYNONYMS:** provisional, conditional, indefinite

▶ **ANTONYMS:** firm, definite

ten|ta|tive|ly /ˈtentətɪvli/

ADVERB ○ *The next round of talks is tentatively scheduled to begin October 21st in Washington.* ○ *Smith was the first to tentatively suggest a labour theory of value.*

▶ **COLLOCATIONS:**
tentatively **agreed/planned/scheduled**
tentatively **suggest** *something*

▶ **SYNONYMS:** provisionally, conditionally, indefinitely

▶ **ANTONYMS:** firmly, definitely

---

term /tɜːm/ (terms)

NOUN A **term** is a period of time. ○ [+ *of*] *Felipe Gonzalez won a fourth term of office in Spain's election.* ○ [+ *of*] *a 12 month term of service* ○ *Offenders will be liable to a seven-year prison term.* ○ [+ *of*] *Premiums are guaranteed throughout the term of the policy.*

▶ **COLLOCATIONS:**
a term **of** *something*
a term of **office/service/employment**
a **jail/prison** term
a term **begins/expires/ends**

▶ **SYNONYMS:** period, duration, session

---

ter|mi|nal /ˈtɜːmɪnəl/   ACADEMIC WORD   MEDICINE   PHYSICS
(terminals)

1 ADJECTIVE A **terminal** illness or disease causes death, often slowly, and cannot be cured. ○ *a patient with terminal cancer* ○ *His illness was terminal.*

▶ **COLLOCATIONS:**
a terminal **illness/disease**
terminal **cancer**

▶ **SYNONYM:** fatal

2 NOUN A **terminal** is a place where vehicles, passengers, or goods begin or end a journey. ○ *Plans are underway for a fifth terminal at Heathrow airport.* ○ *a continental ferry terminal*

t

▶ COLLOCATIONS:
a **ferry/bus/airport** terminal
a **freight/passenger** terminal
build a terminal

▶ SYNONYMS: station, terminus, depot

3 NOUN On a piece of electrical equipment, a **terminal** is one of the points where electricity enters or leaves it. ○ [+ *of*] *the positive terminal of the battery*

▶ COLLOCATION: a terminal **of** *something*

---

ter|mi|nate /ˈtɜːmɪneɪt/   ACADEMIC WORD
(terminates, terminating, terminated)

VERB When you **terminate** something or when it **terminates**, it ends completely. [FORMAL] ○ *the right to terminate an agreement* ○ [+ *at*] *His contract terminates at the end of the season.*

▶ COLLOCATIONS:
terminate **at** *a particular time*
terminate a **contract/agreement/plan**
terminate **employment**
abruptly/immediately/automatically terminate

▶ SYNONYMS: end, discontinue

▶ ANTONYM: begin

ter|mi|na|tion /ˌtɜːmɪˈneɪʃən/

UNCOUNTABLE NOUN ○ [+ *of*] *a dispute which led to the abrupt termination of trade* ○ [+ *of*] *failure to provide reasonable notice of termination of employment*

▶ COLLOCATIONS:
the termination **of** *something*
the termination of **employment/trade**
the termination of a **contract/lease/agreement**
a termination **notice**
a termination **payment/fee/charge**

▶ SYNONYMS: end, cessation, discontinuation

▶ ANTONYM: beginning

---

ter|res|trial /tɪˈrestriəl/   GEOGRAPHY   SCIENCE

ADJECTIVE Terrestrial means relating to the planet Earth rather than to some other part of the universe. ○ *terrestrial life forms* ○ *Although this is intensely hot by terrestrial standards, it is cool by comparison with the Sun's core.* ○ *our terrestrial environment*

▶ ANTONYM: extra-terrestrial

ter|ror|ist /'terərɪst/ (terrorists) `POLITICS`

NOUN A **terrorist** is a person who uses violence, especially murder and bombing, in order to achieve political aims. ○ *One American was killed and three were wounded in terrorist attacks.* ○ *military action against countries that harbour terrorists*

▶ **COLLOCATIONS:**
a **suspected/convicted/wanted/potential** terrorist
harbour terrorists
terrorists **hijack** *someone/something*
terrorists **attack/target** *somewhere*
a terrorist **attack/strike**

▶ **SYNONYM:** guerrilla

ter|ror|ism /'terərɪzəm/

UNCOUNTABLE NOUN ○ *the need to combat international terrorism* ○ *fears about security and terrorism threats*

▶ **COLLOCATIONS:**
combat/fight/defeat/counter terrorism
international/global/domestic terrorism
a terrorism **suspect/charge/threat/expert**
terrorism **fears**

tes|ti|fy /'testɪfaɪ/ (testifies, testifying, testified) `LAW`

VERB When someone **testifies** in a court of law, they give a statement of what they saw someone do or what they know of a situation, after having promised to tell the truth. ○ [+ *that*] *Several eyewitnesses testified that they saw the officers hit Miller in the face.* ○ [+ *to*] *Eva testified to having seen Herndon with his gun on the stairs.* ○ [+ *against*] *He hopes to have his 12-year prison term reduced by testifying against his former colleagues.*

▶ **COLLOCATIONS:**
testify **for/against** *someone*
testify **to/about** *something*
a **witness/eyewitness/expert** testifies
testify **publicly/truthfully**

▶ **SYNONYMS:** witness, declare, certify, state

tes|ti|mo|ny /'testɪməni, AM -məuni/ (testimonies)

NOUN In a court of law, someone's **testimony** is a formal statement that they make about what they saw someone do or what they know of a situation, after having promised to tell the truth. ○ *His testimony was an* *important element of the Prosecution case.* ○ *Prosecutors may try to determine if Robb gave false testimony when he appeared before the grand jury.*

▶ COLLOCATIONS:
present/hear testimony
contradict *someone's* testimony
sworn/written/false testimony
witness/court/expert testimony

▶ SYNONYM: statement

---

test tube /ˈtest tjuːb/ (test tubes) also test-tube SCIENCE

NOUN A **test tube** is a small tube-shaped container made from glass. Test tubes are used in laboratories. ○ *The effect has so far only been seen in test tube experiments.* ○ *Samples are simply mixed together in a test tube.*

▶ COLLOCATIONS:
a **laboratory** test tube
a test tube **study/experiment**

---

tex|ture /ˈtekstʃə/ (textures)

NOUN The **texture** of something is the way that it feels when you touch it, for example how smooth or rough it is. ○ *a cheese with a soft crumbly texture* ○ [+ of] *the grainy texture of the paper*

▶ COLLOCATIONS:
the texture **of** *something*
a **smooth/creamy/soft** texture
a **coarse/grainy** texture
skin/surface texture

---

theme /θiːm/ (themes) ACADEMIC WORD LITERATURE

NOUN A **theme** in a piece of writing, a discussion, or an artist's work is an important idea or subject that runs through it. ○ [+ of] *The theme of the conference is renaissance Europe.* ○ *the novel's central theme*

▶ COLLOCATIONS:
the theme **of** *something*
the **main/central/key/dominant/major** theme
a **common/recurrent/underlying/universal** theme
explore/continue/echo a theme
a theme **emerges/recurs**
a theme **runs through** *something*

▶ SYNONYMS: topic, subject, motif

t

the|mat|ic /θiːˈmætɪk/

ADJECTIVE **Thematic** means concerned with the subject or theme of something, or with themes and topics in general. [FORMAL] ○ *assembling this material into thematic groups* ○ *the whole thematic approach to learning*

the|mati|cal|ly /θiːˈmætɪkli/

ADVERB ○ *a thematically-linked threesome of songs* ○ *Thematically, Miller's work falls into broad categories.*

---

theo|rem /ˈθiːərəm/ (theorems)   `MATHS`

NOUN A **theorem** is a statement in mathematics or logic that can be proved to be true by reasoning. ○ *the central mathematical theorem underpinning the entire theory* ○ *The theorem is very easily proved.*

▶ COLLOCATIONS:
 a **mathematical** theorem
 prove a theorem

---

thera|py /ˈθerəpi/ (therapies)   `MEDICINE`

1 UNCOUNTABLE NOUN **Therapy** is the treatment of someone with mental or physical illness without the use of drugs or operations. ○ *Many women in therapy begin to remember what happened to them in childhood.* ○ *a child receiving speech therapy*

2 NOUN A **therapy** is a particular treatment of someone with a particular illness. ○ *hormonal therapies* ○ *conventional drug therapy*

▶ COLLOCATIONS:
 in therapy
 undergo/receive therapy
 cognitive/behavioural therapy
 complementary/alternative therapy
 physical/occupational/speech therapy
 radiation therapy
▶ PHRASE: hormone replacement therapy
▶ SYNONYMS: treatment, counselling

thera|pist /ˈθerəpɪst/ (therapists)

NOUN A **therapist** is a person who is skilled in a particular type of therapy. ○ *the increasing number of people consulting alternative therapists* ○ *In the view of family therapists, most problems originate in a person's social setting and relationships.*

▶ COLLOCATIONS:
consult a therapist
a **speech/family** therapist
a **behavioural/occupational** therapist

▶ SYNONYM: counsellor

thera|peu|tic /ˌθerəˈpjuːtɪk/

ADJECTIVE **Therapeutic** treatment is designed to treat an illness or to improve a person's health, rather than to prevent an illness. ○ *therapeutic drugs* ○ *therapeutic doses of herbs*

▶ SYNONYM: healing
▶ ANTONYM: preventative

---

there|after /ˌðeərˈɑːftə, -ˈæftə/

ADVERB **Thereafter** means after the event or date mentioned. [FORMAL] ○ *Inflation will fall and thereafter so will interest rates.* ○ *The woman had surgery and died shortly thereafter.*

▶ COLLOCATIONS:
a **year/day** thereafter
shortly/soon thereafter

▶ SYNONYMS: afterwards, subsequently

---

there|by /ˌðeəˈbaɪ/   ACADEMIC WORD

ADVERB You use **thereby** to introduce an important result or consequence of the event or action you have just mentioned. [FORMAL] ○ *Our bodies can sweat, thereby losing heat by evaporation.* ○ *A firm might sometimes sell at a loss to drive a competitor out of business, and thereby increase its market power.*

▶ COLLOCATIONS:
thereby **reduce/increase** something
thereby **avoid/prevent** something

▶ SYNONYM: thus

---

three-dimensional /ˌθriː daɪˈmenʃənəl, AM dɪm-/   MATHS SCIENCE

ADJECTIVE A **three-dimensional** object is solid rather than flat, because it can be measured in three different directions, usually the height, length, and width. The abbreviation **3-D** can also be used. ○ *a three-dimensional model* ○ *the three-dimensional structure of DNA*

▶ **COLLOCATION:** a three-dimensional **model/structure**

▶ **RELATED WORD:** two-dimensional

---

thresh|old /ˈθreʃhəʊld/ (thresholds)

NOUN A **threshold** is an amount, level, or limit on a scale. When the **threshold** is reached, something else happens or changes. ○ [+ *of*] *There are many patients whose threshold of pain is very low.* ○ *The consensus has clearly shifted in favour of raising the nuclear threshold.* ○ [+ *for*] *Fewer than forty per cent voted – the threshold for results to be valid.*

▶ **COLLOCATIONS:**
a threshold **of/for** *something*
a threshold of **tolerance/pain/awareness**
raise/set/reach a threshold
the **current** threshold
a **tax/income** threshold
a **pain/boredom** threshold

▶ **SYNONYMS:** limit, level

---

thrive /θraɪv/ (thrives, thriving, thrived)

VERB If someone or something **thrives**, they do well and are successful, healthy, or strong. ○ *Today his company continues to thrive.* ○ [+ *in*] *Lavender thrives in poor soil.* ○ [V-ing] *the river's thriving population of kingfishers*

▶ **COLLOCATIONS:**
thrive **in** *something*
thrive in a **climate/environment/situation/area**
a **business/industry/company** thrives
plants/wildlife/bacteria thrive

▶ **SYNONYMS:** succeed, blossom, prosper

▶ **ANTONYM:** fail

---

tide /taɪd/ (tides)   GEOGRAPHY

1 NOUN The tide is the regular change in the level of the sea on the shore. ○ *The reserve is inaccessible at high tide.* ○ *Scientists have found proof that strong tides can trigger earthquakes.* ○ *State police say that high tides and severe flooding have damaged beaches.*

2 NOUN A **tide** is a current in the sea that is caused by the regular and continuous movement of large areas of water towards and away from the shore. ○ *Roman vessels used to sail with the tide from Boulogne to Richborough.*

▶ **COLLOCATIONS:**
high/low tide
the **incoming/outgoing** tide
a **strong/flood/spring/rip/neap** tide
the tide **turns/ebbs/flows/recedes**

▶ **SYNONYM:** current

tid|al /ˈtaɪdəl/

ADJECTIVE **Tidal** means relating to or produced by tides. ○ *The tidal stream or current gradually decreases in the shallows.* ○ *the tidal waters of the estuary*

▶ **COLLOCATIONS:**
a tidal **stream/river/current/wave**
tidal **waters**

---

time-consuming /ˈtaɪm kənˌsjuːmɪŋ, AM -ˌsuː-/
also **time consuming**

ADJECTIVE If something is **time-consuming**, it takes a lot of time.
○ [+ to-inf] *It is very time consuming to get such a large quantity of data.*
○ *Starting a new business, however small, is a time-consuming exercise.*

▶ **COLLOCATIONS:**
a time-consuming **process/procedure/method**
a time-consuming **job/task/activity**

▶ **PHRASE:** costly and time-consuming

▶ **SYNONYMS:** arduous, demanding

---

trace /treɪs/ (traces, tracing, traced) ACADEMIC WORD

1 VERB If you **trace** the origin or development of something, you find out or describe how it started or developed. ○ *The exhibition traces the history of graphic design in America from the 19th century to the present.* ○ [+ to] *The psychiatrist successfully traced some of her problems to severe childhood traumas.*

● **Trace back** means the same as **trace**. ○ [+ to] *Britain's Parliament can trace its history back to the English Parliament of the 13th century.* ○ *The traditional format of the almanac can be traced back for at least a thousand years.*

▶ **COLLOCATIONS:**
trace *something* **to** *something*
trace the **origin/history/development/evolution** of *something*
trace *someone's* **ancestry/roots/relatives**

2 NOUN A **trace of** something is a very small amount of it. ○ [+ of] *Wash them in cold water to remove all traces of sand.* ○ [+ of] *The technique could scan luggage at airports for traces of explosives.* ○ [+ of] *said without a trace of irony*

▶ **COLLOCATIONS:**
a trace **of** *something*
a trace of **poison/cocaine/explosives**
a trace of **irony/bitterness**
a **faint/minute** trace
find/contain/remove/leave a trace

▶ **SYNONYMS:** vestige, fragment

---

tran|script /ˈtrænskrɪpt/ (transcripts)

NOUN A **transcript of** a conversation or speech is a written text of it, based on a recording or notes. ○ [+ *of*] *The data collected for each patient included a transcript of the interview and the interviewer's notes.* ○ *reconstructing the case from an array of court transcripts*

▶ **COLLOCATIONS:**
a transcript **of** *something*
a transcript of a **conversation/interview/hearing**
a **court/trial** transcript

tran|scribe /trænˈskraɪb/ (transcribes, transcribing, transcribed)

VERB If you **transcribe** a speech or text, you write it out in a different form from the one in which it exists, for example by writing it out in full from notes or from a tape recording. ○ *She is transcribing, from his dictation, the diaries of Simon Forman.* ○ *Every telephone conversation will be recorded and transcribed.*

▶ **COLLOCATION:** transcribe a **conversation/interview**

---

tran|si|tion /trænˈzɪʃən/ (transitions)　　ACADEMIC WORD

NOUN **Transition** is the process in which something changes from one state to another. ○ [+ *to*] *The transition to a multi-party democracy is proving to be difficult.* ○ [+ *from*] *in order to ensure a smooth transition from one reign to the next* ○ *a period of transition*

▶ **COLLOCATIONS:**
a transition **from/to** *something*
a **smooth/peaceful/seamless/successful** transition
a transition **period/process/phase**
make/facilitate/ensure/ease a transition

▶ **SYNONYMS:** shift, change, passage

tran|si|tion|al /træn'zɪʃənəl/

ADJECTIVE A **transitional** period is one in which things are changing from one state to another. ○ *a transitional period following more than a decade of civil war* ○ *We are still in the transitional stage between the old and new methods.*

▶ **COLLOCATIONS:**
a transitional **period/stage/phase**
a transitional **government/administration**

---

trans|mit /trænz'mɪt/　　ACADEMIC WORD　MEDICINE
(transmits, transmitting, transmitted)

VERB If one person or animal **transmits** a disease to another, they have the disease and cause the other person or animal to have it. [FORMAL] ○ [+ to] *mosquitoes that transmit disease to humans* ○ [+ through] *There was no danger of transmitting the infection through operations.* ○ *the spread of sexually transmitted diseases*

▶ **COLLOCATIONS:**
tramsmit *something* **to** *something/someone*
transmitted **by/through** *something*
transmitted by **mosquitoes/contact/transfusion**
transmit a **disease/infection/virus**
sexually/orally/genetically transmitted

▶ **SYNONYMS:** pass, spread

trans|mis|sion /trænz'mɪʃən/

UNCOUNTABLE NOUN The **transmission** of something is the passing or sending of it to a different person or place. ○ *Heterosexual contact is responsible for the bulk of HIV transmission.* ○ *the fax machine and other forms of electronic data transmission* ○ [+ of] *the transmission of knowledge and skills*

▶ **COLLOCATIONS:**
the transmission **of** *something*
the transmission of a **disease/virus**
data/electricity/radio transmission
human-to-human/airborne/viral transmission

---

trans|plant **(transplants, transplanting, transplanted)**　　MEDICINE

The noun is pronounced /'trænsplɑːnt, -plænt/. The verb is pronounced /træns'plɑːnt, -'plænt/.

1 NOUN A **transplant** is a medical operation in which a part of a person's body is replaced because it is diseased. ○ *several hundred patients awaiting* *bone marrow transplant operations* ○ *the controversy over the sale of human organs for transplant*

▶ COLLOCATIONS:
a **heart/bone marrow/liver** transplant
a **kidney/organ** transplant
a transplant **operation/surgeon/patient/recipient**
undergo/await/receive a transplant

2 VERB If doctors **transplant** an organ such as a heart or a kidney, they use it to replace a patient's diseased organ. ○ *The operation to transplant a kidney is now fairly routine.* ○ *transplanted organs such as hearts and kidneys*

▶ COLLOCATIONS:
transplant a **kidney/heart/organ**
successfully transplant *something*

trans|plan|ta|tion /ˌtrænzplænˈteɪʃən/

UNCOUNTABLE NOUN ○ *a shortage of kidneys for transplantation* ○ *Bone marrow transplantation began 20 years ago.*

▶ COLLOCATIONS:
renal/kidney/bone marrow transplantation
liver/organ transplantation

trau|ma /ˈtrɔːmə, AM ˈtraʊmə/   MEDICINE

UNCOUNTABLE NOUN **Trauma** is a serious injury caused by an accident rather than an illness. ○ *riding accidents involving head trauma* ○ *an ambulance for coronary and trauma patients*

▶ COLLOCATIONS:
head/brain/neck trauma
a trauma **patient/surgeon**
▶ SYNONYM: injury

trea|ty /ˈtriːti/ (treaties)   POLITICS   LAW

NOUN A **treaty** is a written agreement between countries in which they agree to do a particular thing or to help each other. ○ [+ *of*] *the Treaty of Rome, which established the European Community* ○ [+ *on*] *negotiations over a 1992 treaty on global warming* ○ *A peace treaty was signed between France and Russia.*

▶ COLLOCATIONS:
the treaty **of** *something*
a treaty **on** *something*

a **peace/arms/nuclear/climate** treaty
a **draft/formal/global** treaty
negotiate/sign/ratify/approve a treaty
violate/reject a treaty

▶ SYNONYMS: pact, agreement

---

turn|over /ˈtɜːnəʊvə/ (turnovers) [BUSINESS]

NOUN The **turnover** of a company is the value of the goods or services sold during a particular period of time. ○ [+ of] *The company had a turnover of £3.8 million.* ○ *Group turnover rose by 13 per cent to £3.7bn.*

▶ COLLOCATIONS:
a turnover **of** £x
total/annual/average turnover
turnover **rises/grows/falls**

▶ SYNONYM: revenue

---

two-dimensional /ˌtuː daɪˈmenʃənəl, [MATHS] [SCIENCE]
AM dɪm-/ also **two dimensional**

ADJECTIVE A **two-dimensional** object or figure is flat rather than solid so that only its length and width can be measured. ○ *new software, which generates both two-dimensional drawings and three-dimensional images* ○ *The conifers looked like two-dimensional cutouts against the white sky.*

▶ COLLOCATION: a two-dimensional **image/picture/surface**

▶ RELATED WORD: three-dimensional

---

ty|phoon /taɪˈfuːn/ (typhoons) [GEOGRAPHY]

NOUN A **typhoon** is a very violent tropical storm. ○ *large atmospheric disturbances such as typhoons* ○ *a powerful typhoon that killed at least 32 people*

▶ COLLOCATION: a **powerful/deadly** typhoon

▶ SYNONYMS: hurricane, cyclone

---

t

Uu

unani|mous /juːˈnænɪməs/

1 **ADJECTIVE** When a group of people are **unanimous**, they all agree about something or all vote for the same thing. ○ [+ in] *Editors were unanimous in their condemnation of the proposals.* ○ [+ that] *Experts are unanimous that money raised through debt should not be allowed to be used for buyback.*

2 **ADJECTIVE** A **unanimous** vote, decision, or agreement is one in which all the people involved agree. ○ *the unanimous vote for Hungarian membership* ○ *Their decision was unanimous.*

▶ **COLLOCATIONS:**
unanimous **in** *something*
a unanimous **verdict/vote/decision/agreement**
unanimous **support/approval/backing/condemnation**
a **jury/panel/board** is unanimous
experts/critics are unanimous

▶ **SYNONYMS:** common, agreed, shared, universal

▶ **ANTONYM:** divided

unani|mous|ly /juːˈnænɪməsli/

ADVERB ○ *Today its executive committee voted unanimously to reject the proposals.* ○ *The board of ministers unanimously approved the project last week.*

▶ **COLLOCATIONS:**
vote/rule/agree unanimously
unanimously **approve/endorse/recommend** *something*
unanimously **reject** *something*

▶ **SYNONYM:** universally

under|es|ti|mate /ˌʌndərˈestɪmeɪt/ `ACADEMIC WORD`
(underestimates, underestimating, underestimated)

VERB If you **underestimate** something, you do not realize how large or great it is or will be. ○ *Marx clearly underestimated the importance of population growth.* ○ [+ how] *The most common mistake students make in library research is underestimating how long it will take to find the sources they need.*

u

▶ **COLLOCATIONS:**
underestimate the **seriousness/importance** of *something*
underestimate the **extent/complexity** of *something*
grossly/vastly/seriously underestimate
▶ **SYNONYM:** undervalue
▶ **ANTONYMS:** overestimate, exaggerate

---

under|mine /ˌʌndəˈmaɪn/ (undermines, undermining, undermined)

VERB If you **undermine** something such as a system, an argument or a theory, you make it less strong or less secure than it was before, often by a gradual process or by repeated efforts. ○ *Popular culture has helped undermine elitist notions of high culture.* ○ *The technological sophistication of the Bronzes undermined 19th-century Western European assumptions about primitive Africa.* ○ *Western intelligence agencies are accused of trying to undermine the government.*

▶ **COLLOCATIONS:**
undermine a **notion/assumption**
undermine a **government**
undermine **democracy/peace/authority**
threaten to undermine *something*
seriously/fatally/severely undermine
▶ **SYNONYM:** weaken
▶ **ANTONYM:** strengthen

---

under|privi|leged /ˌʌndəˈprɪvɪlɪdʒd/ SOCIOLOGY

ADJECTIVE **Underprivileged** people have less money and fewer possessions and opportunities than other people in their society. ○ *helping underprivileged children to learn to read* ○ *the hideous effects of government cuts on underprivileged families*

• **The underprivileged** are people who are underprivileged. ○ *government plans to make more jobs available to the underprivileged*

▶ **COLLOCATION:** an underprivileged **child/family/background**
▶ **ANTONYMS:** privileged, wealthy

> **EXTEND YOUR VOCABULARY**
>
> In everyday language, you often describe people with very little money or a low standard of living as being **poor**. ○ *The President was born into a poor family and knew poverty throughout his early life.*

However, the word **poor** is quite general and often suggests a
negative judgement. In academic writing, you use more careful
words, such as **underprivileged**, **disadvantaged** or **deprived** to
describe people who have less than others in a society. These words
refer to not only a lack of money and a low standard of living, but also
a lack of opportunities, such as in education and employment.
○ *The authors have been able to draw comparisons between affluent and
disadvantaged areas.* ○ *one of the most socially and economically deprived
parts of London*

un|ethi|cal /ˌʌnˈeθɪkəl/ ACADEMIC WORD

ADJECTIVE If you describe someone's behaviour as **unethical**, you think it is
wrong and unacceptable according to a society's rules or people's beliefs.
○ [+ to-inf] *It would be unethical to expose humans to radiation in a clinical trial.*
○ *to investigate widespread unethical and illegal practices in banking*
○ *accusations of unethical conduct*

▶ **COLLOCATIONS:**
unethical **practices/activity/conduct/behaviour**
highly unethical
something is **considered** unethical

▶ **PHRASE:** illegal and unethical

▶ **SYNONYMS:** immoral, corrupt

▶ **ANTONYM:** ethical

un|fore|seen /ˌʌnfəˈsiːn/

ADJECTIVE If something that has happened was **unforeseen**, it was not
expected to happen or known about beforehand. ○ *Radiation may damage
cells in a way that was previously unforeseen.* ○ *Barring any unforeseen
circumstances, interest rates should remain relatively stable in the medium term.*

▶ **COLLOCATIONS:**
unforeseen **circumstances/consequences**
an unforeseen **event/complication/delay**
something unforeseen

▶ **SYNONYMS:** surprising, unpredicted, unexpected

▶ **ANTONYMS:** foreseen, predicted, expected

uni|form /'juːnɪfɔːm/ ACADEMIC WORD

1 **ADJECTIVE** If something is **uniform**, it does not vary, but is even and regular throughout. ○ *The carbon fibre fabric gives a uniform distribution of heat.* ○ *The price rises will not be uniform across the country.*

2 **ADJECTIVE** If you describe a number of things as **uniform**, you mean that they are all the same. ○ *Along each wall stretched uniform green metal filing cabinets.*

▶ **COLLOCATIONS:**
uniform **thickness/size/colour**
uniform **distribution/consistency**
remarkably uniform

▶ **SYNONYMS:** even, identical

▶ **ANTONYMS:** uneven, different

uni|form|ly /'juːnɪfɔːmli/

ADVERB ○ *a uniformly negative reaction worldwide* ○ *Microwaves heat water uniformly.* ○ *the assumption that stars are uniformly distributed in space*

▶ **COLLOCATIONS:**
uniformly **excellent/negative/positive/grey**
uniformly **distributed/spread**
apply *something* uniformly

▶ **SYNONYM:** evenly

uni|form|ity /ˌjuːnɪˈfɔːmɪti/

UNCOUNTABLE NOUN If there is **uniformity** in something such as a system, organization, or group of countries, the same rules, ideas, or methods are applied in all parts of it. ○ *Spanish liberals sought to create linguistic as well as administrative uniformity.* ○ [+ of] *The strength of the ideology is seen in the remarkable uniformity of attitudes and beliefs.*

▶ **COLLOCATIONS:**
uniformity **of** *something*
impose/ensure/demand/achieve uniformity
national/great/bland uniformity

uni|fy /'juːnɪfaɪ/ (unifies, unifying, unified) ACADEMIC WORD

VERB If someone **unifies** different things or parts, or if the things or parts **unify**, they are brought together to form one thing. ○ *A flexible retirement age is being considered by Ministers to unify men's and women's pension rights.* ○ *The plan has been for the rival armies to demobilise, to unify, and then to hold elections to decide who rules.* ○ [+ with] *the benefits of unifying with the West*

▶ **COLLOCATIONS:**
unify **with** *something*
unify a **nation/party/country/force**
newly unified

▶ **SYNONYMS:** join, unite

▶ **ANTONYM:** separate

uni|fi|ca|tion /juːnɪfɪˈkeɪʃən/

UNCOUNTABLE NOUN **Unification** is the process by which two or more countries join together and become one country. ○ *the process of general European unification* ○ *one of the most difficult obstacles in the unification process*

▶ **COLLOCATIONS:**
unification **of** *countries*
peaceful/rapid/national/political unification
German/European unification
achieve/welcome/celebrate/negotiate unification
the unification **process**

▶ **SYNONYM:** alliance

▶ **ANTONYM:** division

un|prec|edent|ed /ʌnˈpresɪdentɪd/

ADJECTIVE If something is **unprecedented**, it has never happened before. ○ *Such a move is rare, but not unprecedented.* ○ *In 1987 the Socialists took the unprecedented step of appointing a civilian to command the force.* ○ [+ in] *an instant slaughter unprecedented in the history of mankind*

▶ **COLLOCATIONS:**
unprecedented **in** *something*
unprecedented in **history**
an unprecedented **move/step**
historically unprecedented

▶ **SYNONYMS:** unique, unparalleled

un|pre|dict|able /ʌnprɪˈdɪktəbəl/   ACADEMIC WORD

ADJECTIVE If you describe someone or something as **unpredictable**, you mean that you cannot tell what they are going to do or how they are going to behave. ○ *In macular surgery, outcomes are unpredictable.* ○ *Adding more elements into the equation might have unpredictable consequences.* ○ *an unpredictable work environment*

▶ **COLLOCATIONS:**
   a **result/outcome/situation** is unpredictable
   unpredictable **behaviour/weather/consequences**

▶ **SYNONYM:** changeable

▶ **ANTONYM:** predictable

---

un|rest /ˌʌnˈrest/ POLITICS

UNCOUNTABLE NOUN If there is **unrest** in a particular place or society, people are expressing anger and dissatisfaction about something, often by demonstrating or rioting. ○ [+ in] *The real danger is civil unrest in the east of the country.* ○ [+ among] *There is growing unrest among students in several major cities.*

▶ **COLLOCATIONS:**
   unrest **in** *a place*
   unrest **among** *people*
   civil/social/political/industrial unrest
   labour/worker/student unrest
   growing/widespread/violent unrest
   incite/provoke/spark/cause unrest

▶ **SYNONYMS:** instability, discontent

---

un|speci|fied /ʌnˈspesɪfaɪd/ ACADEMIC WORD

ADJECTIVE You say that something is **unspecified** when you are not told exactly what it is. ○ *The government said an unspecified number of bandits were killed.* ○ *He was arrested on unspecified charges.*

→ see note at **insufficient**

▶ **COLLOCATIONS:**
   an unspecified **number/amount/sum**
   an unspecified **date/location/reason**
   unspecified **damages/injuries**
   as yet unspecified

▶ **ANTONYM:** specified

u

---

un|spoiled /ʌnˈspɔɪld/

ADJECTIVE If you describe a place as **unspoiled**, you think it is beautiful because it has not been changed or built on for a long time. [in BRIT, also use **unspoilt**] ○ *The port is quiet and unspoiled.* ○ *a plea for the conservation of unspoiled shorelines*

▶ **COLLOCATIONS:**
unspoiled **beauty/nature/countryside**
an unspoiled **wilderness/island**
an unspoiled **beach/coastline/shoreline**
relatively unspoiled

▶ **SYNONYM:** untouched

▶ **ANTONYM:** spoiled

---

up|bring|ing /ˈʌpbrɪŋɪŋ/ `SOCIOLOGY`

UNCOUNTABLE NOUN Your **upbringing** is the way that your parents treat you and the things that they teach you when you are growing up. ○ *John F. Kennedy, a naval war hero with a privileged upbringing* ○ *[+ as] Proudhon's political ideas were colored by his upbringing as the son of a poor and irresponsible peasant.* ○ *[+ in] his middle-class upbringing in the American Midwest*

▶ **COLLOCATIONS:**
an upbringing **as** *something*
an upbringing **in** *somewhere*
a **good/strict/sheltered/privileged** upbringing
a **traumatic/unconventional** upbringing
a **working-class/middle-class** upbringing
a **Catholic/religious** upbringing

▶ **SYNONYMS:** background, childhood

---

up|hold /ʌpˈhəʊld/ (upholds, upholding, upheld) `LAW`

1 VERB If you **uphold** something such as a law, a principle, or a decision, you support and maintain it. ○ *Our policy has been to uphold the law.* ○ *upholding the artist's right to creative freedom*

2 VERB If a court of law **upholds** a legal decision that has already been made, it decides that it was the correct decision. ○ *The crown court, however, upheld the magistrate's decision.* ○ *The judges unanimously upheld the appeal.*

▶ **COLLOCATIONS:**
uphold the **law**
uphold a **principle/standard/tradition**
uphold a **ruling/conviction/sentence/ban**
a **court/judge** upholds *something*
unanimously/partially uphold

▶ **SYNONYMS:** back, maintain, support

▶ **ANTONYM:** reject

u

util|ity /juːˈtɪlɪti/

UNCOUNTABLE NOUN The **utility** of something is its usefulness. [FORMAL]
  ○ [+ of] *Belief in the utility of higher education is shared by students nationwide.*
  ○ [+ of] *an emphasis on the practical utility of scientific knowledge* ○ *Consumers seek to maximize the utility or satisfaction to be derived from spending a fixed amount of income.*

  ▶ **COLLOCATIONS:**
  the utility **of** *something*
  the utility of a **strategy/approach**
  question/maximize the utility of *something*
  expected/practical utility

  ▶ **SYNONYM:** usefulness

  ▶ **ANTONYM:** uselessness

u

Vv

vac|cine /ˈvæksiːn, AM vækˈsiːn/ (vaccines) `MEDICINE`

NOUN A **vaccine** is a substance containing a harmless form of the germs that cause a particular disease. It is given to people, usually by injection, to prevent them getting that disease. ○ *Anti-malarial vaccines are now undergoing trials.* ○ *Seven million doses of vaccine are annually given to British children.* ○ *people who normally receive the flu vaccine*

▶ **COLLOCATIONS:**
  produce/develop/test a vaccine
  administer/inject a vaccine
  the **flu/smallpox/pneumococcal** vaccine
  the **polio/rubella** vaccine
  a **single/oral/effective** vaccine

vac|ci|nate /ˈvæksɪneɪt/ (vaccinates, vaccinating, vaccinated)

VERB If a person or animal **is vaccinated**, they are given a vaccine, usually by injection, to prevent them from getting a disease. ○ [+ *against*] *Dogs must be vaccinated against distemper.* ○ [+ *against*] *Parents can refuse to have their children vaccinated against certain diseases.* ○ *Measles, mumps and whooping cough are spreading again because children are not being vaccinated.*

▶ **COLLOCATIONS:**
  vaccinated **against** something
  vaccinated against **smallpox/measles/flu/rabies**
  fully vaccinated
  children/adults/animals are vaccinated
  have someone vaccinated

▶ **SYNONYM:** inoculate

vac|ci|na|tion /ˌvæksɪˈneɪʃən/ (vaccinations)

NOUN ○ *The abandonment of routine vaccination has led to a low immunity among the population.* ○ [+ *against*] *Smallpox was the first disease against which vaccination was shown to be effective.* ○ *medics who administer vaccinations*

▶ **COLLOCATIONS:**
  vaccination **against** something
  routine/mandatory vaccination

receive/require/introduce/offer vaccination
a vaccination **programme/campaign**
▶ SYNONYMS: inoculation, injection

---

vacuum /ˈvækjuːm, -juːəm/ (vacuums) `SCIENCE`

NOUN A **vacuum** is a space that contains no air or other gas. ○ *Wind is a current of air caused by a vacuum caused by hot air rising.* ○ *The spinning turbine creates a vacuum.* ○ *The lenses are processed in a vacuum chamber.*

▶ COLLOCATIONS:
    create a vacuum
    a vacuum **flask/tube/chamber**
▶ SYNONYMS: gap, space, void

---

veg|eta|tion /ˌvedʒɪˈteɪʃən/ `BIOLOGY`

UNCOUNTABLE NOUN Plants, trees, and flowers can be referred to as **vegetation**. [FORMAL] ○ *protection of native vegetation* ○ *About 6860 hectares of remnant vegetation were cleared.* ○ *The vegetation cover is much denser in the Subarctic than in the Arctic.*

▶ COLLOCATIONS:
    native/tropical/aquatic/tundra vegetation
    lush/dense/sparse vegetation
    rotting/decaying vegetation
    clear/protect/remove vegetation
    vegetation **cover/management**
▶ SYNONYMS: plant life, flora

---

vein /veɪn/ (veins) `BIOLOGY`

NOUN Your **veins** are the thin tubes in your body through which your blood flows towards your heart. ○ *Many veins are found just under the skin.* ○ [+ on] *enlargement of the external jugular veins on either side of the neck*

▶ COLLOCATIONS:
    a vein **in/on** something
    varicose veins
    the **jugular** vein
    a **broken/severed** vein
    a vein **graft/wall**
▶ PHRASE: deep vein thrombosis
▶ RELATED WORD: artery

V

ver|bal /'vɜːbəl/

LANGUAGE

1 ADJECTIVE You use **verbal** to indicate that something is expressed in speech rather than in writing or action. ○ *fears of physical violence or verbal abuse* ○ *The West must back up its verbal support with substantial economic aid.*

▶ COLLOCATIONS:
  verbal **abuse/support**
  a verbal **assurance/reprimand/attack**
▶ SYNONYMS: oral, spoken
▶ ANTONYMS: written, physical, nonverbal

2 ADJECTIVE You use **verbal** to indicate that something is connected with words and the use of words. ○ *The test has scores for verbal skills, mathematical skills, and abstract reasoning skills.* ○ *the verbal dexterity of writers such as O'Brien and Joyce*

▶ COLLOCATION: verbal **dexterity/fluency/skill**
▶ SYNONYM: linguistic
▶ RELATED WORD: numerical

veto /'viːtəʊ/ (vetoes, vetoing, vetoed)

POLITICS

VERB If someone in authority **vetoes** something, they forbid it, or stop it being put into action. ○ *the power to veto a bill absolutely* ○ *The President vetoed the economic package passed by Congress.*

▶ COLLOCATIONS:
  veto a **bill/resolution/proposal**
  veto a **plan/decision**
  veto **legislation/measures**
  effectively veto *something*
  a **president/governor/country** vetoes
▶ SYNONYMS: block, reject
▶ ANTONYMS: sanction, approve

● **Veto** is also a noun. ○ *The veto was a calculated political risk.* ○ [+ of] *a presidential veto of legislation* ○ *A two-thirds majority was needed to override the veto.*

▶ COLLOCATIONS:
  a veto **of/on** *something*
  a veto of **legislation**
  a veto of a **bill**
  a veto on **reform/tax**
  threaten/exercise/override a veto
  a **presidential/national** veto
  the **power/right** of veto
▶ ANTONYMS: sanction, approval

vi|able /'vaɪəbəl/

ADJECTIVE Something that is **viable** is capable of doing what it is intended to do. ○ *Cash alone will not make Eastern Europe's banks viable.* ○ *commercially viable products* ○ *the argument that plastic is a viable alternative to traditional building materials*

▶ **COLLOCATIONS:**
commercially/economically/financially viable
a viable **alternative/option/solution/proposition**
make *something* viable

▶ **SYNONYMS:** feasible, possible, reasonable

vi|abil|ity /ˌvaɪə'bɪlɪti/

UNCOUNTABLE NOUN ○ [+ *of*] *the shaky financial viability of the nuclear industry* ○ *The philosophy behind the development managers is to ensure long-term viability, profitability and sustainability.*

▶ **COLLOCATIONS:**
the viability **of** *something*
the viability of a **project/scheme/industry**
financial/commercial/economic/long-term viability
assess/ensure/threaten the viability of *something*

▶ **SYNONYM:** feasibility

vio|late /'vaɪəleɪt/ **(violates, violating, violated)** `ACADEMIC WORD` `LAW`

VERB If someone **violates** an agreement, law, or promise, they break it. [FORMAL] ○ *They went to prison because they violated the law.* ○ *They violated the ceasefire agreement.*

▶ **COLLOCATIONS:**
violate the **law/constitution**
violate a **rule/principle/agreement**
violate **probation/copyright**

▶ **SYNONYMS:** breach, break, disobey
▶ **ANTONYM:** obey

vio|la|tion /ˌvaɪə'leɪʃən/ **(violations)**

NOUN ○ [+ *of*] *This could constitute a violation of international law.* ○ [+ *of*] *He was in violation of his contract.* ○ *allegations of human rights violations*

▶ **COLLOCATIONS:**
a violation **of** *something*
in violation **of** *something*
a violation of the **law**

a violation of a **rule/agreement/contract**
a **human rights/copyright/parole** violation
a **gross/alleged/flagrant** violation
constitute a violation
commit/report a violation

---

viv|id /ˈvɪvɪd/ `ARTS`

ADJECTIVE If you describe memories and descriptions as **vivid**, you mean that they are very clear and detailed. ○ *The play is a vivid portrait of black America in 1969.* ○ *The poems are full of vivid imagery.*

▸ **COLLOCATIONS:**
a vivid **description/portrait/portrayal**
vivid **imagery**
a vivid **memory/recollection/dream**

▸ **SYNONYMS:** clear, intense

▸ **ANTONYM:** vague

viv|id|ly /ˈvɪvɪdli/

ADVERB ○ *The two government studies vividly illustrate that racial discrimination remains widespread in urban areas.*

▸ **COLLOCATIONS:**
illustrate/describe *something* vividly
recall/remember *something* vividly

▸ **SYNONYMS:** clearly, strongly, sharply

---

vo|ca|tion|al /vəʊˈkeɪʃənəl/ `EDUCATION`

ADJECTIVE **Vocational** training and skills are the training and skills needed for a particular job or profession. ○ *a course designed to provide vocational training in engineering* ○ *Vocational courses are often given more respect and funding than arts or philosophy.*

▸ **COLLOCATIONS:**
vocational **training/education/skills**
a vocational **qualification/course**

▸ **ANTONYM:** academic

---

vola|tile /ˈvɒlətaɪl, AM -təl/

1 ADJECTIVE A situation that is **volatile** is likely to change suddenly and unexpectedly. ○ *There have been riots before and the situation is volatile.* ○ *The international oil markets have been highly volatile since the early 1970s.* ○ *Armed soldiers guard the streets in this volatile atmosphere.*

v

▶ **COLLOCATIONS:**
a volatile **market/situation/region**
a volatile **mix/mixture**
highly/increasingly/politically volatile

▶ **SYNONYMS:** unstable, unpredictable

▶ **ANTONYMS:** stable, predictable

2 ADJECTIVE A **volatile** liquid or substance is one that will quickly change into a gas. ○ *It's thought that the blast occurred when volatile chemicals exploded.* ○ *volatile organic compounds*

▶ **COLLOCATION:** a volatile **chemical/compound**

vola|til|ity /ˌvɒləˈtɪlɪti/

UNCOUNTABLE NOUN ○ [+ *of*] *He is keen to see a general reduction in arms sales given the volatility of the region.* ○ *current stock market volatility* ○ [+ *in*] *Figure 1.5 reveals increased volatility in exchange rates.*

▶ **COLLOCATIONS:**
volatility **of/in** something
volatility of/in **prices/rates**
volatility of/in the **market**
market/price volatility
reduce/increase/experience volatility

▶ **SYNONYMS:** instability, unpredictability

▶ **ANTONYMS:** stability, predictability

vol|ca|no /vɒlˈkeɪnəʊ/ (volcanoes) `GEOGRAPHY`

NOUN A **volcano** is a mountain from which hot melted rock, gas, steam, and ash from inside the Earth sometimes burst. ○ *The volcano erupted last year killing about 600 people.* ○ *Etna is Europe's most active volcano.*

▶ **COLLOCATIONS:**
a volcano **erupts/smoulders**
a **dormant/active/inactive** volcano
an **extinct/underwater** volcano

vol|can|ic /vɒlˈkænɪk/

ADJECTIVE ○ *Earthquakes and volcanic activity occur at the boundaries between plates.* ○ *fragments of volcanic rock*

▶ **COLLOCATIONS:**
volcanic **eruptions/activity**
volcanic **ash/rock/lava/soil**
a volcanic **island/peak/crater**

Ww

where|by /weəˈbaɪ/

ADVERB A system or action **whereby** something happens is one that makes that thing happen. [FORMAL] ○ *the system whereby Britons choose their family doctors and the government pays those doctors* ○ *a method of soil conservation whereby ploughing is undertaken along contours rather than with the slope*

▶ **COLLOCATIONS:**
a **system/method/means/mechanism** whereby
a **procedure/process/arrangement** whereby

▶ **SYNONYM:** by which

---

white-collar /ˈwaɪtˌkɒlə/ also **white collar**

1 ADJECTIVE White-collar workers work in offices rather than doing physical work such as making things in factories or building things. ○ *White-collar workers now work longer hours.* ○ *Low costs and high levels of efficiency are enticing firms to move white-collar jobs out of Britain.*

▶ **COLLOCATIONS:**
a white-collar **worker/employee/job**
a white-collar **occupation/union**
white-collar **employment**

▶ **SYNONYM:** clerical

▶ **RELATED WORDS:** blue-collar, manual

2 ADJECTIVE White-collar crime is committed by people who work in offices, and involves stealing money secretly from companies or the government, or getting money in an illegal way. ○ *a notorious white-collar criminal who illegally took control of a Gold Coast company* ○ *such white-collar crimes as price fixing and commercial bribery*

▶ **COLLOCATIONS:**
a white-collar **criminal**
white-collar **crime**

w

with|stand /wɪð'stænd/
(withstands, withstanding, withstood)

VERB If something or someone **withstands** a force or action, they survive
it or do not give in to it. [FORMAL] ○ *armoured vehicles designed to withstand
chemical attack* ○ *Such claims have failed to withstand scientific scrutiny.*

▶ **COLLOCATIONS:**
withstand a **challenge/attack/onslaught/earthquake**
withstand **pressure/heat/stress**
withstand **temperatures/scrutiny**

▶ **SYNONYM:** resist

▶ **ANTONYM:** yield to

work|shop /'wɜːkʃɒp/ (workshops) EDUCATION ACADEMIC STUDY

NOUN A **workshop** is a period of discussion or practical work on a
particular subject in which a group of people share their knowledge or
experience. ○ [+ *for*] *Trumpeter Marcus Belgrave ran a jazz workshop for young
artists.* ○ *a one-day performance evaluation workshop* ○ [+ *on*] *Students attend
a variety of workshops on topics ranging from public speaking to managing
stress.*

▶ **COLLOCATIONS:**
a workshop **for** *people*
a workshop **on** *something*
a workshop for **beginners/adults/children/teachers**
a workshop on a **topic/subject**
hold/run/conduct/attend a workshop
a **one-day/two-day/intensive** workshop
a **practical/hands-on/interactive** workshop

▶ **SYNONYMS:** seminar, master class, tutorial

W

XYZ

yield /jiːld/ **(yields, yielding, yielded)**

1 VERB If an area of land **yields** a particular amount of a crop, this is the amount that is produced. You can also say that a number of animals **yield** a particular amount of meat. ○ *Last year 400,000 acres of land yielded a crop worth $1.75 billion.* ○ *The disappointing harvest yielded only 4.5 million tonnes of sugar.*

▶ **COLLOCATIONS:**
yield a **crop/harvest**
yield *x* **tonnes** of *something*

▶ **SYNONYM:** produce

2 NOUN A **yield** is the amount of food produced on an area of land or by a number of animals. ○ [+ *of*] *improving the yield of the crop* ○ [+ *of*] *land with a potential yield of 110 bushels an acre* ○ *Polluted water lessens crop yields.*

▶ **COLLOCATIONS:**
a yield **of** *something/x*
a yield of **crop/wheat/corn/bushels**
a yield of *x* **bushels/tonnes**
a **crop/milk/wheat/rice** yield
a **high/average** yield

▶ **SYNONYMS:** harvest, produce

3 VERB If something **yields** a result or piece of information, it produces it. ○ *This research has been in progress since 1961 and has yielded a great number of positive results.* ○ *Diagnostics could also yield scientific insights leading to new drugs.*

▶ **COLLOCATIONS:**
yield **results/information**
yield **clues/insights**

▶ **SYNONYMS:** produce, generate, allow